AMERICA'S WORKING MAN

AMERICA'S WORKING MAN

Work, Home, and Politics
among
Blue-Collar Property Owners

David Halle

The University of Chicago Press
Chicago and London

The University of Chicago Press, Chicago 60637
The University of Chicago Press, Ltd., London

96 95 94 93 92 91 90 89 88 87   6 5 4 3 2

Library of Congress Cataloging in Publication Data

Halle, David.
  America's working man.

  Bibliography: p.
  Includes index.
    1. Chemical workers—New Jersey.   2. Labor and
laboring classes—United States   3. Social classes—
United States.   4. Class consciousness—United States.
I. Title.
HD8039.C46U624   1984   305.5′62′0973   84–2566
ISBN 0–226–31365–4 (cloth)
ISBN 0–226–31366–2 (paper)

To Carla
and Ritchie
and the memory
of Nicos

Contents

Acknowledgments   ix
Introduction   xi

Part 1: Life outside Work   1
1 The Residential Setting   3
2 Leisure   34
3 Marriage and Family   53

Conclusion to Part 1   74

Part 2: Blue-Collar Work and the Automated Factory   79
4 An Automated Plant: Overview   80
5 The Production Worker in an Automated Plant   105
6 Support Workers: Mechanics, Laboratory Technicians,
     Packagers, Warehouse Workers   127

Conclusion to Part 2   145

Part 3: The Limits of Mobility at Work: Solidarity and Dispute   149
7 Occupational Mobility and Security   151
8 Solidarity and Dispute   171

Conclusion to Part 3   186

Part 4: Politics and Class Consciousness   189
9 Politics and the Structure of Power:
     Democracy and Freedom   191
10 Position in the System of Production: The Concept of the
     Working Man   202
11 Position outside Work: Income Level, Standard of Living,
     and Residential Situation   220
12 Nationalism and Populism   231

Conclusion to Part 4   242

**Part 5: A Sociology of the Mediocre: Religion, Ethnicity, and
National Rituals**   251
13   Religion   253
14   Ethnicity   270
15   National Holidays and Cults   277
16   Conclusion: Class and Politics in America   292

Appendix: Supplementary Tables   303
Notes   305
Bibliography   339
Index   353

Acknowledgments

Among the industrial working class there is a special kind of warmth and friendliness. My major debt is to the men and their wives whose willingness to let me share their lives, and whose kindness and sense of fun, made this research so enjoyable. I am also grateful to local and regional officers of the Oil, Chemical and Atomic Workers Union, who gave me whatever assistance I asked for, and to the management of Imperium Chemical Company, who permitted me to carry out my study without limits or conditions and treated me with unfailing courtesy.

In the Sociology Department at Columbia I wish particularly to thank Herbert Gans and Allan Silver. Each was generous with his time and knowledge and posed challenging questions that helped me see the material in new and stimulating ways. William Kornblum's support and encouragement were invaluable, as was his rich knowledge of blue-collar life. At the start of this research I obtained valuable advice from James Kuhn, B. J. Widick, Eli Ginzberg, and Ivar Berg in the Business School at Columbia. I also received help from Bogden Denitch, Andrew Beveridge, and Conrad Arensberg. To Steven Lukes, my first sociology teacher, I owe a special debt.

Jeanie Attie and Robert Zussman read the manuscript at various stages of its evolution and offered thoughtful comments and critical insight. I am grateful to many other friends and colleagues for their help—Tracy Bolce, Adam Broner, Steve Cohen, Tom DiPrete, Helena Flam, Naomi Gerstel, Abby Ginzberg, Barry Goldberg, Susan Gray, Arno Gruen, Geoffrey Kabat, Mimi Lamb, Marian Landa, Mary Clare Lennon, Louise Mirrer, Stephen Mitchell, Mary Morris, Michael Navas, Kathy Nelson, Clara Rodriguez, Bernice Rogowitz, Peter Schneider, Gel Stevenson, and Nina Swidler.

Anyone needing creative artwork is fortunate to live in New York City. I received the help of several talented people. Brian Lav took all the photographs, with the following exceptions: plates 3, 8, and 20 are by Gary Cumiskey, and plates 5, 6, 7, 19, and 22 are by Marty Cooper; plate 33 is by the author. Josh Brown drew the maps and figures, with the following exceptions: David Hulbert drew figures 3 and 7; José Villegas drew figures 10 and 16; and Michel St. Sulpice drew map 6.

None of the people depicted in the photographs are among the subjects of the research, and their identities are unknown to me.

Introduction

The largest oil refinery on the East Coast lies between residential sections of the cities of Elizabeth and Linden, New Jersey. Owned by Exxon, it occupies two square miles, an extravagant space for an urban area. A series of slender distillation columns push upward to the sky; below are squat, round storage tanks. So as not to absorb heat from the sun, the metal is painted in cool pastels—light blues and silver, pale yellow and pink and faded green. Tanks and cylinders are linked by pipes that twist and weave in graceful curves and angles. Mushrooms of steam spurt from vents in the ground, then drift and quickly disappear.

Nearby are several chemical plants. The space each occupies, a fraction of that taken by the refinery, is a jumble of cylinders and tanks, packed together like jars and bottles on a dressing table. These plants—Engelhard, Allied, Purepac, Apex—line the New Jersey Turnpike, for northern New Jersey contains one of the densest concentrations of chemical production in the world. Along the highway swish plump tank cars carrying raw materials and finished products. The air smells slightly acrid, for chemical plants and oil refineries give off a steady stream of noxious vapors that are often invisible but leave clear odors. Most people who live in the area no longer notice the standard smell, picking up only the unusual.

This book is a study of the entire blue-collar labor force of one of these chemical plants, Imperium Oil and Chemicals.[1] It aims to present a total picture of workers' lives—their jobs, family relations and leisure activities, values and ideology, and their views on religion, ethnicity, politics, and social class.

One question has long dominated discussion of the working class in advanced industrial societies. How far are blue-collar workers "middle class" or "bourgeois"? This debate ranges over all aspects of working-class life and beliefs. There is an "income" debate, in which an image of "affluent" blue-collar workers[2] vies with an image of workers whose earnings fail to cover their basic needs, forcing them to constantly assess "the best strategy for juggling the creditors."[3] There is a "suburbia" debate, in which the view that homeownership and the suburbs operate as a "melting pot" from which everyone emerges as "middle class"[4] competes with findings that working class people in the suburbs "have not, to any marked extent, taken on the patterns of behavior and belief associated with white-collar suburbs."[5] A portrait of blue-collar marriage as resembling middle-class marriage, increasingly centering on the family and home and offering "happiness, enjoyment and relaxation,"[6] is challenged by a portrait of working-class marriage as a "world of pain" marked by meager communication between husband and wife and a limited range of leisure activities.[7] An image of blue-collar workers in automated plants as responsible technicians with interesting jobs[8] is opposed by an image of these same workers as alienated automatons living in "dehumanized prisons of labor" and dominated by management.[9] And the idea that workers perceive the class structure as a graded hierarchy, a fluid system without rigid boundaries,[10] competes with the view that American workers see themselves as a distinct social class with common interests and concerns.[11] Finally, the view that workers are content with the political system is challenged by those who point to widespread mistrust of politicians and political institutions which, if unchecked, could lead to a rejection of the entire system.[12]

This book addresses all the debates just mentioned, which may seem rash. But in a way it is easier to consider all these questions than a few, since many of them are interdependent. For instance, if workers' leisure and family lives are marred because the dull nature of blue-collar jobs leaves them mentally drained, then it is important to study life both at work and at home. Or consider the question of the American worker's image of the class structure. Those who argue that image is a graded hierarchy without clear class distinctions tend to stress the impact of factors outside work, such as income level, consumer goods, and residential setting, while those who insist there *is* a form of class solidarity usually imply that this originates in the work experience.

There is an obvious need for studies that situate the views of blue-collar workers in the context of their entire lives. Yet our knowledge of the working class is fragmented. Most of the best ethnographies deal *either* with work *or* with life outside work. Few studies follow the same group of employees at and away from their jobs. In addition, a number of studies deal with only one stage in the life cycle, for they focus on married workers with young children. This is the time when economic problems are likely to be most severe; there are children to support, and often the wife stays at home to care for them and so cannot take a paid job. The presence of young children also seriously curtails the couple's leisure time. Thus to consider only workers with young children is to risk mistaking one stage of the marital and life cycle for the essence of "blue-collar life."[13]

Studying part of the picture permits great richness and detail. Yet studies of the whole are also important, for it is only in such a context that the parts can be fully understood. As Norbert Elias put it: "Human beings do not consist of separate and independent compartments. What has been taken to pieces for purposes of study, for purposes of study has to be put together again."[14] That is why this book tries to present a complete picture of the lives of the workers it analyzes.

Many previous studies have handled the question of how far the working class is "middle class" by comparing current blue-collar workers with a picture of the working class in the past—the "traditional working class." Has the working class changed over time in a direction that can be called middle class? This strategy raises complex problems, since it entails constructing a picture of the "traditional" or "classical" working class with which to compare modern workers. For instance, what time period is relevant? Should the contemporary working class be compared with the working class in the 1930s, or the 1880s, or some other period? Second, which section of the working class is pertinent? Is it skilled or unskilled workers, new immigrants, or the second, third, and fourth generations that constitute the "traditional working class"? For such reasons I shall analyze the relation of the contemporary working class to the contemporary middle class. How far do the lives and beliefs of the blue-collar workers in this book overlap with those of the middle class?[15]

This raises a related problem. The "middle class" is not a uniform group but consists of various sectors, an "occupational salad" in the words of C. Wright Mills.[16] Out of this salad at least two categories can be distinguished, differing sharply in income level and status. First, there are managers and professionals (such as engineers, lawyers, doctors, and teachers). This group, which in 1980 composed 22 percent of the total labor force in America, I will refer to here as the "upper-white-collar sector." Second, there are clerical, secretarial, and sales workers, most of whom are female and who compose 22 percent of the labor force. They are referred to here as the "lower-white-collar sector." The blue-collar working class I define as consisting of factory workers, skilled workers (such as electricians and welders), transportation workers (such as bus and truck drivers), and (nonfarm) laborers. They compose 32 percent of the labor force (see table 1).[17] Thus the question of how far blue-collar workers are middle class becomes here the question of how far their lives and beliefs overlap with those of the upper- and lower-white-collar sectors.

There is one further complexity. The claim that blue-collar workers are "middle class" or "bourgeois" is ambiguous. It can refer, as in the discussion so far, to a perceived *overlap* between the lives and beliefs of blue-collar workers and those of the middle class. But it can also refer to the claim that blue-collar workers are conservative, or at least *integrated* into the social and political structure. The view

Table 1   The Three Main Occupational Groups, 1980

Occupational Group	Explanation	Percentage of All Workers
Upper white collar	Professionals and managers	22
Lower white collar	Clerical workers, secretaries, and salespeople	22
Blue collar	Skilled workers, factory workers, transport workers, nonfarm laborers	32
Others		24

Source: 1980 Census.

that blue-collar workers are "middle class" in this second sense is usually stated in opposition to Marx's view that the working class is alienated and constitutes a force for radical and even revolutionary change.

The term "embourgeoisement" is often used to refer to *both* versions of the idea that blue-collar workers are middle class. This double use of one term implies that the distinction between the two versions is unimportant. If the lives and beliefs of blue-collar workers overlap with those of the middle class, then they must be integrated into society. But this assumption is incorrect. For example, in America most blue- and white-collar workers mistrust politicians, yet this belief is clearly not a sign of integration. Overlap between classes does not, in itself, entail social or political integration. Blurring this distinction between overlap and integration leads to a common misinterpretation of Goldthorpe's influential study of the English working class, *The Affluent Worker*. Goldthorpe strongly criticizes the idea that the working class is "middle class" in the sense of being integrated into society. *The Affluent Worker* is often, but wrongly, cited as also opposing the view that the working class overlaps with the middle class. Actually, Goldthorpe maintains that there is extensive overlap (arguing that most blue- *and* white-collar employees have an "instrumental" attitude to work and politics and a "privatized" home and leisure life).[18]

Thus the claim that blue-collar workers are "middle class" conceals two distinct questions, both of which this book addresses. First, how far do the lives and beliefs of blue-collar workers overlap with those of the upper- and lower-white-collar sectors? Second, how far are blue-collar workers integrated into, or alienated from, society?

The Research

I chose a group of workers whose position is strategic for these debates, for if any blue-collar group is "middle class" in either of the senses outlined above, then these chemical workers should be. Their wages and benefits are well above the average for blue-collar workers in America, and they are protected by a union. The large chemical complex where they are employed is typical of the kind of technological setting that is said to have transformed blue-collar work. It contains some of the most modern process and batch technology, as well as older equipment. Founded in 1939, it is a profitable concern, as can be seen from the fact that in 1977 the company added a new production center. Imperium Oil and Chemicals, the parent company, is among the five hundred biggest manufacturing concerns in the country, with more than thirty refineries and chemical plants in America and others abroad in Britain, France, and Germany.

Most Imperium workers are homeowners. About half live close to the plant in pre–World War II sections of Elizabeth, Linden, Roselle, and Roselle Park, the kinds of areas often seen as "working-class" or "ethnic" neighborhoods. Most of the other workers have moved to newer outlying suburbs from which they commute to Imperium (map 1). Such areas, containing ranch-style, split-level, or older forms of houses, are typical of suburban development after World War II.

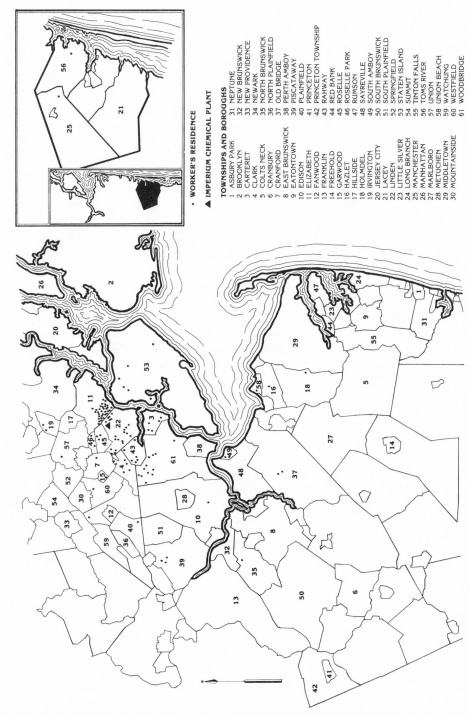

• WORKER'S RESIDENCE

▲ IMPERIUM CHEMICAL PLANT

TOWNSHIPS AND BOROUGHS

1 ASBURY PARK	31 NEPTUNE
2 BROOKLYN	32 NEW BRUNSWICK
3 CARTERET	33 NEW PROVIDENCE
4 CLARK	34 NEWARK
5 COLTS NECK	35 NORTH BRUNSWICK
6 CRANBURY	36 NORTH PLAINFIELD
7 CRANFORD	37 OLD BRIDGE
8 EAST BRUNSWICK	38 PERTH AMBOY
9 EATONTOWN	39 PISCATAWAY
10 EDISON	40 PLAINFIELD
11 ELIZABETH	41 PRINCETON
12 FANWOOD	42 PRINCETON TOWNSHIP
13 FRANKLIN	43 RAHWAY
14 FREEHOLD	44 RED BANK
15 GARWOOD	45 ROSELLE
16 HAZLET	46 ROSELLE PARK
17 HILLSIDE	47 RUMSON
18 HOLMDEL	48 SAYREVILLE
19 IRVINGTON	49 SOUTH AMBOY
20 JERSEY CITY	50 SOUTH BRUNSWICK
21 LACEY	51 SOUTH PLAINFIELD
22 LINDEN	52 SPRINGFIELD
23 LITTLE SILVER	53 STATEN ISLAND
24 LONG BRANCH	54 SUMMIT
25 MANCHESTER	55 TINTON FALLS
26 MANHATTAN	56 TOMS RIVER
27 MARLBORO	57 UNION
28 METUCHEN	58 UNION BEACH
29 MIDDLETOWN	59 WATCHUNG
30 MOUNTAINSIDE	60 WESTFIELD
	61 WOODBRIDGE

Map 1. Where Imperium workers live.

Finally, America has long had a reputation as a society whose working class has been deeply affected by affluence, homeownership, and at least the promise of social mobility. Indeed, for some people "the American worker" is a synonym for a worker who is quiescent and integrated into the class structure.[19] For all these reasons the workers in this study are ideally suited for examining theories about the modern working class being "middle class."

The research took place during a seven-year period, from late 1974 until late 1981. With a total labor force in 1974 of 171 (blue- and white-collar workers) Imperium is slightly larger than the average chemical plant in New Jersey.[20] The total number of blue-collar workers fluctuated. In 1974 there were 121. Over the next three years, because of the economic recession, management allowed the work force to fall by attrition to 115. In 1977 the number of workers rose to 126 as the new plant came into operation. All these workers are men, for blue-collar work is dominated by males.[21] Most wives of Imperium workers are, like many women in America, in lower-white-collar occupations, as secretaries or clerical workers or salespeople. But an interesting and important minority of Imperium wives are professionals or managers.

At the outset I obtained the support of the regional director of the Oil, Chemical and Atomic Workers Union, which represents workers at Imperium. For that reason the local union officers were friendly and helpful. They formally introduced me to men at a union meeting, emphasized that I was not associated with management, and gave me every assistance, including access to union records. Management, having given unconditional permission for my research, never interfered and imposed no restrictions on my movements within the plant. I was able to go anywhere I wished, day and night, throughout the research period.

In the automated setting of a chemical plant workers have ample opportunity to talk. Monitoring an instrument panel, as well as many of the other jobs in these plants, can easily be done without interrupting a conversation.[22] Men spend much of their work time in conversation with each other, and a researcher they trust can provide a welcome diversion. Usually workers were only too glad to spend time talking with me, for they were just as interested in an outsider as I was in them.

Most workers accepted my presence as an independent researcher at face value, confining themselves to occasional satirical comments on the length of my stay such as "That sure ain't no short story you're writing" or "You'd better hurry up. I want to see that study before I retire, and I've only got ten years to go." A few men thought I was a management spy. One told me: "Davey, Jimmy Ryan [another worker] says you must be a spy, otherwise why would you be asking so many questions. If I lose my job because of you I'll come looking for you all over Manhattan with a gun!" Fortunately, as a British citizen I was not a very likely government agent, and as the only person without the funds to come to work by car I was not a very plausible management spy. Anyway, workers have their own information network consisting of links with management's secretaries and with certain supervisors through which they were able to check on my allegiance.

Most views I investigated through long and frequent informal conversations with workers, individually and in groups. I recorded these conversations as soon afterward as possible. When quantitative data on opinions and attitudes are presented here they are based on no less than 75 percent of the entire blue-collar work force in the plant at the time those opinions were collected.[23]

I also used a variety of objective sources of data for each worker. These include information on earnings, age, seniority, job preference, grievance and arbitration records, homeownership, the size and value of men's houses, political party identification, and the occupational composition of the areas where workers live. The main source of data on kinship and on jobs taken by workers who quit was informants. During the research some men turned out to be exceptionally knowledgeable and reliable sources. Whenever information obtained from them was cross-checked, it proved to be accurate.

Some of the data for comparing Imperium workers with the white-collar sectors come from my own research. But for much of the comparison I relied on other studies of white-collar workers and on survey data.

The main method I used to collect data on beliefs and attitudes had some important advantages. Men's opinions were gathered in as natural a setting as possible. Many views workers expressed in conversations between themselves. And even when men were talking specifically to me, their opinions—certainly after the first few meetings—were the result of conversations rather than interviews in any formal sense.

Thus it was possible to gauge which issues men talk about spontaneously. For example, contrary to a common image of the blue-collar worker as being uninterested in politics, these men are vitally concerned with political questions, especially the question of who holds power in America. In addition, it was possible to analyze the language and key terms men use. The concept of the "working man" is central to their image of the class structure, so that an understanding of this term is of crucial importance for grasping that image. Indeed, one of my central findings is that workers' views of the class structure are considerably more complex than is usually thought and that conventional methods of investigating that view cannot do so satisfactorily. Further, the method I used made it possible to explore the informal, less open aspects of workers' lives. Many blue-collar workers inhabit and are familiar with two worlds, both at work and in the domestic setting. At work there is the official version of how the job is done. The actual version of what takes place workers share among themselves but not with management, and usually not with supervision. Despite my generally good relations with the men, it was two years before they began to tell me how work in automated plants is really performed. In their residential life, too, many workers inhabit in part a secret or semisecret world, for a number of their most important leisure activities are of doubtful legal or moral status. These include various forms of gambling, social drinking, and sometimes "womanizing." The absence of any discussion of these two informal worlds makes for a certain flatness in many of the accounts of blue-collar workers on the job and at home.

I would, of course, have discovered much sooner how work in automated plants is really performed had I taken a job as a chemical operator. Not doing so was at first a practical matter. The research began in late 1974, at the same time as the worst economic recession in America since the 1930s. Almost all chemical plants in the region were working a shortened workweek, and some were laying men off. In this climate the chance of obtaining a job was minimal.

Yet for this kind of study working in the plant would not have been the best way of collecting information. I would have been confined in my observations to the area where I worked. I would have had no natural reason to wander around the entire complex, still less to pose the continuous stream of questions I asked workers throughout this study. Nor would I have been able to analyze grievance records or talk with management and supervision outside my work area. Finally, the length of my stay would have been limited. A researcher who takes a job in a plant to gather data is unlikely to be able to spend more than a year in such a total commitment of time and effort. And once the plant has been left there is no legitimate reason to return for more information. I was fortunate enough to find a management that allowed me free access for over six years. In this sense the collection of data was a continuous process. As the writing of this study was progressing, new questions constantly occurred, and I was able to collect the evidence for answering them without difficulty.

Part of my research took place in the plant and in the tavern across the road, where many workers drink and where the local union holds monthly meetings as well as celebrations such as retirement parties. But I also spent considerable time with men in their homes, in various taverns, on social outings such as visits to friends and relatives, fishing trips, football and baseball games, trips to the racetracks, and outings to New York City. I knew the wives of most workers from the annual Christmas party and other social occasions, and some I came to know well.

This study concentrates on one group of workers, but I spent much time doing more general fieldwork. I lived for a year in a section of Elizabeth close to Imperium and also spent long periods in the surrounding townships such as Linden, Roselle, Roselle Park, Rahway, Clark, Piscataway, and Woodbridge, from which many men now commute to work. This was important, for, given the decline of occupational communities that has accompanied the rise of the automobile, a researcher who wants to study the modern working class can no longer confine his attention to a single residential area.

Part 1
Life outside Work

1

The Residential Setting

Among the most striking features of the United States is the high rate of home-ownership. Back in 1906 Werner Sombart drew a contrast with his native Germany: "A well known fact . . . is the way in which the American worker in large cities and industrial areas meets his housing requirements: this has essential differences from that found among continental-European workers, particularly German ones. The German worker in such places usually lives in rented tenements, while his American peer lives correspondingly frequently in single-family or two-family dwellings." By 1975, three-quarters of all AFL-CIO members owned houses.[1]

Yet even before rising interest rates in the late 1970s made purchasing a first home harder, some writers discounted much of the social and political significance of homeownership. They argued that residential America is clearly divided by occupation, into blue-collar and upper-white-collar ("middle-class") areas. In particular they claimed that post–World War II suburbia is divided this way. Thus Richard Hamilton concluded from a review of census data that: "There are not enough 'middle-class' suburbs to allow the assimilation of any significant portion of the blue-collar ranks . . . most of the working-class suburbanites are located in working-class suburbs. The dominant orientations there . . . are quite different from those in the middle-class suburbs." Bennett Berger studied auto workers in a new California suburb and came to the same conclusion.[2]

These are critical issues for class consciousness and class conflict. If blue-collar workers live in their own areas, separate from the middle class and with limited chances for residential mobility, then they are likely to develop a working-class consciousness or strengthen an existing one.

This chapter considers these questions. It examines the kinds of houses workers inhabit (Is there a distinction between a working-class and a middle-class house?), and it examines the class and racial composition of the region and of the various areas where Imperium workers live (Are these working-class or middle-class areas?). A number of parts of the region bear on this question. Places where Imperium workers live include pre– and post–World War II residential and industrial suburbs. Other pertinent areas are the old port of Elizabeth, where many of the parents and grandparents of Imperium workers first settled, and the small number of very expensive areas in the region for "the rich."

Industrial History

Chemical production now dominates the industrial economy of New Jersey,[3] but the modern economic growth of the area was triggered by oil refining. In 1878 a group of domestic refinery owners, desperate to escape Standard Oil's grip on the refining and transportation of oil, began construction of a pipeline from Pennsylvania to the Reading Railroad farther east. Standard responded by building a line right to the North Jersey coast (the Bayonne refinery). Not to be outdone, the independent refiners constructed another pipeline, this time to their own refineries at Bayonne. Abroad, Standard's exports to Europe faced increasing competition from Russian oil. Under pressure to cut costs, in 1909 Standard began production at the Linden refinery, the first United States refinery to use continuous process (rather than batch) methods of distillation.

One result of these battles was the creation of a large number of jobs for refinery workers. The work force, at first mostly German and Irish, in the 1880s and 1890s consisted increasingly of Eastern Europeans—Poles, Russians, Slavs, Hungarians— and Italians. The managers of the refineries had a preference for Eastern Europeans because they were less inclined to industrial militancy than the Irish or English. And most of the jobs in a refinery consisted of unskilled, laboring work. As a history of Standard Oil put it: "Many of these men came straight from Ellis Island to the Bayonne and Bayway (Linden) yards, newly arrived immigrants being preferred because they were docile and not particularly inclined to strike. Slaves were regarded as particularly tractable and efficient in the performance of unskilled tasks."[4]

The labor force at Imperium reflects this period of immigration. Fifty-eight percent are of Polish, Austrian, Czechoslovakian, Hungarian, Rumanian, or Russian origin, and another 8 percent are Italian. Most of the rest are German, Irish, or English. There are two blacks and two Hispanics (see table A1, in the appendix).

Thus most of the men at Imperium were born into the working class. Table 2 shows the main occupations of their fathers. The largest group worked as operators, often in the refinery, or ran drill presses or cranes. The second largest group were

Table 2   Main Occupation of Workers' Fathers

Occupation	Percentage ($N = 90$)
Operator	30
Craftsman or mechanic	25
Own business	22
Laborer	19
Unemployed	3

Source: Fieldwork.

craftsmen—plumbers, carpenters, joiners, iron workers. A third group were labor-ers. Together these working-class occupations account for 74 percent of the total.

Twenty-two percent were self-employed, most in their own businesses. Usually the economics of these operations were too fragile to afford the sons a living. One man had owned a barbershop in which his sons worked for a while, but "during the depression guys couldn't afford to be shaved." Two men owned taverns that closed when a new highway separated them from their customers. Another man was a comedian.

Since their families lived in the area and they were raised there, many workers are part of dense kin and friendship networks. These are essential assets in the job market. To be hired at Imperium, and at many of the plants in the area, the most important condition is to know someone already there. Workers take it for granted that this is how good jobs—in refining or chemical plants or construction or the docks—are obtained. This is why kinship relations at Imperium are close and intricate. Out of a total blue-collar work force of 121 there are twenty-three brothers and seventeen brothers-in-law. Ten men are cousins, twelve fathers or sons, and six uncles or nephews (table 3 and fig. 1).[5] Kin relations also extend into the white-collar work force. Two workers have brothers or brothers-in-law in supervision, one has a brother-in-law who is a company salesman, and two married Imperium secretaries.

The Main Residential Areas

The Old Port

Some of the immigrant parents and grandparents of Imperium workers settled in cities such as Newark and New York, or in places like Scranton, Pennsylvania. But most first settled in the port section of Elizabeth, which contained many of the city's older factories, including a huge Singer sewing machine complex (map 2).

The houses in this port area are small, row houses or detached, on lots generally 25 or 30 feet by 100 feet but sometimes less (plates 1 and 2). As was common in

Table 3   Kin Relations among Workers

Type of Relation	Number	Percentage of Blue-Collar Work Force ($N = 121$)
Brother	23	19
Brother-in-law	17	14
Father/son	12	10
Cousin	10	8
Uncle/nephew	6	5
Total of workers related in at least one of these ways	45	37

Source: Informants and fieldwork.

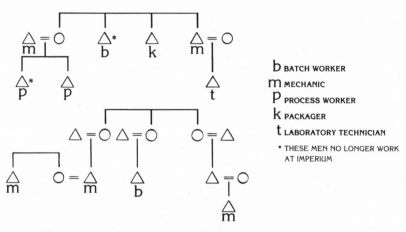

b BATCH WORKER
m MECHANIC
p PROCESS WORKER
k PACKAGER
t LABORATORY TECHNICIAN
• THESE MEN NO LONGER WORK
  AT IMPERIUM

Fig. 1. Two of the more intricate kin networks among workers.

industrializing America, most new immigrants rented rooms in someone else's house. They lodged or else they boarded, with the wife of the homeowner cooking and cleaning for them.[6]

The old port of Elizabeth is now a decaying ghetto, like many in inner-city America. It is inhabited mostly by blacks and Hispanics. No Imperium workers live here any more. Many of the houses are run-down and dilapidated, most industry has closed or moved away, and the huge container port to the north, developed in the 1950s and 1960s, has ended the economic role of the old port. Of the immigrants from Eastern Europe and the earlier Irish and Germans who once dominated the area, only a few remain, and these are mostly elderly.

An adequate discussion of the class structure of these inner-city ghettos, and of other areas in the region, must involve both their actual class composition and the way people perceive that composition. Census data reveal the actual composition of the region. The 1980 census divides the area covered by map 1 into almost three hundred tracts (small subdivisions) and provides data on the occupations of those living within each tract. The category "managerial and professional specialty occupations" comes close to the notion of the upper-white-collar sector used here. In the next few paragraphs, "upper white collar" or "middle class" refers to this category. The combination of two census categories comes close to the idea of blue-collar workers used in this book. These categories are "precision production, craft, and repair occupations" and "operators, fabricators, and laborers." In the next few paragraphs "blue collar" or "working class" refers to the combination of these categories.[7]

Table 4 sets out the occupational composition of selected areas in the region. In general, the percentage of blue-collar residents decreases with distance from the city. Inner-city black and Hispanic areas, such as the old port of Elizabeth, contain the highest average proportion of working class (53 percent), followed by the older industrial suburbs inhabited by some Imperium workers (46 percent), post–World

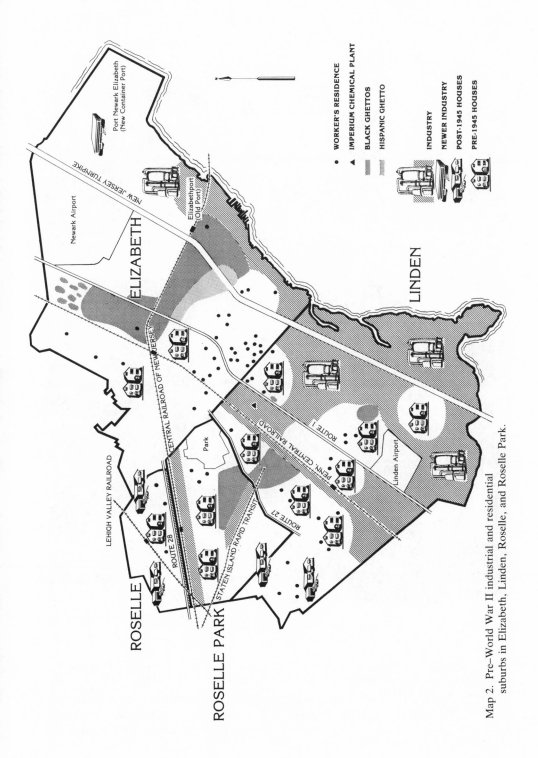

Map 2. Pre–World War II industrial and residential suburbs in Elizabeth, Linden, Roselle, and Roselle Park.

Plates 1 and 2. Houses in the old port of Elizabeth, area of first settlement for many of the parents and grandparents of Imperium workers.

War II automobile townships inhabited by other Imperium workers (30 percent), and the small number of places such as Princeton Township, Colts Neck, and parts of Westfield and Scotch Plains with a reputation for containing the very wealthy (12 percent). By contrast the percentage of middle-class residents increases with distance from the city, from 10 percent in inner-city black and Hispanic areas to 44 percent in the very wealthy areas.

Table 4 Class (Occupational) Composition of Employed Residents in Selected Areas of the Region

Section of the Region	Average Percentage Upper White Collar	Average Percentage Blue Collar
Inner-city black and Hispanic ghettos[a]	10	53
Tracts inhabited by Imperium workers in Pre–World War II industrial suburbs of Linden and Elizabeth[b]	15	46
Tracts inhabited by Imperium workers in areas developed by the automobile after World War II[c]	23	30
Areas with a reputation for containing many wealthy, high-status persons and a large number of custom-built houses on two-thirds of an acre of more[d]	44	12

Sources: Company directory of addresses; census data, 1980.

Note: One-way analysis of variance, on each column, yielded significant F statistics ($p < .001$).

[a]These include the twenty-one heavily black or Hispanic tracts in Elizabeth, Linden, Roselle, Plainfield, Union, and Perth Amboy.

[b]A total of fifteen tracts.

[c]These include a total of thirty-two tracts or undivided townships in Woodbridge, Union, Clark, Cranford, Rahway, Garwood, Piscataway, Scotch Plains, Westfield, Staten Island, Edison, South Amboy, North Brunswick, Old Bridge, Union Beach, Hazlet, Manchester, Toms River, and Lacey.

[d]These include the most expensive sections of Scotch Plains, Plainfield, Summit, Piscataway, and Westfield and all of Princeton Township, Rumson, Little Silver, and Colts Neck—a total of fifteen tracts or townships.

Yet Imperium workers do not view the inner-city areas with the highest proportion of working class and the lowest proportion of upper white collar as working class. Instead, and like most people in the region, they see them as black or Hispanic ghettos. This underlines the danger of relying on the perceptions of those who live in the region to characterize an area without considering census data.

Preautomobile Industrial Suburbs

Thirty-four percent of Imperium workers live within two miles of their jobs, and most of this group are in the industrial suburbs of Elizabeth and Linden (table 5 and map 2). These suburbs are areas of second settlement for Imperium workers. They developed on the edge of the old port area during the late nineteenth century and the

Table 5   Distance of Residence from Imperium

Distance from Imperium	Percentage ($N = 122$)
Within two miles	34
Two to four miles	20
Over four miles	46

Source: Company directory of addresses.

first half of the twentieth. In addition to chemical plants and the oil refinery, they contain a variety of plants. For example, Phelps Dodge produces copper rods, and a large General Motors plant assembles Cadillacs.

Such industrial suburbs were a common feature of the economic growth of the period.[8] They were typically on the outskirts of existing urban areas, for only there were there available the large amounts of space required for new industries such as steel, oil, chemicals, and automobiles. Around these factories, developers and companies built housing for the more privileged of the labor force, who could live close to work. Streetcars allowed others to commute from the port area, and some walked or cycled.

Imperium workers who live in the industrial suburbs of Linden and Elizabeth no longer walk to their jobs. Highways built after World War II have cut off Imperium, and many other plants, from the residential sections, making them inaccessible except by lengthy detours.

These pre–World War II industrial suburbs are typical of areas that outsiders often think of as "working-class neighborhoods." But those who live there are less certain. Indeed, social scientists commonly ask respondents about their class identity—"Are you working class or middle class?"—but they seldom ask them about the class identity of their place of residence—"Do you view the area you live in as working class or middle class?"

Imperium workers sometimes refer to these areas in ethnic terms—for instance, as Polish or Italian—for as areas of second settlement they often contain large concentrations of ethnics. And workers sometimes explain, if asked, that the residential sections of Elizabeth and Linden around the refinery and chemical plants contain a large number of Exxon employees. But few stress occupational segregation as a defining characteristic of these areas, and they rarely refer to them as "working class" or "working men's" districts.

This is understandable, for one in six or seven of the employed residents is upper white collar (table 4). There are teachers, social workers, small businessmen, store owners, and a few local doctors. There is even a contingent—certainly only a handful, but a visible handful—who, dressed in business suits and carrying briefcases, wait each morning on the main streets for the express bus that takes them to office jobs in New York City. (The recent tendency for professionals and managers to view some such areas as fashionable is another reason for workers not to see them as "working class.")

Sixty-nine percent of Imperium workers who live within two miles of their job are homeowners. Most of their houses are modest, though detached and larger than those in the old port area. They stand on lots that average 41 feet by 112 feet (see plate 3 and table A3).

Homeownership

Homeownership is widespread among Imperium workers. Seventy-seven percent own their homes, and another 12 percent live in houses owned by their fathers, fathers-in-law, or brothers (table 6). Marriage usually leads to homeownership. All but two of the married workers over age forty-five own their homes. The younger married men who pay rent do so, in almost all cases, because they cannot yet afford to buy houses. The remaining renters are single—young men, bachelors, widowers, or the divorced.

Homeownership is a major goal, a rarely questioned ambition. And this goal, once achieved, is seldom regretted. Workers associate a variety of benefits with homeownership. There is the freedom to do as they please without the restrictions a landlord might impose. There are the pleasures associated with space and privacy. But when men talk about homeownership it is the economic advantages, in particular the difference between what they paid for their houses and the present market value, that most often comes to mind.[9]

For these men residential property is the most important way of saving, accumulating, and inheriting wealth. Few workers deal in stocks, shares, or securities. Some do have savings accounts. But the regular mortgage payments are an important form of saving, and a house is a solid asset whose value, in these men's experience, is prone to rise. If their parents owned houses, they were almost always the most valuable

Plate 3. Pre–World War II houses in the industrial suburb of Elizabeth.

Table 6   Ownership Status by Distance from Imperium

	Percentage			
Ownership Status	Less Than Two Miles (n = 42)	Two to Four Miles (n = 24)	More Than Four Miles (n = 56)	All (N = 122)
Homeowner	69	79	82	77
Living in home owned by father, father-in-law, or brother	21	12	7	12
Paying rent	10	8	12	11

Sources: Company directory of addresses; property atlases for Union, Middlesex, Monmouth, and Ocean counties; fieldwork.

pieces of property they had to pass on to their children. It is partly because of its central place in their financial situation that most workers are willing to spend considerable amounts of their spare time making repairs or improvements on a house.[10] After their job it is the dominant economic fact in the lives of most workers. The following comments are illustrative.

A worker in his mid-thirties—a second-generation Pole whose father had been a welder in Elizabeth:

> When I was growing up we lived in those flats over there [on the fringe of the port area in the Italian section of southeast Elizabeth]. In the winter all we had was two kerosene heaters, so we froze. And in the summer we were on the third floor and the sun came right in and we roasted.
> I was determined to get my own house. When I was twenty-one I bought a house in Elizabeth for $16,000, and when I was twenty-four a house in Woodbridge for $18,000. Now it's worth $60,000. [In the following paragraphs, workers' estimates of the current values of their homes refer to the period 1975–76; during the next five years values continued to rise sharply, nationwide by 59 percent.]
> The other guys are the same. Most of them lived in apartments when they were growing up. They wanted homes.

A second-generation Polish worker:

> Buy a house. The sooner you do it the better. If you get too old it's too late. I've got a house in Piscataway. I paid $15,000 for it and now it's worth $65,000. And my cousin bought a ranch house in Edison and now it's worth $100,000—mind you, he put in $10,000 in improvements. And even if the value doesn't go up, even if it falls, you always have the house and if you want to retire and move somewhere else you can sell it and have the money—either buy a smaller house or rent a place. But you've always got the money.

A younger, married worker:

> Everyone above age thirty-five is wealthy here [in the plant]. They have
> $50,000 homes. No, I rent. I haven't made it yet.

The purchase of their first homes represented a watershed in most men's
economic position, a major step forward. Many workers tell vivid stories that
illustrate the drama, excitement, and risk associated with raising the cash for the
down payment. One man, for instance, saw this as the acid test of true friendship:

> I count myself lucky. I have three real friends. You know how you can
> tell? When you need money. I borrowed $1,500 from George Test to
> buy my first house in Elizabeth. It was Anne [his wife] who brought up
> the topic with George. He [George] said, "When d'you need it?" and I
> said, "tomorrow," and the next day he came round and he had it all in
> $10 bills! That's a real friend. Five years later he came to me. He
> needed $500 and I gave it him.

A theme often connected with raising the cash for a house is the entry, or reentry, of
the wife into the labor market. For instance, a worker who now lives in Hazlet:

> After the service [Korea] I didn't have nothing. I didn't have enough to
> buy a piss pot. My wife and I were living rent free with my mother-in-
> law. I said to my wife, "You want to live in a house? OK, you go out to
> work for a year and we'll get a house." So she went out to work and
> after one year we had $1,500 to put down, and we bought a house in
> Hazlet. The house cost $12,500 and now it's worth $60,000!

This account needs qualifying, in three ways. First, a very small number of men
do reject homeownership. The two married workers over forty-five years old who
paid rent gave as a reason not having to bother with the physical chores of maintaining a house. As one put it:

> With a house there's all the maintenance to do, taking out the garbage
> and mowing the lawn and cutting flowers; in winter shoveling snow and
> putting down salt on ice, and if someone slips on your ice they'll sue
> you!

A second caveat about the goal of homeownership concerns property taxes.
Almost every worker who owns a home is concerned about rising property taxes.
One, in his mid-fifties, commented angrily:

> Yes, I'm sorry I bought a house. My [property] taxes went up $500 this
> year. I'd be much better off paying rent. It's ridiculous. And I don't
> even use the public schools. My kids went to parochial school, so I'm
> paying twice.

Yet despite widespread unhappiness about the level of property taxes, only one other homeowner said he regretted buying a house.

A third qualification concerns the difficulty of acquiring a first house. This has varied over time, being easier for the generation who received cheap GI mortgages after World War II and much harder for the current cohort faced with high interest rates. Younger Imperium workers who want to buy houses face serious problems. Will homeownership remain a dominant goal among the better-paid working class?

In part this depends on the future cost of houses and mortgages. Yet there are a number of reasons to expect homeownership to remain an important aim even if interest rates stay high over a long period. First, owning a home can be scaled down to less expensive forms. For instance, a row house ("town house") or even a cooperative apartment (which has many of the financial characteristics and advantages of a house) may partially replace the freestanding single-family home as a goal. Indeed, for these reasons builders are already constructing a much higher proportion of town houses in newer developments.[11] (Compare how, with the closing of the frontier in the nineteenth century and the ending of homesteading, the desire to own a single-family, detached house itself in part replaced the desire to own a small farm.)

Second, the current high price of housing most hurts those seeking to buy their first homes. Those who already own property and wish to move can use the increased revenue they obtain from selling their old houses to offset the high cost of a new purchase. A large proportion of the blue-collar working class already own homes, and this includes many younger workers in their thirties and forties.

Third, individual and family effort and sacrifice can increase a worker's ability to raise the cash for a down payment and to finance the mortgage payments on a first house. A man can work overtime or take a second job; his wife can work; they can postpone having children for several years; they can avoid paying rent during the first stage of marriage by living with parents or close kin; and kin or friends may contribute to the down payment by gift, or mortgaging their own houses.[12] Almost all the older Imperium workers who bought homes in an easier housing market used at least one of these methods of boosting their purchasing power. In a tougher housing market workers can use more of them, and they can use each one more extensively. For instance, they may live longer with parents or obtain increased financial help from their families. Using these means, a few of the younger Imperium workers managed to buy their first houses during the current period of high interest rates. This meant increased effort and sacrifice. Yet such effort and sacrifice makes the goal, once achieved, even more satisfying. For these reasons, even if mortgage rates stay high for several years, homeownership is likely to remain an important goal, though in a scaled-down form and achieved by a smaller proportion of workers than in the past.

Preautomobile Residential Suburbs

Other Imperium workers, again mostly homeowners, live in townships such as Roselle, Roselle Park, and Cranford (map 2). These are "residential suburbs," mostly also developed before World War II. Their growth as residential areas was spurred in the nineteenth century by the railroad, which gave wealthy commuters access to commercial and financial centers such as Elizabeth, Newark, and New York City. As a result, they contain some very large older houses. Later, starting about the last quarter of the nineteenth century, the streetcar made them accessible to middle-income persons and triggered the construction of large numbers of moderately priced detached houses. By World War II the shape of these townships was largely fixed—primarily residential and centered on a railroad station and a main thoroughfare for the streetcar, usually running parallel to the railroad.[13]

Most of the houses owned by workers who live here, and the lots they stand on, are similar to those in the industrial suburbs, though slightly larger (the lots average two or three feet wider and eight or ten feet longer; see table A3).

Automobile Suburbs: Industrial and Residential

Almost all Imperium workers organize their lives, including the decision where to live, on the assumption that they will own cars. The only workers without autos are the very few who are either physically unable to drive (one man, for example, has arthritic legs) or whose licenses have been revoked (usually for drunken driving). Even these men still commute to work by car, driven by their wives or riding with fellow workers.

In the 1920s and 1930s commuters in America used autos mostly to help them reach other forms of transport such as the railroad and streetcar. Residential and industrial developments that assume the wide availability of cars began to emerge only after World War II and were triggered by the construction of major highways.[14] The largest group of Imperium workers (46 percent) live in such areas, which are typical of the suburbanization of the period. These workers are more than four miles from Imperium, scattered widely to the south and west around the region (map 1). Most are within twenty miles of work, but a few (five) live fifty or sixty miles to the south, near the shore.

Examples of such auto townships, developed in the 1950s, 1960s, and 1970s, are Edison, Piscataway, and Franklin along Interstate 287 and Old Bridge, Marlboro, Matawan, and Lacey along the Garden State Parkway. Until 1945 and often much later these were mostly rural areas, with small and scattered village settlements. Now their shape bears the impress of the automobile, for they are decentralized, without a dominant "downtown" area. Typically, city hall, usually renamed the "municipal complex," is a newish, sprawling structure surrounded by a large parking lot and hard to reach except by car. If the area contains a shopping mall, that may function as a quasi-center, but encircled by large tracts of parking lot, the mall is not the kind of center the old business district was (plate 4).

Like the areas developed before World War II, these automobile townships range from mostly residential to a mixture of residential and industrial. Some, such as Old Bridge, consist of section after section of development housing (map 3). Others, such as Woodbridge, Edison, Piscataway, and Franklin, contain much

Plate 4. Woodbridge Mall.

housing but also have large sections of newer industry, especially corporate head-quarters, research complexes, office-dominated activities—notably sales and insur-ance—and light industry such as warehousing, assembling, and packaging (map 4).

Most Imperium workers who live more than four miles from work live in such townships. The rest who live more than four miles from work inhabit hybrid townships whose growth was split. As a result of the railroad and streetcar, about half the area was built up before World War II, and in the 1950s and 1960s the automobile triggered the development of the other half where Imperium workers now live. Examples of such townships are Rahway, Clark, Scotch Plains, and Westfield.

How about the class composition of these suburbs? The main problem with the view that they are divided by class is that it ignores the mechanism for distributing housing. It is above all income level (and wealth) that explains the allocation of houses and apartments in America. With the important exception of blacks and those who may resemble them (notably some Hispanics), houses are sold and apartments are rented to those who can afford them.

Yet income level cuts across the distinction between blue- and white-collar workers. Better-paid members of the blue-collar working class earn as much as, or more than, the less-well-paid white-collar workers. In 1981 the average income of Imperium workers was $20,730, of blue-collar auto workers $20,520, and of miners $20,622. This was well above the average ($13,359) for clerical workers, approached the average for accountants ($22,027), and exceeded the average for retail managers ($19,038) (see table 7).[15] When it comes to competing in the market to buy a house or rent an apartment, a teacher, salesman, or small store owner whose annual income in 1981 might have been about $21,000 is in a position similar to that of a blue-collar worker with the same income. And a blue-collar worker whose wife has a full-time job can equal the purchasing power of a junior engineer, accountant, or manager

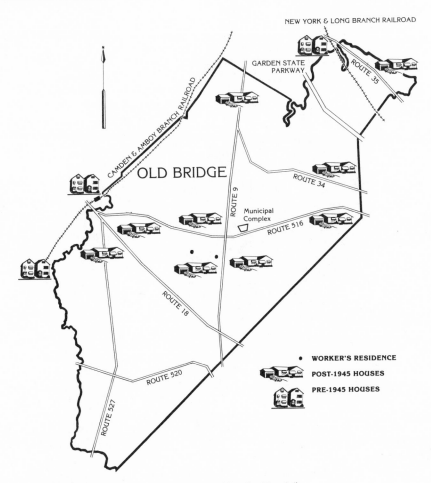

Map 3. Post–World War II auto suburb of Old Bridge (residential).

whose wife stays home. Thus there are strong reasons to expect many post–World War II suburbs to consist of a mix of occupations.

Census data confirm this, for in over two-thirds of the tracts in these auto townships where Imperium workers live the proportion of working class varies from 18 percent to 45 percent, and so does the proportion of middle class.[16] Tracts inhabited by Imperium workers have an average of 30 percent working class and 23 percent middle class.

To *insist* that such areas are definitely and visibly working class is unconvincing, and it is noticeable that Berger and Hamilton's view that they are rests on additional, and questionable, arguments.[17] Yet census data alone cannot settle the matter, for such data cannot determine what degree of imbalance between occupations makes an area "blue collar" or "middle class."

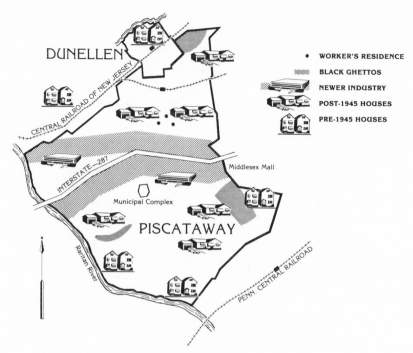

Map 4. Post–World War II auto suburb of Piscataway (residential and industrial).

The central question, rarely asked in other studies, is How do blue-collar workers view the areas they live in? Most Imperium workers definitely see most of these auto townships as occupationally mixed rather than as "working class" or "middle class." This is understandable. When the proportion of upper white collar rises about 18 percent, as it usually does in such areas, then a blue-collar worker is very likely to have an upper-white-collar neighbor (assuming each homeowner has at least five, and more likely seven or eight, close neighbors, one or two on each side and three or four across the street).

Typical are the neighbors of a worker who lives in Rahway. The men include three blue-collar workers (one delivers for a bakery, another works in a factory, and a third is an electrician), an independent truck driver who owns his rig, three small businessmen (a storekeeper, a gas station owner, and a restaurant owner), a schoolteacher, and a real estate agent. The women are mostly clerical and secretarial workers, but there are also a teacher and a beautician. Also typical are the neighbors of a worker who lives in Woodbridge. The men consist of three blue-collar workers, a maintenance supervisor at Newark airport, two small businessmen, and a salesman. Again, the women are mostly in clerical and secretarial jobs, but one is a nurse and another is a teacher.

As a result, there is little reason for a blue-collar homeowner to view these areas, in many of which they or their friends live, as working class. There is if anything even

Table 7   Average Annual Earnings of Selected Blue- and White-Collar Workers, 1981

Occupational Group	Earnings (dollars)
Upper white collar	
Professionals	22,979
Engineers	28,016
Computer specialists	22,882
College teachers	21,061
Accountants	22,027
Managers	24,269
Retail trade managers	19,038
Lower white collar	
Clerical	13,359
Blue collar	
Petrolem refining	23,665
Imperium	20,730
Auto workers	20,520
Mining	20,622

less reason to view them as (occupationally) middle class, for workers are in a better position than almost anyone to know that they contain a significant proportion of blue-collar workers. Instead, most see them as occupationally mixed.[18]

The income overlap between better-paid blue-collar workers and many white-collar employees—the basis for the considerable mixture of occupations in these suburbs—is not new. Such overlap goes back to the nineteenth century. Writers who argue that, despite such income overlaps, residential America was divided by occupation before World War II tend to point to transport needs as the explanation. Although some blue-collar workers could afford to live in white-collar areas, their choices were limited by the need to get to work, by foot, bicycle, or tram. They had to live close to work or to public transportation.[19]

This may explain residential division by occupation in an era when the labor force depended on public transportation, but since World War II workers' widespread ownership of cars has meant that their choice of where to live is no longer limited in this way. (There are, of course, blue-collar workers whose income does not permit them to buy cars. This most poorly paid section of the working class is still dependent on public transportation, which will affect their choice of where to live.)

Houses

People who believe most post–World War II suburbs are clearly divided by class often think they can distinguish a "working-class" from a "middle-class" house. Thus it is important to consider the kinds of houses Imperium workers live in, to see if this distinction is viable.

There are a small number of mobile homes in the region, mostly concentrated in trailer parks (plates 5 and 6). These represent the cheapest form of detached housing. No workers employed at Imperium live in mobile homes.

    The vast majority of houses in the areas the automobile opened up after World War II are "tract" or "development" houses. Builders purchased land, divided it into tracts, and constructed series of houses for sale. Most builders in the region operate on a modest scale, constructing groups of ten, fifty, or a hundred houses at a time. But a few companies, such as Levitt and U.S. Homes, operate on a giant scale, including in one development several thousand houses that by themselves constitute entire townships.

Plates 5 and 6. Mobile homes, the cheapest form of detached housing.

Plate 7. Suburban "town houses" or "row houses."

It is important to consider variations in the size of the tracts, and thus of the houses built on them. There are four main tract sizes. The smallest contain "town houses" or row houses (see plate 7). These tracts are about 20 or 25 feet by 100 feet, like the nineteenth-century row houses in the port section of Elizabeth. Developers did not build many of these town houses after World War II or in the 1950s and 1960s, but, I have pointed out, they are now constructing more in response to the rising cost of land, building, and mortgages.

The remaining three tract sizes all contain detached houses. The smaller tracts of detached houses are about 40 or 50 feet wide and 100 feet long (plates 8 and 9). These are about the same size as those typical of the older, preautomobile industrial and residential suburbs. Medium-sized tracts range from about 60 to 75 feet wide and 100 to 150 feet long (plates 10 and 11). The larger tracts cover about a third of an acre, ranging from 80 to 100 feet wide and 150 to 175 feet long (plates 12 and 13).

Often a builder will include a mix of tract sizes in one development—for instance, mostly small and medium, with perhaps a few large tracts on the corners and a number of row houses. Sometimes builders target a more specific band of the market, constructing on mostly small or mostly large tracts.

The houses of Imperium workers who live in these areas developed by the automobile reflect this variety of tract sizes, except that no workers own row houses. Forty-four percent are built on smaller tracts, 28 percent on medium-sized tracts, and 28 percent on larger tracts, including that of one worker, an exceptional case, who owns a five-acre farm in Piscataway. (As can be seen by comparing plates 12 and 13, there are two main types of house on these larger tracts. One type—plate 13—is much grander than the other. No Imperium workers own the grander type of house.)

Plates 8 and 9. Smaller post–World War II development houses.

The very top of the residential market consists of houses that stand on two-thirds of an acre or more, are architect designed and custom built rather than built by a developer, and are mostly situated in a few exclusive areas (plate 14). Such houses constitute a small fraction of the private detached housing market. Imperium workers cannot afford them, but neither can most other people.

By contrast, the four main types (sizes) of development housing constitute the overwhelming bulk of the private homes built in the region since World War II. They cater to a broad range of incomes and occupations, and the pejorative connotations sometimes associated with the notion of "tract housing" should not obscure this. There is no such thing in post–World War II America as "working-class housing." Instead there are custom-built homes for the rich; there are rental accommodations for the poor or for those who prefer to live in apartments; and there are mobile homes for the poorest of those who can afford houses. For everyone else there are tract houses of various sizes and prices.[20]

Areas for the Rich

A small number of areas, scattered throughout the region in sections developed before and after World War II, contain most of the architect-designed and custom-built houses on two-thirds of an acre or more. These sections are exclusive and very expensive. Examples are the New Dover Road part of Woodbridge, the section of

Plates 10 and 11. Medium-sized post–World War II development houses.

Elizabeth to the southwest of the railroad station, the River Road and Hoes Lane part of Piscataway (which contains a number of fine old mansions), southern Scotch Plains, shading into the southeast of Plainfield, sections of Westfield north of the railroad station, parts of Summit, and most of Rumson, Little Silver, Colts Neck, and Princeton Township.

I pointed out that Imperium workers view those areas containing the highest proportion of blue-collar inhabitants as black (or Hispanic) inner-city ghettos, not as

Plates 12 and 13. Larger post–World War II development houses.

Plate 14. Custom-built houses on more than two-thirds of an acre, the top of the residential housing market.

working class. What about the other extreme, those areas with large architect-designed houses on lavish grounds—areas that also contain the highest proportion of upper-white-collar employees? Imperium workers, and many others in the region, do tend to make a qualitative distinction between such areas and the rest. They view them as exclusive, but the focus of the distinction is income, not occupation. These are seen as the areas where "the rich" live.

Thus Imperium workers do not view the region as primarily divided by occupation into "working-class" areas on the one hand and "middle-class" areas on the other. At one extreme they see certain exclusive areas for the very rich. At the other extreme they see inner-city black or Hispanic ghettos. In between is a vast residential zone that presents workers with a wide range of possibilities depending on how much they can spend and on their taste in house type, lot size, and location. And it is these considerations rather than any single dichotomy between working class and middle class or urban and suburban that informs their perceptions of the region.

Thus the choice of where to live and what kind of property to purchase presents a variety of considerations. Workers think about the price and the age of houses. In general the farther away from urban centers, the newer the houses. In the 1950s and 1960s houses in outlying areas were also cheaper, for land was relatively inexpensive and plentiful there, and building costs were low.

Now economic factors are no longer clear-cut. Building costs have risen sharply, as has the price of land and houses in the outer areas. By 1980 the average market value of the homes owned by workers who lived more than four miles from Imperium was $68,368, compared with $51,738 for the homes of workers in Linden, Elizabeth, and Roselle (table A4). This is a reversal of the relative price of land and houses at the time most workers bought their homes.

Workers also think about the distance of a residential area from their jobs. A ten- or twenty-mile commute is not bothersome, but forty or fifty miles can be a problem in winter and involves getting up earlier in the morning. Older workers are somewhat more reluctant than younger ones to expend energy on a lengthy commute. And for a while the rising price of gasoline was a consideration in determining how far from their place of employment workers will live.

In choosing where to live workers think about property taxes. They are extremely well informed on variations in these taxes by locale. In older urban areas such as Elizabeth or Plainfield taxes tend to be relatively high; in newly developing, outlying areas they are relatively low.

Some workers may move into one of the wealthier townships for the status they believe such a location confers. Thus one man lives in Scotch Plains, another in Cranford, and a third in Westfield. In such cases workers may also be attracted by the idea that these areas contain a higher proportion of upper-white-collar employees, managers and professionals, though this is a question of degree. As I have pointed out, few classify even these areas as middle class by occupation, for they know they contain a significant minority of blue-collar workers.

And of central importance, workers think about the number of blacks and Hispanics in the area. Most are unhappy about being close to a large and expanding inner-city ghetto. As map 5 shows, a number of the workers who live in Elizabeth, Linden, Rahway, and Roselle are close to the centers of black and Hispanic concentration. Although most men are unhappy about living close to an inner-city ghetto, many are not much bothered about living near outlying suburban ghettos that contain a small minority of blacks. Yet some do attach a high priority to being in a township that contains no blacks at all. This, for example, is the main reason 6 workers moved to Clark. As one put it: "Why do I live in Clark? Well, there are no niggers in Clark."

Racial Segregation in the Residential Setting

It is division by race, into black and white areas, that dominates the residential setting far more than division by occupation.[21] And this segregation is accompanied by a mutual fear, for many whites and blacks are clearly wary of straying, at least on foot, into each other's residential strongholds.

Inner-City Ghettos

Most blacks in the region live in older urban ghettos. Whites are well aware of the locations of the nearest inner-city ghetto. (Contrast this with the bewilderment often triggered by asking, "Where does the working class live?")

These inner-city ghettos include most of Newark and much of New Brunswick and Trenton, the old port of Elizabeth and sections southeast of the railroad, the port area of Staten Island, sections of Linden and Roselle, the area surrounding the commercial section of Rahway, large sections of Plainfield that also extend into the northwest part of Scotch Plains, a section of Franklin bordering New Brunswick, and sizable parts of the once-fashionable resort towns of Long Branch and Asbury Park (map 5).

On the edges of these ghettos there are often numbers of Hispanics, and there are large concentrations of Hispanics in Elizabeth and Perth Amboy.

Suburban Black Ghettos

A minority of blacks in the region live in different kinds of ghettos—small settlements within outlying white residential areas. The number of blacks here can vary from a handful to several hundred. Usually these settlements are comparatively old, and may date back to before World War I. In some cases the blacks started out as farmers or farm laborers, and in other cases they worked in local industry or in a service capacity for the surrounding white townships, the women as maids and the men as laborers or mechanics. Originally most of these settlements were isolated from the white residential sections, on the edge of town and separated by areas of undeveloped land. But this isolation decreased as builders purchased more and more land in the region and constructed houses there. Now most are very close to new (post World War II) white single-family housing. They exist as black enclaves in white suburbia (map 5 and plates 15 and 16).[22]

Parts of these black inner-city and "suburban" areas consist of older housing stock that is decaying, but a numerically important section bordering the inner core consists of newer houses, of good quality and well maintained. Some of this housing equals or exceeds the quality of the tract housing constructed after World War II and inhabited by whites. Here live many of the blacks whose income, in a housing market that did not separate black from white, would enable them to live scattered around the region.

There is a third kind of black residential experience, when isolated black families purchase homes in white residential areas. Such families are sprinkled throughout the region. To buy such houses without posing an intolerable threat to their neighbors, blacks usually must be of superior social class—"professionals" of some kind. It is hard to estimate the number of such families, but census data suggest that the vast majority of even black "professionals" live not in such "integrated" situations, but in one of the two "ghettos" (inner-city or suburban), albeit in superior housing within these ghettos.[23]

Each racial group fears the other's residential citadels. Thus almost all Imperium workers speak about Elizabethport, where many were brought up, as having become a very dangerous place in which whites may be mugged, beaten, or murdered. Predominantly black Newark, to the north, is seen as even more dangerous. Some blacks are just as hesitant to enter white neighborhoods on foot. Their caution is understandable. A researcher who inquires about blacks in these areas sooner or later runs across a white homeowner with a story about how he threatened with a shotgun a "nigger" who in some way "stepped out of line." It is true that white homeowners with such stories are a very small minority in the region. But there are

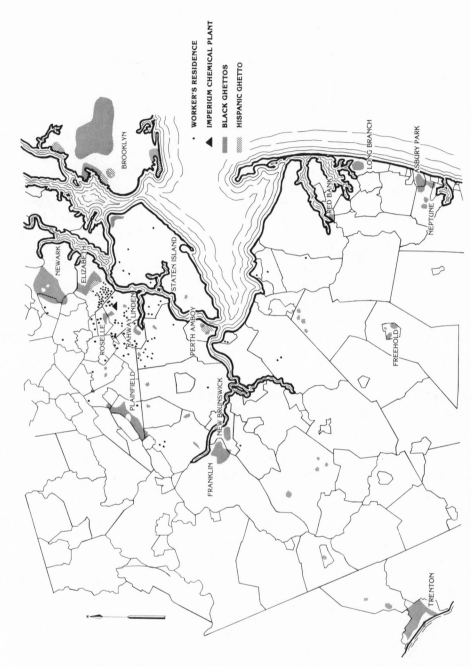

Map 5. Black and Hispanic ghettos in the cities and suburbs.

WORKER'S RESIDENCE

IMPERIUM CHEMICAL PLANT

BLACK GHETTOS

HISPANIC GHETTO

BROOKLYN

NEWARK

ELIZABETH

STATEN ISLAND

ROSELLE

RAHWAY

LINDEN

PERTH AMBOY

PLAINFIELD

NEW BRUNSWICK

FRANKLIN

RED BANK

LONG BRANCH

ASBURY PARK

NEPTUNE

FREEHOLD

TRENTON

certain areas without a single black, and some of their inhabitants are determined to keep it that way. Blacks who enter these places, of which Clark and parts of South Amboy are examples, run a much greater risk.

Physical barriers that keep blacks away from white sections dramatically illustrate the division of the region by race. The ecology of black and white areas, whether inner city or outer suburban, is based on such barriers. The most effective is

Plates 15 and 16. Black suburban ghetto in Piscataway. The black section is a small enclave surrounded by white residential sections.

a large expanse of water. For example, the Arthur Kill River separates blacks in Elizabethport from whites in Staten Island, and the Raritan River separates blacks in New Brunswick from whites in Piscataway. Also very effective is a main highway or a large section of wasteland or farmland (the wasteland can be smaller if it is thickly overgrown with no pathway through it). An example of a main highway is route 22, running through Hillside, which divides blacks to the north from whites to the south.

More minor barriers include sections of light industry, commercial strips or centers, small streams or brooks, parks, and the classic railroad tracks. Railroad tracks are more effective if trains pass regularly than if, as often happens nowadays, they are abandoned or in only occasional use. The effect of these minor barriers is considerably increased when they operate in combination, as they often do through-out the region. In Roselle, for instance, a seldom-used freight railway line, together with light industry and strip commercial development, forms the first line of defense to separate blacks in the southeast from whites in the southwest. A minor thorough-fare operates as a second line of defense against the small number of black home-owners who have penetrated the first line.[24]

In sum, the region divides basically into two housing markets, one for blacks and another, much larger, for whites. Residentially the region *segregates* by race in a way that it manifestly does not do by occupation.[25]

A Second Home and Retirement

Studies of the industrial worker in the 1950s and 1960s show that the drive for homeownership is typical—"getting ahead" outside the plant is usually identified with obtaining a house of one's own. But what happens to a worker's aspirations after his house is bought and all or most of the mortgage is paid off? David Reisman poses, but does not answer, this question in his introduction to Ely Chinoy's classic study of auto workers. Those who play down the importance of residential mobility suggest that at this point workers are stuck. They have exhausted the range of possibilities open to them in the residential setting and are now prone to discontent and class consciousness. For instance, Bennett Berger's study of a group of auto workers who moved from Richmond in California to a new suburb concludes: "In short, these homes in the suburb are for most of the workers the end of the line."[26]

The evidence of Imperium workers does not support such a view. When workers have paid for their houses many think of buying another, though often a modest cottage, as a vacation retreat and for when they retire. The acquisition of a second house is easy to understand given that residential property is the most important way men have of saving and accumulating wealth (plates 17 and 18).

Enough of the older workers have two houses so that this is not a matter of comment or surprise. Men spend an important part of their spare time working on their houses, and when they talk about their hopes for the future they often mention wanting a vacation home to work on too. One third-generation worker of Irish origin had been in the plant since 1939, the date it was founded. He owned two houses, one in Elizabeth and one on the south Jersey shore for his retirement.[27] He summarized the stages men in the plant went through:

> Everyone wanted a home. That was their dream. The average mortgage
> is ten years. After they'd paid that off they bought a second house.
> Then, when their kids got married, some offered to help out with that.
> They got stuck with their kids' mortgages!

Often men finance the mortgage payments on their second home by renting all or a section of it. In this way they become small-scale landlords.

Plates 17 and 18. Vacation and retirement cottages on the Jersey shore.

It is true that only a small minority of workers own two homes. But it is also true that the rest can see that such feats are possible for blue-collar workers.

Until retirement men's residential mobility is limited to a geographic range within reasonable commuting distance of their place of work. But after retirement they can move to the Jersey shore or to another state like Florida or California where the climate is more congenial. Homeownership makes this financially painless. A man can sell his present home and use the proceeds to buy a smaller house or a condominium or a mobile home, often in a "retirement community." Or he can rent an apartment and have the cash from the sale of his house to offset the insecurity involved in leaving friends and kin and moving to a new part of the country (workers who make such a drastic move often have at least one close relative or friend who has been living in the new region for some time and whom, in part, they are joining).

Of the twenty Imperium workers who retired between 1965 and 1980, 40 percent moved to new locations. A number of others seriously considered this, and almost everyone talked about it as theoretically possible, if only to reject the idea at once. Of those who moved, three went to communities on the Jersey shore, one to a farm in Pennsylvania, three to Florida, and one to California. Of these, four moved into houses (one into a farmhouse on four acres of land), two into condominiums in "retirement villages," one into a mobile home in a trailer park, and one into an apartment. Again, the housing market for those who retire presents a range of possibilities that depend on income level and wealth, not occupation.[28]

Once, in the Western world, people died in their homes, among their families and friends. But, as Philippe Ariès has pointed out, dying has increasingly disappeared from the gaze of the family and community, into the institutional context of the hospital and nursing home.[29] This "disappearance of death" takes a special twist in America, where there is a tendency for those of the elderly who can afford it to migrate on retirement. Entering the last phase of their life cycle, many of the aged gather in special communities of their own, sometimes far from their previous places of residence. And the case of Imperium workers suggests this is true of better-paid blue-collar workers as well as upper-white-collar employees.

Conclusion

The region is divided by race much more clearly than by class. Most blacks live in their own sections in a way that blue-collar workers do not. And the residential setting offers Imperium workers the chance for three important kinds of mobility. There is mobility in ownership status, ranging from boarding in someone else's home or renting an apartment to homeownership, perhaps the purchase of a second home for vacation or retirement, and even becoming a minor landlord. There is the social mobility that results from workers' ability to live in areas *they* view as occupationally mixed rather than working class. Finally, there is geographic mobility, from immigrant ghetto to better urban areas to newer outlying suburbs developed after World War II and, on retirement, to other parts of the country such as Florida or California where the climate is kinder to the elderly.

This picture should be qualified. First, it is less applicable to blue-collar workers in modest-paying jobs. Second, workers in pre–World War II industrial suburbs still live in areas that contain many blue-collar employees, often from the same plant (though they tend not to see these areas as "working class"). Further, the residential mobility of Imperium workers should not be exaggerated. There are locations and houses that are beyond their financial reach. And even before the current period of high mortgage rates, accumulating the down payment for a first house could be a long, hard struggle. If mortgage rates stay high for several more years there is a serious question about what will happen to younger Americans (not just blue-collar workers) who once would have bought homes. Yet for workers who already own homes the class structure has, and is seen as having, a certain fluidity in their choice of where and how to live.

2
Leisure

The question of leisure is central to the debate over the degree of overlap between blue- and white-collar lives. Is there a "working-class" leisure distinct from that of the "middle class"? In 1959, in a much-quoted study of buying habits, the Department of Labor suggested that class differences were fading: "The wage earner's way of life is well-nigh indistinguishable from that of his married co-citizens. Their homes, their cars, their baby-sitters, the style of the clothes their wives and children wear, the food they eat, the bank where they establish credit, their days off, the education of their children, their church—all of these are alike and are becoming more nearly identical."[1] Other writers have disputed such a view, modifying it or even claiming that blue-collar leisure is clearly different from that of the middle-class.

There are certain forces that add a distinctive flavor to the leisure lives of workers at Imperium. First, like most blue-collar workers they have a modest level of formal education, typically less than a college degree and in a number of cases no high-school diploma. This has some effect on their choice of leisure interests and on their view of the educational system and of highly educated people.

Second, they have jobs, not careers. Their work is mostly dull, with limited prospects for promotion. As a result they definitely prefer leisure to work. A recurrent theme in the lives of people with careers is the intrusion of work on leisure. They may become so absorbed in work that it displaces much of their leisure time; or they may mix work and leisure to the detriment of the latter (for instance, the "social entertaining" of the business executive). The absence of an absorbing job protects the leisure of blue-collar workers from these consequences.

Third, many of the friends and relatives of Imperium workers are also blue-collar workers. Finally, the pre–World War II suburbs of Linden and Elizabeth continue to provide some basis for a leisure life in an occupational community of blue-collar workers (though, as I pointed out, workers tend not to see these suburbs as "working class").

Yet neither a modest level of education nor a job that is dull and carries limited chances for promotion is confined to blue-collar workers. And though most Imperium workers spend an important part of their leisure with other blue-collar workers, they are all familiar with at least some upper-white-collar people, and they also spend time in settings that are occupationally mixed. In addition, post–World War II suburbs do not provide an occupational community comparable to older industrial areas such as Linden or Elizabeth.

Further, there are other influences on leisure that cut across differences of occupation or education. These include gender, age, position in the marital cycle, and income level. Thus the leisure lives of Imperium workers have distinct features, but these ought not to be overstressed.

The Leisure Culture of Male Friendships

Many of the leisure activities of Imperium workers take place within a culture of male friendships, in which women play little part. The two most prominent features of this culture are social drinking and sports (spectator and participant).

Social Drinking

"Saloons" of a variety of types played a crucial part in the leisure life of urban America, especially for the working classes, during the last quarter of the nineteenth century and at least until World War II (somewhat interrupted by Prohibition).[2] Social drinking, and eating, in a range of taverns, bars, and restaurant-taverns still plays an important part in workers' lives, though much less than during the heyday of the saloon. Many young single men and older workers who have retired spend several hours a day in the tavern. Married workers divide about equally into those who spend almost as much time in the tavern as when they were single and those who enter only occasionally, preferring to go straight home after work.

The number of taverns gives an idea of their importance, though the handful of customers in some indicates that their role has declined. For instance, southern Elizabeth contains one tavern for every seventy adult males. Nor are bars confined to the older, urban regions. They are also numerous in the more recently developed outlying areas, although they are less concentrated and are more likely to be located along main roads. Most workers who enjoy drinking and who live in these newer areas drive to taverns within a few miles of their home in addition to continuing to drink at bars close to their place of work.

The taverns in the region can be divided into two main types. There are occupational bars close to work sites. The social class of the customers reflects the nature of the work site. For instance, taverns close to factories in older urban areas are heavily patronized by blue-collar workers and first-line supervisors.[3]

Within fifty yards of Imperium are six such taverns, serving the various factories close by. One of these occupational taverns, Lesniak's, is directly opposite Imperium and is frequented by many of the chemical workers during lunch and before and after work. The union local, composed of Imperium workers, holds its monthly meetings there, as well as special events such as parties for workers who are retiring.

Customers of occupational taverns or tavern-restaurants in the newer suburban areas are mostly white-collar workers, for the industry there is dominated by offices. These tavern-restaurants tend to be large establishments with spacious parking lots, generous bars, and roomy eating areas with attractive tables. The restaurant section usually has a menu that reflects the broad income range within the white-collar sector. There are cheaper items for those with modest budgets, especially lower-white-collar workers, and there are expensive items for those with more money to spend, especially upper-white-collar managers and professionals. Blue-collar workers who eat lunch in these places tend to sit at the bar, distinctive in their work clothes.

The second main type of tavern is the "neighborhood" tavern, which serves people who live in the immediate vicinity. The customers reflect the class composition of the neighborhood. Those in the older urban areas have higher proportions of blue-collar workers than those in newer suburban sections (plates 19 and 20).

Occupational and neighborhood taverns are the main, but not the only types. There are, for instance, go-go bars throughout the region, catering to a mixture of occupations (plate 21). And there are the fancier restaurants, again situated throughout the region but especially near main highways, to which Imperium workers go from time to time, usually with their wives or girl friends (plate 22). Such restaurants, catering to anyone who wants to have a "night out," serve a variety of occupations and have a visibly classless tone. An outsider can rarely infer the customers' occupations from their attire, for all are dressed to "go out" (casual, casual-smart, or smart, depending on taste). Many young single Imperium workers go to New York City as often as every month. With a group of male friends they visit bars and night spots. Sometimes they take their girl friends with them and, for a special evening, go to the theater (plate 23). Nearly always this means a lavish and

Plate 19. Neighborhood tavern in pre–World War II industrial suburb of Elizabeth.

Plate 20. Neighborhood tavern in post–World War II auto township of Piscataway.

Plate 21. Go-go bar. The customers are a mix of occupations—men in suits and men in work clothes.

Plate 22. A moderately expensive restaurant where residents of the region, of various occupations, go for a night out.

Plate 23. Theater district in New York City.

colorful musical rather than a serious drama. The older married workers also go to New York City with their wives, but much less often (perhaps once a year).

Thus social drinking and eating take Imperium workers through a range of establishments that vary in their class composition. When they drink in occupational taverns outside the plant most of the other customers are also blue-collar workers. When they drink in neighborhood taverns where they or their friends live, the class composition of the customers is more varied. In general, the farther the tavern is from the inner city, the lower the proportion of blue-collar workers and the higher the proportion of upper-white-collar employees. And when workers go out to eat in fancy restaurants or visit New York City, the other customers or spectators are a mix of social classes.

Sports

It is hard to exaggerate the importance of various kinds of sports in the lives of most of these chemical workers. More than half are enthusiastic fishermen and hunters, and this is true regardless of age or marital status. Some belong to clubs. In the fishing season groups of twenty or thirty men from such clubs, well supplied with beer and sandwiches, leave on a rented bus for a weekend in Boston or a day off the south Jersey shore. Hunting clubs organize weekends in lodges in south Jersey or take bear-hunting trips to Maine that last several days (plate 24). Some of these fishing and hunting clubs are run by the taverns, and a few taverns still sponsor football and softball teams. In the football season busloads of men go to games in cities like Pittsburgh and Washington.

Plate 24. The Linden Hunting Club after the annual meeting.

Plate 25. Fishing off the Jersey shore.

Other men prefer smaller groups. Six Imperium workers own fishing boats in which they regularly take groups of three, four, or five fellow workers or friends (plate 25). Often men rent boats. Many workers who hunt make trips with a few friends, usually to Maine. Partly because of their interest in hunting and fishing, men have a tendency to develop a keen interest in gastronomy, for the culmination of a hunting or fishing trip is eating the catch.[4] Some workers are accomplished chefs, exchanging recipes for items like lobster or bluefish.

Younger workers who played football or baseball at school often continue to play, joining local clubs. Few men play football beyond their late twenties, but the active life of a baseball player is longer, especially since men can, and often do, switch to the physically easier game of softball. As men get older they substitute other sports for the more energetic ones of their youth. Golf is rapidly growing in popularity among these chemical workers. There are several fine public courses in the region. Many workers in their mid-thirties and above play, and for a few, especially among the bachelors and divorced, it is a passion that absorbs the bulk of their spare time during the season. Bowling is also fairly popular among workers of all ages regardless of marital status.

Interest in spectator sports is very high. Much time during the evening and on weekends is spent viewing games on television. Men also watch sports live. For basketball they go to Madison Square Garden in New York City (the Knicks) or to the Meadowlands in New Jersey (the Nets). They also go to the Meadowlands to see the Giants play football, or to New York City to watch the Jets (football) or Mets (baseball) at Shea Stadium or the New York Yankees at Yankee Stadium (plate 26). Sometimes a group will take barbecue equipment to a baseball or football game and enjoy a leisurely "tailgate party" in the parking lot before the game (plate 27).

Gambling is an important pastime, often related to sporting events. There are two racetracks within commuting distance—the Meadowlands, an easy fifteen-minute trip from work up the New Jersey Turnpike to the north, and Monmouth racetrack farther south. About 20 percent of these chemical workers go to the races once a week or oftener, usually after work. Playing the numbers is also common. At least 70 percent of the men place bets every day with "runners" at work.[5] Also widespread, and illegal, is betting on the outcome of football, basketball, and

Plate 26. Baseball at Yankee Stadium.

Plate 27. Giants Stadium, New Jersey: a tailgate party in the parking lot before the football game.

baseball games. Large numbers of workers have contacts with a vast network of underground bookies who handle such bets. The legal New Jersey lottery is extremely popular too. Many workers buy several tickets each day at their local stores.

The common observation that blue-collar workers spend a great deal of time watching television is usually taken to imply that their leisure is passive and dull. But much of this television viewing involves watching sports, and it should be understood in this context. Televised sporting events are merely the most passive part of a general interest in sports that is far from passive, takes many forms, and constitutes some of the most important contours of men's leisure life.

Interest in sport tends to cut across class lines. It is true that certain of the activities of Imperium workers, such as playing the numbers, are more frequent among those who are poor or of moderate income than among those who are rich. And some ways of organizing leisure—for instance, large groups of men renting a bus for a fishing trip or to attend a football game—reflect an older style that is historically rooted in the neighborhood life of working-class communities. Further, certain pastimes associated with the very wealthy, such as sailing, are unusual among Imperium workers (although other such pastimes, such as golf, are now common). Yet in other ways the sporting activities of Imperium workers transcend occupation.

The most comprehensive national survey of the way Americans use their time is by John Robinson. His results support this conclusion. Sport in America divides as much by gender as by class (although this division should not be taken too far; women are becoming more involved, as spectators and players, in some sports once confined to men). Sport tends to separate male from female as much as blue-collar from upper-white-collar.[6]

Leisure and Marriage

The previous chapter pointed out that within a few years of marrying workers tend to acquire houses and children. The combination of a mortgage, young children, and a wife who does not work creates financial difficulties for almost everyone. Most men in this situation work as many hours of overtime as they can.[7] One obvious but important change in their leisure is that they have less of it. In addition, there is a pull to stay around the house, especially since the presence of young children obliges parents to spend considerable time at home. If there is any period in a man's life, barring an old age burdened by physical disablement, when his leisure life might be expected to be most curtailed, it is this one. For that reason, studies that concentrate on couples with young children risk mistaking one stage in the life cycle, a stage when leisure is particularly restricted, for the essence of leisure among the working class.

Nowadays the home provides all the physical amenities of the tavern, if not its social attractions. Almost all the houses I visited had large color television sets, usually prominently displayed in the living room. Most men have another set in the bedroom. One family—husband, wife, and four children—have five televisions. Stereo equipment, comfortable sofas and chairs, and dishwashers are practically universal. Most workers have barbecue grills and lawn chairs in their backyard, and a few have raised swimming pools.[8]

Maintaining and improving a house also involves considerable time and energy. It is common for men to allocate half of a two- or three-week vacation to a project around the house. There are routine activities such as gardening and painting as well as special changes and remodeling. Many of the homeowners are involved in a constant series of such projects. In part this is work that must be done and, unlike better-paid employees of the white-collar sector, men cannot afford to hire people to do it for them. But partly men do this work because it is activity they understand and enjoy. Most of the houses they own were originally built by developers in a small number of standard forms. Workers often alter these houses not only to meet their needs when they first move in but also to fit the changing shape of their families. And through friends and kin they are frequently in contact with a network of people, employees or small entrepreneurs, who handle the materials they need for these projects. In this way they obtain special deals. Above all, men maintain and improve the house because of its central place in their efforts to save and accumulate wealth.

Typical is one worker, in his late thirties with several children. During four years he made the following changes to his house. He spackled the walls of his living room and then, two years later, covered them with wood paneling bought in a special deal from a friend who knew a lumber merchant. He sold his sofa and easy chairs and bought replacements. He put new tile on the upstairs bathroom floor and walls, and carpeted the walls of his downstairs bathroom. In the "den" where he keeps the bar and stereo system, he built a "lounging pit" from a design in a popular architecture magazine and covered it with a new carpet. His elder son did the carpentry for the pit, and the carpets for the den and bathroom were fitted by a friend, a chemical worker who had once been employed installing carpets. He installed a decorated door to replace the plain one leading from the den to the garden; and when his dog destroyed the new door, he installed another. Outside he built a formal pathway to his front door, replacing the muddy walkway with steppingstones surrounded by large decorative pebbles and flanked by railroad ties. The entire family spent two days laying the pebbles, which, like the railroad ties, had been obtained from a friend in a special deal. In another deal, involving a friend of his wife's cousin, he purchased a raised swimming pool, which took up almost his entire backyard, and installed it with the help of his sons and two friends. He bought a new barbecue grill to replace the old model, and he constructed a wooden picket fence around the back yard. Future plans include building a roof over the swimming pool (a somewhat speculative idea) and demolishing the partition between the kitchen and dining room. These projects clearly absorb a vast number of hours and considerable creative energy.

Partly because of this growth of the home as a leisure center, and partly because of younger workers' moving to outlying areas, many of the taverns in older, pre–World War II urban areas are not as full as they once were. The tavern remains an important social center, but it has lost its dominance of working-class leisure. Some in the older urban areas have an air of decay—not enough customers and dilapidated furniture. There clearly are now more taverns in the older industrial and residential suburbs of Elizabeth and Linden than demand justifies. Many of their owners are old, and the taverns they run are not likely to remain open after they retire or die.[9]

For young married men children's activities at school can absorb an important part of leisure time. Here too sport is crucial. The men, and sometimes their wives, are often ardent fans of their own children's sporting and sport-related activities. They watch them, usually over the weekend, play on school football, soccer, or baseball teams (plates 28 and 29). This is the most important way workers relate to their children's lives at school. They may be, and usually are, concerned about academic performance, but in this area they often feel out of their depth. It is through competitive sports that men can take a direct interest in school life, an interest that focuses more on sons than on daughters (however many men watch their daughters play sports such as basketball and perform as cheerleaders or play in the school band that provides halftime entertainment at the football game).

The two activities in which husband and wife are most likely to participate jointly, apart from enjoying amenities in the house and events centering on the children at school, are going out to eat and visiting friends and relatives. The older workers often belong to ethnic social clubs such as the Polish National Home or to fraternal orders such as the Knights of Columbus. These usually hold regular dances, and some have dinner dances as often as every week. Several of the older workers and their wives regularly attend these social affairs.

If young children, a nonworking wife, and a mortgage impose certain general constraints on men's leisure, there is still room for considerable variation. Married workers in this study split into two roughly equal groups. There are those who, within the limits just outlined, continue to participate actively in the shared male culture. They drink in taverns, play sports and attend sporting events, fish and hunt, and visit their friends. Nor do they necessarily discontinue liaisons with other women. But the second group of married workers do spend more time with their families. They tend not to stop at the tavern after work or to spend much of their leisure time with male friends from work or the community.

The Leisure Life of Older Workers

As workers get older their leisure life enters a third stage, entirely overlooked by studies that focus on couples with young children. Their children grow up and become financially independent, their wives usually take jobs, and their mortgages are paid off or close to it. This means a dramatic improvement in men's economic situation.[10] Further, at work they have accumulated considerable seniority, which usually means they can bid into more desirable kinds of jobs. And, of crucial importance, they get five or six weeks of paid vacation each year.

At this point men are free to travel, and they do so—with their wives if the marriage is still viable. The most popular vacation spots are Las Vegas and Florida. Some workers fly to Las Vegas three or four times a year. It is common for men whose children have moved to different parts of the country to visit them regularly, perhaps once a year. But workers also vacation abroad. They visit their countries of

Plates 28 and 29. High-school football, Linden township.

Plate 30. Embarking for a cruise from the Forty-fifth Street pier in Manhattan.

origin, or they may return to areas where they were stationed during World War II. Cruises are popular (plate 30). Men may visit the Bahamas or Jamaica, Hawaii or Spain. One worker recently returned from a vacation tour to mainland China. These trips are becoming the newest status symbols. As one man's wife, in her mid-fifties, put it, reflecting on the increasing tendency of older workers to travel: "Trips are the big thing now. People are very jealous of each other. One guy will say, 'I went to Hawaii,' so the next week the other guy will be planning to go on a cruise to the Bahamas or somewhere."

As workers grow older there is also some tendency for the different leisure styles that existed when they had young children to converge. Men who after marriage retained strong links with the male culture may in later life be less attached to that culture. Partly this is because with age they become less vigorous. Active participation in sports decreases, and sometimes men develop physical ailments that hamper their movement. Partly it is because men's male buddies tend to decrease in number. They may die or become seriously ill or move to another part of America. At the same time, the second group—those men whose leisure revolved around home and family—find that their children have grown up; and usually their wives now have jobs.

Social Relations

A primary foundation of the solidarity so characteristic of working-class culture in the past was a common economic insecurity. Ties of friendship and kinship were critical in an era without government unemployment insurance, Social Security, or medical insurance, and with limited or nonexistent pensions, medical insurance, or job security from the company. Such ties provided a degree of protection against the numerous economic catastrophes to which everyone was vulnerable.

Now the network of social relations that provided such support has declined considerably in importance. The development of government welfare and insurance programs (such as Unemployment Insurance, Social Security, Aid to Families with Dependent Children, and food stamps), and company-financed fringe benefits such as medical insurance and pensions, together with a steady income from a stable job, have removed much of the economic rationale for those old relations of cooperation and solidarity. People help each other less, mostly because there is less need to do so.[11]

The financial security of the more privileged sector of the industrial work force should not be exaggerated. Catastrophes such as a plant closure can and do occur. And a worker with young children, mortgage payments, and a wife who stays home is often in considerable economic difficulty. But compared with the period before the mid-1930s, when job security and welfare and insurance programs were minimal, there has been a dramatic change whose main direct effect is the weakening of traditional relations of solidarity and cooperation outside work.

Thus the network of exchange relations between friends, neighbors, and kin plays, and is perceived to play, a much-reduced role. This is apparent, and generally regretted, by workers who still live in the old industrial community as well as by those who have moved to outlying areas. Men complain that "people are more selfish," "neighbors don't help each other the way they used to," "families aren't close anymore," "families don't stick together," "kids go their own way." "kids don't stick with the family," "people have drifted apart."

Of course these traditional exchanges were often unequal and, especially in the context of the family, sometimes suffused with tension, exploitation, and struggles for power. Now greater financial independence makes possible greater social and personal independence. Young people who have left school and cannot find work, or who lose a job, can eke out an admittedly sparse existence on government programs as an alternative to being supported by parents or kin. Parents who retire or are retired from the labor market can live on a pension and Social Security without their children being "forced" to support them.

But while this financial independence has eliminated some of the more obvious sources of interpersonal and interfamilial tensions, it has also eroded an important part of the basis for solidarity between kin, neighbors, and friends.

During the period of this research a number of personal tragedies occurred. For a while one of the best-liked workers, a former union officer, was at home dying of cancer. From time to time men would refer to him with bitterness and regret, for many suspected his sickness was caused by the chemicals to which he, and they, had been exposed.[12] When he died there was sadness in the plant for several days. Men would cluster quietly in groups, grieving over his loss. A collection raised more than $1,000 for his family, and the union sent a lavish wreath to his funeral. But this was largely symbolic—a genuine expression of regret. Most of his long illness had been financed by medical insurance and his company pension.

The father-in-law of another chemical worker was cleaning a machine in the auto plant where he worked. The safety switch jumped, and the machine cut off his hand. On hearing the news, his son-in-law left work and spent several hours at the hospital. He then called the insurance company and began arranging to file a claim. Instead of moving in with him, his father-in-law now collects a disability pension from the government and the company.

Cultural patterns whose major source has faded may still exert their influence long afterward. The working-class homeowner in a newer residential area who sits on his front steps drinking beer with his neighbor is in some respects repeating former patterns. But this social friendliness is not the same as the massive reality of economic interdependence that dominated social relations in the past.

The Structural Bases for Differences in Leisure

Yet there are two forces that affect the leisure lives of these workers—their relatively low level of formal education, and the effects of a job that is mostly dull and carries limited promotion prospects.

The Effect of Education

Blue-collar workers usually lack college degrees and often have no high-school diplomas. This raises a number of points.

Few Imperium workers have much interest in certain pursuits associated with the educational elite and "high culture." These include classical music, ballet, opera, and serious drama, as well as "heavy" reading in literature, art, and the natural and social sciences. For example, though most workers read at least one newspaper every day, these are popular tabloids such as the *Daily News* and *New York Post*, not "quality" papers like the *New York Times*. Their taste in films, on television or at the movie theater, centers on the action oriented—thrillers, spectaculars, and westerns—rather than on films that are more serious, like those of Bergman, or that move at a slower pace, like those of Fellini. And occasional visits to the theater are to spectacular musicals, not sober dramas.

Yet the difference between the cultural pursuits of these workers and those of most college-educated Americans ought not to be overstressed. It is true that educational level is the most important determinant of interest in "high culture." Those with college degrees are more likely than those without to have *some* interest in "high culture." Yet only a minority of even the college-educated population spend *much* of their leisure in these ways. Harold Wilensky studied the cultural interests of men drawn from a variety of occupations. He found that, though only 1 percent of blue-collar workers read a "quality" newspaper every day, only 11 percent of engineers did so either. Even among professors and lawyers, a highly educated group of upper-white-collar workers, only a minority read a "quality" newspaper (42 percent of all professors and 36 percent of all lawyers).[13]

The tendency of blue-collar workers to lack a college education has another consequence. It can lead to a certain defensiveness and to some feeling of unease and inadequacy when faced with highly educated persons and with school personnel. Most workers are sensitive about their lack of formal education. It is one of the topics they are least likely to be candid about. Time and again a man who had said he had a high-school diploma would later reveal that he had dropped out of high school. In general school was a humiliating experience during which most men were classified as "nonacademic." There are exceptions. A few workers did well, especially at mathematics and science. Usually they became mechanics. They either went straight from high school to technical school and then into blue-collar jobs, or they entered the blue-collar labor force and later attended technical school at night. But for most workers, including many of the mechanics, school was a period when their self-esteem was under continual attack.

How did they cope with this? Some simply accepted the school's assessment of their intellect. As one, in his late forties, explained:

> I was a real dummy. When I was at school if we got a question right we
> moved forward a chair in class and if we got a question wrong we
> moved back a chair. I was always at the back.

More commonly men distance themselves from the school's judgment. Sometimes they accept personal responsibility for academic failure but explain that the problem was they did not work hard enough: "I was lazy at school," "I fucked up," "I didn't study," "I wasn't interested," "I should have worked harder." Such explanations, true or false, are clearly easier for a man to accept than is the idea that his intellect is inferior.

But the most frequent way men account for their failure in school is by blaming the curriculum and the teachers. The curriculum was irrelevant and the teachers were inept, malevolent, or exploitative. Consider the following, from a worker in his late forties, a mechanic:

> What was school like? It was horrible, horrible! Those teachers, they
> didn't care. One said to me, "You're going to end up in a factory any-
> way, what are you wasting your time here for?"
>   They [the teachers] were cuckoos. They gave you *Romeo and Juliet*
> to read, and I looked at it and I said, "What is this! What has this got
> to do with me?" I looked on the flyleaf. You know, back then they
> passed books down from one class to the next, so you could see who'd
> had your book two or three years ago. And I saw Joe Smith's name
> from three years ago. I knew he was digging ditches now, so I said to
> myself, "This book didn't do anything for him. What's it going to do for
> me?"

Another mechanic, in his early forties, also had difficulty taking the Shakespearean component of the curriculum seriously:

> I was kicked out [of school]. Why? Because I laughed at *Macbeth*. I
> thought it was funny. I passed the course, but the teacher told me I
> couldn't graduate. I got angry. I told her I'd push her through the wall,
> but she wouldn't let me graduate, so I had to go to summer school to
> graduate.

This experience can impart a certain flavor to men's leisure lives. For instance, there may be tensions as they follow, or attempt to follow, the academic part of their children's schooling. A father who urges his children to study hard but whose own reading is limited to casual perusal of popular newspapers and magazines and light books is sending out double messages, as many children perceive. Further, a number of men's children protest that since their fathers did not study in school, why should they? To this the main logical response is that *if* their fathers had studied harder they would now have better jobs. This entails a continual self-deprecation that few men enjoy.[14]

Thus comparative lack of education imparts a tone to many men's leisure lives. Yet this should be qualified in two ways. First, a minority of workers have avoided being scarred by the educational system (such as some of the mechanics) or have overcome its effects. Second, this effect is not confined to blue-collar workers but is likely to be shared by many of those with modest educational attainment, including most lower-white-collar employees.

The Effect of Work and Work Relations

The second influence on the leisure life of these blue-collar workers is their jobs. For most, except the mechanics, the work itself is uninteresting, as I will argue in part 2. And it is unlikely to lead to promotion out of the blue-collar ranks. Men have jobs, not careers. As a result, work is not a central interest. The difference between work and leisure is clear, as is men's preference for the latter. Many workers compensate for the dullness of their jobs by seeking leisure that is varied and exciting. And they seek friends with whom they can enjoy that leisure: they tend to be "person oriented."[15]

The best evidence for this relation between the nature of their jobs on the one hand and their leisure and friendships on the other is men's drive for leisure *at work*. They enliven the time they spend at their jobs with a vibrant series of (mostly informal) leisure activities, revolving around male friendships. This is the focus of their time and energy within the plant (see chap. 6).[16]

By contrast, work may mar the leisure lives of those for whom it is a central interest, especially those with careers. They may allow work, because of its intrinsic interest or because they wish to further a career, to supplant leisure time, becoming "workaholics." As a manager interviewed in Young and Willmott's study of marriage and the family in England put it: "There is a total commitment to my job. I'd almost say that my work is my leisure." Those for whom work is a central interest may also mix work relations with leisure relations, and this can lead to a decline in the quality of their social life (for instance, the manager who does a great deal of business-related entertaining). Or they may allow work to intrude on and interfere with leisure. Consider in this light these comments from a computer manager: "I quite often get a phone call when I'm sitting at home. . . . If the computer goes on the blink at 10 P.M. they ring up and ask me what the hell they should do. Sometimes I have to go back."[17]

Many of these ways in which work can mar leisure are related to the conventional idea of a career. As a study of couples where both spouses have careers put it: "One usually is expected to be single-minded about pursuing a career, and to subordinate the rest of one's activities to it."[18]

Since they lack absorbing jobs that are part of careers, these blue-collar workers are mostly free from these consequences. They can focus their time and energy on leisure and friendships outside and, if possible, at work. If men do not live for their work, they are more likely to live for their leisure.

Yet having a dull job with few prospects for promotion is not confined to blue-collar workers. It includes part of the lower-white-collar sector (clerical workers and secretaries), and it also includes, though perhaps to a lesser degree, a proportion of those in upper-white-collar occupations such as teachers, accountants, and lower- and middle-level managers who find their jobs of limited interest and who have risen as high as they are likely to. They too tend to focus on friendships at work, (hence, for instance, friendship groups among secretaries).[19]

Further, there are a number of ways a work setting can affect leisure that cut across social class. For instance, there is shift work. Some work sites, including the plant where Imperium workers are employed, operate continuously, twenty-four hours a day, seven days a week. Those employed at such sites must work shifts. Shift work has an obvious impact on social life, for it requires a pattern of work, sleep, and leisure that is different from the dominant pattern in the rest of society. Examples of settings requiring shift work are blue-collar occupations such as oil refineries and chemical plants and police and fire departments, but also white-collar settings such as hospitals (affecting professionals and lower-level professionals such as doctors and nurses as well as nonprofessional employees). Other work settings require extensive long-distance travel, which affects leisure and marital relations. Examples are blue-collar truck drivers and white-collar airline pilots, flight attendants, business executives, and entertainment figures. The effect on leisure of shift work or extensive travel may be as important as the effect of a dull job versus one that is of central interest.

Conclusion

Among Imperium workers, much of what might be called "working-class" leisure results from the following forces. A dull job with limited chance for promotion leads to an emphasis on leisure and friendships at and outside work, to relations that are "person oriented" rather than oriented toward the pursuit of a career. A comparative lack of formal education leads to an unease and defensiveness about education and the highly educated and is associated with lack of interest in "high culture," though the interest displayed by most better-educated persons should not be exaggerated. In addition, many Imperium workers spend important parts of their leisure with other workers, and those in older, industrial suburbs still live in occupational communities close to other workers, which provides some basis for a joint leisure life. (Though this is much less clearly true of workers in post–World War II suburbs. Further, the automobile and government and employer insurance or welfare programs have changed even these older communities.)

These forces impart a flavor to a leisure life that, in other important respects, cuts across occupation and social class. Social drinking in the tavern, watching and playing sports, going out to eat, spending time around the house, raising children and following their progress at school, going to a musical on special occasions, and, especially in later life, traveling; these are activities that clearly absorb the time of many American men including those in upper-white-collar occupations. Robinson's national survey of how Americans spend their time supports this conclusion about the limited impact of occupation on the way people spend their leisure, as do several other studies.[20] This is why the attempt to specify a "working-class" leisure is not easy.

3
Marriage and Family

Modern marriage is distinguished above all by an ideal—that husband and wife should be each other's closest companion as well as sexual partner. As one study put it: "Among the many curious features of modern woman's life is one that would have thoroughly offended St. Paul, bewildered Tristan and amused Don Juan—namely the fact that she is her husband's best friend and he is hers."[1]

Before this ideal became dominant, a person's loyalties and affections were spread over a number of people and objects—for instance, parents and other relatives, friends, fellow workers, the land, animals, God, and the saints. The contemporary view, by contrast, contains the expectation that the nuclear couple and their children should "be the object of a passionate and exclusive love," and that the family and home should be a "place of refuge," a warm shelter from the outside world. This places a heavy burden on the psychic resources of husband and wife.[2]

At the same time, the American family has lost many of its material functions. Once, in an agricultural setting, its male and female members had important productive roles at home. Now paid labor ("work") typically takes place away from the home, which has become the sphere of unpaid and therefore undervalued "housework." Once responsibility for educating the children lay mostly with parents. Now it lies with the school. Once care of the very sick took place within the family. Now it is the domain of the hospital and nursing home.[3]

This is ironic. As the important material aspects of the lives of family members increasingly are handled outside the home, the expectation has grown that their deepest emotional relations should occur within. As a result, the principle of the *modern nuclear family* can conflict with other principles of how to live interpersonal life—for instance, *relations based on work*, and *relations with friends* of the same and of the opposite sex. This often causes problems for husbands and wives nowadays whatever their social class, though occupation and education may influence the form such conflicts take.[4]

This perspective on the modern family implies some similarity between social classes—between marriages of blue- and white-collar workers. So does Mira Komarovsky in her classic study *Blue-Collar Marriage*. She points to differences, but also to similarities, as does Caplow's recent account of families in Middletown. Such is also the view that the marital lives of Imperium workers suggest.

Yet two studies of the marriages of American blue-collar workers stress the way these marriages are unlike those of the middle class. For instance, one begins by asking the reader, assumed to be middle class, to make the imaginative effort to enter an unfamiliar world: "The reader's present life (and family background) are probably far removed from the world in which working-class wives and their families live their daily lives." In a more recent study Lillian Rubin argues that marriages of blue-collar workers are distinct from those of the middle class above all because of the misery that pervades them. They are, as she puts it, "worlds of pain."[5]

Such a view goes too far for the workers in this study. There *are* features of these blue-collar husbands that add a distinct flavor to their marriages. They have somewhat low status as "factory workers" and modest levels of formal education. And they have jobs, not careers. The impact of these features should not be ignored (though, as I noted in the discussion of leisure, they are not confined to blue-collar workers). Yet for a balanced picture it is important to place these distinguishing features in the context of certain similarities between these marriages and those of the middle class.

There are several reasons for the divergence between my findings and studies that stress mainly *differences* between marriages of blue- and white-collar workers. First, men at Imperium represent economically more privileged blue-collar workers. For the same reason their wives too could be expected to have jobs and education above the average for wives of blue-collar workers. My study is designed to consider theories of possible overlap between blue- and white-collar workers, which is why it is appropriate to consider a group of workers at a point in the class structure where overlap is most likely. However, care should be taken when generalizing from their marriages to those of blue-collar workers in inferior jobs.

Second, studies that stress the difference between "blue-collar" (or "working-class") and "middle-class" marriages contain three related features that understate certain overlaps, at least nowadays. First, they focus on couples with young children. As a result they take for the essence of working-class marriage what may be the effects of one stage of the marital cycle, a stage where leisure life is most curtailed, the wife is least likely to be employed, and economic problems are likely to be greatest. Second, they exclude couples with more than a high-school education, thus overlooking an important minority of educated wives of blue-collar workers who do not fit conventional stereotypes of the working-class wife. Third, they ignore the wife's occupation when defining the social class of the marriage. Thus they define a "working-class" or "blue-collar" marriage as one where the *husband* is a blue-collar worker, regardless of the wife's occupation.[6] This implies that marriages in America can easily be divided by occupation into two main types, "blue collar" and "middle class." But the entry of large numbers of wives into the labor market after World War II complicates this distinction. Indeed, the three selection criteria I have pointed to are mostly based on the assumption that the paid employment of wives is of secondary importance. This assumption was more plausible in the past, so in part my findings reflect changes over time.

Marital Contentment and Discontent

During the long time I knew them, I talked with almost all these workers about marriage and family life. Seventy-nine were willing to discuss these questions at enough length for me to feel justified in including their views in the analysis that follows. Of this group, 59 are currently married, and the rest are divorced, separated, or bachelors.[7]

Almost all the married men have in mind a general judgment about the quality of their marriages—the extent to which marriage is a source of satisfaction. The basic question underlying this judgment is whether they are glad or sorry to be married. This is a question that naturally occurs to everyone, for the existence of divorced persons among their fellow workers, kin, or friends is a constant reminder that marriages can be terminated.[8]

Thirty-five percent say they are glad to be married and speak with enthusiasm about their wives. Another 25% have mixed feelings. Some have gone through a long period of very serious difficulty, often coming close to divorce. Others experience major problems, but also important satisfactions, in their marriages. The third and largest group, 40% of the husbands, are unhappily married. Relations with their wives are in general a source of considerable frustration and anger. When this unhappily married group is combined with those men who have serious reservations about their marriage and with those who are divorced, it is clear why there is a certain routine hostility toward wives. For example, throughout the plant the same joke often recurs when groups of workers discuss their wives: "My wife? I auctioned her off last week . . . to the lowest bidder! And there still weren't any takers!"

What reasons do those men give who do not, or did not, get along with their wives? What problems have they encountered?

The Principle of the Modern Nuclear Family versus Other Principles

The modern marital ideal of shared companionship as well as shared sex is one of which all these workers are aware and to which most subscribe. But in practice many find it hard to achieve. Thus the most frequent problem in these marriages is conflict between spending leisure time with wives and spending it in other ways.

Leisure Relations with Male Friends

The main, but not the only, reason for this conflict is the lack of common leisure interests. An important part of men's leisure activities are of a kind not easily shared with women, as the previous chapter pointed out. This motif touches most men's marriages, and for at least half it creates serious problems, constituting a recurring source of dispute, anger, and resentment.[9] Consider these examples.

A wife in her late forties:

> I never see Jimmy [her husband]. He's out a lot, and when he's home
> he likes to watch sports on TV. And I hate sports, especially football.

We used to argue a lot about which programs to watch, so for his
fiftieth birthday my mother bought us another television. But now it's
worse, because when he's home he just shuts himself in the bedroom
watching football. I don't see him at all.

A worker in his mid-forties:

Susan [his wife] keeps saying, "Why don't we go away together? Just
you and I." But that's boring. I like to go fishing and drink a few beers
when I'm on vacation, but she doesn't want to do that. She doesn't like
to fish, and she thinks I drink too much.

A wife in her mid-forties:

A lot of these guys leave everything to their wife. They're out a lot
drinking with other guys. They're not responsible. They let the wife take
care of the kids.

The two commonest joint leisure activities for husband and wife are eating at
restaurants and visiting friends. But visiting friends is often a joint activity only in a
formal sense. On such occasions the company tends to divide along gender lines. The
men do talk with the women, but they spend far more time talking with each other.
Mindful of this dominant problem, those workers who are happily married
commonly stress the importance of spending leisure time with their wives. This is
widely viewed as the key to marital harmony. Apart from the "personalities" of the
husband and wife, it is almost the only explanation men who are happily married give
for why some marriages are satisfactory while others are not. Typical in this regard is
a worker in his early forties:

Yes, I like marriage. What makes a good marriage? Well, you have to
care for each other. You can't spend all your time working and drinking. You have to have time for each other. You have to appreciate her.

Another man, in his late forties, made the same point more vehemently:

I don't care what they [the other workers] say, marriage is a beautiful
thing. But you have to work at it. You can't just leave your wife alone,
like a lot of these guys. A lot of them are animals. All they want to do
is earn money, eat, drink, and have a good time.
I'll tell you what makes a good marriage. It's when you do things
together. Like, my wife comes fishing [he is an enthusiastic fisherman
and has his own boat]. She likes it, and she likes to be with me.

Indeed, despite the difficulties just outlined, there is a sizable group of marriages
(just under half) for whom the lack of shared leisure time is not a serious problem.

For some that is because the husbands have given up their contacts with the male leisure culture. They come home after work and, as they sometimes put it, "don't socialize with the other guys." Others develop leisure pursuits that they can share with their wives. Dancing is a common one. For instance, one couple in their late forties are enthusiastic square dancers. They belong to two clubs and for the past seven years have gone dancing once a week. Two other couples belong to a Polish social club in Piscataway, some distance from where they live, that holds dinner dances every second Saturday. They are regular attenders. Another man is an officer of the Polish National Home and is responsible for hiring the "Friday night" band. Most Fridays he is there, dancing with his wife.

The limited nature of their shared leisure pursuits is not a problem for some couples because they are willing to allow each other considerable latitude. The wife does not mind if her husband spends several hours a day in the tavern, and the husband is content to let his wife spend time with her female friends or kin.

Some couples enjoy joint leisure activities and still allow each other room for their own interests, including tolerating extramarital affairs. One worker, who likes to go drinking and play cards with his friends, explained the understanding he had with his wife, and its limits:

> We [his wife and he] do a lot together. We both bowl, and we go out to eat together, and go to parties. I'm happy.
> My wife is very liberal. She doesn't bother if I'm out, and I don't bother if she's out. I know she's with her girl friends or something. She doesn't mind if I come home late unless it's very late, maybe 2:00 or 3:00 in the morning. Then the next day she'll say something like "Where were you?" And I'll say, "I have a right to stay out," and we'll argue. Maybe it'll last two days. I know she has a legal [he means moral] case, but I argue, and she does. It's like we're letting the other know we care.
> There are some things you can't do. Like my wife doesn't mind if my friends come over to play cards so long as it's not every night. Once or twice a week is OK, but not every night. Then she'll say, "No way!" because she has to clean up afterward, sweep and clean away cigarette butts and all that. That's a lot of work.

Work and Workaholism

A desire to spend leisure time with male friends is the main reason workers may not be with their wives as much as the wives might like. But it is not the only reason. Some men are "workaholics." They will repeatedly, over many years, spend as much extra time in the factory as they can. Many workers are tempted by offers of overtime and the additional money it brings, but only a few will, throughout their lives, work overtime on every possible occasion. After twenty years of marriage, the wife of such a workaholic took a job where she met another man, and she left her husband.

Sexual Friendships with Other Women

Other men spend less time with their wives because they are having extramarital affairs. Given the geographic separation of work and home, this is not difficult. There are the cocktail lounges—Snug Harbor Inn, the Quiet Retreat, motels like Howard Johnson's—strung out along the highways and safely isolated from domestic life. Also, as men get older, the gender ratio becomes increasingly favorable. Heart disease, and illnesses associated with the work environment or with excessive drinking, reduce the number of men much faster than that of women. For a worker in his forties and older there is a plentiful supply of available women—divorced, widowed, or never married. And a widow is quite likely to bring with her a house and her dead husband's pension. Weekly dances held at neighborhood social clubs such as the Polish National Home are an easy way for older men to meet women, who considerably outnumber men on such occasions.

Thus for many of these workers the principle of the nuclear family conflicts with the principle of male friendships, and for some it conflicts with the principle of work or with the principle of sexual friendships with other women. The modern marital ideal that husband and wife should be each other's closest friend as well as sexual partner is hard to achieve regardless of occupation. As with leisure, occupation may make some difference to the way couples experience this ideal. But if it does, it separates not working class from middle class, but those with jobs from those for whom work is a central interest, especially those with careers. And those with jobs include not only most blue-collar workers, but also most lower-white-collar workers and a portion of the upper-white-collar sector.

For these blue-collar workers, in jobs, not careers, friendships at work—"buddies"—are vital, for it is such camaraderie that makes a dull setting tolerable. A work context involving cooperation and a union strengthens such ties. There is some tendency for this work-related culture to spill over into life outside work and to compete and interfere with wives' claims on a share of their husbands' leisure time. (This tendency should not be exaggerated. As I have pointed out, about half the married workers go straight home after work. And not all blue-collar settings involve cooperation and dense friendships at work.)

Further, the wife of a professional or of a manager with a career may also resent her husband's spending leisure time with his work associates. But her hostility may be tempered by the realization that there is often a payoff in terms of promotion and therefore extra income and status for the family. The spouse of a blue-collar worker, by contrast, sees no such dividends in her husband's spending leisure time with his male friends. From her point of view it is pure loss. (She is, however, more likely to accept his working overtime, since this does mean extra money for the family.) Thus for these blue-collar workers it is the principle of male friendships that is most likely to conflict with the principle of the nuclear family.

On the other hand, absorbing work and a career can intrude on marital life just as, in the previous chapter, we saw how they intruded on leisure, in a variety of ways most of those in "jobs" are largely free of. Here it is the principle of work and work-based relations that is the main point of conflict with the principle of the nuclear family. First, a person's time and energy may be focused on work, leaving only a residue for the spouse. As a business executive quoted in an English study put it: "We [his wife and he] have organized around the necessity of my job. There was a point in our married life when my wife felt that the demands of my job tended to conflict with married life. We managed to sort that out. My wife realized that I couldn't be complete without being absorbed in my work and that there would be even greater conflict were this not so."[10]

Second, the husband's job may set the framework within which his wife's leisure takes place and may limit its extent. For instance, the wife may be "required" to act as an ancillary, unpaid worker (An example is the salesman's wife who types, stuffs envelopes, and answers the telephone for her husband.) Or the husband's job may disrupt the wife's leisure time. (As in the expectation, common in the world of business, that managers' wives will follow their husbands around the country, and even the world, as they are promoted and simultaneously transferred.) Or the husband's job may blur the distinction between work relations and leisure relations, to the detriment of the latter. (For example, "social entertaining" may be required outside work hours. At its worst the wife may have to play the "hostess" role, providing food and hospitality to work associates. At best she may simply have to accompany her husband in a variety of social situations.) As Kanter points out in her discussion of wives whose husbands were employed as managers by a large corporation: "The public consequences of relationships made it difficult for some wives to have anything but a superficial friendship with anyone in the corporate network. Yet, since so much of their time was consumed by company-related entertainment, they had little chance for other friendships, and reported considerable loneliness."[11]

If their spouses' careers expose the wives of many upper-white-collar workers to these troubles, then their husbands' lack of careers protects the wives of blue-collar workers from similar difficulties.[12] Thus the difference between a career and a job may change the likely order of conflict between the principle of the nuclear family and other principles. For those in careers it may be the principle of work that interferes most often with the principle of the nuclear family. For blue-collar workers in jobs it may be the principle of male friendships that most commonly interferes.

The Social Status of the Husband

The second commonest problem, cited by 30 percent of the married men, concerns a tendency of some of the wives to complain that their husbands' social status is too low. This typically conveys a number of ideas. There is the obvious truth that blue-collar workers lack a college degree and whatever status this confers. There is the related notion that they lack the qualifications and aspirations for the kind of jobs that require college education and beyond, notably upper-white-collar jobs. One worker expressed this as follows:

> You know, women are terrible. Here I am, just a working slob, and I've got a house and the mortgage all paid off. And still my wife says I should be looking higher. And *she* doesn't work. I hate work.

Another worker, in his mid-fifties, commented:

> I've got a $60,000 house, but my wife isn't satisfied. She says she doesn't like "factory work." A lot of these guys' wives aren't satisfied.

One worker, discussing the problem, explained:

> Luckily my wife doesn't mind my job. She's a simple country girl. She was born on a farm.

There is also the view that workers lack the social tastes, interests, and skills that education is supposed to confer. Particularly prone to give offense is men's earthy language and forthright manner. Consider the following example of a worker who is very sociable and well liked, but blunt with his language. His wife finds this embarrassing in front of other people and inappropriate for the children. He related a typical incident:

> I tell Jane [his wife] I am what I am, but she gets big ideas. My friends call her "the princess."
>   Yesterday I was tired. I got home around 11:30 [A.M., after working the midnight shift] and I met Jane and Deirdre [one of his daughters]. They wanted to get something from the store. So I gave them a lift, and Deirdre met a friend of hers and started chattering. You know, I was tired—I'd been working since 8:00 the night before. So I said, Deirdre, get the *fucking hell* in here!"
>   Well, after they came out of the store they'd obviously been talking, because Jane said, "Deirdre was talking to her friend about. . . . " I said I didn't care. As far as I was concerned the matter was closed. But she kept yammering on. I called her just now [on the telephone], and she still says I shouldn't have used that language in front of Deirdre's friend.
>   So I'm in a bind. I know what's waiting for me back home. She'll start to yell at me and turn the children against me.

Tastes that are perceived as unrefined are also a source of argument. A second-generation Italian worker in his early forties was angry about a recent incident. He and his wife had gone out to dinner at a New York restaurant with some friends. The others had ordered moderately exotic dishes, but he preferred simple Italian food and told the others so as he ordered spaghetti and meatballs. To his annoyance his wife publicly rebuked him, complaining that whenever he went out he embarrassed her.

These issues are particularly explosive since the overwhelming majority of workers are very sensitive about their lack of formal education.

Again this discussion illustrates the interplay between themes that are distinctive of the marriages of blue-collar workers and themes that are not. Much blue-collar work does carry less social status than upper-white-collar employment and, in some people's eyes, than lower-white-collar work, which is at least performed in the clean surroundings of the "office." Imperium workers are well aware of the low status associated with "factory work," as their occasional references to themselves as "factory stiffs" or "just working slobs" indicate. And there is a clear tendency for blue-collar workers to have less education than upper-white-collar workers. Given the high value attached to education in America, this often creates defensiveness and a feeling of inadequacy and failure.

Further, employed wives of blue-collar workers tend to have jobs that arguably carry higher status than their husbands' jobs. Most blue-collar workers' wives, if employed, are in clerical and secretarial jobs that, though typically poorly paid, are still "office jobs," not factory jobs. And a minority are in upper-white-collar managerial or professional employment (the question of the occupation of wives in America is explored in detail later in the chapter).

The impact of this is softened because the income of men at Imperium usually exceeds their wives'. Given the importance of income as a determinant of status in the United States, this clearly offsets a tendency of husbands to feel inferior, even if from other points of view their occupation carries lower status. Indeed, workers often pointedly contrast their income with that of white-collar occupations. Consider this example of a mechanic who had left school in ninth grade: "[Proudly] My daughter told her teachers how much her father earned without an education! They didn't believe it, so I Xeroxed a pay stub for her to show them!"

Still, in a society that has for so long stressed that occupation is of primary importance for the husband but only secondary for the wife, the relatively low status of "factory work" as compared with white-collar "office work" can create special problems for the marriages of blue-collar workers. And their modest education, while itself constituting a source of unease among blue-collar workers, may diminish their chance of having certain skills needed to handle such difficulties.[13]

At the same time the difficulties created in these marriages by the tendency for wives to feel dissatisfied with their husbands' job, education, or social demeanor should not be exaggerated. About a third of the married men find this a problem, but that leaves a larger group who do not.

An interesting case is a worker whose wife has a Ph.D. and is a college professor in New Jersey. Of all these marriages this is the one where the educational and occupational imbalance between husband and wife is the greatest. The wife commented, with obvious affection for her husband:

> Statistics show that marriages in which the wife has more education than
> the husband don't last, but we're the exception that proves the rule.

When they first married neither had more than a high-school diploma. Her husband described what happened:

> Jenny [his wife] used to work as a medical secretary. Finally she got
> bored. She said she wanted to get a B.A. I was surprised. She was in
> the top salary grade, getting almost as much as me. But I said OK.
> Then she said. "You can't do anything with a B.A." So she went for
> her master's. She used to work and study, but I said it was too much for

her. I offered to pay for her while she went to school. Then she said, "You can't do anything with a master's," so she wanted to go for her Ph.D. I said, "Oh!" [runs his hands through his hair in a mock gesture of horror.] So I paid for that too.

Despite an occasional joke about the length and expense of his wife's education, he is obviously proud of her achievements. And though they allow each other freedom to conduct their own lives, they also move with a certain enjoyment in the social worlds of both spouses. She sometimes spends time at the tavern where her husband does much of his drinking, and she is popular with his friends. To their delight she tells obscene jokes that any of the men would be proud to have originated. And he enjoys mixing with his wife's friends. As he put it:

I've got used to meeting all these people—doctors, nuclear physicists, chemists. I was uncomfortable for the first two years, but now I can mix with all of them, and here I am, just a factory stiff![14]

The occupational imbalance between this couple is clearly an extreme case, but their ability to prevent it from disrupting their marriage is not. This suggests that complaints about the husband's social demeanor, or his lack of education or occupational status, may have as much to do with psychological as sociological factors. In part it is the personalities of some spouses that explain why they run into a problem here. The low status of "factory work" becomes an excuse for concealing these psychic dynamics, especially since spouses could focus on the husbands' superior income rather than the inferior status of factory work.

Problem Drinking

Heavy drinking that constitutes or verges on alcoholism is the third most frequent difficulty men cite in their marriages. Seventeen workers mentioned it as a problem.

These men commonly make a distinction between an alcoholic and a heavy drinker. An "alcoholic" is someone whose drinking persistently interferes with his ability to come to work or to perform minimally on the job. A "heavy drinker," on the other hand, enjoys spending time in the tavern and drinking beer at home but can usually still perform the routine activities of living and working. But this is a distinction men's wives do not always appreciate. As one man complained:

Mary [his wife] reads a guy in the newspaper who says if you need a cocktail before dinner every night then you're an alcoholic, and she believes it. Then she yells at me because I have a beer before dinner.

Excessive drinking is, of course, likely to be a symptom of some other problem. But, whatever its origin, it can become a serious and very ugly difficulty of its own within a marriage. The following cases are illustrative.

A worker in his early fifties:

Drunkenness is a big problem here. I drank myself for a long time when
I was working in the fasic plant [the process plant involving shift work].
It messed up my homelife. My wife nearly left me. She said if I didn't
stop drinking she would leave. And my eldest son—I think it had a
really bad effect on him. He had a drug problem for a long time—still
does. I still have a problem. You know, if I go over the road [to the
tavern close to work] it's very hard to leave.

A young worker in his early thirties explained how he came to beat up his wife:

The other day I beat my wife up—put her in the hospital. She accused
me of drinking and going with another woman. A few months ago she
threw me out of the house because of drinking. But [angry at this false
accusation] cheating on my wife! Never! If she doesn't want to give it
[sex] to me then I'll wait, and if she gets tired of me then I'll get a divorce—but cheating on my wife, never.

Mostly it is the men who drink too heavily (for their spouses' liking) but
sometimes it is the women. A worker in his late forties explained how his marriage
ended and how, as he later discovered, his wife had been a secret alcoholic:

I should never have got married. I don't know why I did it. I guess it
was pity. I broke up with her a couple of times before we got married.
    It [the marriage] lasted from the time I was twenty-six to thirty-two.
She wasn't clean. She was untidy. I couldn't stand that. And, well, there
was something more important. She had a psychological problem—she
drank, hard alcohol. I found out later. I never knew at the time. She
hid it, but she drank all day.

Those workers who regularly drink beyond their capacity to control their behavior are fairly quickly fired.[15] They are the ones who consistently fail to get to work
on time or are consistently too drunk to make a contribution to the job. This leaves a
group who sometimes (perhaps once a month) become dangerously drunk. Several
years ago one such man, after an evening in the tavern, drove his car under a truck.
His face had to be remodeled by a plastic surgeon. Another worker crashed into a
bridge after leaving the tavern. When the police arrived he was so drunk he urinated
all over their car, and he lost his driver's license for a year.
    Heavy drinking and problem drinking ("alcoholism") are obviously not con-
fined to blue-collar workers, nor are they most concentrated among them. The most
comprehensive studies of American drinking practices are the series of national
probability samples by Don Cahalan and associates. Their findings indicate a number of social variables and contexts that make heavy drinking more likely. (A "heavy
drinker" is defined as someone who drinks nearly every day with five or more drinks
per occasion at least once in a while, or about once weekly with five or more drinks
on most occasions.) Men are more likely to be heavy drinkers than women, and
people below age fifty are more likely than older people. Those in cities and suburbs

are more likely to be heavy drinkers than those in rural areas. Catholics account for an above-average proportion of heavy drinkers, and conservative Protestant denominations that preach against the use of alcohol include fewer than average.[16] As regards the influence of occupation, heavy drinking is about as widespread among managers and professionals as among blue-collar workers. This makes sense. Beer and the tavern are part of traditional working-class culture, but the world of business and management also involves considerable drinking, though with differences of nuance—less beer in the tavern, more drinks over expense-account meals.

A heavy drinker is not the same as an "alcoholic," though they are not unrelated since a heavy-drinking milieu is more likely to produce "drinking problems." Defining an "alcoholic" is very hard. It is not only these blue-collar workers and their wives who have trouble agreeing on a definition. As a result Cahalan, like many other writers, prefers to refer to "problem drinkers," defined as those whose drinking is associated with physical, psychological, or sociological problems. Examples are problems with health or injuries, psychological dependence, difficulty with spouse, relatives, or friends, and trouble on the job or with the police. Drinking problems are fairly evenly distributed among social classes except that they are more prevalent among the poor (not the same as stably employed blue-collar workers).

So far this chapter has explored the main difficulties that occur in these marriages. There are several reasons for focusing on difficulties. First, more marriages have problems than do not. Second, workers tend to be more articulate about their difficulties, for difficulties provoke thought and reflection. Workers are less likely to be able to explain why their marriages are successful than why they are not. Apart from pointing to the reverse of the reason why marriages are not successful (the husband spends time with his wife instead of ignoring her, or neither spouse drinks excessively, or the wife does not complain about her husband's lack of education and social standing), workers offer only personality traits as explanation of successful marriages (their spouses are "considerate" or "unselfish" or "easygoing").

Yet there is a theme that persistently occurs when workers are discussing the benefits of being married. They often stress the idea that their wives rescued them from the wild life-style of the male culture, a life-style they believe would in the end have been their downfall. Their wives and the responsibility of marriage, provided discipline and order in their lives. The following cases exemplify this theme.

A worker in his early fifties, on his twenty-fifth wedding anniversary:

Oh yes, I'm glad I married. My wife straightened me out. Otherwise I would have been a complete bum.

A worker in his late fifties:

Marriage? Well, it's discipline. You know, a wife will straighten a guy out. She'll make sure he comes home instead of going out drinking every night, and he'll start to think of his responsibilities.

You know, in the morning when the alarm goes off she'll say, "It's 6:30, time to go to work!" If he's by himself a guy will go [violently flattens an imaginary alarm clock with his hand] when the clock goes off. And if he does it three or four times he'll lose his job. Lots of guys have lost their jobs like that.

A man, now in his late thirties, who married when he was the eighteen-year-old leader of a motorcycle gang:

If I hadn't got married I would have been in jail by now.

The case of a worker who married relatively late illustrates this view in more detail:

I got married when I was thirty-eight [five years earlier]. I never thought I would. I'd been going with this girl, on and off, for ten years. I kept putting her off, telling her we'd get engaged in a couple of years and then breaking up, and then seeing her again.

She's [his wife] a nurse. She put me straight, otherwise I would have been very sick. I'd go out drinking every night with other guys—spend the whole night in the gin mill. I was pretty far gone, and what do you think her parents thought, with her going with a drunk guy like me? But after we were married they were marvelous. They never mention that early period.

Wives

Before World War II employers discriminated in favor of single women, often firing those who got married. But since then there has been a huge influx of married women into the labor market, in full- or part-time jobs. Between 1950 and 1976 the number of people employed in civilian jobs rose by 33 million, of whom 20 million were women. And 60 percent of these women were married.[17]

Imperium wives reflect these tendencies. Fewer than a third are not in paid jobs. Most of this group have young children. They remain at home because they believe children in their early years need a mother's constant attention, or because they cannot find anyone else to care for their children during the day.

The Housewives

Only a very small number of wives of Imperium workers are committed housewives in the sense that they deliberately remain out of the labor market even after their children have grown up. And those in this group tend to be defensive, aware that they are a beleagered and dwindling minority and feeling a need to explain and justify themselves. One such woman, in her early forties with three grown children, commented:

I don't work. I don't want to work. We were discussing it last night with some people, and two of the women said, "Don't you want to be something, to make something of yourself?" But I think they're deluding themselves. How are they "being something?" [a reference to the kind of clerical and secretarial jobs her friends have]. I like not working. I don't think I could ever go to work at 9:00 and leave at 4:00. I don't have the discipline. Sometimes I feel sorry for Tony [her husband] when he has to get up at 5:00 in the morning in winter and leave the warm bed.

Some of these marriages provide satisfaction to both partners. But others illustrate all the problems such marriages bring among the "middle class" too—an excessively controlling husband and a depressed wife whose resentment against her husband appears in all kinds of ways. The following account, by a mechanic in his mid-fifties, is an example. Husband and wife often quarrel, and they stopped having sex four years ago:

> I don't know what she's [his wife] got to complain about. She has a house and clothes and a car. I gave her all those things. And she doesn't work.
>   We had some good years at the start, but not after the kids came along, and now she's sick. She's got sugar [diabetes], so she can't do much. It's her fault. There's sugar in her family and I used to say to her, "Be careful, don't eat sugar," but she wouldn't listen. She said, "I don't get pleasure from hardly anything else, so why shouldn't I eat?" She used to eat those chocolate layer cakes all the time.
>   I honestly don't give a shit anymore [about the marriage]. My wife won't give me sex anymore. [Regretfully] When the young ones [children] come along then you're caught. Then you have to stay. But until the kids come along you're a free agent. You can always split.

The Employed Wives

Of those Imperium wives (more than two-thirds) with full- or part-time jobs, the largest number work in lower-white-collar occupations, as secretaries or in clerical or retail settings (see table 8). A number of those in clerical jobs are bank tellers or enter data into computers. Retail jobs commonly involve selling in a store.

The second largest group of Imperium wives have upper-white-collar jobs as professionals or managers. Most of this group are in the less-well-paid professions. Four are schoolteachers and four are nurses. There is one college professor, a social worker, and a middle-level manager in a hospital. These women together constitute a sizable block who have training and education that ranges from one or two years beyond high school for the nurses to at least a B.A. for the teachers and a Ph.D. for the college professor. It is this group of wives of blue-collar workers, more likely than the others to possess a certain kind of energy and ambition, that are systematically overlooked by studies of "working-class" marriage that consider only couples where neither has more than a high-school education.

In addition to such lower- and upper-white-collar occupations, a small number

Table 8   Occupation of the Men's Wives

Occupation[a]	Number
Professional or managerial (mostly teachers and nurses)	12
Clerical (includes secretarial) and sales	19
Blue collar	6
Service workers	9
Housewives	19
Total	65

Source: Fieldwork.

[a]Includes those who currently work in an occupation or have been employed in that occupation within the past two years.

of men's wives (six) are blue-collar workers. They have jobs that involve tending machines or packaging goods.

Census data make it possible to compare the occupations of Imperium wives with those of wives of men in a variety of occupations.[18] The jobs women have in America display certain overlaps that transcend the occupations of their husbands, especially in the middle range of the class structure. For instance, clerical work (this includes secretarial jobs) is strikingly common among wives. A third of the women married to professionals hold such jobs, as do 45 percent of the women married to better-paid managers. Indeed, clerical work is the commonest employment of wives in America. Thus most of the new jobs created since 1950, jobs filled mainly by the vast influx of married women into the labor market, have been clerical and in the retail sector. In a society that has for so long implied that a female's major role is as wife and mother, this clustering of women in dull and low-paying clerical work should be no surprise.[19]

Still, an important minority of wives are in professions especially teaching, nursing, and social work (though far fewer are managers). Almost half of the better-paid professional men are married to other professionals, as are 23 percent of the better-paid managers. And 13 percent of wives of skilled blue-collar workers are professionals. Here it is important to remember that Imperium wives are likely to have education and jobs that are above the average for wives of blue-collar workers. This explains why upper-white-collar work is their second-commonest occupation, whereas for wives of blue-collar workers in general it ranks after blue-collar work.

There are, then, certain broad similarities in the labor-market position of wives of better-paid blue-collar workers and wives of men in the lower and middle ranges of the managerial and professional sector. There are, of course, forces that tend to increase the difference between these two groups of wives. Studies of spouse selection point to the tendency for people to marry partners with similar social and educational backgrounds. Thus wives of upper-white collar-workers are more likely to have upper-white-collar fathers than are wives of blue-collar workers (though it is not unusual for women from upper-white-collar families to marry blue-collar work-ers, especially the better-paid ones).[20] Professional men (but not managerial men) are as likely to marry women in professions as to marry women in lower-white-collar jobs. Further, studies suggest a strain toward "status consistency" within marriage. In particular, wives will be under pressure to avoid certain jobs that are incompatible with the status of their husbands' jobs. For instance, wives of upper-white-collar men are very unlikely to be blue-collar workers, in part because for many such husbands it is awkward to have a blue-collar wife. It is less appropriate for the wife of an engineer or a manager to work in a factory than for the wife of a factory worker to do so.[21]

Finally, marriage to a blue-collar worker involves certain concerns that wives of white-collar men are more likely to be free of. Much blue-collar work is dangerous, and this is certainly true of many of the jobs at Imperium (see parts 2 and 3). Wives of Imperium workers often express anxiety about their husband's physical well-being. Some are resigned, others wish their husbands could find safer jobs.

Still, the preceding discussion suggests areas of overlap between the labor market position of wives of better-paid blue-collar workers and wives of white-collar men in middle-level jobs. There are two reasons why this overlap is not always noticed. First, the studies that stress differences between wives of blue-collar and upper-white-collar workers consider only those wives of blue-collar workers who have children and no more than a high-school education. Focusing on women with young children ensures a disproportionately large number of housewives or women in part-time employment, and ruling out those with more than a high school educa-tion omits the interesting minority of blue-collar wives in upper-white-collar occupa-tions.

Second, studies that stress differences between blue-collar and middle-class marriages typically ignore the wife's occupation when defining the class character of the marriage. Marriages where the husband is a blue-collar worker are usually called blue-collar or working-class marriages regardless of the wife's occupation. And marriages where the husband has an upper-white-collar occupation are usually called middle-class marriages regardless of the wife's occupation. This practice avoids the complications, and some blurring of class lines, that result from taking the wife's occupation seriously.

It is hard to justify ignoring the wife's occupation in a period when women increasingly view themselves as serious contenders in the labor market. Ironically, these very studies that ignore the wife's occupation when defining the social class of the marriage tend to report that, if she has a job, it is usually important to her. In any case, it is inconsistent to argue that the distinction between blue-collar and middle-class *occupations* is basic for understanding marriage in America and then to assume, before beginning the study, that the occupation of the husband is central while that of the wife is irrelevant to the class character of the marriage.[22]

The Children

What about the occupational attainment of the children of Imperium workers? Table 9 shows the occupations of those of the men's children who are no longer in school or

Table 9   Occupations of the Men's Children

Occupations of Sons	Number	Occupations of Daughters	Number
Professional or managerial	9	Professional or managerial (mostly teachers and nurses)	11
Clerical and sales	5	Clerical and sales	15
Blue collar	24	Service workers	7
Armed services (army, navy, air force)	5	Own business	2
		Housewives	12
		Total	47
Service workers (includes three policemen or firemen)	6		
Unemployed	4		
Total	53		

Source: Fieldwork.

college. The largest group of their sons are in blue-collar jobs (including six who work at Imperium), and a majority are if we include the military, police, and firemen as blue collar. Most of the daughters, like the men's wives, are in clerical or retail jobs or are housewives looking after young children. A minority of the men's children are in professions or are managers. One son has a Ph.D. in educational psychology and works as a guidance counselor at a state college. Another is a middle-level manager for Ford. He worked for some years in Detroit, was transferred to England for a while, and is now a manager in Chicago. A third son graduated from the University of Wisconsin and works as a reporter for United Press International in Manhattan. He specializes in sports reporting and travels to major events abroad, such as the Olympics, and at home, such as the Super Bowl and the World Series. For many of these chemical workers his job seems as close to paradise as a man can get on earth. Another worker's son is a disk jockey for the glamorous Manhattan discotheque Studio 54. Among the daughters, most of the professionals are, like the men's wives, schoolteachers and nurses. Two of the teachers have doctorates.

The symbolic importance of these occupations should not be underestimated. It is true that only a minority of the men's children are in professions (and none are lawyers or doctors, the goal of so many children of the white-collar professional sector). But workers talk to each other about their children. The UPI correspondent was covering the Olympic Games in Munich when the Israeli athletes were massacred. His concerned father telephoned Germany to find out whether his son was safe. Through this channel most of the other chemical workers heard a detailed account of the dramatic events. In 1978 the New York police raided Studio 54, the Manhattan discotheque, and claimed to have found cocaine in the possession of one of the owners. This was widely reported in the media. The chemical worker whose son is chief disk jockey there was able to give his father the "inside" story of the raid, and his father's work friends heard the report at second hand. The man whose son was a manager for Ford in England gave his friends periodic assessments of the state of the English economy and the condition of the British working class.

In this way, most workers come to believe that the class structure of America offers a degree of opportunity. They see that some men's children have attained significant advancement.[23] It is true that workers often comment on the difficulty they have, or will have, in paying for a college education for their children. But they know that students who do well in high school can attend inexpensive state or city colleges. During the entire period that I knew them, I never heard a single worker suggest that his own occupation or modest education might seriously diminish the occupational chances of his children.

Marriage after the Children Have Left Home

The Companionate Marriage

As men grow older their marital and leisure lives enter a third stage marked by a much-improved economic situation. Their children have grown up, their wives usually take jobs, and their mortgages are almost or completely paid off. At work men have accumulated twenty or thirty years of seniority, which protects them against cutbacks in the labor force (though not against a plant closure) and entitles them to several weeks' annual vacation, as well as to a pension when they retire.

At the same time, physical health becomes more important. Workers begin to develop ailments that slow their mobility. By this time, too, everyone knows fellow workers who have died suddenly, and the lesson of life's brevity is not lost. As they enter their late forties, sometimes even earlier, and regardless of their current health, workers often remark that they do not know how much longer they have to live—they might die tomorrow.

In this third stage there is a tendency for some of the married workers who once spent most of their leisure with male friends to now spend more time with their wives. Often this is either because physical ailments curtail men's sporting activities, or because their buddies have died or moved away, or because they fear being alone in old age. The worker who married in his late thirties explained:

> We [he and his girl friend] decided to get married very suddenly. My buddies were shocked. They reckoned she must be pregnant. They couldn't understand why I did it. But I just figured I wasn't getting any younger, and I didn't want to be sitting by myself when I got older, so I did it for companionship.

Often men and their wives in this stage resolve to make the best of the remainder of their lives. In this context the wife becomes more of a companion. Joint travel, in America and abroad, adds color and interest to the marital relation. A worker in his mid-fifties commented on his own marriage and on that of the other older workers:

> We used to argue a lot. She said I was always out with my friends. We came close to splitting up, but finally we decided life was too short to argue. Now we spend more time together.

> You know, with most of them [the older workers] it isn't even what
> you might call love. It's . . . well, when you've been with someone for a
> long time you get like this [locks his hands together].

Such marriages come to resemble those where husband and wife have always
spent considerable time together, for there too the spouses tend to rely on each other
for companionship as they grow older. One worker in his early fifties, whose
marriage had always been happy, commented on this change. His younger son was in
college:

> You know, before we got married I used to like to go out with my wife.
> We'd eat and have a couple of drinks. Then after we got married we
> figured "Why not stay home?" So we didn't bother to go out for drinks.
> We'd have our drinks at home. But we used to socialize. I couldn't im-
> agine not going out Saturday night. My wife had four or five girl friends
> and I had my friends, and we'd do a lot in couples. We'd go out, we'd
> eat, and we'd all take along the kids.
>   But then gradually it began to stop. You know, people got involved
> in their own families. Gradually you saw less of each other. You know,
> one night you'd ask one couple and they'd be caught up with something
> with the kids, maybe something at school. And then they'd ask you and
> you'd be doing something and someone would get offended and you'd
> stop seeing each other. It happened to everyone I know. I don't know
> why, it's a pity. I guess you slow up. Like the last few years on Saturday
> evening we'll watch TV.

Another worker, in his late fifties, observed:

> After the age of forty-five there's no love left. Love has disappeared.
> It's not love. It's companionship.

This tendency for husband and wife, as they grow older, to see each other
increasingly as companions is not confined to the marriages of blue-collar workers.
For instance, Clifford Sager, a psychoanalyst and marital therapist, distinguishes a
number of standard styles of interaction between spouses. One of these styles is the
"companionate" marriage, which is common among older couples regardless of
social class.[24]

It should not be surprising that when these workers are older such differences as
once existed between their marriages and those of the white-collar sector decrease.
Retirement removes perhaps the main factor that differentiates marriages, the
occupation of the husband. Both blue- and white-collar spouses become preoccupied
with a similar series of problems entailing financial security, physical health, and
making the most of their remaining years.

The Discontented

At the same time, some couples finally split up. With the children grown, an
important reason for remaining in an unhappy marriage disappears. Whether they

are happily or unhappily married, most men derive considerable pleasure from watching their young children develop and from spending time with them. A divorce would risk loss, or considerable reduction, of this contact, since custody usually goes to the wife. Workers who are divorced often speak with regret about their inability to see their young children as much as they would like. Some have lost all contact except for occasional formal matters. Men who have stayed in unhappy marriages to enjoy their children have less incentive to remain after the children leave home.

The absence of young children also removes certain economic barriers to divorce. Wives no longer must stay home to care for them, so they can obtain full-time jobs, and thus economic independence. The children's growing up frees the husband in a different way. He no longer has to fear heavy child support payments if he quits the marriage.

Yet by no means all the workers who are unhappily married obtain a divorce when the children have left home. Forty percent of Imperium husbands are definitely unhappily married, and the children of half of this group are no longer in high school. These husbands consistently fail to get along with their wives. Why do they stay married?

For both husbands and wives there is a psychological dimension—fear of change, fear of independence. And there are still economic considerations. For the wives there are doubts whether they can maintain the same standard of living. As one commented about some of the Imperium wives who were unhappily married and did not have jobs:

> They're scared. They don't know what they can do. You take a woman in her fifties, and she hasn't done anything [hasn't had a job] all her life. What's she going to do? And if they [husband and wife] break up she *may* get something [alimony and property settlement], but she doesn't know, she can't be certain.

There is also a very important economic reason why many of these men remain in unhappy marriages. They are afraid of alimony payments and property division. In particular, men are very reluctant to lose their houses. In New Jersey, when marriages end in divorce property is usually divided equally between the husband and the wife. In addition, the husband must often pay alimony. Ironically, the house, which represented economic independence, becomes a source of marital dependence.

Desertion, a traditional method of at least avoiding alimony payments, is not feasible since men are to a large extent locked into their jobs.[25] Occasionally unhappily married workers do talk of disappearing out West as a way of freeing themselves without incurring crippling financial penalties. But reluctance to give up their relatively well-paying jobs and their seniority and pensions is a very strong deterrent to desertion.

These cases are illustrative. A worker in his late thirties, discussing his extramarital affair:

When you're married everything changes. Women get bolder, more domineering. They figure they've got you now. It's quite different from before you were married, like night and day. And if you don't like it they say, "OK, go ahead! Get the lawyer [a common euphemism for divorce]." Because they'll get half of what you've got. You don't always think of it like that, but you know it's there.

A worker in his mid-forties, whose wife would no longer have sex with him:

When you get married you lose your freedom. And the divorce laws in New Jersey are brutal. Take Bill [a divorced worker in the plant]. He's still paying six years later [after the divorce], and if he doesn't she sends the police around. And he lost his house. He can only afford a room in Elizabeth.

A worker in his late thirties:

I can't afford a divorce. New Jersey is brutal. They'll stick me for $200 a week. You know, Freddy [a friend of his] was earning $90 a week in a warehouse in Linden and when he split they [the courts] took $60. He couldn't live on $30.

A year later, discussing his deteriorating marriage:

I'll tell you one thing. She [his wife] ain't going to win. I paid for that house, and it's mine! Mine! She didn't contribute a nickel to the cost of the mortgage payments. So I'm not going to the lawyer first. She can go. In New Jersey everything is split down the middle. I reckon I can take this for five more years. Then there'll only be the two youngsters around and I can split. Maybe I'll go to Las Vegas. But how can I give up my job and seniority and pension and shit?

The division of property in a divorce is often the occasion for bitter, ugly dispute between husband and wife. It is a time when the ideological expectation that the home is a sphere of "love," rather than of monetary relations, is most brutally torn apart.

This motif illustrates a subtle way such men's position in the class structure, their level of income and wealth (but not their occupation), influences their married life. Since they have relatively well-paying jobs and usually houses, they have real assets to lose in any divorce settlement. And desertion, the solution of the poor, is no help since it would cost them all their assets instead of the half they would lose in a divorce. They would have to quit their jobs and leave their houses to escape legal retaliation. At the same time their income is not high enough for them to recover easily from a divorce settlement. At their income level alimony and property division are severe economic blows.

Conclusion to Part 1

The lives of these blue-collar workers outside the workplace display several notice-able features. Because they often have jobs that are not absorbing, many stress friendships at and outside work and protect and enlarge their opportunities for leisure. In this sense they tend to be "person oriented." They have less education and lower-status jobs than most upper-white-collar employees, which may produce a defensiveness about education, some sense of social inferiority, the absence of certain tastes and interests associated with a college education, and marital tension, especially if their wives have more education and are in good white-collar jobs.

Moreover, there are ways the class structure reproduces itself. Blue-collar workers are more likely than upper-white-collar workers to have blue-collar fathers. And their children are less likely than the children of upper-white-collar men to attain high-status jobs or to marry women whose fathers have high-status jobs.

There are ways the class structure reinforces as well as reproduces itself. Many of the friends of Imperium workers are also blue-collar workers. And men in the pre–World War II industrial suburbs of Elizabeth and Linden inhabit areas where numbers of fellow workers from Imperium also live (although government and company insurance and welfare programs, and six-lane highways, have eroded an important part of the solidarity that once characterized these communities). Further, there are some pressures on people to select spouses from similar backgrounds and to avoid certain kinds of incongruous occupational mixtures. A factory worker's wife can more easily take a blue-collar job or one of the inferior lower-white-collar jobs than can the wife of a manager or professional.

These forces do affect the residential, marital, and leisure lives of blue-collar-workers. If there is a "working-class culture" outside the workplace, then these are its ingredients, though a modest job, a modest level of education, an occupationally modest family of origin, and the absence of a career are not confined to blue-collar workers. Clearly some of these characteristics are often present in those who occupy lower-white collar jobs and may, in a limited way, characterize some of those in upper-white-collar jobs.

Consider now the main overlaps between the lives of blue-collar and upper-white-collar employees outside the workplace. Better-paid blue-collar workers earn as much as or more than many white-collar-workers. This enables workers at Imperium to move from older neighborhoods to areas that contain a greater occupational mix, especially to post–World War II suburbs in which their close neighbors are rarely other Imperium workers. And their income enables better-paid blue-collar workers to buy the same houses and consumer goods and services as many white-collar employees and engage in many of the same leisure activities. There is no such thing in post–World War II America as a "blue-collar house," any more than there is a blue-collar car, stereo, or television. Instead, there are products that vary by size, quality, and price. Certainly inflation and high interest rates have eroded the standard of living of the blue-collar working class, but they also affect the white-collar sectors. Real income may fall in America, yet the overlap between classes remains. And if the suburban detached house becomes too expensive, effort will focus on more modest prizes such as a suburban town house or a condominium. Goals may be trimmed, but they will be trimmed more or less uniformly.

Life outside work bears the mark of other forces, in addition to income level, that cut across collar color. Residential America is visibly divided by *race*, into black and Hispanic areas on the one hand and white areas on the other. This is potentially explosive. There are also differences of *gender*. For example, interest in sports such as football, baseball, hunting, and fishing is concentrated among males (though some women do follow such sports and though other sports such as jogging or swimming are less divided by gender). Gender operates in another way. Many wives in America share certain similarities that transcend their husband's occupations. They are concentrated in unpaid housework, poorly paid clerical and service jobs, and certain professions such as teaching, nursing, and social work. And they, rather than their husbands, tend to be responsible for most of the housework and child care. Finally, there is the effect of *age* and *stage in the marital cycle*. For example, the presence of young children often curtails the leisure lives of parents (though usually more for the mother than the father).

It is important to remember that Imperium workers are representative of neither extreme of the class structure outside the workplace. Their economic position is better than the average for blue-collar workers and well below that of the rich and the higher levels of the professional and managerial strata. Thus, poorer blue-collar workers are less likely to be able to live in occupationally mixed post–World War II suburbs, and their wives are less likely to have upper-white-collar jobs. On the other hand, the richer professionals and managers are more likely to live in architect-designed houses or houses on large expanses of land. And they are more likely to hire full-time help with child care. Yet for blue- and white-collar people between these extremes, overlaps outside work are numerous and important.

Finally, to mention such overlaps is not to imply that life outside work is integrated. For example, in their marriages both blue- and white-collar Americans face the task of reconciling the principle at the heart of the modern nuclear family— the idea of husband, wife, and children as each other's closest friends, a cohesive emotional unit based on relations of "love" rather than the often exploitative relations seen as pervading the outside world—with other principles of interpersonal life and with reality. The principle of the modern nuclear family coexists uneasily with the principle of *work* and *work relations* (for those in careers, for example, leading especially to conflicts between absorbing work and homelife; for those with jobs perhaps leading to conflicts between friendships at work and homelife; and, for anyone working shifts, leading to possible difficulties at home). It coexists uneasily with the principle of *friendships of the same sex*, men with men and women with women (leading to conflicts over how much leisure time spouses will spend together and how much separately with their own friends). And it coexists uneasily with the principle of *friendships between men and women*, including sexual relations (the problem of extramarital affairs).

Part 4 will systematically examine the question of beliefs in general. For the moment it is enough to say that the confused and often contradictory beliefs many Americans have about how to live their interpersonal lives, the dilemmas aroused when the principle of the nuclear family conflicts with other principles, can be called a "contradictory cosmology." This "contradictory cosmology" creates difficulties for many marriages regardless of social class.

If taken no further, the debate over the lives of blue-collar workers outside the workplace cannot be resolved. Some people will point to overlaps with the white-collar sectors and announce the disappearance of working-class culture. Others will stress differences and insist on its survival.

Yet the debate can be taken further. Most observers study the home, leisure, and marital relations of blue-collar workers less for their intrinsic interest than for their possible impact on working-class consciousness and political behavior. Now Imperium workers seldom see their lives outside the workplace as distinctly "working class." I pointed this out in detail in the discussion of their residential lives, where I noted that, especially in post–World War II suburbs, they rarely see themselves as living in "working-class areas." I also mentioned that, in reviewing the jobs of their own children or the children of their blue-collar friends, they notice the minority who have upper-white-collar jobs as much as the majority who do not. This point is generally true for other aspects of the lives of Imperium workers away from their jobs. They rarely see these as distinctly "working class." They are, of course, aware that above all their modest levels of education distinguish them from most upper-white-collar people. But most are well aware of other features of their lives that overlap with those of many white-collar employees.

This should not be glossed over. There is a danger that snobbishness on the part of outside observers, many of whom come from the most privileged sections of American society, may lead them to overlook the way blue-collar workers view their achievements beyond the workplace. An outsider may examine the neighbors of workers in post–World War II suburbia and notice that none of them are lawyers or doctors. Most Imperium workers are aware of this, but they also notice that they do have neighbors who are teachers or social workers or small businessmen. Outsiders may stress the fact that many Imperium workers spend time in occupational taverns with other blue-collar workers. Imperium workers are aware of this, but they also notice that when they go out to eat in certain restaurants, or visit New York City, or play golf, the context is occupationally mixed. Outsiders may classify their marriages as "blue collar," but to most workers it is obvious that some of the successes and failures of their marital lives resemble those of white-collar people they know or hear about in the media.

Above all, most workers contrast what they see as a certain fluidity in their lives outside the workplace with their considerably more restricted lives at work. Nor is this necessarily the result of "false consciousness" or the "hegemony of ruling class ideas," for it has some real basis. In part 4 I will argue that this view is reflected in an image Imperium workers have of their position in the class structure *outside work*. Most do not see this class structure as a graduated and benevolent hierarchy, but they do see it as having some fluidity in its middle range.

However, first it is important to consider *life at work*, for this is viewed as more distinct (again, with good reason) and is reflected in a conception Imperium workers have of their position in the class structure at work.

Part 2

Blue-Collar Work and the Automated Factory

The main reason for studying this chemical plant is that much of it is highly automated. This presents a chance to examine the argument of those who claim such
plants have transformed blue-collar work. The second reason for studying Imperium
is that it also contains various more traditional blue-collar jobs, which makes it
possible to place the discussion of automated plants in the context of blue-collar
work in general. Among the kinds of employees represented at Imperium are
operators who monitor instrument panels (the work often seen as characterizing
automated plants), skilled maintenance workers (such as electricians, welders, and
plumbers), assembly-line workers, physical laborers, warehouse workers, and
laboratory technicians.

4

An Automated Plant: Overview

Chemical plants, together with oil refineries, power plants, atomic plants, and certain steel plants, are often highly automated. Other industries such as automobile manufacturing are, through the introduction of robots, moving in a similar direction. There are two main pictures of work in these settings. One group argues that highly automated plants have radically transformed blue-collar factory work. The scope of the suggested transformation varies, but the following are the main claims that have been made.

The work is interesting, since monitoring an instrument panel—the main job in such plants—requires skill and intelligence. At the same time, workers are free to proceed at their own pace; unlike assembly workers they are not tied to the rhythm of a machine. And the operator's job requires responsibility, since an error can lead to the destruction of very expensive machinery. For this reason he feels pride in his work. In general, it is argued, the chemical operator looks increasingly unlike the conventional picture of the blue-collar industrial worker and increasingly like the standard image of a white-collar professional.[1]

There is also a very different picture of workers in a highly automated plant—that they are dominated and controlled by management. Around the turn of the century, management destroyed the old craft unions in the steel, oil, and chemical industries and reorganized factories according to Frederick Taylor's principles of "scientific management." The essence of these principles was that management should itself determine the best method of performing the job, then prescribe precisely how workers should proceed. As a result of this reorganization, it is claimed, workers in automated plants are effectively docile servants dominated by management in highly "Taylorized" work settings. Their situation is similar to that of most blue-collar workers, including the assembly worker in an auto plant—the classic symbol of the oppressed employee.[2]

Despite the importance of the subject, the evidence on which these two competing pictures are based is slender. For instance, the more optimistic view relies almost entirely on survey data. This is risky. I have pointed out that many blue-collar workers are skilled at living with two worlds at work. There is the official version of how the job is done. This is for management and outsiders. And there is another, more accurate version of what takes place, which workers keep to themselves. A classic, if extreme, example of these two worlds and the care with which workers keep them apart is the case of a supervisor of mines in England. In a government inquiry into safety on the the job he was asked to give a simple account of how the work was performed. He could not do this, he replied, for whenever he approached miners put down their tools, resuming work only when he had gone. For such reasons, survey data without fieldwork may mistake the official version for the actual practice.[3] The more pessimistic view is based on still fewer data. Braverman's very influential account, for instance, is mostly supposition. In fact, there are remarkably few comprehensive studies of work in automated plants in the United States that bear on this debate.[4]

The evidence I have gathered suggests that neither picture of the worker in a highly automated plant is correct. The job is not, as the first view would maintain, interesting and satisfying, nor does the responsibility involved afford men much sense of pride. On the contrary, the work is dull because it is repetitive, and it is also dangerous. In addition, a form of shift work is involved that disrupts men's social lives and disturbs their bodies. Chemical workers are not like white-collar professionals.

Yet the second picture of the worker in an automated plant is also misleading. Men in these jobs are not mindless automatons, dominated by management in highly "Taylorized" work settings. For there are certain features of such settings that enable workers to assume a degree of control, sometimes considerable, over their work situation. Because the work is dull, men mostly use this control to create for themselves time and space in which to enjoy a variety of social activities while at work. These *are* blue-collar workers, but their situation does not correspond to the conventional view of the assembly worker, the common paradigm of the blue-collar worker.

Work in the Plant

Production Workers

It is important at the start to consider exactly what work in an automated plant entails. Failure to do this is responsible for some of the commoner misconception about such plants. This chapter, then, begins with an overview of the various kinds of work in an automated plant. It also contains a sketch of the blue-collar job hierarchies, information on earnings, an outline of job preferences within the plant, and a definition of automation. The chapter ends with a detailed account of four kinds of production situations that involve monitoring by the operators, the activity on which the debate over automated plants has focused. This is essential background for the next chapter, which considers how blue-collar workers in automated plants perceive their jobs.

The plant contains five main production centers (see map 6). Two of these are what engineers call "continuous process plants," for the same product is produced in a continuous flow, twenty-four hours a day, seven days a week. One of these, the "fasic plant," produces "fasic anhydride" (not the real product),[5] and the other consists of turbines and boilers that produce steam for the entire complex.

The other three production centers involve "batch production." In this kind of process there is a clear gap after each lot of product is turned out, and a batch plant may produce, in sequence, a series of different products. The three batch plants all

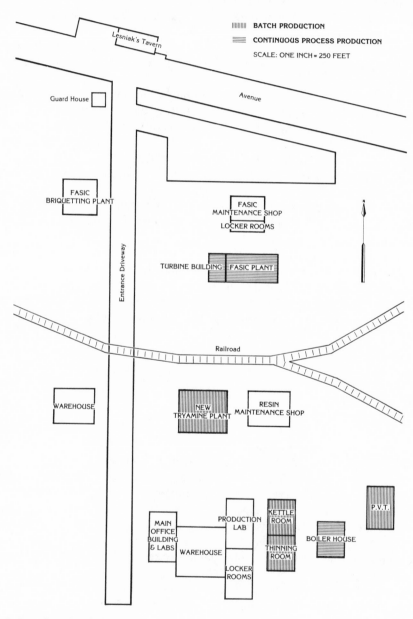

Map 6. Imperium chemical plant.

produce resins. One is called "the kettle room," another "the PVT plant." The third, which opened in late 1977, is a "tryamine" plant, the most modern in the United States. There are, then, two main groups involved in production—*process workers* and *batch workers*.

Support Workers

Highly automated plants are sometimes thought of as ghostly places run by a handful of men. This may be true at night, but it is not so during the day. As Bright put it, if automated plants require so few workers, "why, then, are there so many cars in the parking lot?"[6] The answer is that a whole range of functions are performed in support of production workers.

There are four groups of blue-collar support workers—mechanics, warehouse workers, laboratory technicians, and packagers. *Mechanics* service the production centers, repairing machinery when it fails and sometimes installing new machinery. *Warehouse workers* handle the tank cars that bring raw ingredients into the plant and that ship out the finished product. These workers also take finished material in drums from the production centers for storage in the warehouses, from which they are loaded onto delivery trucks. *Laboratory technicians* test the various resins as they are being produced in the batch plants to see if they meet specifications. *Packagers* operate a machine that turns liquid fasic anhydride into flakes that are stored in canvas bags to await customer delivery.

The Nonunion Labor Force

All the workers described above belong to the union. The remaining personnel consist of supervisors, management, clerical and secretarial workers, chemists, engineers, and salesmen. With the exception of some first-line supervisors, they operate out of the main office building and are white collar. Most of the clerical and secretarial workers are female, but the rest of the white-collar workers are male. The entire plant work force is summarized in table 10.

Blue-Collar Job Hierarchies

In each work area men are divided into crews organized in a hierarchy (table 11). Usually there are three levels, though in the laboratory and packaging plant there are only two. The terms for these levels vary. In production (process and batch) a worker moves from "helper" to "assistant" to "chief," while in other areas the chief is called a "leader." As a worker moves up, so does his hourly rate. For instance, in the process plant an assistant receives twenty-seven cents an hour more than a helper, and a chief thirty-nine cents more than an assistant. Positions above chief or leader entail entering supervision and leaving the union. Mechanics receive the highest

Table 10   Imperium Work Force

Work Group	Number
Blue collar	121
Production workers	
Process workers	24
Batch workers	34
Support workers	
Mechanics	24
Warehouse workers	26
Laboratory technicians	6
Packagers	7
White collar	55
Support workers	
Management	5
Production supervisors	15
Chemists and engineers	4
Clerical and secretarial	25
Salesmen	6
Total	176

basic hourly rate, followed by laboratory workers and process workers, with packagers at the bottom.

Those groups directly involved in production—process and batch workers and laboratory techicians—work shifts. (Packagers sometimes work an afternoon shift.) For doing so they receive a premium, which in 1983 was twenty-five cents an hour for the afternoon shift and forty cents for the midnight shift. Because of the premium, the actual average hourly rate of mechanics, process workers, and laboratory workers is very similar, followed by batch workers, warehouse workers, and packagers (table 11).

Average Annual Earnings and Overtime

The average yearly earnings for each area are shown in table 12. Process workers earned $30,589, more than any other group. They were followed by laboratory workers $28,392 and batch workers $28,309. Warehouse workers earned less than any other group $24,167.

The main explanation for differences in the average earnings of work groups in the plant is the availability of overtime. Men are paid time and a half for the first four hours worked beyond their normal schedule and double time for any additional hours. Average earnings and hours of overtime are very closely correlated (table 12). It is because process workers put in an average of seventeen hours a week overtime that they earned so much more than other men. As we will see (chap. 5), a guaranteed minimum of eight hours a week of overtime is built into the schedule of

Table 11   Blue-Collar Job Hierarchies and the Wage Structure, 1983

Work Group	Basic Hourly Rate (dollars)	Basic Hourly Rate Plus Average Shift Premium
Process workers		
Chief	10.31	10.53
Assistant	9.92	10.14
Helper	9.65	9.87
Batch workers		
Chief	10.22	10.44
Assistant	9.92	10.14
Helper	9.65	9.87
Laboratory workers		
Leader	10.37	10.59
Technician	10.22	10.44
Packagers (briquetter workers)		
Leader	9.83	—
Helper	9.65	—
Mechanics		
Leader	10.51	—
Class A	10.39	—
Apprentice	9.72	—
Warehouse workers		
Leader	10.22	—
Assistant	9.97	—
Helper	9.65	—

Source: Contract.

process workers but no other group. Warehouse workers, with less overtime than any other group (6.5 hours a week), have the lowest earnings.

Throughout the plant men often comment on the difference overtime makes in their earnings. "It's overtime where you make your money" is a common remark, and they consider overtime almost a right—part of the job. During recessions when overtime is scarce, they become angry and disgruntled.

The ample availability of overtime is closely connected with the technology of an automated plant. Since production proceeds around the clock in shifts, a man can do his own job for eight hours, then stay on to replace another worker on the next shift who may be sick or on vacation. And because it takes at least a week, and usually longer, to learn each of the jobs in the plant it is not practical for the company to employ a utility man, as is done on the assembly line in an auto plant, to fill in for absent workers. So at Imperium the place of an absent worker is taken by another man from the same work area but a different shift, who then earns overtime. This is

Table 12   Average Earnings and Overtime, 1983

Work Group	Average Yearly Earnings[a] (dollars)	Average Weekly Hours of Overtime
Process workers	30,589	17[b]
Laboratory workers	28,392	9.25
Batch workers	28,309	10.8
Mechanics	27,420	9.0
Packagers	25,603	8.5
Warehouse workers	24,167	6.5
Overall average	27,716	

Source: Figures given to union by management. The figures for each work group are based on 1976 data. To bring them up to date and into line with data in table 11, I have raised them by 69 percent—the average increase since 1976 in the hourly wage rate at Imperium.

[a]Before tax.

[b]This includes the sixth day of each shift, for which process workers automatically receive overtime.

why shift workers (process and batch operators and laboratory technicians) can accumulate so many hours of overtime.

Overtime is also frequent among mechanics. Problems in the machinery that occur after the day shift has ended often must be fixed at once, which usually means calling in mechanics. There are two men to cover the afternoon and midnight shifts, but they are general mechanics. If the problem is at all complex, the day mechanics who are expert in that area must be called in and paid at the overtime rate.

Only among warehouse workers are opportunities for overtime not plentiful. This is because work can be done only when trucks arrive to deliver or pick up material, which is mostly during the day.

Job Preference

Movement among jobs in the plant, both up a work hierarchy and between different work areas, is determined by plantwide seniority. Vacant positions are posted on a bulletin board and men "bid" for them, with the jobs going to the applicants having the greatest seniority. There are two conditions. First, unless the vacant job is at the lowest level in the work hierarchy a man must have had experience in the job immediately below the one for which he is bidding. For instance, if a worker bids for the job of chief operator in the process plant he must at some time have worked as an assistant operator there. But he may bid for the helper's job without ever having worked in the process plant. Second, applicants for the job of apprentice mechanic must also pass a general intelligence test and a test in mathematics. Among those who pass the test, the job goes to the worker with most seniority.

Under this system men can and do move freely between different kinds of work in the plant. Most have spent time in several areas, and some have done every job in the plant. The greater a man's seniority, the more choice he has between jobs and the closer he can come to obtaining the one he wants most. An indicator of men's preferences between various jobs can, then, be obtained by comparing the seniority levels of workers in different areas of the plant. An area where average seniority is high is more desirable than one in which it is low.[7]

The outstanding advantage of this method of indicating job preferences is that it records what workers do, rather that what they say they will do or what they say they would like to do. It gives a clear picture of the way men act when faced with concrete choices between different jobs.

Table 13 ranks jobs by the average seniority of workers in them. The warehouse and maintenance are the two most popular jobs in the plant. Men there have an average seniority of 25.4 and 22.2 years respectively. Next in popularity come jobs in the batch plant, as operator or laboratory technician. The least desirable jobs are process operator (the job some people argue has transformed blue-collar work for the better) and packaging. Ironically, the second most unpopular job (process operator) carries the highest earnings potential. The reasons for this will be explained later.

This ranking reflects the popularity of jobs given the characteristics of the Imperium labor force, including an average age of forty-eight. This is not high for such plants, for workers tend to stay in these jobs. But from fieldwork it is clear that a decisive determinant of a man's choice of job is position in the life cycle. When workers assess a job they consider how it rates on five main characteristics. How much does it pay? How much physical discomfort does it involve? To what extent does it interfere with social life outside and inside the plant? How secure is it? How interesting is it? The relative importance men attach to these factors alters with age—with their position in the life cycle.

A young unmarried man will tend to place a premium on a job that does not interfere with his social life. A married man with a young family will probably give high priority to a job that pays well, for he is likely to be on the financial treadmill entailed by mortgage payments and a wife who does not work. An older man with his family grown and mortgage fully paid off is probably more concerned with job

Table 13   Job Preference as Measured by Average Seniority

Work Group	Average Years of Seniority	Work Group	Average Years of Seniority
Warehouse workers	25.4	Batch workers	17.1
Maintenance workers	22.2	Process workers	13.5
Laboratory workers	17.3	Packagers	11.0

Sources for tables 13 and 14: Company list of employees by current job; seniority and age list in appendix C of contract between Imperium and local — of the Oil, Chemical and Atomic Workers Union.

Note: One-way analysis of variance; $F = 9.3$, $p < .001$ $(N = 121)$.

security, avoiding physical discomfort, and enjoying his social life inside and outside the plant.

Given the average age of the work force, the overall ranking of jobs at Imperium is likely to reflect disproportionately the preference of older men. To reveal the job preferences of younger men the work force was divided into two groups, older and younger. Age forty-nine was taken as the dividing point, since at this age there is a good chance that a man will be done with mortgage payments and that his children have entered jobs.

The results are displayed in table 14. Younger men are less enthusiastic about the relatively low-paying warehouse jobs, though they still prefer them to working as packagers or as process or batch operators. These relative rankings will be explained later.

The Concept of Automation

A study of workers in an automated plant cannot avoid defining "automation," for the concept is not at all clear. A conveyor belt, a washing machine, a distillation process in an oil refinery, and a computer-guided missile are all automated machines, but they differ in important ways. How are these differences to be captured?[8]

The central idea underlying the concept of automation is that of a machine doing work once performed by man. As automation increases, machinery takes over more and more of the worker's role. The concept of automation can, then, best be clarified by classifying different types of machines.

A machine may be defined as a "combination of members so arranged that natural forces can be compelled through them to do work by yielding certain prescribed motions."[9] As machinery becomes more advanced, additional constraints to motion are added so that eventually all but the desired motions are eliminated. Chains of interacting parts are developed, gradually providing more precise and

Table 14   Job Preference as Measured by Average Seniority for Younger and Older Workers

Work Group	Average Years of Seniority	Work Group	Average Years of Seniority
Younger workers[a]		*Older workers*	
Maintenance	20.2	Warehouse	28.0
Warehouse	19.9	Maintenance	23.3
Laboratory	16.4	Laboratory	22.0
Batch	16.2	Batch	18.7
Process	12.2	Process	17.4
Packaging	10.2	Packaging	13.0

[a]Younger workers are those age forty-nine and below in 1977.

more continuous control of motion. Increasing constraint becomes the criterion of mechanical perfection.

Using increasing constraint to motion as the criterion, levels of mechanization can be distinguished and arranged in a hierarchy, from the least to the most automated (fig. 2). The lowest level of mechanization is the human hand, followed by hand tools (level 2). Some of the most skillful work is performed at this level, which includes the work of the surgeon, violinist, and sculptor.

At level 3 a powered tool is used, such as a portable drill or welding torch. Much maintenance work is performed at levels 2 and 3. At level 3 the machine adds force but not control. Control is added at level 4, where a physical framework guides and limits the action of the tool, such as in a drill press or lathe or forklift truck or electric typewriter. The machine performs only within fixed limits, and the operator controls the amount, direction, and duration of its action. At level 5 the machine performs a single action within definite limits of space, speed, and time without human assistance. An example is a conveyor belt. Level 6 consists of machines that perform a series of such actions, rather than just one, such as a washing machine or a single robot that, for instance, welds or paints on an assembly line.

At level 7 the control of the machinery is geographically separated from the production machinery, and this remote control makes it possible to direct several machines from one central location or control room. Level 8 eliminates the need for human intervention to start the machine.

Levels 9 through 11 provide information on the progress of the production process. Level 9 signals values such as temperature and pressure, as on control panels in a chemical plant or oil refinery. Level 10 contains a measuring device that signals when the measured characteristic reaches a certain limit. For instance, in a chemical plant a bell may ring when pressure approaches some danger point. Level 11 records the information signaled at level 9. Thus a mechanical pen might mark the value of temperature or pressure on a moving chart.

Levels 12 to 14 include machines that modify their own actions in accordance with the information they collect. At level 12 a signal directs the machine to follow a new pattern of operation. For instance, the machine might pack a certain number of items into a container and then switch to another container. At level 13 the machine discards products that do not meet certain specifications. At levels 15 through 17 the machine corrects its own performance after, during, or before operation. Level 17 is found in computer-guided missiles that anticipate and adjust to required actions.

Computers merit special mention, given the recent explosive growth in their use. Computers are tools that can combine with other machines to operate at a variety of levels of mechanization. For example, a digital watch, like a conventional watch, operates at mechanization level 5. By contrast, in space flights computers combine with other machinery so that most of the flight operates at mechanization level 17.

It is therefore apparent that the term "automation" covers a wide range of situations and levels. In this book, where I describe production processes in detail I will provide a "mechanization profile" that breaks a production process into its various components and shows the level of automation at which each component operates.

Initiating Control Source	Type of Machine Response	Power Source	Level Number	Level of Mechanization
From a variable in the environment	Responds with action — Modifies own action over a wide range of variation	Mechanical (Nonmanual)	17	Anticipates action required and adjusts to provide it
			16	Corrects performance while operating
			15	Corrects performance after operating
	Responds with action — Selects from a limited range of possible pre-fixed actions		14	Identifies and selects appropriate set of actions
			13	Segregates or rejects according to measurement
			12	Changes speed, position, direction according to measurement signal
	Responds with signal		11	Records performance
			10	Signals preselected values of measurement (includes error detection)
			9	Measures characteristic of work
From a control mechanism that directs a predetermined pattern of action	Fixed within the machine		8	Actuated by introduction of work piece or material
			7	Power tool system, remote controlled
			6	Power tool, program control (sequence of fixed functions)
			5	Power tool, fixed cycle (single function)
From man	Variable		4	Power tool, hand control
			3	Powered hand tool
		Manual	2	Hand tool
			1	Hand

Fig. 2. Levels of mechanization. From James Bright, *Automation and Management* (Boston: Division of Research, Graduate School of Business Administration, Harvard University, 1958), exhibit 4-2, p. 45. Reprinted by permission. Subsequent mechanization profiles are also based on Bright's scheme.

Four Kinds of Monitoring

Those who stress the special nature of work in automated plants focus on the task of monitoring instrument panels. It is important to consider a variety of monitoring situations, since there are differences between them, and some writers (for instance Blauner and Woodward) have suggested that the distinction between monitoring in process and in batch production is significant. In the following discussion I will distinguish four situations involving monitoring and describe two of these in detail so as to give a picture of what production in such plants entails. I will argue that the distinction between process and batch plants is important from the workers' point of view less because of differences in the intrinsic interest of the job than because of differences in the kind of shift work the two production techniques entail.

Monitoring Type 1: Crew Process Production—The Fasic Plant

The fasic plant consists of clusters of cylindrical tanks—large fat ones for storing benzene and thin, sleek ones within which production takes place. These are grouped around the main distillation column, sixty feet tall. The cylinders, painted pink and blue and silver, are sheathed by pipes from which valves protrude at frequent intervals. The whole plant hisses softly with the sound of slowly escaping steam.

The work crew—chief, assistant, and helper—monitors and directs most of the production process from a control room at one end of the plant. It is a small area, about eighteen feet by ten, dominated by an instrument panel that stretches most of its length (fig. 3). The panel is divided into two main sections, which contain banks of instruments to measure performance during the stages of production. Most of the measurements concern temperature or pressure. Behind the instrument panel the men have installed a small stove and refrigerator. To the side are a card table, radio, and television set.

What does a process worker's job involve? There are two main stages in the production of fasic anhydride. First, benzene and air are mixed at high temperature in the presence of a catalyst to form fasic acid. Second, fasic acid with xylene added is distilled, producing fasic anhydride. This process is outlined in figure 4. The helper controls the first stage, the assistant controls the second, and the chief is responsible for the entire operation.

Stage A: The Helper
The helper begins the process outside the control room by opening a main valve on the benzene storage tank (M-1). From within the control room he monitors the flow of benzene and filtered air, making sure they enter a heated tank (M-2) in fixed proportion. The tank, which contains the catalyst (vanadium pentoxide), is kept at 4,000°C by regulating valves. The resulting mixture of fasic acid and carbon dioxide passes through a condenser that cools it to 54°C and the carbon dioxide is dried off in an absorption column. The liquid fasic acid is stored in a tank (M-3) that the helper

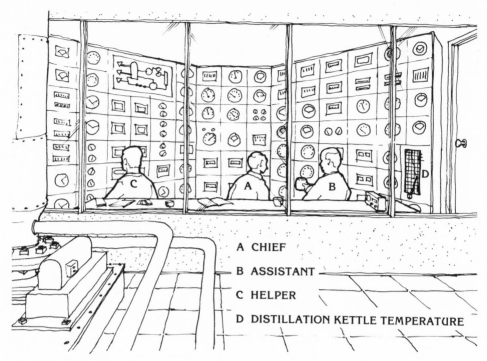

Fig. 3. Control room of the process (fasic) plant.

has opened by going outside and turning a valve. The process continues day and night.

Most of this time the helper spends in the control room watching temperature dials and pressure gauges. At intervals he goes outside to turn a valve. But there is additional manual work. Even automatic valves sometimes stick and must be shifted by hand.

When a new shipment of benzene arrives it is the helper's job to pump it from tank cars into storage tanks (M-1). He does this by clambering up a ladder on the side of one of the tanks, which are twenty feet high, opening a valve, and hooking a pipe from the top of the tank car into the valve. He starts a pump, which shuts off after a predetermined amount of benzene has passed into the storage tank. It takes up to two hours to fill a storage tank, and during this time the helper must keep an eye on the pump in case something goes wrong. This task is not complicated, but benzene is highly flammable.

Once a year the work crew must change the catalyst. This involves removing the base of the tank and scraping out the catalyst and fasic acid that have become caked all around the inside. The job is done with hand tools, and men must wear gas masks to prevent the fasic acid from corroding their lungs.

Stage B: The Assistant
The assistant controls the distillation of the fasic acid produced in the helper's stage of the process. He begins by opening valves on the fasic acid storage tank (M-3) and

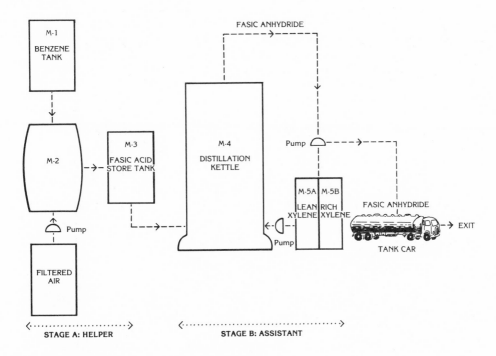

Fig. 4. The process production of fasic anhydride.

on the xylene tanks outside (M-5A and B); allowing the mixture to enter the distillation kettle (M-4). He heats the kettle to 120°C, again by regulating valves on the kettle, outside the control room.

Inside the control room he monitors the kettle's temperature, recorded on a chart. This chart is the key to the entire distillation process. It is prominently displayed in the assistant's section of the control room (fig. 3D), and on it he notes the main stages as they are reached.

Figure 5 reproduces a typical chart. Each row indicates an hour. The chart moves slowly, and a pen resting on it indicates the kettle's temperature over time. The resulting temperature line, drawn from bottom to top, can be seen in column B. In column C are the assistant's notes indicating the main stages as they are reached. In column A he records the quantities of fasic anhydride that have been distilled.

Distillation proceeds as follows. First, when the temperature reaches 100°C the water begins to evaporate. The assistant notes on the chart "10.55 [time]. Water starting off." When he sees the temperature rise above 100°C he knows all the water has gone. He opens the valves outside connecting the storage tank for lean xylene (fig. 4. M-5A) with the distillation column, writing on the chart "13.30. All water off. Go M-5A." At 120°C only rich xylene is left in the distillation kettle. The assistant switches storage tanks, again by opening valves outside the control room. When the temperature reaches 140°C the assistant knows most of the xylene has evaporated. He goes outside, opens a small valve at the base of the distillation kettle, and takes a sample of liquid in a beaker. He stirs it with a thermometer, cooling the liquid by

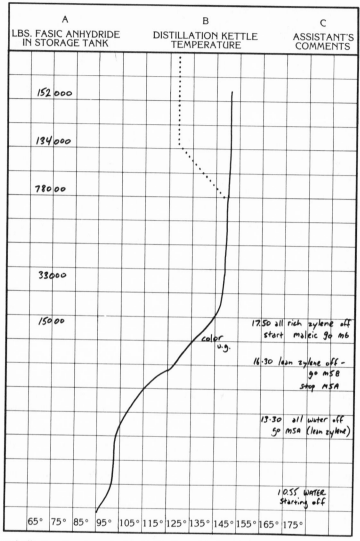

Fig. 5. Chart indicating the stages in the distillation of fasic anhydride.

running cold water over the outside of the beaker. When the liquid crystallizes, turning cloudy at a temperature of 52°C, it is pure fasic anhydride.

The assistant closes by hand the valve to the xylene tank and opens the valve to the fasic anhydride storage tank, writing on the chart, "17.50. All rich xylene off. Start fasic. Go M-6." Fasic anhydride is distilled at a rate of 15,000 pounds an hour, and periodically the assistant notes on the chart the quantity of fasic distilled (fig. 5, col. A).

At the top of the distillation column is a vacuum system. This speeds and helps control the process by drawing vapors up the column and lowering the boiling point of the various liquids. So long as this is operating as it should, distillation proceeds smoothly. But if vacuum fails the process can become difficult to control. An assistant: "If you've got good vacuum it's very hard to fuck up. But you've got to watch out. Last night it was 11:30 and we were about to go home. Then suddenly we lost vacuum and everyone had to run like hell."

Distillation in the fasic plant occurs roughly every thirty hours. The same chart, with the same marginal notes from the assistant, is reproduced about 292 times a year. Figure 6 summarizes the entire process in a mechanization or automation profile.[10]

Monitoring Type 2: Solitary Process Production—The Boiler Rooms

The two boiler and turbine rooms, which supply steam and power for the rest of the plant, illustrate a second type of process production. Instead of a crew, there is a single operator who sits in a glass booth that protects him from the noise of the machinery. Here he monitors instrument panels that display temperature and pressure.

The state of New Jersey requires boiler operators to have a license that shows they have received technical and practical training. To obtain this license, men go to a training school. There is a hierarchy of licenses, from "black seal" (the lowest level) through blue, red, and gold (the highest level). Different levels indicate the capacity of boiler a man is competent to handle. Imperium hires only men with at least a blue seal.

The boilers combine fuel (hot gases), air, and water to make steam. All of this is done automatically. A continuous supply of fuel is pumped in, controlled by a pressure regulator. The correct air and fuel rate is produced by a preset control, and the water supply is determined by a feed-water regulator.

There are a variety of automatic safety devices. There are valves to let steam out if pressure rises too high. If the water supply falls dangerously low, a device cuts off the flame that ignites the fuel. And there is a light-sensitive device to close down the whole boiler should the flame go out or the fuel supply fail.

The operator's task is to monitor the process in case the automatic machinery fails. Should this happen, there are hand controls for shutting down production.

Monitoring Type 3: Crew Batch Production—The Kettle Room

The batch plant contains three production centers. One makes a variety of liquid plastics. The other produces alkyds, used as a base for paints and varnishes. The third produces tryamine. Since the production processes in the first two batch plants are very similar, only the alkyd center will be discussed in detail.

In some ways batch production in a chemical plant is like cooking on a very large scale, and this is reflected in the language men use to describe the process. The "kettle room," as the alkyd production center is called, contains six kettles—giant vats in which the chemicals are "cooked" (fig. 7). These are 20 to 30 feet high, with a

Initiating Control Source	Type of Machine Response			Power Source	Level Number	Level of Mechanization	1 Unload benzene—hook up pipe	2 Monitor pump	3 Open valves on benzene tank	4 Monitor formation of fasic acid	5 Alter valves outside control room	6 Open valves on fasic acid tanks	7 Monitor distillation process	8 Alter valves outside control room	9 Test a sample
From a variable in the environment	Responds with action	Modifies own action over a wide range of variation		Mechanical (Nonmanual)	17	Anticipates action required and adjusts to provide it									
					16	Corrects performance while operating									
					15	Corrects performance after operating									
		Selects from a limited range of possible pre-fixed actions			14	Identifies and selects appropriate set of actions									
					13	Segregates or rejects according to measurement									
	Responds with signal				12	Changes speed, position, direction according to measurement signal	●								
					11	Records performance			●				●		
					10	Signals preselected values of measurement (includes error detection)									
					9	Measures characteristic of work									
From a control mechanism that directs a predetermined pattern of action	Fixed within the machine				8	Actuated by introduction of work piece or material									
					7	Power tool system, remote controlled									
					6	Power tool, program control (sequence of fixed functions)									
					5	Power tool, fixed cycle (single function)									
From man	Variable				4	Power tool, hand control									
					3	Powered handtool									
				Manual	2	Hand tool									●
					1	Hand	●	●		●	●	●		●	

Fig. 6. Mechanization level of stages in the process production of fasic anhydride. Workers responsible for each stage: stages 1–5, helper; 6–9, assistant; 1–9, chief.

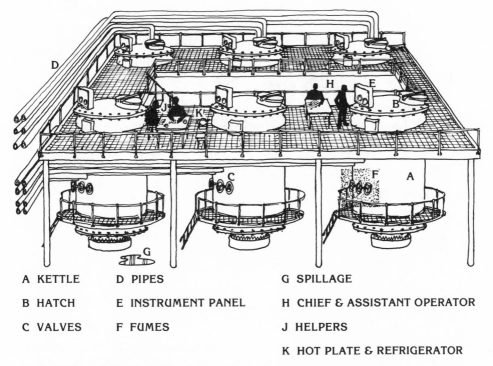

A	KETTLE	D	PIPES	G	SPILLAGE
B	HATCH	E	INSTRUMENT PANEL	H	CHIEF & ASSISTANT OPERATOR
C	VALVES	F	FUMES	J	HELPERS
				K	HOT PLATE & REFRIGERATOR

Fig. 7. Batch production in the kettle room.

capacity of up to ten thousand gallons. Most of the ground floor is filled with the bodies of the kettles, under each of which are heating elements.

Twenty feet above the ground is a second floor, through which the kettles' noses protrude a few feet. The "cook" is controlled here. Alongside the nose of each kettle is a control panel showing temperature and pressure. Here workers monitor production and add new ingredients through a hatch at the top.

At intervals during the cook workers take samples to the laboratory. When the technicians there indicate that the alkyd is ready, it is pumped into the thinning room next door. A separate work crew then adds chemical inhibitors that prevent the alkyd from solidifying under normal conditions. Again samples are taken to the laboratory, and when the product is ready it is pumped out into tank cars or individual drums. These stages in alkyd production are diagramed in figure 8. Three work crews are involved in the process—in the kettle room, the thinning room, and the laboratory. Each crew has its own hierarchy—three levels in the production rooms, two levels in the laboratory.

Batch Operators: The Helpers
Helpers in the batch plant are very much like manual laborers. They are not permitted to touch the controls on the kettles, and they play no part in the monitoring. Their job is strictly delineated. They are responsible for transporting raw

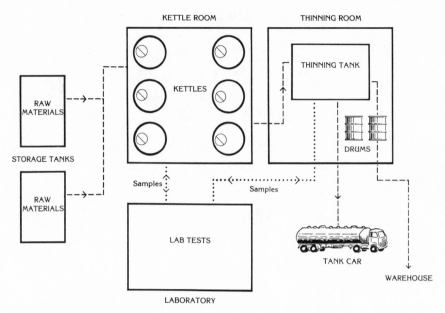

Fig. 8. Stages in batch production.

materials to the kettles. Sometimes this involves only opening a valve on one of the storage tanks outside the kettle room, for the more commonly used liquid ingredients are brought from the storage tanks by pipes that lead directly into the kettles. When the chief or assistant wants to add an ingredient from these tanks he sends the helper to open the appropriate valve. The helper does this by hand, then starts a pump that transfers a set quantity of the ingredient into the kettle.

But solid ingredients, and those liquids less frequently used, must be transported by tow motor to the kettle room and hoisted on lifts to the upper level. Helpers open the hatch in the kettle's nose by hand and pour in the ingredients. This involves a fair amount of manual labor—sometimes large chunks of solid ingredients have to be hacked into smaller pieces that can fit through the hatch. Some spillage of chemicals, which can be dangerous, is hard to avoid.

The only time the helper need be on the second level is when he is hoisting up ingredients or pouring them into the kettles. The bulk of the work on the upper level consists of monitoring the control panels, which helpers are not allowed to touch. For a long time, to emphasize the helpers' lowly status as laborers, chiefs and assistants refused to allow them onto the upper level. A worker who used to be a helper explained how this changed: "They didn't used to let you up on the platform. You were garbage. So you'd sit downstairs behind the kettle like a jerk in cold weather, freezing. When young blood came in they put a stop to that. They told the chiefs they'd throw 'em off the platform." Now helpers sit upstairs, but at a separate table from the chief and assistant (fig. 7).

Chief and Assistant

The chief and his assistant direct the cooking of the batch. As with the distillation of fasic acid in the process plant, they follow a clearly laid out pattern. At the start of a new batch the supervisor of the alkyd plant gives them a formula card and a chart. A typical formula card is illustrated in figure 9. It lists the ingredients and their quantities and the main stages in the cook. Each stage corresponds either to the addition of a new ingredient or to a change in temperature. The worker pins this card to the control panel next to the kettle.

Figure 10 shows a typical chart. The chief or assistant fits this to a time clock on the instrument panel and the clock rotates the chart, one segment each hour. A pen traces the kettle's temperature.

Workers regulate the heat of the kettle so that the recorded temperature line stays as close as possible to a "model" temperature line drawn beforehand by the supervisor. Spaced along this line are letters (A, B, C, D . . .) that correspond to stages on the formula card. When the pen reaches such a marked stage workers consult the formula card for appropriate instructions, which usually involve further ingredients and a change of temperature. When the batch is finished the chart, with the temperature line, is placed in the supervisor's office. Like the distillation chart in the process plant, it is an important device to let management check that the men did what they were supposed to do.

The chief and his assistant are responsible for making sure production proceeds in accordance with these guides. They are also responsible for anticipating explosions. On each of the six kettles, alongside the temperature chart, is a pressure gauge that warns if there is danger of explosion. As in the process plant, disks built into the kettles give way when pressure exceeds a certain point, allowing the contents to escape into the air. Although this prevents a major explosion that could destroy the entire plant, it entails a smaller explosion that showers chemicals all over the work area. And sometimes these chemicals ignite.

Stage	Ingredient (code no.)	Pounds	Comments
A	32415	5,000	Heat to 70 [degrees]
B	54130	6,000	Add glycol: heat to 200
C	34679	3,000	
D			Reduce heat to 150
E			Reduce heat to 100

Fig. 9. Formula card for batch production.

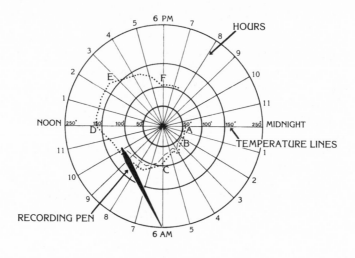

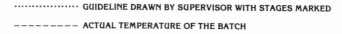

Fig. 10. Chart indicating the desired, and the actual, temperature of a batch.

The chief or his assistant checks the gauges on the six kettles at regular intervals, about every ten minutes. This involves patrolling a distance of roughly one hundred feet. Since pressure can build up very rapidly, each kettle has an alarm system set to go off at a certain pressure.

When the last stage of the chart has been reached, the helper draws a sample from the base of the kettle and takes it to the laboratory. There other workers test the product for acidity and viscosity. Usually these items need adjusting, and the workers in the laboratory issue appropriate instructions to the chief and assistant in the kettle room. They may, for instance, tell the chief to add fifty pounds of glycerine and "put it on sparge" for an hour. "Sparge" involves releasing a stream of carbon monoxide gas from the bottom of the kettle, which helps mix the glycerine with the rest of the chemicals.

When tests indicate that the correct acidity and viscosity have been reached, the laboratory technicians tell the chief in the kettle room to "press out." He opens a valve and starts a pump to transfer the contents of the kettle into a tank in the thinning room next door. Figure 11 is a mechanization profile for the kettle room crew.

The work in the thinning room is a combination of monitoring the thinning process and then, when the product is ready, pumping it into either tank cars or drums. Only one control panel has to be monitored (by contrast with the kettle room, where there are six panels, one on each kettle). The chief can do this alone. The assistant and helper are responsible for pumping or drumming. Pumping involves only hooking a pump to the top of a tank car and setting an automatic gauge.

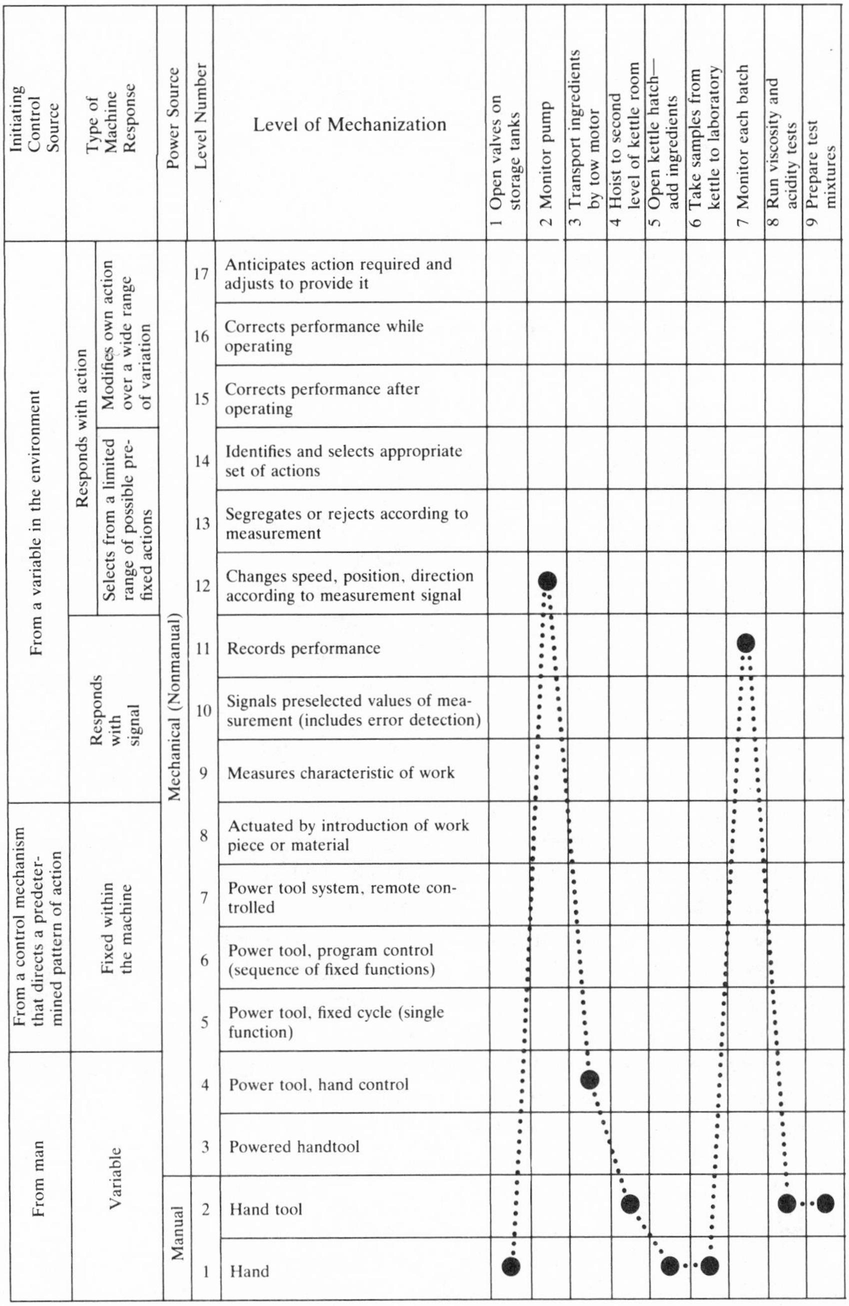

Level Number	Level of Mechanization
17	Anticipates action required and adjusts to provide it
16	Corrects performance while operating
15	Corrects performance after operating
14	Identifies and selects appropriate set of actions
13	Segregates or rejects according to measurement
12	Changes speed, position, direction according to measurement signal
11	Records performance
10	Signals preselected values of measurement (includes error detection)
9	Measures characteristic of work
8	Actuated by introduction of work piece or material
7	Power tool system, remote controlled
6	Power tool, program control (sequence of fixed functions)
5	Power tool, fixed cycle (single function)
4	Power tool, hand control
3	Powered handtool
2	Hand tool
1	Hand

Column headers (stages): 1 Open valves on storage tanks; 2 Monitor pump; 3 Transport ingredients by tow motor; 4 Hoist to second level of kettle room; 5 Open kettle hatch—add ingredients; 6 Take samples from kettle to laboratory; 7 Monitor each batch; 8 Run viscosity and acidity tests; 9 Prepare test mixtures.

Left categories: Initiating Control Source; Type of Machine Response; Power Source. From a variable in the environment / Responds with action (Modifies own action over a wide range of variation; Selects from a limited range of possible pre-fixed actions; Responds with signal) — Mechanical (Nonmanual). From a control mechanism that directs a predetermined pattern of action / Fixed within the machine. From man / Variable — Manual.

Fig. 11. Mechanization level of stages in the batch production of resins. Cooking the resin. Workers responsible for each stage: stages 1–6, helpers; 7, assistant and chief; 8–9, laboratory workers.

The main work comes when the resin must be pumped into individual drums—tedious and dangerous physical labor. It involves placing a heavy drum under a nozzle from which the alkyd is poured, waiting until the drum is full, then capping it and easing it on a set of rollers to the entrance, where it is picked up on forklift trucks by warehouse workers. (Figure 12 is an automation profile for production in the thinning room.)

Monitoring Type 4: Highly Automated Batch Production—The Tryamine Plant

The tryamine plant began production in late 1977. It was said to be the most modern of its type in the country. Workers joked about this, for instance complaining that the company should have installed escalators instead of stairs to take them to the second level.

The plant is very similar to the kettle room (monitoring type 3), with the following main differences. Much of the information on the control panel is digitally displayed. This includes information about pressure, temperature, quantity, and time. Further, instead of being on top of the kettle, the instrument panel is in a control room built to one side of the second floor. There is also a freight elevator. In the kettle room those ingredients that are not brought directly to the kettles by feed pipes must be hoisted up to the second floor, then poured in. In the new plant they can be taken up by elevator. Finally, the process of adding such ingredients has been made cleaner, for there is a screw device that funnels them into the kettles. This decreases the fumes workers are exposed to as they add ingredients. Otherwise the new tryamine plant is just like the kettle room. Production involves a crew of chief, assistant, and helper, and batches are tested in the laboratory as they cook. The final product is shipped out either in drums or in tank cars.

Production could be automated even further. For instance, a computer could link measuring devices with the machine controls. It would analyze the measurement data and adjust the controls in accordance with program instructions—the formula for each batch. Such instructions could be inserted as cassettes, a different cassette for each type of product. This degree of automation—mechanization level 16 or 17—exists in very few plants. It means retooling with largely untried equipment costing millions of dollars, and the cost savings are minimal since it is still necessary to have a crew of operators to handle minor and major equipment failures. Compare the way the automatic pilot on airplanes has not eliminated the need for human pilots but has just made the job duller.

Conclusion

All four kinds of monitoring work in the plant (process and batch) share certain features.

1. Production is basically repetitive. This is obviously the case in process production. In the fasic plant (monitoring type 1, crew process production) the same production cycle involving distillation recurs about every thirty hours throughout the

Initiating Control Source	Type of Machine Response			Power Source	Level Number	Level of Mechanization	10 Monitor thinning process	11 Run viscosity and acidity tests	12 Pump resin into drums	13 Roll drums to end of thinning room	14 Pump product into tank cars—hook up pump	15 Monitor pump	16 Clean filter press
From a variable in the environment	Responds with action	Modifies own action over a wide range of variation		Mechanical (Nonmanual)	17	Anticipates action required and adjusts to provide it							
					16	Corrects performance while operating							
					15	Corrects performance after operating							
		Selects from a limited range of possible pre-fixed actions			14	Identifies and selects appropriate set of actions							
					13	Segregates or rejects according to measurement							
					12	Changes speed, position, direction according to measurement signal						●	
	Responds with signal				11	Records performance	●		●				
					10	Signals preselected values of measurement (includes error detection)							
					9	Measures characteristic of work							
From a control mechanism that directs a predetermined pattern of action		Fixed within the machine			8	Actuated by introduction of work piece or material							
					7	Power tool system, remote controlled							
					6	Power tool, program control (sequence of fixed functions)							
					5	Power tool, fixed cycle (single function)							
From man		Variable			4	Power tool, hand control							
					3	Powered hand tool							
			Manual		2	Hand tool	●						
					1	Hand			●	●			●

Fig. 12. Mechanization level of stages in the batch production of resins. The thinning process. Workers responsible for each stage: stage 10, chief; 11, laboratory workers; 12–16, assistants and helpers.

year. The boiler rooms (monitoring type 2, solitary process production) offer even less diversity, for there is not even a cycle of events. Production is a single unchanging flow. In batch production (monitoring types 3 and 4) there is somewhat more variety. Men make different kinds of batches using different formulas, ingredients, and methods of production. But the general procedure—following formula cards and charts—does not change.

2. Accounts of automated plants usually imply that the work is all watching dials and gauges. But this is misleading, for even jobs that mostly involve monitoring do require manual work. Some valves need to be opened by hand outside the control room, either because they are too important in the production process to be left to an automatic switch that might not work or because the automated switch is broken. Sometimes chemicals leak onto the floor and must be cleaned up. And every so often parts of the machinery must be cleaned out from the inside by operators. Sometimes when I explained to process workers that I was interested in studying a highly automated plant I would get an ironic laugh: "Automated plants! Ha! You're in the wrong place. This isn't automated. I had to go out just now and put in a new valve by hand."

In addition to the manual component of basically monitoring jobs, there are some jobs that consist almost entirely of manual or laboring work. A production process that is highly automated might require manual labor when certain raw materials are added or when the product is "packed" in drums or bags. This is an important feature that is obscured by the tendency to study part of a plant or a selected group of workers."[11]

3. The job is dangerous. It involves powerful machinery that can explode, and the raw materials that are routinely handled are often toxic and flammable.

4. Both process production and batch production involve shift work around the clock, because a chemical process can take thirty hours or more to complete and cannot usually be interrupted midway without spoiling the product.

5

The Production Worker in an Automated Plant

Excluding the tryamine plant (monitoring type 4), there are fifty-eight workers directly involved in production (men in the tryamine plant are considered separately because the newness of the plant involves all kinds of special factors concerned with teething problems in the machinery).

Four of the fifty-eight workers were unwilling to discuss their jobs and twelve, mostly helpers, do work that is almost entirely manual labor—transporting raw materials, breaking them up, pouring them into kettles. Their job involves little or no monitoring. None of these laborers liked their work. Comments ranged from "The helpers are just a pair of hands; they do whatever the chief or assistant tells them," to the following from a man who was once a helper:

> It's hard, brutal work in poor air and bad fumes. There is tremendous heat from the kettles. No brains or talent are required. You blindly follow orders from insecure, unfeeling, insensitive clods. You smash up material with sledgehammers in bad heat like a convict, constantly worried about being caught sneaking a smoke or standing still. It's great to develop muscles or petrify brains.

The remaining forty-two men do work that *is* mostly monitoring an instrument panel. By far the largest number, thirty-two, did not enjoy the work or find it interesting. Another four were hard to classify, sometimes saying they liked the work and sometimes disliking and even detesting it. Only six said they found the work interesting.

Job Interest

Most men find the work dull because it is largely routine and repetitive. With some modifications the same procedure occurs again and again. In this connection it is important to distinguish the period while workers are learning the job from the time afterward.

Learning the Job

The learning period may be long—up to six months or a year, especially for the boiler operators (monitoring type 2). During this time men often do find the work absorbing.

For most workers the hardest part of learning the job is remembering which valves control which flow. The processing equipment in the fasic plant, for example, consists of several large tanks and columns linked by a maze of pipes. A man may find himself sixty feet above the ground, at the top of the distillation column, staring at several valves. Each valve is attached to a different pipe, and each pipe weaves around the structure and away through a cloud of vapor toward one of the neighboring tanks. Which valve controls which process? In other sections of the plant men can sometimes figure this out by following each pipe to its destination. An assistant in the batch plant explained:

> When I wasn't sure I had the right valve I used to walk along the pipe until I found where it went to.

But on top of the distillation column this is not possible, since the pipes disappear behind tanks and stairways. Learning which valve controls which flow is a large part of mastering the job of an assistant in the process plant and of production throughout the entire plant. A young assistant commented:

> There's a lot to learn here. You can read all you want in books, but you have to do the job to understand it. There are still things I don't know, like about some of the valves. I have to ask Bill [the chief].

A new assistant in the batch plant:

> All those valves! It drives you bananas. And if you open the wrong one you can ruin the entire batch. That's $40,000.

The Job Once Learned

But once the heart of the job has been learned variety is mostly infrequent and unwelcome, for it usually indicates a problem, and therefore some danger, in the production process. It may take men up to a year to fully understand their jobs, but they commonly spend ten, fifteen, or twenty years in the same job or a very similar one. The following comments illustrate the way most men view their work:

> **Researcher:** I'm interested in whether with automation jobs become more or less interesting.

> **Boiler operator** [monitoring type 2, solitary process production] in his late forties: Oh, definitely less interesting. This job is very boring, very boring, especially on the midnight shift. I do a lot of reading. There's a lot of guys

who can't stand it in here, just looking at four walls [gazes around the small booth where he is sitting]. They get out. I would have got out of this racket long ago, but I've got a bad back, I had an operation, and if you're fifty and you've had an operation on your back they don't want to look at you anywhere else.

Boiler operator in his mid-forties: Actually this is a pretty boring job. When things are going smoothly there's nothing to do. All it really is is watching dials and gauges. Well, I read and stuff.

A process worker [monitoring type 1, process production with a crew] in his mid-thirties: In the beginning it was interesting, but after it got dull. It's the same shit, day in, day out. It's boring. There's no variety.

A batch worker in his late forties has a reputation as one of the most conscientious workers in the plant. He never drinks and is rarely absent from work. Does he find the work interesting? "It's a job." The question is inappropriate, for the answer is obvious. He really wants to be a policeman so he can "move around and meet interesting people." Other men make life in the plant bearable by indulging in a wide range of social activities at work. How does this man make his job more tolerable?

You see, I'm a Pentecostal Christian. There's a spiritual life and a material one. I concentrate on the spiritual life. God put me here for a purpose. No, I don't know what that purpose is, but he has a plan. Sometimes when I get close to him I see glimmers of it. That's why I don't mind it in here.

A batch worker in his early thirties:

[Angrily] It's boring shit. You're doing the same thing all the time.

Operators in the tryamine plant fell into the same pattern, but it took longer because the plant had all kinds of extra problems connected with its newness. These problems extended the period during which the job offered some variety.

How about the small number (six) who said the work was interesting? Two were younger men, recently hired and still learning the job. For instance, an eighteen-year old had been an assistant in the fasic plant for just five weeks:

This is complicated—the valves and all that. The first two weeks, they were breaking me in. They said, "just concentrate on one thing at a time." I'm still learning things—this is interesting. It's a challenge. I reckon if I can do this I can do any job in the plant. It's just like distilling alcohol—we used to do a lot of that at home.

Yes, I saw *Star Wars*. I like science fiction. I suppose these are the jobs of the future, monitoring, automated jobs. That's what it's all going to be like [leans back in his chair pensively, looks balefully at the control panel]. I tell you, there's going to be a lot of fat guys. Funny how they try and make jobs more simple all the time. This job isn't hard. They say after six months or a year you have it mastered. I guess you don't have to pay a machine.

I want to be an instrument mechanic. There'll be a vacancy soon and I'll try for it. It's day work.

Another man, a boiler operator (monitoring type 2), was classified as liking the work because he insisted that he did, though when asked to explain why he always gave as reasons the fact that he could do *other* things while at work. For instance:

I enjoy the work. I don't mind being alone. There's always something to do. I often bring in parts of my car to work on, and guys ask me to fix their air conditioners.

The rest who liked the work said they enjoyed the variety.

Four men could not be classified, since they sometimes said they liked the work and sometimes said they disliked or hated it. For instance, a chief operator in the fasic plant had been there for twenty-six years. He was recognized as the fasic expert and liked the status and prestige this recognition conferred. Did he enjoy the work? That depended on which day I talked to him.

I've been here over twenty years. It's more interesting than the resin section. You're more alert. Over there there are long periods when you aren't doing anything. I prefer to be alert.

A few months later he was sitting in the tavern.

[Angrily] Do you think I'd be here [at work] if I didn't have to be? It's a wasteland here. Why do you think I drink? There's nothing else to do.

The Social Relations of Monitoring

Since few men find the work interesting, they spend as much as possible of their time in the plant amusing themselves in other ways. These will be discussed later. But in this context there is an important distinction between the boiler operators (monitoring type 2, solitary process production) and the other three types of monitoring. It is apparent from this and other studies that the number in a work crew is an important dimension along which automated plants vary. Some require only one worker. In others a crew consists of three, four, or five.[1]

In those types of monitoring that require only one worker, the range of social activities available is very limited. Sitting alone for eight hours a day, with only an occasional visit from other workers, can be a depressing experience. It is generally recognized at Imperium that the job of boiler operator carries with it that special drawback. As the supervisor of the boiler operators put it:

It takes a very special kind of guy to work in the boiler room. I studied while I was there [for his blue and red engineering seals], so I didn't mind the loneliness. And the social life didn't bother me. I never was much of a socialite, so I don't mind not seeing friends. My wife does all the socializing.

The other kinds of monitoring that involve working with two or three others are better, but even a three- or four-man crew can be very confining. A control room is a small space for three people to spend eight hours. Workers sit with two others, whose company they may or may not enjoy. (The batch plants are pleasanter in this respect, since men can patrol the upper floor.)

Especially on the afternoon and midnight shifts, this can easily induce claustrophobia. Inside, the giant control panel vibrates and sometimes rattles, and outside the process machinery hisses and steams. Sometimes wisps of vapor drift across the windows of the control room. In the evening the white-collar staff and most workers have gone home. Stepping out of the control room at night, a worker sees the massive series of tanks and cylinders, brightly lit. The other view, facing the refinery, consists of railroad tracks and empty marshland. In the background is a column of burning gas—waste product from the refinery. A chief:

Sometimes I've hated a guy I'm with so much that I'm all eaten up inside. But what can you do?

A chief and a helper in the fasic plant were known by everyone to detest each other. During a typical evening in the control room the chief spent several hours telling the assistant about his experiences during World War II as a gunner on a destroyer. This was not the first time he had recounted these stories, and the helper sat in silence, glowering at his section of the control panel. His lower lip quivered with resentment at having to listen to the stories yet again. Afterwards he explained.

These older guys think everyone wants to hear their bullshit about the war. He didn't do anything anyway—just sat behind a gun.

Some workers have spent two or three years together in a control room without speaking except for strictly work-related purposes. In any work situation there will be people who do not get along, but the confined setting of a control room, together with shift work, exacerbates the problem.[2]

Work and Danger

In addition to being dull for most men, the job is also dangerous. This characteristic of work in an automated setting such as a chemical plant or refinery or atomic plant has often been noted. For instance, a standard text designed to inform management on how to plan, construct, and run a chemical plant discusses the question of the work force as follows: "The labor attitudes to be considered primarily involve the availability of people who will work hard and continuously and do not "loaf" on the job. In many chemical plants maloperations can result in fires or explosions and a lackadaisical attitude cannot be tolerated."[3]

The dangers take two forms. First, there are those that are slow but cumulative in effect. There is continual seepage of dangerous chemicals into the air the men breathe. When tank cars are loaded and unloaded, drums filled, hatches on kettles opened to add ingredients, and valves adjusted or opened to take samples, chemicals escape into the atmosphere. Ventilation systems that convey the most dangerous fumes away from the immediate work area deposit those fumes into the air around the plant. The result is that, even if men work some distance from a production center, the air they breathe is likely to contain a mixture of noxious substances.

Every so often a valve leaks, or someone forgets to close a valve, and a pool of chemicals, often toxic, forms on the floor. The work crew has to clean up this mess, sometimes wading ankle deep in chemicals to do so. Table 15 lists some of the ingredients most commonly used in production in the plant, and their effects on men exposed to them. The following comments illustrate these hazards. An assistant in the batch plant:

> You're breathing in all those chemicals, so you get all shriveled up, like Joey. You know he looks like an old man. He's all hunched up, and he's only forty.

A chief:

> It's hot in there [the kettle room]. Some of those kettles are 180 degrees, and there's all sorts of chemicals around. They dry you out. Often I've come out so dry I couldn't blow my nose. I wanted to pick it but there wasn't anything there. Big business—they've got you over a barrel.

A helper:

> I've been here when they put in large amounts of asbestos and the place is white with fumes. Chemical workers don't live long. You're bound to pick up something.

When workers in the batch plant (monitoring types 3 and 4) are filling drums with finished resin, they paste a label on each drum that warns the consumer, in some detail, of the health hazards of exposure to the product. This is part of the Occupational Safety and Health Administration's (OSHA's) safety requirements. There is an irony here, since it is impossible for the men who fill the drums to avoid inhaling some vapors from the product as they paste on label after label explaining the danger of such inhalation. Figure 13 shows a typical label.

These hazards are gradual in their effect on men's health. But, in addition to the slow seepage of chemicals into the air or onto the ground, workers are vulnerable to disasters that are more dramatic in form and catastrophic in effect.

Some of the substances used in production, if leaked in large quantities, will kill

Table 15 The Effects of Exposure to Some Substances Commonly Used in Production

Substance	Use in the Plant	Effects of Exposure
Gases Carbon monoxide	Released in a stream from the bottom of a kettle to mix ingredients	Very toxic. Attaches to hemoglobin in the body, diminishing the supply of oxygen.
Dusts Asbestos	Ingredients in some resins	Very fine, almost indestructible fibers that easily enter the lungs and may remain there indefinitely. Carcinogen.
Organic chemicals Benzene	The main ingredient in fasic anhydride (process plant)	Very toxic. Acts on the nervous system causing drowsiness and loss of consciousness. Affects the bone marrow, destroying its ability to produce blood cells. Associated with leukemia.
Glycol	Reduces the acidity and viscosity of resins	Skin irritant. Can affect the nervous system and cause liver, kidney, and blood damage.
Fasic anhydride	Produced in process plant	Can cause severe burns, especially to the eyes, and corrode the respiratory system.
Methyl ethyl ketone	Solvent in resin production	In high concentrations, can have a narcotic effect.
Styrene	Ingredient in some resins	Skin irritant. Causes headaches, nausea, and liver damage. Affects the nervous system.
Xylene	Used in the process plant	Same effects as benzene but milder.
Metals Cobalt	Ingredient in some resins	Skin irritant.

Sources: Jeanne M. Stellman and Susan M. Daum, *Work Is Dangerous to Your Health* (New York: Pantheon, 1970). Howard H. Fawcett and W. S. Wood, *Safety and Accident Prevention in Chemical Operations* (New York: John Wiley, 1965).

FOR INDUSTRIAL USE ONLY

OSHA **T43**

SYNTHETIC RESIN SOLUTION

CONTAINS FORMALDEHYDE and/or UREA and/or PHENOL and/or FURFURYL ALCOHOL and/or ORGANIC ACIDS

WARNING! HARMFUL IF INHALED OR SWALLOWED. MAY CAUSE IRRITATION OF SKIN, EYES, NOSE, OR THROAT.

Avoid prolonged or repeated breathing of vapors or spray mist. Keep container closed. Use with adequate ventilation. Do not get in eyes, on skin, on clothing. Wash thoroughly after handling. Wash contaminated clothing before re-use. Discard contaminated shoes.

FIRST AID: On contact, flush eyes or skin with plenty of water for at least 15 minutes. If inhaled, remove to fresh air, give artificial respiration if breathing is difficult.

IF SWALLOWED: Give a tablespoon of salt in a glass of warm water and repeat until vomit fluid is clear. Give milk or white of egg beaten in water. **CALL A PHYSICIAN.**

See MCA Chemical Safety Data Sheets SD-1 Formaldehyde and SD-4 Phenol

KEEP OUT OF REACH OF CHILDREN

Fig. 13. Occupational Safety and Health Administration label of the kind workers apply to all drums in the batch plants.

at once. In 1974 a pipe carrying carbon monoxide through a control room in the batch plant sprang a leak. The three-man crew inside was already delirious when, by chance, a mechanic came by and saw them on the floor.

The constant danger of fire and explosion has already been mentioned. In addition to hazards from their own plant, men are exposed to the consequences of a disaster in a neighboring plant. A few years ago there was a massive explosion in the refinery next door. So great was the impact that store windows were blown out in Elizabeth, a mile away. At Imperium, much closer, the blast from the explosion was tremendous. All the windows in the main office building were blown at high speed across rooms and into the rear walls. Anyone in their path would have been cut to pieces. Luckily it was 5:00 A.M.

These comments illustrate something of the way men view and experience such dangers. A boiler operator (monitoring type 2, solitary process production):

> This is a dangerous job. I'm not ashamed to say sometimes when I'm here by myself I'm scared.
> What they kept telling us at school, over and over again, is that machines can go wrong. The instructor told one story about a fireman [boiler operator]. He left his boiler for a while, I don't know why. And when he came back it was red hot. The valve to cut off the heat when the water drops wasn't working.
> So he did the right thing. He cut off the fuel—but it killed him. Suddenly it started shooting water into the boiler and it blew up—blew him against the wall and the wall came down on him. He did the right thing, shutting it down, but it killed him.

As was mentioned, in the fasic plant (monitoring type 1) every year the crew must clean out the catalyst, using hand tools. A younger worker, in his early thirties, went too close to the area where his crew was scraping out the acid. He was not wearing a mask, and he inhaled enough fasic fumes to ruin his lungs. He will be on disability pension for the rest of his life. Another man, who now works in the warehouse, also had an accident during recatalyzation. He was more fortunate:

> My mask was defective, and I breathed in a whole lot of fasic. When
> I took off my mask the other guys started laughing at me. I couldn't
> understand what they were laughing at. Then I looked in a mirror and
> my face was all green. I lost my voice for three weeks. That fasic eats
> you away. You don't live long as a chemical worker.

A chief in the kettle room (monitoring type 3, batch production with a crew) described what happens when the alarm indicating a pressure buildup goes off:

> When we hear the alarm we run to the kettle and try and clear up the
> shit. And if we can't do anything we run—get the hell out.
>   Usually pressure goes up in a couple of minutes, so there's really
> nothing you can do about it. And when a disk blows, the product goes
> all over the place.

On one occasion a kettle burst into flames, throwing its contents over a wide area. One worker was standing by a second-floor window in a locker room next to the kettle room. He described his experience:

> There was an explosion, and I saw this ball of flame coming through the
> window. I put up my hands to protect my eyes. My hands were burned
> black—even now they look like bird's claws. I was three years in the
> hospital and two years in a rehabilitation center.

The mechanic who found the crew exposed to a carbon monoxide leak described what he saw:

> Those guys didn't know what they were doing. Fred was so bad that he
> fell down in his own vomit, and when I got him up he didn't know what
> was going on. Another minute and it would have been history for him.

One of the crew involved explained:

> I had a headache for a week. I thought I must have got the flu or some-
> thing.

In 1955 three men did die. One worker was overcome by fumes inside a kettle he was inspecting. Another went in to assist him and also collapsed. A third worker was then lowered on a harness, but when he collapsed the harness slipped off, and all three died. Men refused to work for four days after that until the company had installed extra safety equipment and better gas masks, and for many the incident is still a bitter memory for which they have not forgiven the company.

For all these reasons, men believe working at Imperium shortens their lives. Throughout the plant they make the same comment: "Chemical workers don't live long." Often they become very angry as they talk about the damage being done to their bodies. The following examples are illustrative.

A young assistant operator in the process plant had been spattered with acid during an explosion a few years earlier. His father had worked for twenty years at Imperium and now, at the age of sixty-five, was dying of cancer. The operator:

> Ideally I'd like to see this whole joint closed down. The company sucks. It's all unsafe—the fumes and all that.

A former president of the union, who worked as an operator in the thinning room, explained why he gave up attempts to make working conditions safer:

> The whole safety program is a joke. We used to have meetings, and if we suggested anything that cost more than a hundred dollars the company would say, "No, that's too expensive." I said, "What is this? Nothing is a safety problem if it costs more than a hundred dollars?" So after a while I told them their whole safety program was a bunch of shit and I refused to sit on the safety committee any more.

An older man in the warehouse, who had worked at the plant since it was founded:

> There must be something wrong. This plant has been going since 1939 and there's only seven guys of pensionable age.
> Take that inert gas machine and the mystery connected with that—it killed three guys. There was Jimmy Sullivan, our first [union] president. He was a strong, healthy guy, and then he worked down there for a few months and went out sick and never came back. And Al—he worked there. He used to be as strong as a horse, and now he's got cancer.

The new tryamine plant exposed operators to an additional danger—untried technology. For instance, after a year of operation an urgent directive came from company headquarters. Their research chemists had realized that a combination of ingredients used in the plant was highly explosive and should be discontinued at once. Such are some of the benefits to operators of working on the frontiers of new technology! Compare the dubious privilege of being an operator in a nuclear power plant.

A job in a chemical plant, oil refinery, or power plant where the consequences of an error can be disastrous puts considerable responsibility on the operator. It is commonly argued that a worker placed in such a position of importance is likely to feel a sense of satisfaction and well-being.[4]

But this very much overstates the case. The dangerous nature of the job at Imperium does have the effect of removing from the arena a complaint commonly heard from, for instance, workers on an assembly line. Unlike assembly workers, men at Imperium do not grumble that any child could do their job.[5]

But there is little evidence that the danger of the work has any positive effect beyond this. On the contrary, most men consider the hazards of their work a major disadvantage. A dangerous job is a dangerous job, and the responsibility is cold comfort.

Shift Work

In addition to the dullness and hazards of the job there is a further drawback. Production in such plants entails shift work. And rotating shifts—the kind most commonly used in these settings—disrupt most men's social life and disturb the regular functioning of their bodies. At the same time the form of rotating shift employed in process production has one important difference from the form employed in the batch plants. For in process, but not batch production workers rarely have their weekends free. It is this, rather than differences in the intrinsic interest of the job, that most men perceive as the major distinction beween process and batch production.

Why does process production entail shift work? The answer is that in neither plant can it be neatly fitted into the period from 8:00 A.M. to 4:00 P.M. For instance, since the production cycle in the fasic plant is about thirty hours, it cannot be halted when men go home in the evening. In addition, after a thirty-hour cycle is complete another begins at once. Breaks cannot be taken between cycles, for it takes two days to fully stop the plant (including allowing machinery and materials to cool) and another three to get it running smoothly again. For this reason the fasic plant and the boiler rooms that provide it with steam entail shift work throughout the week *and* the weekend.

Batch production is different. It too requires shift work through the week, twenty-four hours a day, since a chemical batch may take from four hours to three days to complete and cannot easily be interrupted midway without spoiling the product. But there is the very important difference that men usually have their weekends free because production is halted after each batch. Beginning a new batch is no harder whether the period between batches is an hour or two days. Natural break periods are in a sense, built into batch production, and with careful planning the end of a batch can be made to coincide with Friday afternoon.

In both process and batch plants men work rotating shifts. A day is divided into three shifts—day (8:00 A.M. to 4:00 P.M.), afternoon (4:00 P.M. to midnight), and midnight (midnight to 8:00 A.M.). Crews rotate shifts from day to afternoon to midnight, working six days (process production) or five days (batch production) on each shift followed by two days off. Men in process production are paid overtime for the sixth day of each shift. The cycle of work and days off is outlined in tables 16 and 17.

Most men hate rotating shifts. It interferes with their social life, imposing a rhythm at odds with that of their friends and families. Batch workers have two weekend days when their leisure time coincides with other people's, but only four of the days process workers have off in every forty-eight-day cycle are on the weekend.

Shift work upsets men's biological rhythm as well as their social rhythm. They continually complain that rotating work schedules every week upsets their sleep, bowels, and appetites.[6] This is more than just inconvenient or unpleasant. Medical studies have shown that life expectancy is significantly related to factors that shift work makes very difficult, such as regular meals and adequate sleep.[7] These comments are typical of the way men see shift work.

A crew in the fasic control room:

Chief [in his mid-fifties]: Shift work stinks. I'll tell you, shift work is fine if you don't like your wife and family and you don't want to see your relatives. Otherwise it's terrible. You miss too much. Like, I've got young kids and I don't see them.

Anyone will tell you, 90 percent of the guys who work shifts do it for the money. We do it for the almighty dollar. And once you begin it's hard to stop. You get caught up in expenses.

In a year or two, when my family is grown up, I'll bid into the warehouse [a day job]. Because when your kids have gone you're saving money—your phone bill is less and your electricity is less. So you come out about the same

Table 16   Cycle of Work and Days off for a Crew Rotating Shifts in the Process Plant (Forty-eight-Day Cycle)

Shift	Hours Worked	Days Worked	Days Off
Day	8:00 A.M. to 4:00 P.M.	Monday–Saturday	Sunday/Monday
Afternoon	4:00 P.M. to midnight	Tuesday–Sunday	Monday/Tuesday
Midnight	Midnight to 8:00 A.M.	Wednesday–Monday	Tuesday/Wednesday
Day	8:00 A.M. to 4:00 P.M.	Thursday–Tuesday	Wednesday/Thursday
Afternoon	4:00 P.M. to midnight	Friday–Wednesday	Thursday/Friday
Midnight	Midnight to 8:00 A.M.	Saturday–Thursday	Friday/Saturday
Day	8:00 A.M. to 4:00 P.M.	Sunday–Friday	Saturday/Sunday

Table 17   Cycle of Work and Days off for a Crew Rotating Shifts in the Batch Plant (Twenty-one-Day Cycle)

Shift	Hours Worked	Days Worked	Days Off
Day	8:00 A.M. to 4:00 P.M.	Monday–Friday	Saturday/Sunday
Afternoon	4:00 P.M. to midnight	Monday–Friday	Saturday/Sunday
Midnight	Midnight to 8:00 A.M.	Monday–Friday	Saturday/Sunday

in a day job. But until then you have to do it. You've got family responsibilities.

And holidays! You've got no fucking holidays. Like the Christmas party—where was I? I was here! That's where I was. Now this Christmas isn't so bad. I'm on days, so I can be home for Christmas dinner. But the guys on afternoons—they don't have no Christmas.

Assistant [in late forties, joining in]: Yes, if guys are truthful the reason they work shifts is the money [holds his fingers up, rubbing them against his thumb].

Now, my wife is at home with the kids. She doesn't work. You can only work shifts if you know your wife is tied down with the kids. Otherwise she'll be out fucking around, and that's no good. You're working afternoons and midnights, and she's out fucking around.

Chief [in the background, gloomily]: Shift work is fucking terrible, fucking terrible.

Assistant [continuing]: But you *can* spend time with your family. You can see your kids during the day. The only problem's the occasions—weddings, christenings, forget them. You can't go. Yes, the only reason to work shifts is the money.

Helper [in his mid-thirties]: Yes, I was over there [the kettle room] for five years, but I couldn't afford it. So I transferred here. I'm sending my daughter to parochial school, and I can't afford it unless I do this.

Chief [still in the background, but now shouting angrily]: Shift work stinks, it stinks!

Helper [continuing]: It's crazy. Like I worked until 4:00 this morning—I stayed overtime. And then I got up at 7:00 to take my daughter to school. It's crazy, but I can't afford to go back over there.

For boiler operators (monitoring type 2, solitary process production) the problems of shift work are compounded by working alone, one man in a glass booth. They are in an isolated and lonely situation. A boiler operator [in his late forties]:

The midnight shift bothers me. Then it's hard to get to sleep. I learned just to lie there in bed and not think of anything. And it ruins your appetite. You know, after the midnight shift you're eating dinner at 8:00 in the morning.

It's lonely here too. That's why when I see someone I talk my head off.

A batch worker [in his late thirties]:

I hate shift work. I'm forty. I've been doing it for seventeen years, and I'm aiming to get on steady days. I want to be with my family—like tonight my oldest girl is playing a basketball match and I can't go. I'm her greatest fan, and I'm stuck here.

I hate this afternoon shift. I hate it. I never get to see my family. It's all messages—a note on the table, a few words on the tape recorder. I didn't like it even when my wife wasn't working [she is a secretary in the Elizabeth school system].

The other day I woke up at 11:00 [A.M.]. There was no one there. At 12:30 the twins came home for lunch and at 1:00 they were gone, and there was I, out on the carpet like this [slumps down in his chair] watching television.

In this context the difference between process and batch shift work is very important. Batch workers do at least have their weekends to enjoy with friends and family. Often men with enough seniority to transfer into a day job (warehouse or maintenance) will remain in production because they can earn more money there, but they make a sharp distinction between process and batch production. Choosing to work a few years in the process plants is acceptable if a man is young and wishes, for instance, to accumulate money for a down payment on a house or some similar reason. But those who choose to stay longer than a few years in the process plant are a clear minority among younger and older workers.

A system of fixed shifts (each crew staying permanently on *one* shift) would be better for men's physical health. But if they were allowed to choose a shift according to seniority then the afternoon and midnight crews might contain mostly newer and less experienced men. This could be dangerous or even disastrous. Anyway, most men are not willing to stay on the afternoon or midnight shift for long.

Imperium tried increasing the period between rotations from one to two or three weeks, but men did not want to spend that long on a shift they disliked. A personnel manager interviewed for a study of shift work during World War II put it succinctly: "It takes a week to get used to a new shift and three weeks to get really settled. Then if you have monthly rotation you have to get unsettled again. If you rotate once a week you never really get settled, so there's no problem."[8]

Weekly rotation is the system men dislike least, since it enables them to lead a social life that is nearer that of the community than any other system. They prefer to salvage their social life rather than their biological life.

Most men, then, dislike rotating shifts and work in monitoring jobs either because they can earn more money there than anywhere else in the plant or because they do not have enough seniority to transfer into day jobs.

At the same time they usually acknowledge there are some advantages to shift work. And there is a small minority of men who, because of these advantages, prefer rotating shifts to day work. First, they can more easily have extramarital affairs. If a worker wishes to spend the night with another woman he can always tell his wife he is working the midnight shift. Rotating shift work not only provides the perfect excuse for not coming home at night, it also increases the range of possible liaisons. After the midnight shift a man can visit a married woman at her home during the day when her husband is at work. Or he can visit a widow or divorcee, who may not want her children to know about her affairs, after the afternoon shift when the children are asleep. Finally, a man who rotates shifts can more easily have simultaneous affairs. A boiler operator explained that he was sleeping with three women:

One is married. I try and hit her when I'm on the midnight shift. I see her in the morning. The other is divorced. I get her on the afternoon shift when her kids are at school. And the single one I hit whenever I can.

A small number said shift work helped their marriages:

I like shift work. I've always done it. Hell, the old lady and I get sick of each other if we're together all the time.

This man believed the quality of the time he and his wife spent together was enhanced by infrequency. A larger group, men with unhappy marriages, valued shift work *because* they saw less of their wives. A process worker:

As I drove into my driveway this morning my wife was leaving for work. We waved from our cars: "Bye-bye." "Bye-bye." We haven't seen each other for weeks. It's better that way. Then you can't fight.

Another group who prefer shift work are those who enjoy having weekdays free. Some men like to spend time decorating or improving their houses during the day when the children are at school. Some men with children too young to go to school take trips with their families during the day. And in the summer men on the afternoon or evening shift can spend the day at the beach or fishing or hunting.

Still, despite these side benefits, for most men shift work is a disaster, setting the rhythm of their social lives at odds with that of their families and friends and disturbing the normal functioning of their bodies.

Special Knowledge and the Battle for Control

In one crucial respect, the analysis presented so far of how men perform their work is misleading. It implies that they simply follow, as closely as they can, a set of instructions and procedures. But this is true only in part. For there is a power struggle, waged every day, between workers and management for control of the work situation. Men in the batch plants and to a lesser extent in the fasic plant have seized from management considerable control over the organization of work.

This is possible because men possess a series of devices they often refer to as their "secrets." These devices have to do with special knowledge of the production process. There is a ritual quality to these "secrets." Management is well aware of their existence. The details may not be apparent, but the general form is. When workers and supervision interact they behave on the assumption that these secrets exist but talk to each other and outsiders as if they did not.

These devices or secrets are of three kinds. First there is knowledge about the quirks and peculiarities of the machinery. A distillation kettle might take longer than expected to heat to a certain temperature. A particular valve might be especially prone to stick. And equipment is subject to a variety of modifications once in operation, many of which are thought too minor to be recorded. Over time these small changes accumulate, and the equipment moves a considerable distance from the design. The operation of the equipment then has to be learned on the job rather than from a manual. As a chemical engineer, quoted in another study, said:

> I spent two weeks in the plant trying to separate the essentials of the process from the witchcraft. I know I didn't completely succeed, but I was afraid to go further.[9]

An Imperium process worker (monitoring type 1):

> It's like learning about movie making. They can teach you all about the general principles at schools, but once you get out there you find it's quite different. Management knows the general principles, but the men know the everyday running side.

An Imperium batch worker:

> There's nothing like experience. All those books and shit. You can have the biggest fucking degree in chemistry, but you come in here and you won't know your ass from your elbow. It ain't like they say it is.

Second, workers know about the behavior of the machinery in the gray zone between normal operation and catastrophe. When temperature or pressure moves to dangerous levels, the assistant or chief must make some rapid decisions. Most important is whether to shut down production at once or try to ease things back to normal. In making this decision a worker with experience of similar situations will know which procedures work and which do not. At least as important is knowledge of the gray area—of where the danger zone starts. The instruction manual may state that certain levels of pressure and temperature are dangerous, but given the variability of equipment even on installation and the modifications it undergoes over time, this information is unlikely to be precise. It may be possible to operate quite safely within a formally designated danger zone, and there may be danger areas that are not formally designated. An assistant in the fasic plant:

> When the water has been driven off and you're down to pure xylene, if you let the temperature rise too much you'll get gases sucked up by the vacuum, and the whole thing will blow up. The supervisor will look at the temperature and say, "Do this," but he's only guessing. He doesn't really know. He has to rely on you.

All this can be discovered only by experience, and it is workers who have the experience. Since their information has sometimes been gathered at some physical risk to themselves, it is not surprising that they are reluctant to share it with management.

Third, and most important, workers have devised a series of shortcuts to make the work easier, and a related set of ways to control the work pace. This is especially true in the batch plants, where the variety of products provides greater opportunity for such activity.

In theory, the laboratory technicians in the batch plants control the entire process, for they test the product. They decide when it is ready, and they tell the chiefs what adjustments to make. For this reason their basic hourly wage is higher than that of batch and process workers. But in fact the control laboratory technicians can exercise is strictly limited—production workers have their own ideas about what they should be doing.

Workers have a whole range of shortcuts. For instance, in the batch plant the formula card might specify that the ingredients in stage C should be cooled gradually over a four-hour period from 100° to 50°C. This involves fairly close monitoring, since heat must be reduced slowly so that the temperature line on the production chart follows the line drawn by the supervisor. Men have discovered that if they cool the product in two hours instead of four the outcome is just as satisfactory as far as the laboratory tests are concerned, so for the remaining two hours they can leave the kettle at a constant temperature of 50°C and relax. The production chart, whose temperature line would show the supervisor what had been done, can easily be altered. An assistant explained:

> If you discover you can do something quicker than the chart says, you don't want the company to know or they'll cut the time. The chart is a record of what you've done. But you can fix it. If you don't want them to know about something you can just stop the needle for a while. This way you have time free.

Sometimes men discover they can eliminate an entire stage without any apparent difference in the product. If the stage involves inconvenient work and the laboratory technicians do not notice its absence, then men may omit that stage in future batches. In many cases workers come across such devices by accident. A chief forgets to do something the formula card says he should do—cooling slowly or adding an ingredient—and the laboratory does not comment, so the "accident" becomes a technical discovery, a useful component of the men's practical knowledge. An assistant commented:

> The formula tells you a certain material is necessary. Perhaps you're supposed to add twenty-five pounds of cobalt. And one day the chief forgets to put it in, and it works OK.
>   If it's a pain in the ass to put in the material he won't do it next time. The fucking thing is cooking at 250 degrees and they want you to unbolt a manhole and put in some garbage—it's dangerous.

The drive to increase the proportion of free time at work begins as soon as a new product is introduced. When a resin is to be produced that has not been made in the plant before, one of the chemists from Imperium's laboratory in Sterling Forest comes down to supervise the process. A chief commented:

Some guy in an experimental laboratory in Sterling Forest figures it out over a pressure cooker. When they get it here the guy will stay for one whole cook. Then the next time you do it you're on your own. You start to look for easier ways to do it.

When a batch is pumped from the kettle room into the thinning room it passes through a filter press to remove impurities. The thinning room crew used to change the filter paper for every batch, but they discovered this was not always necessary. The chiefs found that if on combining a sample from the batch to be filtered with a sample from the last batch the mixture did not turn milky, then they could use the old filter paper without harming the product. An assistant explained:

It's a pain to change the filter—they're papers. You have to open it up and put new papers in. It's hot and sticky and it stinks. So we do this test, and now we only have to change the papers once a week. We save the company a lot of money, but we don't tell them because they don't give you any credit—they'll give you a lousy hundred dollars—and they cut the time they allow you for it.

The same fight for control over the production process goes on after the alkyd is pumped into the thinning room, for when the alkyd has been thinned it must be pumped into individual drums. Drumming entails continual physical effort, exposure to dangerous chemicals, and the possibility of injury if a drum slips. Thus workers aim to prolong the thinning process so as to lessen the amount of drumming they do each week.

The easiest way to do this is to ignore or modify instructions from the laboratory technicians. For instance, the technicians may tell the men in the thinning room to add fifty pounds of styrene and then heat for two hours. At the end of two hours the product should be ready for drumming. To postpone this, men may add only a few pounds of styrene, so that after two hours the tests indicate that more styrene, and more monitoring, is necessary. Or workers may apply less heat than required, slowing down the whole process. A laboratory technician commented:

The hardest part of my job is you have to be a psychologist and politician. If the batches were run by those formulas they give you, we'd never have enough storage tanks. These guys could do it in no time.

It depends what day it is. If it's Wednesday the guys in production will go slow. They don't want to start a new batch. You take a sample and tell 'em to add styrene, and then if you take another sample and it's still the same you know they threw the bag away. Now on Friday they'll go fast because they want to go home. They decide how long it's going to take. Bobby [a chief], for instance; he'll say to me, "Kid [the speaker is thirty-six], it'll be ready at 7:00 P.M.," and at 7:00 P.M. it's ready.

A crucial factor that helps men impose their own rhythm on the work is that no two batches ever take the same time to cook, even if they are from the identical formula. The same alkyd can vary by several hours in the time needed to prepare it, because the ingredients are never of exactly the same quality. Ingredients that are nominally identical vary in strength and consistency. Two fifty-pound loads of cobalt will not have the same potency. This gives a certain unpredictability to production. As an assistant put it:

> Every batch is like a newborn baby. They are all different, with different problems.

A particular process might usually take two hours, but if it takes four hours on a certain cook, supervision cannot be certain whether it was because workers dawdled, reducing the heat or the quantity added, or whether the material was below strength.

This unpredictability gives workers an important lever.

Men use their "secrets" for two related purposes.[10] The first is to accumulate power or leverage against supervision. If only workers understand certain aspects of production, then the supervisor is dependent on their goodwill. And if he is dependent on their goodwill, men can control him and keep him at a distance. As an assistant put it:

> Guys will try to make sure the supervisor doesn't know more than them. If he does, then he can get on your back and ride you. But if you know more than him you can keep him away.

And if the supervisor exerts what workers consider excess pressure, they can retaliate by slowing down. An assistant explained:

> The chiefs know so much the supervisors don't know. You ask any supervisor. If it's Friday they'll [workers] get a batch out in four hours that usually takes ten. Sometimes supervisors try and run a batch straight down the line exactly like it says in the formula, and it'll take three days. And the guys here can do it in three hours. It's not like the formula says.
>
> Every supervisor knows the guys on Friday run a batch that usually takes ten hours in four, but they don't dare say anything because next time the guys will take till Saturday afternoon and then the supervisor gets called into the office: "How come this happened?" and all that, and he's sweating.[11]

Workers even conceal special pieces of information from each other. The reason is the same—power. A worker who has some useful piece of knowledge that other men do not have has a lever to use to whatever end he wishes.

A chief:

> When you find something out you don't tell anyone, not even a friend. He may tell someone else and then they'll use it against you. You know, if something goes wrong they'll say you didn't do it like you're supposed to.

That's how everyone learned as they came up the ranks. They had to find out for themselves. The chief tells you stuff, but just enough to get the job done. He doesn't tell you the other things he knows.
Guys reckon that's how they learned, so why shouldn't you. That's why they say it's dog eat dog here.

An assistant:

Ritchie is the best chief here. He's been there twenty years or more and he knows everything. He'll spend two days telling you everything. Most chiefs won't do that. They won't tell you what they know because they'll figure then you may learn a little more and you'll have something over them.

The special practical knowledge men possess becomes critical during a strike. The company usually tries to run the plant itself, using supervisors and management from this and other plants. Workers claim that management, lacking the practical information vital for success, invariably mishandles the job. A process operator commented on the last time management tried to run the plant:

We would sit in here [the tavern across the road from the plant] laughing. We could tell from the way the steam was rising from the fasic plant that they were fucking up. They can't run it without us.

The second purpose to which men put the knowledge they accumulate is to increase their opportunities for free time and social activity at work. In a chemical plant, because of the nature of the technological process, a certain proportion of men's time at work is not filled and cannot be filled. For instance, production workers must check instrument panels at regular intervals, perhaps every ten minutes. They are not expected, and could not reasonably be expected, to watch the panels all the time. If it takes one minute to check a panel, the nine minutes between checks are the workers' own. During normal times there are long periods when little work is required. A major aim of most of the production workers is to increase these periods and convert them into time that is entirely free. The wide range of devices for doing this has been described.

Why does this situation persist? Management knows that the formulas from the company laboratories in Sterling Forest will need all kinds of modifications in the specific conditions of the plant. This is the difference between trying a formula in an experimental laboratory and putting it into production—the machinery and conditions are not the same. And only the workers can discover in precisely what ways the formula is inadequate for plant production, for according to the contract between union and management, supervision is not permitted to participate in production. In this way management has little choice but to rely on workers' expertise.

In return management obtains regular production. Workers do not usually produce as rapidly as they could, preferring to spend on social activities the time they save by shortcuts. But batches do meet specifications, which would not always be the case if production workers rigidly followed the formulas.

Conclusion

Most men find the work that characterizes automated plants—process and batch—dull and uninteresting, for it is inherently repetitive. Process production involves an unchanging flow or the continual reproduction of the same cycle. Batch production is slightly more varied but involves repeating the same kinds of activities.

In addition, the job is dangerous. Workers are continuously exposed to harmful chemicals and to the possibility of explosion and fire.

Being an operator in an automated plant is in some ways like being a soldier on guard duty in an area the enemy rarely enters. Lengthy periods of inactivity are punctuated by occasional bursts of danger during which a man may be injured or even die. Few find this interesting or enjoyable.

Nor is it easy for production workers to take pride in the results of their labor. The typical product of a chemical plant is a liquid that smells unpleasant and gives off harmful vapors. The worker last glimpses his work disappearing into a drum or the belly of a tank car. In another plant this liquid may be converted into paint for new automobiles or made into fiberglass to be molded into a boat's hull. But the connection between the resin they produce and a brightly painted car on the highway or a yacht on the Jersey shore is not one that chemical workers make with any frequency, or one that appears to give them any pleasure.

Further, the job entails shift work. And "rotating shifts," the commonest schedule in such plants, disturbs men's bodies and disrupts their social lives. But batch plants, unlike process plants, enable workers' days off to coincide with the weekend. This is, from the workers' point of view, the only really important difference between batch and process technology. The claim that process production offers considerably better working conditions than batch production is based on mistaking contingent for inherent features of plants. For instance, process plants are not necessarily cleaner or newer or pleasanter than batch plants. The tryamine plant (monitoring type 4, highly automated batch production) installed in 1977 was shiny and bright. The process plant Mann studied was dusty and dirty.[12]

It is because of the kind of shifts they must work that those who choose to work in the process plant are a clear minority among younger and older workers (table 14). This is why, for both groups, only the packaging plant is a less desirable job. Of 114 men who had enough seniority to work in the process plant if they wished, only 16 percent (19) did so.

The other workers think men who choose to work for many years in the process plant have a misguided set of priorities. They are seen as social dullards—as a group who are prepared to put aside their connections with friends and family for the sake of cash.

This judgment is relative. Men acknowledge that a job will involve some social sacrifices. They accept younger workers' staying a few years in the process plant to accumulate a cash reserve, possibly for a down payment on a house. And, though many men prefer not to, others might choose to work as operators in the batch plant, where earnings are still high, even though this entails shift work, since they still have weekends free. But to continue for more than a few years as a process operator is poor judgment, a mistaken subservience to mammon, a waste of a man's life. Workers who have transferred from the process plant tend to speak with slight contempt, even pity, of the men who choose to stay there. "It's the money," they say, sometimes with a smile at the folly of human greed. Two workers from the batch plant were sitting in Lesniak's one evening discussing the process workers:

> They're all horse's asses over there. No life. They're dull. You never see them over here [Lesniak's]. There's a world of difference between them and guys on the resin side.

Finally, it is apparent that these men do not view their work with the enthusiasm that conventional accounts (Blauner, Woodward, Touraine, Mallet) imply. But neither do they fit the picture offered by more recent critics of that conventional view (for instance, Braverman). They are not Taylorized automatons, operating in a work setting dominated by management. On the contrary, they have seized a fair degree of control over their work. It is true that management has attempted, in part according to Taylor's principles, to specify precisely what each worker should do. But for the reasons just described there are clear limits on how far this can be implemented. Taylorism is a management ideal that, I suggest, is less completely realized than is usually thought.[13]

6

Support Workers: Mechanics, Laboratory Technicians, Packagers, Warehouse Workers

So far we have considered process and batch operators, who are directly involved in production and are the focus of the debate over blue-collar work in automated plants. Four groups of *support workers*—mechanics, laboratory technicians, packagers, and warehouse workers—throw further light on blue-collar work in general as well as on work in automated plants.

Mechanics are the only group who enjoy their work, and they illustrate the limited ability of factories to offer interesting jobs. Laboratory technicians underline the difference between the kind of knowledge blue-collar workers have and the knowledge possessed by people with formal training in science. The packagers are assembly-line workers—for many people the paradigm of the blue-collar worker. And the warehouse underlines the extent to which, given the context and nature of their jobs, most men would rather engage in social activities than work.

Mechanics: Interesting Jobs

Responsibility for the regular service and repair an automated plant requires lies with the mechanics. They are divided into two maintenance shops that cover the process and batch sections. Like other groups, the mechanics are organized in a hierarchy, moving up from "apprentice" to "class A" to "leader." Certain men are certified or licensed as having special skills, such as electrician or welder or insulator, but even if they are not so designated most mechanics have a particular area of concentration. One man, for instance, might specialize in pumps, another in boilers, a third in fitting pipes or servicing valves.

The mechanics are the one group of workers at Imperium among whom most are enthusiastic about their work. Fourteen of the twenty-one mechanics who talked about this said they liked what they did. They found the work interesting and obtained a sense of accomplishment for it. These comments are typical:

> You get a certain sense of achievement here. Something breaks down and you mend it. I used to be an assistant in the fasic plant. I made

$17,000 there last year [1973]. Now I'm a shift mechanic. I prefer it—
the money is less, but the money isn't everything.

I like working on machinery, running pipe. It's not the same thing every
day.

I've been at Imperium thirty years, but only ten as a mechanic. I went
through the apprentice program; before that I worked as an operator in
the fasic plant. I like this much better. It was monotonous over there—
you did the same thing over and over. Now this job is interesting: you
are always doing something different.

I love this—it's interesting—it's a challenge.

A good mechanic acquires a reputation for expertise in a certain area. There are
workers who are generally acknowledged to know more than anyone in the plant
about fixing pumps, or welding, or boiler systems, or electrical circuits. And they
take obvious pride in the status such expertise confers. Three of the best mechanics
were sitting in Lesniak's one evening. One of them commented:

I know pumps. I can fix any kind of pump you like. When Fred Leiter
[the maintenance supervisor] wants a pump fixed he comes to me. John
here, he knows turbines—he's fantastic on turbines. And Ritchie [the
third mechanic] does welding. He's a fucking good welder.

At one time there was a problem with a turbine. The company tried for several
months to get it correctly aligned, but without success. Finally they called in a
specialist engineer from outside, who diagnosed the trouble as a cracked case. The
worker who was considered the plant's expert on turbines commented on the
incident:

They couldn't get it aligned. They've been trying for months. At first
they blamed me, and I felt bad. I knew it wasn't me, but they thought it
was, so I felt bad. Finally they called in these guys from the New York
Institute and they're terrific. They said it was a cracked case. We're
working on it now, aligning it to two-thousands of an inch.

For a week this mechanic, who did not graduate from high school, was working
on the alignment problem along with expert engineers with degrees. He derived
enormous pleasure and satisfaction from this experience.
    Occasionally Imperium would ask one of the better mechanics to train men in a
new plant the company was setting up. For instance, one man was asked to go to
Chicago for two months to "break in" the mechanics in a new fasic plant. Though he
declined, he took much pride in the recognition the offer implied.
    This picture needs to be qualified. A few mechanics were recognized to be
incompetent. Men would explain that, for instance, a particular welder "doesn't
know his ass from his elbow."

And six mechanics disliked their work, all giving the same reason—danger and dirt. Mechanics are called in when machinery is not working as it should, and in a chemical plant this is always dangerous. A pipe carrying carbon monoxide may be leaking. A faulty valve might be giving off a stream of fasic anhydride.

Much of the time a mechanic works outside, and in winter this can be cold and wet. Sometimes a man must lie in a pool of chemicals and mud to reach a faulty piece of machinery. The following are explanations given by men who do not enjoy being mechanics:

> Maintenance is the hardest job in the plant. You're crawling under pipes, and you're out in the snow and rain.
> One time they sent me climbing up this tower on top of the phthalic plant. It was way up, and swaying in the wind. I got to the top and was hanging on with one arm looking for the electric plug for my tools. I couldn't find it so I yelled down, but I was so high no one noticed. I climbed down and they told me to use the electric light socket, so I went back up and was stretching up to unscrew the bulb, holding on to the side with one hand, swaying with the wind and scared to death. That's when I decided to try and get out of maintenance.

> I hate the work. I'm a pipe fitter. It's messy—you're under pipes in all kinds of sludge. The only good thing about the job is it's steady days.

> I was working in the fasic plant doing shift work. I hated it. So I decided to "better myself." I went through the apprentice mechanics program. It was hard work. For four years I scarcely saw my wife. Being a mechanic isn't what I really wanted to do. I'm thirty-six, and I still don't know what I really want, but it was the best I could do to provide for my family.

The other mechanics agree that the job is dangerous and dirty, but they still enjoy it. Most are fatalistic. Maintenance work is fairly interesting, day work, and well paid, and if it is also dangerous that is a price men in their situation have to pay. A young welder:

> I like the work, so long as supervision leaves you alone, and mostly they do since they don't know how to do the job.
> But it can be dangerous. There's benzene around here, and with the sparks from the welding torches it can be history for you!
> Once I got blown up. They told us they'd cleared out the benzene feed line for twenty-four hours, but something had gone wrong. I was three flights up on the distillation column, and when I applied the torch I got blown right up. Luckily I landed on the only place that wouldn't have meant falling all the way down. When I came to, the first thing I did was to feel if my nuts were still there!

Almost all the mechanics who enjoy what they do first became interested in this kind of work when they were young. Many began with working on cars:

> How did I first become interested in maintenance work? When I was a
> kid I took an old car apart and put it together again and it ran!

And over half were first taught mechanical work by their fathers, either working
around the house or on the car or, if their fathers were mechanics by trade, watching
them at work:

> When I was six, my father used to take me along with him to the shop
> during lunch hour—he was a carpenter, a plumber, and a joiner. He'd
> say "watch this." Well I caught on pretty fast.
>
> When I was seven in kindergarten at Saint Hedwig's it was the
> depression. There were a couple of leaks in the pipes, and the priest
> didn't know what to do—he couldn't afford a plumber. I said, "Let me
> take a look at it, Father." I knew those fittings, because I'd watched my
> father. So I went home and got some new ones. I fixed it in two hours.
>
> After that I did all the plumbing. The priest kept me back three
> years in kindergarten to do the plumbing. He said, "the nun says you
> don't attend history and your geography is poor." I said, "Father, I
> don't do so bad at geography, and I don't attend history because I'm
> doing the plumbing." Finally he admitted he was keeping me back for
> the plumbing.

Some men could not remember when they had not been mechanics in some way.
"I've always been mechanical" is a characteristic comment. And one man even
argued that mechanical aptitude and interest were inherited traits: "You've either
got being a mechanic in your blood or you don't."

Qualifying as a Mechanic

Until the early fifties the selection and training of mechanics was informal. A man
who wished to work as a mechanic, and who seemed to have some relevant experience or aptitude, would be given a practical test such as fixing a valve or pipe in the
plant. If he passed, he became a mechanic at Imperium. One man, who is now the
acknowledged expert on mending pumps, explained:

> I joined Imperium when I was fifteen [1944]. At first I washed bottles.
> Then an opening came up in maintenance, so they said, "Look, try
> welding this pipe." Well, I knew how to do it because my father taught
> me welding, so I got the job.

In the fifties the union pushed for, and obtained, a formal apprentice program
that would enable workers at Imperium to become licensed mechanics. If a vacancy
in maintenance occurs, any worker in the plant may apply. To qualify, he must be
under forty-five years of age and must pass a general intelligence test and a test in
mathematics. If more workers pass the test than there are vacancies, then apprenticeships are handed out in order of seniority. After becoming an apprentice, a

worker attends evening classes at a vocational school for four years and works in the plant during the day. On completing this program he receives a certificate from the Department of Labor's Bureau of Apprenticeship and Training. About half the present mechanics at Imperium went through this program; the rest either were accepted before it was instituted or could demonstrate other employment as a mechanic that the company accepted as evidence of competence. For instance, one man who had been an electrician for the New Jersey Power Company for several years, was accepted in this last category.

Once men have completed their apprenticeships, the certificate they obtain from the Department of Labor is a decisive asset in the job market. Most employers accept it as clear evidence of mechanical competence, while work experience alone may or may not be accepted. This is one of the main reasons the mechanics are noticeably less dependent on the company than are other workers.[1]

At a union meeting, some men who had failed the qualifying tests for apprenticeship raised the question whether the company was on solid legal ground in requiring such tests. One worker said he had heard that their legality was being challenged in the courts, and this led to a discussion of the desirability of the whole apprentice program. A union officer acknowledged that the union could probably force the company to drop both the tests and the program, but he pointed out that if a mechanic wished to leave Imperium for another job he would be much better off having obtained the "piece of paper," as men referred to certification:

> It depends what you want to do. If you're going to die at fucking Imperium you don't need it, but if you go somewhere else, you do.

For a number of men who would like to become mechanics the qualifying tests, in particular the mathematics test, constitute a formidable obstacle. The harder questions involve dividing and multiplying fractions and using percentages. For a worker who left school in ninth or tenth grade ten or twenty years ago, dividing 5 9/11 by 3 5/8 can be forbidding. An assistant in the batch plant who very much wanted to become a mechanic was preparing for the test. He was an intelligent and articulate man, but he had a mental block when it came to mathematics. He explained:

> I fucked around in school. I just wanted to get out. Now I'm sorry. That's why I yell at my kids so much—I don't want them to make the same mistake I did.

Nor, once the tests have been passed, is the period at school easy. For a man who has worked eight hours in a factory, spending the next three or four in a classroom can be torture. One mechanic commented:

> It was hell. For four years I didn't see my family.

At a union meeting the president of the local reminded men that a vacancy for mechanic existed and urged them to apply for it. But he warned:

No one should apply for this if they haven't got the smarts. The school
is tough and the exams aren't easy. Don't think you're going to be able
to bullshit your way through—they've got engineers with degrees
teaching down there.

It is ironic though not, on reflection, surprising that the only workers who enjoy
their work are those called in when the machinery breaks down, for mechanization
involves the increasing imposition of constraints on the motion of a machine. At low
mechanization levels, such as a power drill, the worker operating the machine has
many options. The circular motion of the drill bit comes from the machine, but
direction is imposed by the operator. As automation increases, more of those
options are built into the machine, which is why in many settings only the mechanics
who repair the machinery (and the engineers who design it) enjoy their work.[2]

For younger and older men, maintenance, together with the warehouse, is the
most popular area to work in. It does not involve shifts, carries an earnings potential
as high as jobs in the batch plant, is interesting for most men, and gives a worker an
edge in the outside job market.

The Packaging Plant: Assembly-Line Work

Most of the product of the fasic plant is shipped out in liquid form in tank cars. But
there is also a demand for the product in solid form (briquettes), so a packaging plant
is connected with the fasic plant. This involves repetitive assembly-line work, packing briquettes into bags. It is the least popular job at Imperium (table 13). No one
with high seniority chooses to work there, for the job is boring, very dangerous, and
relatively badly paid.

The packaging plant has three levels. Liquid fasic anhydride is pumped from the
process plant to the third floor, where it is cooled until it forms flakes. The flakes pass
down to the second floor, where a machine molds them into small bars called
briquettes.[3] These briquettes in turn descend to the first floor, where a helper holds a
bag under an outlet until it is filled. He ties the bag closed and places it on a conveyer
belt. Another helper removes the bags and stacks them in a warehouse. The two
helpers alternate jobs every few hours, bagging and stacking, stacking and bagging.
This is the kind of activity an auto worker on an assembly line performs. It is routine,
repetitive, and demands the worker's constant presence by the machinery. Helpers
repeat the same task every few minutes throughout the day. No skill is needed.
Figure 14 outlines these stages, and figure 15 is a mechanization profile for the
packaging plant.

The hourly rate is lower than for any other job, a reflection of the workers' lack
of skill, and there is little chance for earning large sums through overtime, since the
plant works only two shifts—day and afternoon.

Further, the work is more obviously dangerous than any other job in the plant.
When the briquettes drop into the bags they create fasic anhydride dust. The
ventilation system that is supposed to dispose of this works poorly, so the helper who
is holding the bags must wear a gas mask. But the dust floats around the entire

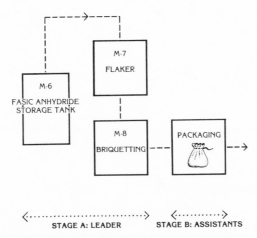

Fig. 14. Packaging of fasic anhydride.

briquetter plant, not just the bagging machine, making for extremely unhealthful working conditions. Men tell stories of serious damage to their respiratory systems. The following exchange at a union meeting gives some indication of working conditions in the briquetter plant, and of men's anger at the situation:

Helper [angrily]: This has been going on for five years. Why can't we have a new section in the air pipe? This one is obviously corroded, so we breathe in the fasic.

Union president: When we bring it up, Frank [the plant manager] says they're not sure how long they're going to keep bagging. It's not economical. They may just pump it [the liquid fasic] into tank cars and send the bagging out to Tenneco or something.

Helper [yelling]: Meanwhile, we're breathing all this dust and shit, and when you breathe it in the moisture in your nasal passages turns the dust to acid and eats you away.

Union president: It may be that in the end we'll have to close down the bagging altogether—call in OSHA and get rid of the whole thing. I'm telling you, if we call in OSHA that briquetter plant is a goner.

Helper [bitterly]: And while we're bagging we can read the labels on the bags and it says, "don't breathe the fasic—it's very dangerous." And it's all over the place.

Laboratory Technicians: Knowledge

What knowledge of chemistry do workers in a chemical plant possess? Surely they know less than a professional chemist, but how much less? Is the difference only

Initiating Control Source	Type of Machine Response		Power Source	Level Number	Level of Mechanization	1 Monitor cooling machine	2 Monitor briquetter	3 Place bags under briquetter—remove when full	4 Place bags on conveyer belt	5 Transfer bags from conveyer to warehouse
From a variable in the environment	Responds with action	Modifies own action over a wide range of variation	Mechanical (Nonmanual)	17	Anticipates action required and adjusts to provide it					
				16	Corrects performance while operating					
				15	Corrects performance after operating					
		Selects from a limited range of possible pre-fixed actions		14	Identifies and selects appropriate set of actions					
				13	Segregates or rejects according to measurement					
				12	Changes speed, position, direction according to measurement signal					
	Responds with signal			11	Records performance	●	●			
				10	Signals preselected values of measurement (includes errer dectetion					
				9	Measures characteristic of work					
From a control mechanism that directs a predetermined pattern of action	Fixed within the machine			8	Actuated by introduction of work piece or material					
				7	Power tool system, remote controlled					
				6	Power tool, program control (sequence of fixed functions)					
				5	Power tool, fixed cycle (single function)					
From man	Variable			4	Power tool, hand control					
				3	Powered tool					
			Manual	2	Hand tool					
				1	Hand			●	●	●

Fig. 15. Mechanization level of stages in the production of solid fasic anhydride (briquetting). Workers responsible for each stage: stages 1–2, leader; 3–5, helpers.

quantitative, or is it qualitative? Is a job as a blue-collar worker in an automated plant an alternative, though slower, way of acquiring the scientific knowledge of an upper-white-collar chemist? Among blue-collar workers at Imperium the activities of the laboratory technicians seem most like those of a chemist, so examining their job should throw light on these questions.

There are four laboratories connected with production at Imperium. The central research laboratory for the entire company is at Sterling Forest. There trained chemists develop new resins and calculate the ingredients and instructions for their preparation. The formulas workers use in the batch plant were developed there.

Within the plant there are three laboratories. One, in the central administration building, is operated by a man known as the "plant chemist," who holds a degree in chemistry. He checks and refines the formulas used in the plant, and answers customers' queries. He is almost never seen in the production centers, and few workers have ever met him.

There is a very small laboratory in the process plant—a couple of sinks and a few pieces of equipment in an area ten feet square. The supervisor of the process plant sometimes runs checks there on the composition of the fasic anhydride, but these checks are routine. Since only one product is turned out, the same one workers have been producing for twenty-five years, there are few surprises. The assistant runs very simple tests on the fasic anhydride as it is being distilled—he checks the color by looking at it and tests the freezing point by stirring it with a thermometer.

The largest laboratory is the production laboratory for the batch plant (fig. 16), where tests are run on samples of each batch as it cooks. The men here are part of the union, not supervision. A crew consists of only two workers. There is a technician who runs tests and gives the production workers instructions on how to bring the batch up to specifications. And there is a leader who also runs tests, prepares some of the chemical material for the test, and makes sure the technician does his job. The leader is responsible for ensuring that the chemical composition of each batch meets certain standards and requirements, so in a sense he is responsible for production throughout the batch plant.

When workers in the kettle room have carried out all the instructions on the production chart, a helper brings a sample of the product to the laboratory. The laboratory technician begins by testing whether the product meets the specified viscosity. He pours part of the sample into a test tube, to within half an inch of the top, corks the tube, and places it in a rack next to another sealed tube that is the standard or model for that type of resin. The standard tube contains the resin at the desired viscosity. It too has a small amount of air at the top. The technician turns both tubes upside down at the same time and watches the air bubble rise in each (fig. 16). If the bubble in the sample tube reaches the top before the bubble in the standard, then the sample is not viscous enough and the product needs more cooking. When the sample bubble reaches the top at the same time as the standard bubble, then the correct viscosity has been attained. Because of this test other workers call the laboratory technicians "bubble watchers."

After testing for viscosity the technician uses the rest of the sample to test for acidity. He weighs a flask, adds the sample liquid, and reweighs to calculate the

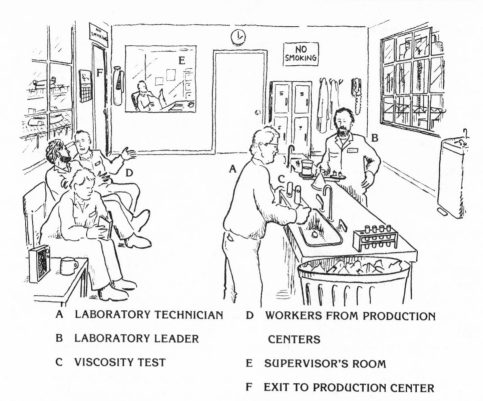

A LABORATORY TECHNICIAN   D WORKERS FROM PRODUCTION

B LABORATORY LEADER   CENTERS

C VISCOSITY TEST   E SUPERVISOR'S ROOM

                                            F EXIT TO PRODUCTION CENTER

Fig. 16. Laboratory technicians.

weight of liquid he has added. He places a measuring rod in the flask and slowly pours in a mixture that has been made up by the laboratory leader and has a precalculated number. When the liquid turns pink he checks the measuring rod to see how many cubic centimeters of mixture he has added. He uses a calculator to multiply the number of cubic centimeters of mixture it took to turn the liquid in the flask pink by the number assigned to the mixture by the laboratory leader, then divides this by the quantity of fluid in the flask before the mixture was added. The result is the sample's acidity. If this is higher than specified, it is necessary to add glycol and continue cooking.

But the technician must also bear in mind the viscosity specification. He must make sure that whatever instructions he issues for reducing the acidity of the cook are not inconsistent with obtaining the desired viscosity. He does this by consulting "the book." This is a large notebook that contains a record of every batch produced at Imperium, together with what was added to bring the batch to the correct specifications. When one book is filled a new one is begun.

The technician looks through the book until he finds a case where, with the same product, the viscosity and acidity were close to that of the current sample. He sees what was added and what happened. When he finds a case where what was added led to the desired viscosity and acidity, he instructs the operators to duplicate that case. A laboratory technician:

> It's all by experience, by what's in the book. We have years of knowledge in this book.
> Let's say the acidity is supposed to be thirty-one and the viscosity twenty-four, and when you do the test you find the acidity is thirty-five and the viscosity twenty-nine. Then you look through the book, and you find last time when you had an acidity of thirty-four point five and a viscosity of thirty you added fifty pounds of glycerine and put on a twenty-minute sparge, and the acidity came down to twenty-nine and the viscosity to twenty-two. So you tell the chief to try it for twenty minutes, and then you take another sample until you get it right.

Thus the work of laboratory technicians, like process and batch workers, consists of learning a set of procedures (tests for viscosity and acidity) and following a model ("the book"). These tests are routine. Technicians repeat them perhaps fifty times a week. Using the book involves an element of judgment, but mostly it is routine. Other workers speak disparagingly of the laboratory technicians' job.

> It's easy. There's nothing to it.

> It's just watching bubbles all day.

The idea that laboratory technicians will acquire a knowledge of formal chemistry in the course of their work is no more plausible than to suppose that bank tellers will learn the principles of Keynesian economics.

Where knowledge of chemistry is concerned, the basic division within the plant is not between those who have worked there a long time and those who have not, nor is it between those who work in a laboratory and those who do not. The basic division is between the men who have degrees in chemistry and the rest, including the supervisors and workers. Only three men have degrees in chemistry—the plant manager, a man who works in the small laboratory in the process plant, and the "plant chemist" referred to earlier.

It is important to be precise about the nature of this division. The essential difference is not that these three men possess the scientific spirit of inquiry and understand scientific method, for in their perennial search for methods of cutting production time, workers display these qualities too. Nor is it that workers cannot think abstractly, for they are comfortable with abstract terms such as viscosity and distillation. Neither do the men with degrees necessarily have more knowledge, for workers in the plant may know a great deal. If the difference is stated in these ways it is easy to suppose there is no great gulf between the two groups, so that as a worker gradually acquires more knowledge, or learns to think more abstractly and with a greater sense of inquiry, he will approach the knowledge of a trained chemist.

The essential difference between these groups lies in the way they acquired their

knowledge. Workers picked it up on the job, taught by other workers—they were
shown valves and kettles and instrument panels and charts. The men with degrees,
on the other hand, learned from books. They have the ability to read a text on some
aspect of chemistry and absorb the information it contains. They understand the
language in which chemistry is written and can therefore easily expand and refine
their knowledge. They can situate and understand the chemical operations performed in the plant within the context of the principles of chemistry. The other men
are confined to what can be explained to them by workers in the plant. This is what
creates the absolute gulf between the very small number of men with formal training
in chemistry and everyone else.

Work and Play

Most men would rather play than work for Imperium. This is certainly true for
production workers, packagers, and warehouse workers, who do not find their jobs
interesting. Even the mechanics, most of whom like their work, enjoy social activities. Throughout the plant men struggle to increase the proportion of time they can
spend on social activities rather than work.

When a new worker enters the plant he is "broken in." Partly this consists of
being taught the job by his fellow workers, but partly it consists in being introduced
to the struggle for free time. Men are taught, often in vivid fashion, that extended
play is both possible and preferable to work. This is an account of an apprentice
mechanic's first day:

> When I was new here, the guys sent me over to be George's assistant.
> He was the carpenter. I figured he was going to teach me how to be a
> carpenter.
>
> I arrived and he said, "So you're my assistant? See that stool? Sit
> on it. See that hole in the wall? Look through it. Now, if you see any-
> one coming, wake me up!" And then he started snoozing, right there.
> That's how I got broken in.

Another man described his early experience as a warehouse worker:

> On my first day, at 10:00 in the morning, Fred and Billy and Big Walter
> [other workers] got up and said to Happy—he was the leader—and
> George and Fats [also workers], "Bye, Happy and George and Fats,"
> and to me, "Come along. Follow us." I was new and didn't know any-
> thing. I followed them. They went out the back and along the railroad
> tracks and then through a gap in the fence and into the Blue Moon!
> And we stayed there for two hours drinking until noon. Then they got
> up and went back through the fence and along the railroad tracks and
> into the warehouse: "Hi, Happy and George and Fats." "Hi, Fred and
> Billy and Walter."

After lunch it was the same. And it was the same every day for the whole week. I'd get home drunk every night and my wife would say, "Where've you been?" And I said, "Working," but she wouldn't believe me until I showed her my paycheck at the end of the week.

After 5:00 P.M. management goes home, leaving a skeleton staff of two or three supervisors for the entire plant. At this point an informal but binding understanding that operates between workers and management becomes very clear. Management will permit workers to spend as much time on social activities as is consistent with getting the work done. So long as production is maintained, workers can organize it and themselves—with a few limits—as they wish. The supervisors' behavior is constrained in highly ritual fashion. They are supposed to keep to areas that do not intrude on workers' freedom to relax and engage in social activities. Usually this means a supervisor must remain within a certain distance of his room or office, so that workers know exactly where they can expect him to be. He is permitted to patrol the plant, provided he takes care to let workers know when—only ritual patrols are acceptable. A weighman in the guard room enlightened a new guard one night:

Here comes the Greek [the resin supervisor]. It's 7:00 [evening]. That's when he comes round. You won't see him again tonight.

One of the worst breaches of etiquette is for a supervisor to move in unexpected ways. Workers have horror stories concerning such men:

There was one guy—he was a real bastard—he was loony toons. He got promoted and it went to his head. He'd do terrible things. He'd drop in unexpectedly at night to check up on you. If he'd find a guy sleeping he'd raise hell. What does it matter so long as you get the work done? At the beginning of the shift they give you a list of work for eight hours. What does it matter if you work like crazy and get it all done in half an hour? Finally the company got rid of him, we complained so much. They shipped him South to one of their plants there.

Supervisors who do not respect the informal contract between management and workers are not likely to keep their jobs long. For, as I have explained, men in production—especially batch operators—have wrested a fair degree of control over the work process from management. And if they feel a particular supervisor is being uncooperative they can slow down the work in his section of the plant. They can also use the union to complain to management. Since management needs men's cooperation for production, and since in the end management does not really care what happens in the plant so long as production is maintained, an offensive supervisor is usually removed. Anyway, if an evening supervisor does not get on with workers he has no other social resource. To spend night after night in isolation is a miserable fate.[4] For all these reasons management and supervision tacitly permit workers considerable latitude.

In 1971 the manager of the process plant was promoted to manage the entire plant. After a honeymoon period of three years he decided, for some reason, to take a tough line with the work force and began trying to enforce certain rules. Many workers were outraged. He was a "petty Hitler," a "no-good," a "tyrant." A batch worker:

> Hey, yesterday Frank Leiter [the plant manager] caught Bobby and Mousy going out for lunch without clocking out. Well, what could they say? They were outside the plant and he'd seen their cards. But the guys begin to lose respect for you if you're plant manager and you begin to bother with that kind of thing. You could at least send out a flunky.

This new tough policy lasted a few months, after which plant life returned to normal.

What do men do with this free time they accumulate at work? Partly that depends on the work area—on the space available, the closeness of supervision, and the proximity of a production center. But there are some activities in which almost everyone participates. With a few exceptions men work in groups and usually spend much of the day in conversation. No sections of the plant are unpleasantly noisy, and no one's mobility is so limited that he cannot choose with whom, in his work crew, he wishes to talk.

Many men's work, in theory at least, involves visits to other work groups. And since men have a legitimate reason for such visits they can always use this to explain their conversations with different groups. For instance, workers in the kettle room can talk with men in the thinning room or the laboratory or with the mechanics for that section of the plant. The laboratory is a social center for the batch plant since men bring their samples there and wait for instructions on how to proceed. Men from the batch plant tend to gather in the laboratory to chat and to get away from the chemical fumes. Workers from the warehouse are continually driving back and forth between the batch plant and the warehouse as they transport finished drums of material. Table 18 shows the range of legitimate visits each work group can make. From this point of view members of the process crew are among the least privileged,

Table 18   Work Groups Classified by Factors Expanding the Scope for Social Activities

Work Group	Degree of Supervision	Extent Work Demands Regular Attention	Other Work Groups That Can Legitimately Be Visited
Process workers	H[a]	H	—
Batch workers	L	M	Laboratory workers
Laboratory workers	H	M	Batch workers
Packagers	L	H	—
Mechanics	M	M	Other mechanics, process and batch workers
Warehouse workers	L	L	Process and batch workers

[a]H, M, and L refer to high, medium, and low.

since they must spend most of the shift together in the control room, with little opportunity for making social calls.

Men talk about work, sports, fishing, hunting, food, politics, sex, and local gossip, including each other. An index of workers' gregariousness is the speed with which such gossip travels. An operator in the batch plant complained:

> Guys talk in this plant. You tell a guy something on Tuesday and he promises not to say and by Wednesday it's all over the plant. So me and Tommy play games. We start false rumors.

A guard on the midnight shift who is employed by a security agency under contract to Imperium complained about the chemical workers:

> These guys are a real pain in the ass. After midnight there's nothing for me to do here, so I like to snooze. But they'll come in [to the guard-house] and bullshit for ten minutes and wake you up. And then just after you've gone to sleep another guy will come in and bullshit and so on. Sometimes there's four or five in here bullshitting.

Gambling is an important activity at Imperium. There are enough men who play the numbers game to require three runners in the plant—workers who gather bets and place them with an outside organization. The plant is divided into territories so that one runner who works in the warehouse collects bets from warehouse workers, another collects from men connected with the batch plant—operators, mechanics, and laboratory technicians—and the third, one of the process plant maintenance crew, collects from the process section—operators and maintenance men. Men bet on horses and spend considerable time and energy discussing the merits of entrants in the races at the Meadowlands.

Within the plant workers spend much time playing cards. The process crew, on the afternoon and midnight shifts, plays throughout the night on a table set up in front of the control panel. Men play in the warehouse and the maintenance shops as well as in the laboratory. Card games are ideally suited to this kind of work, for the usual number of players, three to five, is the same as the number of men in a typical work crew. More important, the rhythm of the card games fits with the rhythm of work. A game may last five or ten minutes, at the end of which a man can check the control panel and resume a new round of cards.

Men are constantly reading newspapers or magazines, for like card games these fill in short gaps between work. The commonest newspapers are the *Daily News* and the *Elizabeth Journal*; typical magazines are *Playboy*, *Hustler*, and the *National Enquirer*. A few men read more intensively. A chief in the batch plant spent three years alongside the control panels studying to be a Catholic priest, and a young worker in the process plant took a degree in chemistry. He did all his reading at work.

In every section except the packaging plant, men have installed cooking facilities—a refrigerator and a stove or hot plate—on which they prepare meals each day. Usually these are not very elaborate, for most groups are too near chemical fumes for leisurely eating to be pleasant. But the workers in the warehouse, which is far from centers of production, cook on a grand scale. Each day they prepare a large meal, the menu for which is enthusiastically debated the day before. About 11:00 A.M. they all sit down for lunch prepared by two workers who particularly enjoy cooking. Men invite friends from throughout the plant. The following comments are typical:

> Today we had ham and tomato salad with baked potatoes. George brought the ham in from down the shore, and Freddie gave us the tomatoes. They're from a farm down in South Jersey where he lives. Tomorrow we're having onions, peppers, and sausage.
>   Last week we had meatballs and spaghetti on Tuesday and kielbasa and sauerkraut on Wednesday. We got through fifteen pounds of potatoes. But you make too many enemies. Guys in the plant say, "Why didn't you invite me?"

In some sections of the plant workers have television sets. And, to make life in the plant more interesting, men are capable of considerable ingenuity. For a while production workers used to show pornographic movies in the laboratory on the midnight shift. The worker who obtained the films explained:

> I have a friend who makes them fuck films in Florida. We used to have a different fuck film every Monday night on the midnight shift. He lent me a copy of *Deep Throat* and *The Devil in Miss Jones*.

Occasionally men engage in more practical activity. A helper in the process plant described such a program:

> Before I got married I used to be a pimp. You know, I'd fix guys up. I'm fixing some guys up at Imperium on Friday—twenty-five dollars apiece in the briquetter room. At night there's no one there.

The Case of the Warehouse

The commonest attitude toward work is illustrated by the warehouse. Older men especially are eager to move there from other sections of the plant (except from maintenance). Warehouse work is mostly trivial, and there is little opportunity for overtime,[5] so annual earnings are less than in most other areas. But it is day work, is easy, and allows plenty of opportunity for social activity, which is why it is so popular.
     Workers in this department handle incoming raw materials and the outgoing products of the batch plants. Three kinds of work are involved.

Warehouse Workers

Most men operate out of the warehouse, and their job is to transport drums of resin from the batch plants to the warehouse. The drums are carried, four at a time, on forklift trucks. From the warehouse they are collected in trucks sent by customers. Driving a forklift truck is simple, involves little physical effort, and allows workers to move back and forth between production centers in the warehouse so that they can chat with men in various sections of the plant. There are long periods when there are no drums to be moved and no customers' trucks waiting to be loaded. During this time men can sit in a section at the back of the warehouse and talk or play cards or read or watch television or cook. Since the warehouse is a long way from the production centers, the concentration of chemical fumes is lower than in other areas. As one man commented, when asked whether he had considered leaving Imperium for another job:

> Oh! This is a perfect job—it couldn't be better. Well, you've seen how it is.

A weighman (see below) angrily chided the workers in the warehouse during the height of the 1974 recession when there was fear the company would lay men off:

> The men are to blame. They're bleeding the job. The guys in the warehouse sit by the door smoking, so when the big shots from White Plains come down they're going to see them and think, "What kind of place is this?" So they'll lay men off.

Tank Car Handlers

The second type of warehouse workers are "tank car handlers" who load and unload the tank cars within the plant.

The work is light and easy, involving hooking up and unhooking pumps between tank cars and storage tanks. Work is scheduled during the day, so there is no need for shift work. Yet there is often opportunity for men to earn overtime by staying a few hours past 4:00 P.M., since tank cars sometimes arrive after this time. A worker has the advantage of a day job with the opportunities of earning overtime that are usually associated with shift work.

Still, the job has a drawback. Tank car handlers are constantly exposed to fumes from the materials they load and unload. For that reason a few men with enough seniority to become tank car handlers prefer to work elsewhere in the warehouse; others are less choosy. A tank car handler:

> The best job is tank car handler. The fumes? No, you don't think about it. Benzene, acid, I've handled it all. You tell yourself it's just like pumping water at home.

Weighmen

Two men (one on the day shift, one on the afternoon shift) work in the guardhouse, recording the quantity of raw material that tank cars bring in and finished products they take out. Tank cars stop outside the guardhouse on a large scale. The weighman notes their weight, which takes about two minutes; since tank cars enter and leave roughly every half-hour, the worker has considerable spare time. Since anyone who enters the plant goes through the guardhouse, much of this time is spent in conversation, and this is one of the most sociable areas of the plant. The job itself is totally uninteresting. As one of the men who worked there commented: "It's boring— there's no action." But the work is extremely easy and away from chemical fumes and therefore, for older men, is one of the most desired jobs in the plant.

Conclusion to Part 2

I chose to study an automated plant in part because such plants are considered the most favorable kind of industrial setting. Yet, with the exception of the mechanics, few Imperium workers find their jobs interesting or satisfying. And the monitoring work that characterizes automated plants involves some serious drawbacks—rotating shifts and often dangerous conditions. If this is the case for industrial workers in the most favorable circumstances, then the prospect of providing interesting and satisfying work in factories is slight. Factories require some mechanics, who mostly enjoy what they do. But work connected with machinery (above the level of hand tools or hand-powered tools) is likely to be dull because the essence of automation is increasing constraints on the motion of machinery. Attending to, acting as an adjunct to, or monitoring such machinery is not likely to be interesting for most workers.[1] As I have pointed out, it is in general only when the machinery is not running smoothly that work connected with it becomes interesting, which is why only mechanics who service machinery and engineers who design it generally enjoy their work.

It has often been noted that the qualities blue-collar workers value in a job (apart from pay and security) are variety, freedom from supervision, and the ability to work at their own pace. The mistake has been to suppose that factory jobs, with the exception of maintenance work, can provide these qualities. When men at Imperium think of variety and freedom it is the kind enjoyed by a long-distance truck driver who travels to different places and meets new people, choosing his route and his hours. Or by someone who owns his business and answers to no boss or supervisor. Or by the policeman who knows everyone in the area and goes wherever he wishes.[2]

Images of the Industrial Worker

At the beginning of part 2 I pointed out that there are two images of workers in automated plants. The first, common in industrial sociology, is based on a stereotype of the white-collar professional. It sees men in automated plants as model workers in a model work situation. They are interested in, even enthusiastic about, their work. They perform responsible tasks from which they obtain a sense of satisfaction.

The second image is based on the assembly worker in an auto plant. Like assembly workers, employees in automated plants are assumed to be downtrodden and controlled. Management has planned and organized the tasks they must perform, removing any chance for individual initiative and skill. Every stage of the job is supervised and controlled. The principles of Frederick Taylor's scientific management govern the workplace. That modern industry is "Taylorized" is one of the clichés of industrial sociology.

The evidence of this study suggests that neither picture is accurate. Except for mechanics, few men find the work interesting or satisfying. On the contrary, it is mostly dull and tedious because it is inherently repetitive. This is why the first image is mistaken.

The second image contains a more accurate view of the character of work in automated plants but mistakes the character of those who work there. Faced with tedious tasks, men expend considerable ingenuity, with fair success, to make life at work more tolerable. This involves wresting from management a degree of control over the work situation in order to create time and space for social activities on the job. The rhetoric may be Frederick Taylor's, but the practice is different.

This book, then, suggests a third image of the industrial worker. Faced with uninteresting tasks, workers use a variety of means to increase their control of the situation. On a minor scale they are "operators" in the popular sense of the term. They become well versed in concealing information and practices from management so as to manipulate them. The distinction between rhetoric and practice is one they are experienced in maintaining.

This view has a familiar ring, but not from industrial sociology. There is a popular image of privates in the United States Army—an image supported by television shows such as "Sergeant Bilko" and "Hogan's Heroes"—that is very similar. These men spend much of their time and energy scheming to wrest effective control of their lives from "authority" in order to reduce the work load and have as good a time as possible given they are in the army. This image of the noncommissioned soldier is accepted and enjoyed. It is not clear why, then, it should be thought that these men, on entering or returning to the industrial work force, should behave any differently. For privates in the army and industrial workers are the same men. In each case lack of educational qualifications mainly accounts for their position.[3]

This raises a further question. For what proportion of the industrial work force is this third picture accurate? The question is hard to answer, for if workers have wrested some control from management neither party is likely to be eager to reveal the fact. Supervision and plant management do not want their superiors to know they do not control the work situation, and workers do not want to draw attention to the extent to which official work guidelines are violated.

But there is reason to think this picture not only may be accurate for workers in automated plants but may even represent the most common situation among unionized, blue-collar workers in general. First, according to Frederick Taylor, it was the dominant practice among blue-collar workers in the United States when he wrote

(1911). Indeed, it was the situation "scientific management" was designed to remedy. Second, it has been suggested that even assembly-line workers resemble this picture at least as much as they resemble the picture of downtrodden automatons. Even assembly workers can, through the threat of walkouts and wildcat strikes, establish some control over the work situation.[4] And anyway assembly workers are not typical even of the auto industry. Thus not more than 25 percent of General Motors's total blue-collar work force in 1974 could be classified as assembly-line workers.[5] On close examination, then, assembly workers in auto plants—the classic site of the "worker as robot" image—and chemical workers in automated plants—the classic site of the "responsible" worker image—both resemble the third image suggested here. Perhaps in that case so does a large sector of the industrial work force.[6]

Part 3

The Limits of Mobility at Work: Solidarity and Dispute

What opportunities do these workers have for promotion within the plant, what are their chances on the outside labor market, and how much job security do they possess? These aspects of occupational mobility are important for the debate over the relation between blue-collar and upper- and lower-white-collar work and for class identity and consciousness. The better the chance of moving upward at work and the more secure their jobs, the more workers possess "careers," perhaps analogous to those of upper-white-collar managers and professionals, and the less likely they are to be conscious of class and to feel solidarity with each other.

There is a view that blue-collar jobs within automated plants enable workers to pursue careers in some ways like those of white-collar managers or professionals because the jobs are arranged in a hierarchy corresponding to increasing levels of skill and therefore of responsibility. As a worker is promoted his knowledge grows, and so does his chance of moving even higher. Nor do such automated plants close down, since management is unlikely to make the heavy investment they require unless the long-term economic picture is favorable. In any case, since workers have valuable marketable skills, they can easily find jobs elsewhere.[1]

This view is misleading. Lack of the appropriate educational qualifications mars workers' chances on the internal and external labor market, holding them back at most of the crucial points. They can move up the blue-collar job hierarchy and into the ranks of supervision. But without college degrees they are unlikely to rise above second-line supervision.

In a classic study Ely Chinoy compared the plight of the auto worker seeking to reach the upper levels of management to that of the traveler who asked a farmer the way to his destination. The pragmatic farmer replied, "If I were you I wouldn't start from here in the first place." Despite the organization of blue-collar jobs in a hierarchy, the chemical worker is little better placed than most blue-collar workers to make a career in management.[2] For the same reason, most desirable newer white-collar occupations are closed to Imperium workers. In such occupations educational qualifications are typically essential for entry and promotion. As a result, the occupational mobility of workers in automated plants is not basically different from that of most blue-collar workers.

7
Occupational Mobility and Security

The Internal Labor Market

Blue-Collar Job Hierarchies

Control of the work force—making sure men act as management wishes them to act—is a battle that is constantly waged. It is part of the everyday life of the plant. Workers have a number of weapons in this fight—their union, the ability to strike, and informal influence over the production process (including "their secrets"). Among the weapons management has is the division of work groups into blue-collar hierarchies. Most work areas are divided into three levels ("helper," "assistant," and "chief" or "leader"), though in the laboratory and packaging plant there are only two. Such job hierarchies exist in most highly automated plants and—though usually in nonunion settings—may consist of up to five levels.

These hierarchies are designed to serve two purposes for management, both connected with weakening blue-collar solidarity. First, a worker can be assigned the responsibility for ensuring that the man below him does his job, and the blame if that job is not done. Second, the hierarchy is supposed to act as an incentive. Workers lower down the ladder will, it is hoped, be encouraged in their tasks by the knowledge that they can ascend the hierarchy as vacancies occur. And the more steps in the ladder, the more occasions when men can feel a sense of progress.

Some people argue that job hierarchies in automated plants exist for technological reasons, with the production process creating a series of jobs that require increasing degrees of skill and knowledge. This argument ascribes too much to technology. In contexts such as chemical plants and oil refineries the hierarchical division of labor is a creation of management, not technology, and is designed to control social, not technical forces.[1]

Most of the jobs at Imperium can be learned in a few months, and there is no reason, from the point of view of job requirements, why work crews should not consist of men at the same level of pay, status, and authority. The one area where this is not true is maintenance, for a skilled mechanic needs considerable training. Yet the organization of mechanics at Imperium demonstrates the function of the work hierarchies as instruments of social control. To become a mechanic, a worker goes through a formal training program that involves four years of daytime work and evening study at college. During this time he is classified as an apprentice. The division between mechanics and apprentices is based on real differences of skill and knowledge. But mechanics too must be controlled, which is why the position of "leader" has been created. The leader's task is to make sure the other mechanics do their work, and his job is clearly analogous to the position of the chief in production crews.

The following comments illustrate these dual functions, openly recognized by workers and management, of the work hierarchies as devices for assigning responsibility (and blame) and providing an incentive to those below.

The supervisor in charge of the process plant:

> As far as I'm concerned, having a chief, assistant, and helper is a bribe. It gives you something to offer the guy in the middle, something to encourage him.

A chief in the batch plant:

> It's really the chief's job to keep them in order; you have to keep them on a chain. For instance, you may have two guys who fight—they don't get on. Then you send one of them outside on some project and keep the other up here [in the control room].

The same process operates lower down the hierarchy. Assistants are supposed to guarantee the performance of helpers. Another chief in the batch plant:

> We used to have one chief, one assistant, and three helpers in a crew. But it didn't work. You'd send the three helpers out to do a job, and the assistant would stay here in the control room. But you'd get jealousy among the helpers. One of them would always take off—go drinking or something. And then the other would, and you'd be left with one guy— he can't do all the work. So if you send out an assistant he's responsible. You can say to him, "Hey, why didn't this get done?"

But hierarchies are only a limited success as devices to undermine blue-collar solidarity. First, workers will not always behave like foremen. Pressure in a work crew accumulates around the chief or leader; men lower down, such as assistants, may be assigned responsibility for specific tasks, but the chief is responsible for all the work of the crew. Yet the chief is also a worker, a member of the union. Management encourages chiefs to think of themselves as supervisors, but the union applies equal pressure on chiefs to remember that they are not. A union officer:

> The chiefs do the supervisor's job. Of course they don't all act for the company. Some are with us, where they should be. They try and fuck the company.

Tension between some chiefs and the union became acute during a recession. Union officers wanted the chiefs in the batch plant to drastically slow down production so as to increase the days of work available. Since demand for resins had fallen, men were working only a three- or four-day week. At a union meeting an officer reported that some of the chiefs were being uncooperative:

> I've been doing what I can, but some of the chiefs are hardhearted scumbags. I said to Joe [a chief], "Some of these guys are only working three days a week, and that isn't right." He looked at me and said, "Are you telling me to slow down?" Well, what could I say? I couldn't actually tell him to slow down.

A chief explained the ambiguity of his position:

> As chief, you're right in between the company and the union.
> Once a helper got drunk and messed up the job, and he blamed me. They [supervision] came to me, and I said, "Look, the guy can't even stand up. And you're blaming me."
> But it's very hard to prove a guy is drunk. The union files a grievance and says you're not a doctor. Sometimes I say to a supervisor, "This man's drunk—I'm sending him home," and the supervisor says he's not drunk. And often as not you'll find him asleep by the wall with his tongue hanging out!
> You're in a bind. You can't turn the guy in to management because then the union ostracizes you, and you're finished. They won't work with you. And if you go to the union they say, "What can we do? It's not our job."

Chiefs and leaders must adopt some kind of compromise between the desires of the men in their crew and those of management. If they push the interests of management too hard, the workers will find ways of taking revenge. One chief, for instance, tried to exert more authority than the men in his crew thought appropriate. To retaliate they used to creep up behind him in the control room and bang pieces of corrugated iron. His nerves soon deteriorated, and to escape he bid into a low-paying job sweeping up in the yard. His fate was an object lesson to other chiefs not to antagonize their crews.

A young worker had just become a chief in the batch plant. After mastering the job, he began to throw his weight around, to the growing annoyance of his crew. One evening a helper was sitting in the tavern complaining about this to an older, more experienced worker:

> **Helper**: You know he [the chief] says, "I'm the chief. I do what I want. I don't fill drums, I don't clean up. I just turn valves." So he doesn't help us, and then he comes out here for four hours. I wouldn't mind that, but then when I go to sleep he wakes me up and says I should clean the filter press,

and he and Fred [the assistant] are already up! And he keeps his pillow next to where I sleep so when he goes to get his pillow he wakes me up.

Older worker: You've got to put a stop to it right away. You have to say to him, "Unfortunately, we've all got to work for a living, so we'd better all work together." Otherwise this shit will never stop. He'll be doing the same thing for the next ten years.

Helper: Well, if he's going to wake me up I'm going to make sure I wake him up.

Older worker [later, explaining to the researcher]: You know, sooner or later they'll [the other crew members] fuck him [the chief]—open a valve when he's not around so the whole batch runs out and he's responsible. Then he'll learn. And if he doesn't they'll do it again, and pretty soon the company will move him down, tell him he can't do the job.[2]

On the other hand, a chief cannot be so lax that the work is not done at all. Because of these difficulties many workers, in all areas of the plant, have turned down the opportunity to rise to the top of the nonsupervisory hierarchy. This is the second reason such hierarchies are of limited success in weakening blue-collar solidarity.

This reluctance of many workers to ascend the blue-collar hierarchy can be seen by comparing the seniority of chiefs and leaders with that of the men they oversee, for since promotion up the blue-collar hierarchy is determined entirely by seniority, any worker with more years in the plant than his chief has turned down the chance of moving up. There are twenty-four chiefs or leaders in the plant. There are another twenty-six workers who have more seniority than their chiefs or leaders, so that of the fifty men who have had a chance to take the top positions in their work crews

Table 19 Workers' Willingness to Take Top Jobs in the Blue-Collar Work Hierarchy

	Total Plant	Production Workers[a]	Support Workers[b]
Number of chiefs or leaders	24	16	8
Number who declined to become chief or leader[c]	26	21	5
Percentage of workers who had the chance to become chief or leader and declined that chance	52	57	38

[a]Process and batch workers.
[b]Mechanics, laboratory workers, warehouse workers, and packagers.
[c]Measured by the number of workers with more seniority than their chiefs or leaders.

twenty-six (52 percent) have declined. Table 19 lays out this information for the plant as a whole and for production and support workers separately.[3]

The men who declined to become chiefs or leaders did so because they have no interest in exercising authority, at least within the work crew. Nor do they wish to take responsibility for production—they do not want to be concerned about whether the chemical reactions are occurring in the right way. They prefer to take a detached attitude to their jobs—to treat work as an intrusion into their social life both inside and outside the plant. They will do their jobs, but they also enjoy the various social activities that go on in the workplace.

Supervision in Automated Production

What about supervisors? In automated plants are they more like advisers, ready to offer technical help and assistance, as is often maintained, or are they disciplinarians?

Each production crew in the process plant has a supervisor who rotates shifts along with the workers. In the batch plant there is always one supervisor on duty responsible for both production centers and the laboratory. Mechanics and warehouse workers also have a supervisor (see fig. 17). These men, all nonunion, constitute first-line supervision.

It is true they are not obtrusive. There is nothing comparable to the foreman on an assembly line who has workers under constant surveillance. The higher-level supervisors tend to keep away from the main production centers, and most of the first line are careful not to give the impression of acting as sentinels. During the day they spend very little time in the control rooms directly observing workers. Mostly they sit in their offices or chat with upper-level supervisors. In the process plant at night supervisors spend more time in the control room, but that is because there is no one else they can talk with. Workers generally agree that:

> Imperium [supervision and management] don't bother you. They leave
> you alone so long as you're doing your job.

And on the whole higher-level supervisors do possess considerable knowledge and are consulted by workers when problems arise beyond the latter's competence.

But the primary function of first-line supervisors is surveillance, however discreetly they perform this function. Workers constantly refer to line supervisors as "watchdogs." As one operator put it:

> They're watchdogs to make sure the guys don't go outside to Lesniak's.

Another operator explained:

> The supervisors are there to make sure the guys don't drink or fuck
> around. It would be cheaper to hire four Doberman pinschers. It would

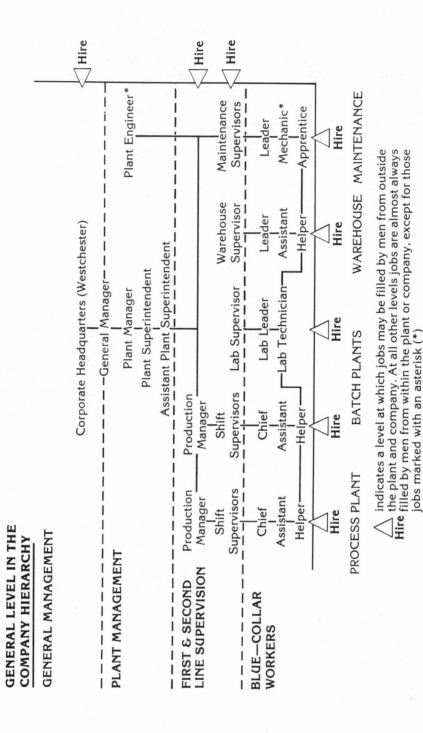

Fig. 17. The internal labor market.

only cost you sixty dollars a year in dog food, instead of paying for all these guys.

Since line supervisors are often workers who have been promoted, they may possess at least as much technical knowledge about the job as the men they supervise. But this is not a condition for obtaining the job. Some patently know less than the workers, which makes it clear that their main function is surveillance rather than technical assistance. An operator commented:

> The supervisor usually knows less than the chief. Generally when there's a problem he says to the chief, "Handle it the way you usually do!"
> Anyway, when there's a problem he can't make a decision. He has to ask higher up.

Sometimes management even asks the workers to train the person who will supervise them. Not suprisingly, men resent such an assignment. A chief in the process plant explained his reaction when the head of production asked him to train a line supervisor hired from outside:

> Fred Hauser said to me, "Here, show this guy what to do." I said, "He can follow me around, but I'm not showing him anything, and if a wrench should accidently hit him it's not my fault."
> Watchdogs—that's what supervisors are.

A Career in Supervision?

What about moving into supervision and management at Imperium? How eager are workers to do this, and what are their chances of success? About half the workers, as shown in table 19, do not want promotions to the top of even the blue-collar hierarchy. They turn down the chance to become a chief or leader—nonsupervisory positions entailing union membership—because they do not want the bother of disciplining other men.

Of those workers who have taken the job of chief or leader, another half would turn down, and in some cases have turned down, offers of promotion into supervision. The main reason is that on entering supervision workers lose the protection of the union. So long as they remain within the range of jobs entailing union membership men will be fired only for blatant violations of company rules. The union contests every firing in arbitration, and the company knows it must build an overwhelming case to be successful. But supervisors can be fired at management's whim. Workers enjoy the independence provided by their job security and are reluctant to exchange it for the sycophantic behavior they perceive a supervisory position as requiring. One of the best mechanics in the plant commented:

> They've asked me lots of times to go into supervision, but I like to speak my mind. I like to say what I think to people, and those guys can't do that.

An example of what he had in mind occurred during a lengthy dispute the mechanics were having with management over whether they or outside contractors should do certain work. A warehouse supervisor approached him.

> **Supervisor**: You fucking cocksucker, I hear you've been making trouble again.
>
> **Mechanic**: You fucking cuntlapper, what's it got to do with you?

And men who enter supervision are sometimes caught in a conflict between their old friends and the pressure to demonstrate their new loyalties to management. They risk alienating their former workmates. A union officer spoke angrily about a worker who had just taken a supervisory job:

> Take Vic. A guy who's been a member of the union for twenty-five years [and then entered supervision]. We've been trying for years to get an extra man in the thinning room, and Vic goes and tells them [management] that there are two guys sleeping and another fucking around. So we go in to Frank Leiter [the plant manager] and ask for another man, and he says, "Vic says you don't need anyone else. There are two guys who sleep all the time."
> Well, the guys will still speak to him, but they'll do everything possible to fuck him behind his back.

Workers tell grisly stories, with relish, to illustrate the fate of supervisors or management the company wished to dispose of. In these stories unwanted supervisors are usually "shipped down to one of the company's plants in the South," while managers are "promoted" to White Plains (company headquarters) and then fired. This perception of the insecurity and competitiveness that pervades the levels of supervision and management in a large corporation is not inaccurate, as Kanter's study of such a corporation shows.[4]

Still, promotion to supervision is attractive to about 25 percent of the blue-collar force. Figure 17 shows the number and type of positions available. At levels marked with an arrow jobs are given to men either within or outside the plant. Other levels are filled almost entirely by promotions from within.

There are fourteen first- and second-line supervisors. Nine of these men had once been union members. The rest were hired from outside. The ratio of such positions to blue-collar jobs in the plant is about one to nine, which is probably better than in the auto industry (in the auto plant studied by Ely Chinoy the comparable ratio was one to seventeen). If a worker wishes to become a supervisor he stands a reasonable chance of success, though he may have to wait twenty years.

But promotion any higher than second-line supervision is very unlikely, for at that level jobs go to men with degrees. A number of studies have shown that this is true for most blue-collar workers. At Imperium the only exception was the assistant plant superintendent. Workers often say of a man who has just taken a job in supervision: "He thinks he's going to be company president. But he ain't going nowhere."[5]

Job Security

Some authors writing about workers in process plants have argued that the job is very secure, since a company will not make the heavy capital investment such plants require unless market conditions are favorable and are likely to continue so. A job in a highly automated plant is a job for life.[6] So how likely is a worker to lose his job? There are three main ways this may happen. It is important to distinguish between them, since they have different causes and may affect different age groups.

Closure of Automated Plants

The first way is if the plant closes. This, of course, affects everyone. How likely are automated plants to close?

Table 20 ranks New Jersey manufacturing industries by the percentage of the labor force in each industry laid off from 1970 to 1982 because of plant closure. Workers in chemical production were less likely than any other group to lose their jobs because of a plant closure. Still, forty-nine chemical plants did close during that time, as did a few refineries.

In general the older a worker the more serious it is if he loses his job. Above a certain age it is a catastrophe, for a man is then too old to obtain a comparable position elsewhere. Men at Imperium have a clear idea of the age beyond which chemical workers will not be hired by another company. Throughout the plant men

Table 20   Plant Closures in New Jersey Manufacturing Industries, 1970–82

Industry	Number of Plant Closures[a]	Number of Workers Laid Off	Annual Average Percentage of Workers Laid off in Each Industry
Textiles	48	7,002	2.2
Transportation equipment	10	5,774	2.1
Primary metals	40	8,902	1.8
Rubber and plastics	47	5,793	1.2
Apparel	55	9,855	1.2
Furniture	7	1,400	1.2
Food	57	6,920	1.0
Electrical machinery	85	10,254	0.8
Petroleum and coal	5	1,083	0.7
Printing and publishing	20	2,628	0.4
CHEMICALS	49	5,527	0.3

Source: New Jersey Department of Labor and Industry.
[a]These figures exclude layoffs involving fewer than ten persons.

say no one will employ them after the age of fifty. Their views on the subject are well informed since, in addition to personal experience of the labor market, most have a wide variety of contacts with other workers in the region.

Further support for the view that chemical workers are not hired beyond the age of fifty comes from examining data on the ages at which men were hired at Imperium. (See table 21). Workers are most likely to be hired between the ages of twenty and twenty-nine and very unlikely to be hired beyond the age of forty-five. This is why older workers are more likely to leave their wives than to leave Imperium. None of the thirty-four men who left voluntarily between 1960 and 1977 was more than fifty-two (see table 22).

Since older workers are so dependent on the company, even the slightest doubt about the future of the plant is enough to cause fear. Because plants do close, that doubt is always present, and so is the fear. And when times are bad fear turns to panic. The recession that began in 1974 triggered such a mood. Men were angry, morose, and scared. As the union president put it:

> We're really sweating. You know, a plant shutdown is the worst catastrophe for a working man.

Table 21   Ages of Workers When Hired

Age	Percentage	Age	Percentage
16–19	7	40–45	5
20–29	57	50–59	0
30–39	31	60–65	0

Source: Age list in appendix C of contract (*N* = 121).

Table 22   Workers Who Quit, 1960–77

Occupations for Which Workers Quit	Number	Average Age
Own business[a]	10	41 (30–52)[b]
Mechanic (not self-employed)	9	33 (20–44)
Truck driver	7	32 (29–50)
Policeman or fireman	4	26 (20–31)
Other	4	
Total	34	

Sources: Informants and contract.

[a]Includes four mechanics who started businesses in which they used their mechanical expertise.

[b]Age range.

In 1977 Imperium constructed a new production center in the plant. Men were pleased but still very cautious. A mechanic expressed the common view:

> I've heard of companies spending millions of dollars on a new plant and then tearing it all down because it's cheaper to produce somewhere else.

This fear is translated into a hesitancy about pushing certain demands. For instance, the older men are reluctant to complain too much about safety and health conditions lest the company decide that the cost of meeting men's demands no longer makes production profitable. A young assistant whose face had been covered with fasic acid and whose father was dying of cancer after working twenty years at Imperium commented bitterly:

> The older guys are frightened. They're just thinking about keeping their own jobs. I'd like to get rid of them and get in some younger guys so we can fight the company.

Yet the logic of the older men's position is strong, for they are not privy to the profit and loss accounts of the company. They do not know how marginal an operation their plant may be and so can never be sure that a demand involving considerable expense will not induce the company to close the plant. This may be very unlikely, but so long as it is possible it can always be argued that the catastrophic consequences of a plant closure are not worth even a slight risk from posing major demands. A young union official who was often critical of the older men's limited militancy could still see a certain logic in the argument, for occasionally he would expound a modified version of it himself:

> Sure, it would be easy to call in OSHA to inspect the plant, and they'd come around and close the place down. But then you've lost your job, and what's the use of that?[7]

Firings

The second way a worker may lose his job is to be fired. For workers in general the likelihood of this happening, leaving aside personal factors, probably depends mostly on whether there is a union and how strong it is.

It is hard to be fired from Imperium. As men say, "the company is very lenient." Much of this leniency reflects the fact that if a man is fired the union always takes his case to independent arbitration, since otherwise a worker might sue the union for negligence. Because the company knows it must prove to an arbitrator the justice of every firing, few workers are fired. Table 23 gives information on firings from 1965 to 1977.

Despite the official reasons for each firing, generally there is only one reason—heavy drinking that persistently and obviously interferes with work. The official categories "insubordination" and "lateness or absenteeism" are usually related to drunkenness. For instance, after a night in the tavern one man drove his car around

Table 23   Information on Firings, 1965–77

	Number of Cases
Total firings	13
Official reason for firing	
Insubordination	4
Excessive absenteeism	
or lateness	8
Drunkenness	1
Age of men fired	
20–29	4
30–39	5
40–49	2
50–65	2
Seniority of men fired	
0–9 years	7
10–19 years	5
20–30 years	1

Sources: Union records; contract.

the plant at high speed and, when the guard closed the entrance gate, drove in over the railway tracks. He was fired for insubordination because he had entered the plant in his car though forbidden to do so by the guard.

Even a worker with a serious drinking problem is unlikely to be fired unless he becomes impossible to deal with. If a man comes to work obviously drunk and is perceived as such by the supervisor, he may be sent home. More frequently his fellow workers will cover up for him.

Yet the possibility of being fired for drink-related problems, albeit slim, operates to create a certain fear among the older men who drink heavily. Some of them are unable to control their drinking habits and know that, if the company wished, it could fire them and have some chance of winning the inevitable arbitration case. A union official commented:

> Sure, these guys get all fired up and holler and shout at meetings, but really they're scared. Take Frank. He's got a bullshit line, but he's scared shitless. Why? Well, he takes time off and shit. He drinks—he can't help it. So he's frightened the company could fire him.

Partial Reductions in the Labor Force

Men may lose their jobs because the entire plant closes or because they are fired. This can happen to workers at all ages. There is a third possibility. A man may be laid off because the size of the work force in the plant is reduced, though the plant itself remains in operation. Such partial reductions primarily affect the younger workers, for most industries with unions have a clause in the contract that specifies that any layoffs should be in reverse order of seniority. The newer and usually younger worker acts as a cushion to protect older men.

Temporary Layoffs

Reductions of this kind are of two main types. First there are those in industries that are particularly apt to hire and fire as the economy grows or moves into recession. Such layoffs are usually temporary. A worker laid off in a recession is likely to be rehired when economic growth resumes. The auto industry is notoriously such an industry, which accounts for its being at the top of table 24, where manufacturing industries are ranked by the percentage of their work force laid off owing to a reduction in the number of workers employed at a plant.

Two main factors determine the extent to which an industry will shed labor temporarily during a recession. The first is the time it takes workers to learn the job. If the job can be learned quickly, then there is little cost to the company in laying off workers and training new men when the recession ends. Since most jobs on the assembly line in the auto industry can be learned in a few hours, there is no reason for the company to keep men for whom there is no work. By contrast, in oil refining and the chemical industry it takes weeks and even months to master a job, and companies are therefore more likely to retain men through a recession. The second reason accounting for the differences in how likely industries are to shed labor during a recession is technological. In certain industries the manufacture of a product can be

Table 24 New Jersey Manufacturing Industries: Partial Reductions in Plant Labor Force and Movement of Plants within New Jersey, 1970–82

Industry	Number of Plants Concerned	Number of Workers Laid Off[a]	Annual Average Percentage of Workers Laid off in Each Industry
Transportation equipment	12	4,199	1.5
Rubber and plastics	13	999	1.3
Primary metals	19	3,653	1.0
Food	34	4,930	0.7
Petroleum and coal	6	742	0.5
Electrical machinery	51	5,770	0.5
CHEMICALS	35	4,621	0.3
Apparel	12	1,661	0.2
Textiles	6	739	0.2
Printing and publishing	12	1,050	0.2
Furniture	3	165	0.1

Source: New Jersey Department of Labor and Industry.

[a]These figures exclude layoffs involving fewer than ten persons.

interrupted at any time and resumed later without cost. Production in an auto plant can, for instance, be halted at 4:00 P.M. and resumed the next morning. During a recession the auto industry can, and does, lay off an entire shift (the afternoon or midnight shift) in order to reduce, but not halt, production. By contrast, in the oil and chemical industry production must continue twenty-four hours a day if there is to be production at all. A batch of resin may take three days to cook and cannot be abandoned midway. Neither can the distillation process involved in refining or in certain chemical processes be completed in neat eight-hour periods. It is therefore not possible in these industries to reduce production by laying off an entire shift. In general either everyone works or no one does, and production is halted entirely.

Layoffs Resulting from Increases
in Efficiency

The second type of layoff involving a reduction in the total size of the labor force at the plant results from increases in efficiency, so that the same production can be achieved with less labor. It is sometimes argued that this kind of layoff rarely occurs in highly automated industries such as chemicals or oil refining, since the work force there has already been reduced to a minimum. This is mostly true of production workers, not of support workers. For the past twenty-five years in these industries there has been a movement to reduce the size of the maintenance force. This has taken the form of attempting to lower the number of full-time speciality maintenance positions such as carpenter or insulator, for which men must be hired even if there is not work for them to do all the time. Instead companies prefer to encourage the idea that a worker is a general mechanic who can be assigned to a variety of tasks as they arise.[8]

No mechanics have been fired from Imperium for this reason, but sometimes when a man retires he is not replaced. Mechanics are uneasily aware that there is pressure to reduce their numbers. One of the maintenance supervisors commented, with a touch of sadism:

> Of course the guys are worried about automation. They didn't use to think it was possible. Now they say to me jokingly, "You're not going to send a robot out there are you?"

And in the warehouse there are often opportunities for major reductions in the work force. A warehouse leader:

> The company will do anything it can to reduce the need for human labor. I used to have twenty-six guys working under me here. Then almost all the stuff went out in drums. Now the company is trying to get customers to take it in tank cars. It reduces the need for labor. What Imperium does is they offer customers a discount if they'll build their own storage tanks and take the stuff in tank cars. Anyway, it keeps better in storage tanks. You can control the temperature.

It is such reductions in the supporting work force that probably account for why the chemical and oil refining industries appear higher in table 24 (partial reductions in labor force) than in table 20 (plant closures). And from 1961 to 1973 the total work force in all refineries in the United States dropped from 106,000 to 88,000, though during the same period the amount of crude oil processed yearly rose from 2,987 to 4,537 million barrels. In the chemical industry between 1948 and 1967 total employment rose by only 39.2 percent (700,000 to 974,400) while the industry output increased by 366 percent.[9]

What writers have said about job security in highly automated plants can now be assessed against Imperium workers' views about the security of their jobs. Highly automated plants are unlikely to close down; but chemical plants and oil refineries do close. Workers protected by a union are unlikely to be fired, except for persistent drunkenness; but some workers cannot stop drinking heavily, especially on the night shifts that process plants entail. Since these plants are already highly automated, men are not often laid off because the company has introduced a more efficient way of doing the work; but, at least among support workers, this does happen.

Workers in highly automated plants can lose their jobs. And since after the age of forty-five men rarely obtain a comparable position, many older workers fear the possibility of being laid off or fired. In normal times they are scared, and in bad times they panic.

The External Labor Market

Jobs for Which Men Leave

With the exception of mechanics, workers who leave Imperium are a small minority (fewer than 2 percent a year). From 1960 to 1977, thirty-four workers quit. Table 22 shows which jobs or occupations they went into. There are only four main kinds of jobs for which workers will be tempted to leave the company. The largest group (29 percent) started their own businesses. The next largest group (26 percent) took maintenance jobs. Another group became truck drivers (21 percent), and the fourth group became firemen or policemen. Of the remaining four men, one got a job organizing for the international union, one worked in a warehouse, one became a janitor in a local school, and one's whereabouts are unknown.

Except for the mechanics, none of these men took other factory jobs. It does not make sense for workers to leave Imperium to work in another factory. *As industrial work goes*, their jobs are well paid, secure, and not intolerably dull. Almost all Imperium workers will at some time remark that their jobs compare favorably with most jobs they could reasonably hope to get. They do not mean they enjoy the work or like the job, but they know that men without degrees and often without high-school diplomas have a limited range of choices, most of which are worse than being a chemical worker. Imperium is as good a place as any to fulfill their destiny, if that destiny is factory work.[10] If workers leave Imperium, it is to escape the constraints of the factory altogether. Running one's own business, driving a truck, and being a policeman all, in different ways, give men greater freedom and control and variety.

Police work is seen as one of the most desirable jobs, conferring status, good pay and job security, and, most important, unlimited opportunity to meet people. One man commented:

> I would like to have been a cop. You can go anywhere and you get to know everyone. And it's exciting. I would have been a great cop.

Nor has it escaped men's attention that many police forces permit men to retire on half-pay after twenty years. As one worker remarked:

> My ideal job? Being a policeman. I would have been on pension now!

A truck driver has mobility, the freedom to meet and chat with people, and— special attraction—a job that is impossible to supervise. Until a few years ago Imperium had its own trucks that made deliveries in the region. Truck driver was the most sought-after job in the plant. One worker explained why:

> It was good work—hard at times, easy at others. You went to other plants to deliver and saw different people. You were your own boss. There were no fumes and no heat. It was fairly safe. You arranged your own route and loaded the truck correspondingly. There was responsibility and challenge. There were periods of solitude and thinking while driving, and periods of talking and meeting with all kinds of people. There was some overtime, and you were home every night.

Running one's own business has the attraction of "being your own boss." Just as important, it offers men the only chance they have, aside from gambling, to become wealthy—rich enough to stop working. One of the ten men who left to establish his own business is seen by Imperium workers as definitely having made it—they speak of him with admiration, respect, and envy. He is living out the American dream. After working for a few years at Imperium as a helper in the process plant, he used his savings to buy a White Diamond hamburger store near the plant, and he now owns two more in Linden and Rahway. When workers talk about men who left to run their own businesses, they usually mention him as someone who did it successfully.

But they know of more attempts that ended in failure. One man started a contracting business and lost $3,000 when his partner disappeared with his capital. Another man bought an ice cream store in Baltimore but gave up when he found he had to work too many hours to make money. To leave the security of a regular income from Imperium for the hazards of self-employment takes courage.

As well as courage, men need capital to start a business and experience to build up the knowledge, contacts, and confidence that give their venture some chance of success. For these reasons the average age of men who left Imperium to start a business was higher (forty-one) than that of men who left to work for other employers.

Of the men who began businesses, three bought taverns or fast-food stores. Three men went into the auto business, one repairing and one racing cars, and one operating a gas station. Three men bought stores selling merchandise like cameras or picture frames, and one man began his own welding business (table A5).

Mechanics are much more likely to leave Imperium than any other workers, whether to enter another factory or not (see table 25). Partly this is because their skills are more easily transferable to other activities.[11] Eleven of the fifteen mechanics who left Imperium entered occupations where their skills were important or essential. And mechanics leave more often because a man who has the determination and talent to complete a tough apprenticeship is more likely to have the qualities to escape factory work entirely.

Seven of the men who took maintenance jobs did enter factories. They left Imperium either because they were offered more money or because they wished to move out of the region. Since skilled mechanics are in short supply, they might be attracted from Imperium by a better-paying or easier job.

Workers at Imperium do not dream of jobs that are far beyond their reach. As Bennett Berger put it: "It is only children whose functional stratification perspective includes a whole society: it is only they who find it difficult to choose between being a cowboy and being president." Workers think about jobs they could have or could have had if things had been slightly different—starting their own business, driving a truck—something that offers variety, freedom from supervision and factory routine, and some chance for creativity. One man wanted to coach school sports, since sport was his consuming passion. Another spoke of the building trades as offering an avenue for self-expression through work. Only the mechanics ever cited their current job as their ideal.[12]

The one white-collar professional job some men fantasize about is working as a full-time organizer for the international union. For men who are involved in the local union this can be an attractive possibility, since union organizers are well paid, move around, meet people, have a certain status and prestige (they wear suits), and are doing something they consider important. The current union president explained why he would like such a job:

> The pay is good. So are the conditions. You're your own boss. The
> work is clean. You earn much more money. It's interesting, challenging,

Table 25   Last Job at Imperium of Workers Who Quit

Last Job	Number
Mechanic	15
Process or batch worker	5
Warehouse worker	4
Packager	1
Laboratory worker	1
No information	8
Total	34

Source: Informants.

progressive work improving people's lives, getting them benefits, prescribing ideas, learning more.

But these jobs are hard to get. Another union officer at Imperium who would also like a job with the international explained the difficulties:

> You need a big local, so they take some notice of you. And you have to kiss ass a lot—show up at all those meetings and do favors for guys. That's what Mike did [a former president of the Imperium local who got a job with the international], and it worked.

That men do not dream about other upper-white-collar jobs should be no surprise. For they are the areas in which formal educational qualifications are important for entry and promotion. Such qualifications represent an overwhelming barrier to men's real chances in the white-collar labor market and to their aspirations. Some men lack the desire to obtain a B.A. or a B.Sc. Others, as a result of their early experiences in the educational system, are convinced they lack the talent. Only working for the union—a white-collar job where for very specific reasons formal education is less essential an asset—affords men a chance for a white-collar career.

Imperium workers sometimes refer to themselves derogatorily as "factory stiffs." They don't want to work in a factory at all, but they know other factory jobs are likely to be worse. The following comments illustrate this attitude. A warehouse worker had tried every job in the plant, including maintenance:

> When I came here in 1947 I thought this place was paradise. Before, I'd been working in a terrible job handling pipes, one after the other. And before then in a plant handling asbestos. I'd begun to cough—the money was good and I was going with a girl and I wanted to get married, but I couldn't take the fumes. So I left and came here. There, when they said take a ten-minute coffee break they meant ten minutes. Here if you took half an hour for coffee no one minded.
>
> People stay in these jobs. They don't leave. The odd guy goes to Exxon, but most people stay.
>
> I think I can do something better, more important, than shipping drums. I feel that maybe somewhere there is a better, more interesting job for me in another, better part of the United States or Canada. I also feel that maybe I should stay where I am.

A batch worker in his early thirties left Imperium to start a construction business. It failed. He tried to get a job in city government, but his friends there, whom he had counted on to pull strings, let him down. He returned to Imperium but was still trying to leave, this time by starting a chauffeur business. He explained his earlier disappointments and fears:

> Me, I've missed the boat. It's too late. I'll be a factory stiff all my life.
>
> Of course the grass is always greener on the other side. From what I've heard about other jobs this ain't bad. Supervision doesn't bother you, and the work isn't hard. For what you do the money isn't bad.

With the exception of most mechanics, workers who stay realize they are wasting much of their lives, but they do not see or are unwilling to risk an alternative. The same phrases constantly recur when older workers talk about other possibilities: "It's too late," "I had my chances," "I've missed the boat."

The American Dream

It is important to note that like most Americans these workers typically believe that their position in the class structure is of their own doing. They are factory workers because they want to be or, if they do not want to be, because they "missed the boat." They "had their chances." If they regret their position, they tend to blame not their class origins but themselves. Usually they focus on their relation to the educational system. They were not smart enough in school or, more commonly, they did not work hard enough—did not bother to go to college or, in many cases, to graduate from high school. After failing to take advantage of the educational system, many men still consider that, had they had the courage, they could have opened a small business. The vast majority do believe in the American dream—that with hard work a man can transcend his social class.[13]

I mentioned earlier that the wife of one of these chemical workers, in her early thirties, had returned to college. She obtained a B.A., then an M.A., then a Ph.D. She is now chairman of an academic department in a university in New Jersey. Her husband kept many of these chemical workers informed of her progress. And every year they heard for themselves when they met her at the Christmas party. In a society where such feats of *individual* upward mobility are possible, the American dream, whatever its sociological truth, is an idea whose grip upon the popular mind is understandably strong. But, as I will argue in part 4, it is a serious mistake to suppose that belief in this dream means workers do not have a very clearly defined notion of the class structure in America. The dream is only a part, albeit an important part, of their vision of the class structure.

The Barrier of Education

There is a theme that recurs throughout this discussion of workers' chances on the internal and external labor market. It is lack of the appropriate educational qualifications that holds men back at most decisive points. Since they have no training in the formal language of chemistry, they are unable to go beyond what they can learn from experience in the plant. They cannot situate their own practical knowledge of chemical operations within the context of formal chemistry and the chemical industry. They are confined to watching and learning how specific production processes operate.

They can move up the blue-collar job hierarchy and into the ranks of supervisors. But without a degree they are very unlikely to rise above second-line supervision. And for the same reason, the majority of the desirable newer white-collar

occupations are closed to them, for these are occupations where educational qualifications are typically essential for entry and promotion.

The infrequency with which even better-placed blue-collar workers develop
aspirations for such white-collar occupations has often been associated with the
tendency for such workers to be isolated geographically and socially from upper-
white-collar workers. In many cases, it is argued, the neighbors and acquaintances of
industrial workers in the suburbs are other industrial workers or lower-white-collar
workers such as clerical workers or salespeople.[14]

But there are several reasons to think this is not the most important explanation
for men's lowered aspirations. Above all, part 1 of this book has disputed the view
that, outside work, the blue-collar working class is clearly separate and isolated from
the upper- and lower-white-collar sectors. Through their wives, children, friends,
and neighbors, workers, at least from time to time, come to know upper-white-collar
professionals and managers. Further, they do not need to meet such people to learn
about jobs that may be preferable to their own. They read in newspapers and
magazines that teachers have longer vacations and better working hours; or that
lawyers and doctors command large incomes and great prestige; or that salesmen
travel around in their work instead of being confined to one place. It is not mainly
because they are insulated from professionals and managers that blue-collar workers
do not aspire to their jobs. It is because most lack, and feel they cannot obtain, the
educational qualifications that are vital for entry into such occupations.

8
Solidarity and Dispute

Outside work, in the residential setting, the network of mutual support that was once a classic feature of working-class communities has declined, as chapter 2 pointed out. Company and government now supply many of the economic benefits once provided, in more limited form, by friends, family, and voluntary associations. With the weakening of this network, relations outside work have faded as an important source of the emphasis on values such as generosity and cooperation.

But for many blue-collar workers the workplace remains an arena that generates solidarity and cooperation. This solidarity has five possible sources, all of which are present among Imperium workers. There is the need to *help each other* in order to perform the job. At Imperium, with a few exceptions such as the boiler operators, men all work in crews and have an interest in cooperating to complete their tasks as easily as possible and to impose their own norms over those of management. Second, every man knows that in a *dangerous situation* he might be dependent on others for help and even for his life. Third, since men must spend many hours in each other's company at work, they have a strong incentive to make the most of that company, to create an active *social life on the job*. Fourth, there is the *limited chance for mobility*, for entering management or obtaining better jobs elsewhere. With minor modifications, such as the ability to move up a blue-collar job hierarchy, most men are stuck as blue-collar workers, especially as they get older. Finally, they are all *union members*, subject to the same contract and to the direction of supervisors and management. Many of their grievances at work are handled by the union, and when it is time to negotiate a new contract they will, if necessary, all strike together. These five conditions, at least three of which are present in many blue-collar settings, combine to create a firm basis for cooperation and solidarity.

Yet such solidarity should not be exaggerated or romanticized, for it is also punctuated by conflict and dispute. Relations among rank-and-file workers, and between rank-and-file workers and the union, are not always harmonious.[1]

Disputes between Workers

All kinds of disputes occur between workers. One man may think another does not pull his weight or may dislike his personality. There are disputes resulting from the hierarchical division of labor; a chief might have behaved autocratically toward his crew or have refused to teach them anything about the job beyond the minimum. The use of the principle of seniority to determine promotions and layoffs leads to tension between older and younger workers. There are racial disputes, minor at Imperium because of the very small number of black workers. And there are tensions between union officers and the rank and file. Some men dislike each other so much that they have not spoken for years.

The following wrangle at a union meeting is an example of the heated open arguments that can take place. Under discussion was a decision, voted on at the previous meeting and now implemented, that the day shift for production workers and laboratory technicians (the groups who rotate shifts) should run from 7:00 A.M. to 3:00 P.M. instead of 8:00 A.M. to 4:00 P.M.

> **Laboratory technician** [who wants to return to the 8:00 A.M. to 4:00 P.M. schedule]: That new schedule was voted on at the last union meeting—I wasn't there. Why should mechanics and warehouse men [day workers] vote on an issue that doesn't affect them? I've got a list of guys who want to go back to the old system, and there's twenty-seven guys. [He had gone around the plant with his own informal survey.]

> **Union Officer**: Frank Leiter [the plant manager] says he's waiting for a decision from the guys—he wants a vote on it. He'll do it whatever way we vote.

> **Laboratory technician**: There's the list—twenty-seven guys for, seven against. What's wrong with that? Half the guys can't come to a union meeting to vote. Last time the mechanics and shit voted, and it doesn't affect them.

> **Second union officer** [becomes very angry at what he sees as an example of workers' abuse of the union; they cannot be bothered to attend union meetings, then criticize the executive for decisions made at such meetings]: What I want to say is, I'm sick of guys making snide comments about the union in the shower room—sniggering and shit. [His voice rises to a yell and, jigging up and down in rage, he advances menacingly down the room toward the laboratory technician.] The place for all that is here, in the union meeting, not in private. If they've got anything to say, it should be here.

> **Laboratory technician** [he is also a shop steward]: What's wrong with the shop steward going around asking the guys?

> **Batch worker** [who favors the system recently introduced, 7:00 A.M. to 3:00 P.M., and has been feuding all evening with the next speaker, a process worker. Now he becomes furious, since he perceives the laboratory technician and the process worker as in alliance to restore the old system]: You stupid nitwit [to laboratory technician]. We decide on things here.

> **Process worker**: We could have a special meeting. I admit I voted for the new system, but now I've tried it I want to go back to the old.

Batch worker [yelling]: I don't want no special fucking meeting. Here is the place to settle it. I can fix you [to the process worker]. You and your smart talk. I can get you.

Laboratory technician [to the batch worker]: You idiot. You don't talk to me like that. [Forms the loose cloth of his work suit at his crotch into the shape of a penis and wags it at the batch worker.] And I don't give a fuck for you.

Third union officer [also furious, like the previous union officer, at workers complaining about decisions made at union meetings that he assumes they were too lazy to attend]: I'm not having any referenda or anything like that [taking a couple of paces forward, his face scarlet with rage]. We settle things here, in the union meeting.

One of the commonest disputes concerns the fair distribution of overtime. Overtime is supposed to be allocated equally by rotation. The supervisor is expected to offer the opportunity to that man in the work area whose last offer was least recent, provided he is qualified to do the job. But this principle, "equalization of overtime," as it is called, is often hard to apply without controversy. For instance, if a chief is out sick, is only another chief qualified to substitute, or can the assistant do so? This may depend on the particular people concerned. Among the mechanics there is often much uncertainty over who is qualified to do what and over the precise job description of a piece of work.

Table 26 is a random sample of eighty-five grievances that men filed with the union against the company over the period 1965–80. The largest number (forty) concern the distribution of overtime. Twenty-six of these specified, in some detail, the nature of the dispute, and twenty-one of this group involved complaints by a union member that overtime had been distributed unfairly to another union member.

An example is a grievance filed by fourteen mechanics complaining that the company "violated overtime rules in the contract by continually working the same maintenance men on overtime without regard to all other men in maintenance." The company claimed the other mechanics could not do this kind of work, a claim the

Table 26   Sample of Grievances, 1965–80

Nature of Grievance	Number
Overtime distribution	40
Company not paying the correct rate for the job, undermanning a job, or not providing work when it is supposed to	27
Unfair suspension or discharge	7
Discipline	7
Working conditions	4
Total	85

Source: Union records.

latter hotly disputed. The result was a great deal of jealousy and bad feeling between the two groups of mechanics. The following discussion of the issue at a union meeting gives an indication of the heat generated:

> **Union officer**: There's the issue of mechanics' overtime. Frank Habatz [the chief engineer] has had the same guys on a job for a long time. He won't rotate the job. He has a few favorites there. I said to him, "You've created a monster. When I went into the maintenance shop the two groups weren't speaking. We've created a monster there."
>
> **Batch worker**: Those guys shouldn't have accepted it [the overtime]. That's the trouble. When there's plenty of overtime it's all right, but in a slack period the company plays guys off. The guys are to blame. They shouldn't have accepted it.
>
> **Process worker**: I heard they did offer overtime to the other guys and they refused.
>
> **Mechanic** [angrily]: No, they gave us one day, throwing us a bone. Well, it was only one day. So we told them they could stick it up their ass. We refused.

Another instance of such disputes is the following incident between two groups of batch workers. One man described what happened:

> I didn't tell you how we got the overtime. Freddy Baier [the supervisor] asked me and Teddy to stay overtime on Tuesday—he couldn't get anyone else—cleaning out a tank car. The anhydride had crystallized, and you have to hack it out with a pick. It's tough work.
>   Well, Wednesday we waited till 3:30 [P.M.], and he didn't ask us to stay. He'd asked those other guys. So when he came round I said: "You cocksucking trader. We helped you out on Tuesday when no one else would stay, and then you go and give the work to those other guys." So he said, "Oh, no! It was equalization of overtime" and all that shit.
>   Well, Teddy and I had decided if he asked us to stay tonight [Thursday] we wouldn't. Well, he came over to me this afternoon and said, "Bill, there's twelve drums of coconut oil to be emptied. Will you stay?"
>   Now, that was different. That coconut oil only takes fifteen minutes, and we get paid for four hours. He [the supervisor] made a point of telling me it was only twelve drums. So I said yes.
>   Now those other guys are green with envy.

The Worker and the Union

For Imperium workers their local union is an important expression of the interests they have in common and in opposition to those of management and the company. In this sense the union reflects and fosters solidarity among the blue-collar work force.

Yet the relation between rank-and-file workers and the union officers is uneasy. Indeed, the general attitude of the former toward their union combines strong suspicion with an equally strong conviction that without the union they would be at the mercy of a potentially arbitrary and capricious management. Workers are wary of the union but absolutely convinced of its necessity. This dominant attitude is captured by a phrase workers constantly use to sum up their views. "Unions," they say, "are a necessary evil." Fifty-seven percent at some time used this way of describing unions, and there were certainly more who would have agreed.

The union at Imperium dates from 1944. At that time, as a result of a dispute with management over the payment of wartime production bonuses, workers voted to affiliate with the Gas, Coke and Chemical Workers–CIO, which, now called the Oil, Chemical and Atomic Workers Union, has represented them ever since. Meetings of the local are held every month in a back room of the tavern across the road from the plant. Attendance averages about 20 percent, considerably higher than the 5 percent that is the average attendance at local union meetings in America.[2] (When the local union officers are negotiating a contract with management, attendance at union meetings rises to 70 percent or higher.) Elections for officers of the local are held every two years. If an officer is seen as performing satisfactorily he is usually reelected unopposed. But when an officer has generated wide discontent—for instance, by excessive arrogance or clear nonperformance of his duties—then the rank and file or other officers usually run a rival candidate, and this can lead to a vigorous and democratic campaign.

As most workers see it, unions are necessary because they provide security and protection and obtain better pay and working conditions. Security was mentioned by 77 percent as the main advantage a union offers, 34 percent mentioned better pay and working conditions, and 28 percent talked about the value of solidarity in facing management.

But unions are seen as having several drawbacks. There is a belief that they may make excessive demands that lead to a plant shutdown (mentioned by thirty men), can slow an ambitious worker's chances of promotion (mentioned by twenty-five men), and sometimes protect the job of a worker whom everyone knows is incompetent (mentioned by twenty men). Above all, unions are an evil because, in most men's eyes, they are corrupt: 65 percent mentioned corruption as a major disadvantage of unions. They consider national union leaders in America to be corrupt on a large scale, and a smaller group believes their local union is corrupt in a more minor way.

The corruption of national unions has to do with a variety of allegations. There are tangible charges, such as a belief that unnecessarily high union dues go to support an extravagant life-style for the union hierarchy. There is a belief that union leaders get a "cut" from every contract negotiated. And there are intangible suspicions such as the view that the union hierarchy is a part of the power structure that runs America (chap. 9 discusses this view in more detail).

The alleged corruption of the local union has to do with a series of concrete grievances. After each meeting beer and sandwiches are served, paid for by the local. Many of those workers who do not usually attend consider this a waste of money, and some think the union officers get a kickback from the tavern owner. The officers reply, with some justification, that without refreshments attendance would be lower.

Every month the union officers meet with management to exchange grievances, and afterward the officers go to lunch, paid for by the local. And four times a year the president and treasurer of the local attend a regional conference of the international union, held over a three-day weekend at a New York hotel. Further, the president of the local receives a small salary (about $200 a year) to compensate for the time he spends on union business. All these benefits, none of which are concealed, provide opportunities for the rank and file to feel resentful of their officers.

In the early 1950s Sayles and Strauss studied twenty union locals. The attitudes they found among the rank and file resemble those among Imperium workers. The overwhelming majority supported the union's economic activities as useful and necessary and were convinced they needed the union for protection. But they were not emotionally involved with the union, feared that accepting the union's help was an indication of their inadequacy, and were suspicious of union officers, believing— usually unjustifiably—that they must be getting something extra out of it.[3] The cases below illustrate this general attitude among Imperium workers.

A warehouse worker in his late fifties:

> Unions are very important. You need the union against management. Still, they can go too far. They want the earth, and then all that happens is the company puts a padlock on. Like in the civil service. They've got all those fantastic benefits and things. And then they lay people off.

A process worker in his early thirties:

> Unions are a necessary evil. You need them for protection. But they get a ten cents an hour raise on wages and then raise union dues a dollar.

A laboratory technician, a shop steward in his late thirties:

> Unions are necessary, but they're an evil. Because often the union is forced to fight for a guy deep down they know is no good. And it gives the union a bad name. They're necessary, otherwise some of the companies would throw a guy out. It's happened before. Seniority is the heart of the union. Without seniority the union might as well cash in its money. You can't do anything.

A worker in his early sixties:

> Nowadays with unions its all material things. In the old days some guys were very involved with ideas and stars up there [raises his hand above his head]. Now Dubinsky, he was a jewel. In those days the business agent got around the same money as everyone else. And he had all that responsibility. Now the business agent gets three times as much as the rest.

At its 1975 annual convention, the international union voted to tie union dues to workers' wages, thus providing for automatic dues increases. This was done for two reasons. First, it spared each local from having to ratify every increase and avoided the bitter dispute that always accompanied such a request. Second, it introduced a progressive element into the dues structure, since locals whose wages were lower paid lower dues. In addition to this automatic increase, the proceeds of which went to the international, the Imperium local proposed to raise dues to meet increases in its own costs.

The news of these proposed increases was met with predictable hostility when union officers introduced the proposal for ratification by the local:

> **Union president**: And now we come to what we've all been waiting for— union dues. At the convention they decided to raise "per capita" dues ninety-five cents—that's the part that goes to the international. And we, the committee, want to raise local dues ninety-five cents too [dues currently were $8.10 a month, of which $5.00 went to the international and $3.10 to the local]. We're [the local] going under. You hear the [treasurer's] reports every month. It's getting lower and lower. Without that increase I don't know what we're going to do. We may as well forget the union [the local].
>
> Jesus, d'you think I like having to come to you like this? It's terrible. In ancient times the kings used to execute the guys who brought bad news. But it wasn't their fault, and it's not my fault. I don't like telling you this.

The representative of the international union, who serviced this and neighboring locals, then made a rambling speech in support of the proposal. He stressed the way the cost of living for union representatives was rising, that the international did not make a profit, that locals without the international were useless, that the move was unavoidable:

> **International representative**: I've been in the union movement thirty-five years, and every time we take a dues increase back to the membership everyone in the plant gets upset. We can't go on upsetting the membership. Now if prices settle down, you can go to a convention and throw the whole thing out.
>
> **A mechanic** [angry and determined]: Wait a bit. Some guys here are only working three and four days [the effects of recession], and you're asking them to pay $10.00. This has got to stop. Everyone's doing this to us. The federal government raises income taxes, the property taxes go up, prices go up, and now the union is doing it to us. And it's discriminating against the older guys. We're an older union. We've been going twenty-five or thirty-five years, and we've fought hard for what we've got. And now we have to pay $5.95 and these new locals pay $3.50. The way I see it, we older unions are getting stuck up the ass.

Union treasurer [angrily raising his voice]: Len, come May [contract negotiation time] you're going to want an increase, aren't you? And what are you going to do? How are you going to do it without a union? Without this increase we're going under.

Mechanic [also angry]: Why are you pointing at me? You know all the other guys—what they'd say [a reference to the workers not present at the meeting]. They wouldn't want this.

Union president: This meeting represents those guys who're interested. I'll tell you, I know what guys say in private. They don't say it to me, but they said it behind my back and people tell me. They say the local spends too much money. They say we spend too much money on Sullivan's [the union president] trips and on the committee's lunches and on refreshments at meetings. Well I'll tell you straight, I'm not ashamed of any of that. I think the president, the guy who sits up here, should go to the conventions. He should have the trips. It could be someone else next year. The trips should go with the job, and I ain't afraid to say so.

And the refreshments. We should have refreshments for the guys who come—these are the guys who're interested. And the lunches. They don't cost that much—forty-five or fifty dollars. And most of the time now we don't go to Lesniak's. We go to the Blue Oasis, and I think they give good value.

After much argument the motion to raise local dues was carried by a two to one margin.

It would be a mistake to infer from this, or from the existence of disputes between workers, that men's support of the union in crucial disputes with management, especially over the terms of a new contract, is unsteady. For when men say a union is necessary it is such occasions they often have in mind. Fifteen contracts have been negotiated with the company since 1952, and seven were preceded by strikes. Strike votes are usually unanimous or very close to unanimous, and in the heat and uncertainty of last-minute negotiations anticompany feeling and solidarity with fellow workers can run high.

Some union officers remember with chagrin one contract, negotiated in the 1960s. As the contract was about to expire the company made what it, and the union officers, understood to be their "real" offer on wages. The union officers took the proposal to a meeting of the local, held the same evening in the tavern, and recommended acceptance. Because the talks had dragged on longer than expected, the rank and file, who had been waiting in the tavern for the final offer, had become very angry with the company and had drunk liberal quantities of beer and whiskey. Under the combined effect of anger and alcohol, they resoundingly rejected the company's offer, precipitating a lengthy strike that ended when they received a token one-cent-an-hour increase. To avoid a repetition of this fiasco, votes to ratify a contract are now held on Sunday mornings if possible and somewhere that does not serve liquor.

Early in 1976 the union officers requested from the rank and file, and received, a unanimous strike vote. This was a lever to strengthen their position in negotiations with the company over a new contract. The motion was resoundingly passed despite the fact that the plant, and the entire region, was seriously affected by the economic recession. A union officer commented:

> Sure, they'll all vote for a strike. Well, they don't want to seem like
> they're letting down the other guys. A guy'll vote for a strike and then
> go home and pray it doesn't happen.

Once a strike has begun, and the company is trying to run the plant itself (with the help of extra supervisory personnel drafted in from other plants in the region), men can act with considerable vigor in defense of their interests. The most violent strike occurred in the late 1960s when the work force was reinforced by some younger men recently returned from Vietnam. A young process worker:

> The last strike was wild. We used commando tactics. We snuck through
> the fence with wire cutters and shut down the pumps while the guard
> wasn't looking. Or they'd [workers] start a fire in the garbage cans down
> at the entrance, and while management were all rushing down there six
> guys snuck in here [the control room for the fasic plant] and fiddled with
> all the valves and levers.
>   A lot of these guys were wild. They'd come through the hedge—the
> guard would see 'em—and they'd throw rocks at him. He'd run away,
> and they'd throw firecrackers inside.
>   The first four weeks we were just playing around, but after that, I'm
> telling you, if it had gone another week they would have blown up the
> whole plant.

There was at least one case of arson. A union officer:

> The company brought in a bus for extra supervisory people drawn from
> all over the company. Some of our guys got mad. They'd sit in the
> tavern and watch these people doing our work. So after a few drinks
> some of them burned down the guardhouse. They wrecked our guard-
> house; [with quiet satisfaction] it was unrecognizable.

A manager:

> It was rough during the strike. There were lots of younger guys, and
> they don't care—they have no benefits, no seniority, no stake. They'd
> just as soon close the place down.
>   During the strike the only way we could get raw materials in was by
> railroad. You know, the railroad is railroad property. They're [workers]
> not allowed to touch it. Still, we had a guy up front of the train riding
> shotgun just in case.
>   It's amazing how guys change. You can be real friendly with a guy

and then during a strike it gets nasty. That strike broke up families—
you had supervisors and workers from the same family on different
sides. They [workers] heaved boulders, not stones, through our car
windshields. Some of the supervisors were frightened of being molested.

Joking Relations: Solidarity and Dispute

Joking relations—ritual insults—are central in understanding and summarizing interpersonal relations among these workers. Joking relations reflect the strong underlying basis for solidarity as well as the existence of tensions and dispute. Radcliffe-
Brown gave the classic definition of a joking relation: "a relation between two
persons in which one is by custom permitted, and in some instances required, to tease
or make fun of the other, who in turn is required to take no offence."[4]
It is hard to exaggerate the importance of these relations in the everyday life of
the plant. They heavily flavor social interaction, and most, though not all, men
routinely engage in them. Consider this example. A group of workers were playing
cards in the locker room. Several others were watching.

> **First worker** [remarking loudly about a second worker]: He gave me six fish
> once, and they all fitted into one frying pan! [Laughter from the others.
> Having discovered a winning line, the speaker repeats it.] Yes, he gave me
> six fish, and they all fitted into one frying pan! [Further laughter from the
> others.]
>
> **Second worker**: I gave you seven.
>
> **First worker**: Yes, and they all fitted into one pan! [Louder laughter from
> the audience.]

Workers call these interactions "ball busting" or "ball breaking."

Joking Relations and Values

Joking relations among Imperium workers operate on three levels. First, and most
important, they are ritual statements and affirmations of values.[5] A joking relation
consists of an "insult" that is offered in "jest." There is ambiguity and uncertainty
concerning the intention of the insulter. Sometimes there is an intent to affront,
more usually there is not. But regardless of intention there is little or no uncertainty
about the nature of the jibe. *If* intended seriously, the remark is insulting. Thus the
themes underlying these insults illustrate the values workers have in common.
Take, as an example, the banter over the fish. It is, on the surface and to an
outsider, unclear whether one worker who accuses another of being stingy or cheap
really intends the accusation. But what is agreed is that stinginess or cheapness are
vices and their opposite, generosity, is valued. Unless a man believes cheapness is
wrong, and that the recipient of the jibe believes it is wrong, there is little point in

suggesting, as a ritual insult, that someone is cheap. These interactions, in which the same themes recur again and again, are then a ritual way men reaffirm certain values, and they can be studied to ascertain those values.

Table 27 shows the main issues around which insults at Imperium revolve. The data were collected by noting the themes underlying *all* the insults exchanged over a given period of time, at various places within the production complex and in the taverns where workers from the plant drink. These themes, inverted, are an indicator of the values both of the person who gives the insult and of the recipient.

Friendship and Generosity
Friendship and generosity are the most frequently mentioned values underlying the insults men exchange. Apart from being expressed in joking relations, gestures of such values are built into men's drinking lives by the custom of paying in turn for rounds of drinks. It does not matter that most men are quick to notice if someone does not reciprocate, for what is important here is the symbolic gesture of friendship and generosity. And in continually repeated joking relations that involve the themes of generosity and friendship, men express the importance of these values. The banter about the fish is one example. The following is another. A group of batch workers were sitting in the local tavern one evening. A chief operator had brought some doughnuts to work earlier in the day and passed them around. In his absence workers were discussing the quality of his generosity.

First worker: He must have kept them a week before he brought them in.

Second worker: Yes, they had green hairs growing out of them. [Smiles from the others. Another worker comes in and also makes a derogatory remark about the doughnuts, whereupon the two earlier speakers repeat their

Table 27   Themes Underlying Ritual Insults

Theme of Insult	Value Affirmed in Insult	Number
Cheapness ($n = 28$) Breaking the rules of friendship ($n = 16$)	Friendship and generosity	44
Homosexuality ($n = 21$) Sexual incompetence ($n = 7$) Cowardice ($n = 7$)	Masculinity	35
Ethnicity ($n = 16$)	Minor importance of ethnicity	16
Stupidity ($n = 8$)	Intelligence	8
Physical unattractiveness and personal hygiene ($n = 8$)	Physical attractiveness	8
Other		7
Total		118

comments. At this point the chief operator who supplied the doughnuts enters.]

First worker: Hey, those doughnuts, you kept them a week before you brought them in, didn't you?

Second worker: Yes, they had yellow hairs on them.

Chief operator [smiling slightly]: You mean cocksucker [stressing now the value of masculinity; turns to the second worker], when did you ever buy anyone anything? And there was one missing before I took them out—you took it, didn't you?

In this interchange it is unclear if the generosity of the donor is really being questioned. But what is clear is that all the participants agree that generosity is a virtue and cheapness a vice, and their joking exchange reaffirms and strengthens this view.

Masculinity

Masculinity is the second commonest theme underlying these joking relations. This often takes the form of banter about homosexuality. The following is an example. A group of four workers are sitting and talking. One gets up and goes to the bathroom. A minute or so later a second, Freddy, also moves toward the bathroom. His friends comment:

First friend: Hey Freddy, got your knee pads with you?

Second friend: Hey Freddy, got your napkin ready?

Exchanges around the same theme are constantly repeated among men. What does this mean? The blue-collar worker's ritual rejection of homosexuality has been much misunderstood by the casual observer. There is a common stereotype of the blue-collar worker as an insensitive homosexual hater. But this is misleading. It overlooks what men do, as opposed to what they say. Blue-collar workers typically spend much more time in close contact with other males than do white-collar employees. At Imperium, for instance, the work setting—crews operating shifts in enclosed areas such as a control room—entails considerable casual physical and emotional closeness. Men are often physically intimate in a nonsexual way. They put their arms around each other and touch each other in genuine gestures of affection. On one occasion two close friends, who had temporarily squabbled, kissed on the mouth in a spontaneous demonstration of the underlying strength of their ties. Men spend the afternoon and evening shift together for years at a time. After work they undress and shower in the locker room. They know each other and help each other.

In this context the routine joking and ritual affirmation of heterosexuality constitute a device that makes possible real intimacy between males in a society such as the United States whose dominant cultural values discourage such intimacy. Men can, through ritual accusations of homosexuality, reassure themselves and discount the possibility that their friendships are suspect. This is surely also the explanation of the widespread practice among the working class of "goosing"—tweaking a man's testicles or pinching his buttocks. If men can touch each other's genitals without going any further, this provides a reassurance that the relation is based on real friendship rather than sexual attraction.[6]

The claim, often made about noncommissioned soldiers in the army as well as about blue-collar workers, that banter about homosexuality indicates a fear of homosexuality is in one sense correct. But it is very one-dimensional if taken to indicate a lack of intimacy between soldiers or workers. It is because of the depth of their intimacy that these men feel a need to reassure themselves of its nonsexual character.

Consider another interchange, which expresses friendship, generosity, masculinity, and another value—physical attractiveness. Two days after the annual Christmas party—an elaborate dinner dance financed by the company but run by the union—a group of mechanics were sitting in the maintenance shop discussing the party:

> **First mechanic** [to second mechanic]: Why were you so quiet at the party? Hey [to the other mechanics], his mouth was like this [clamps his jaw to his upper lip]. [The second mechanic is notorious among other workers for his heavy drinking and imaginative use of crude language. Like most of the other men, he brought his wife to the party. During the evening he drank only moderately and restrained his language. Everyone knew this was because his wife was there, and it was about his restrained masculinity that the first mechanic was teasing him.]

> **Second mechanic**: You! You didn't even bring your wife. He was afraid someone was going to take his wife, that's why he didn't bring her, you cocksucking dwarf: [Masculinity and the value of physical attractiveness—the recipient of this remark is five feet six inches tall.]
>
> And you [turns to a third mechanic], you were too mean to come out with me today to lunch. [Friendship and generosity.] And there's another mean cocksucker [turns to the fourth mechanic]. He wouldn't drink with me last night. He was scared he'd have to buy me a drink. [The other mechanics smile happily at these provocations.]

Joking Relations as Mediators of Disputes

In the context of disputes such as those discussed earlier, joking relations have a second meaning. As Radcliffe-Brown pointed out, they mediate strife. They provide a "modus vivendi" among men who sometimes quarrel but who, because of their situation, must somehow put aside personal differences in order to work together.[7] Joking relations achieve this effect through the ambiguity or unclarity that surrounds the intention of the person who issues the insult. Is he serious when he, for instance, accuses another worker of cheapness, or is he "just joking"? Since all agree cheapness is wrong, the *value* underlying the insult is clear, but the intention of the insulter is not.

The ambiguity inherent in joking relations serves to blur the distinction between real and feigned hostility, so that men can become quite angry and insult each other without committing themselves to a final break. And after a quarrel a context of joking relations enables normal relations to be reestablished, if men wish, with minimal loss of face for those involved. Two of the men most skillful at joking relations explained how they function to mediate strife:

> You see, no one's perfect. And if you're working with a guy all day
> there are bound to be quarrels. So you call him names, and if he takes
> it the wrong way, well that's too bad. Some guys fight and some guys
> don't speak at all, but what kind of way is that?[8]

> You know it's [ball busting] a roundabout way of telling a guy you don't
> like him. It's a nice way of telling a guy.
>   He'll have done something—you know, these things have a long his-
> tory. Maybe sometime a guy will have fucked you. And so this is a way
> of letting him know. Sure, you often don't mean it. Like I just called
> Steve a "fat fuck." That doesn't mean anything. But when you mean it
> a guy knows. You just get a sense. Like the guys are always breaking
> Bobby Wojek's balls. He knows they mean it. He's a scumbag. I've
> worked with him. I know him well.

Joking Relations and Struggles for Power

In a setting such as an industrial plant there is a special kind of equality that results from the similarity of the circumstances men find themselves in. They are all blue-collar workers, subject to the same management and the same contract, doing the same kind of work, and advancement to better jobs within the plant depends very largely on the impersonal rules of seniority. Most of the ways men can distinguish themselves from one another are a result of interpersonal skills. In this connection joking relations have a third meaning. They reflect and constitute a continual jockeying for power and status.[9] Imaginative insults have an intrinsic value of their own. There is a marked tendency for those men who are the most popular or have the highest status to be the most imaginative and provocative in their jibes. Many of the union officers, who are elected to their positions by the rank and file, are talented "jokers." In part their skill at joking relations accounts for their popularity. In part their popularity gives them the confidence to be skillful at joking relations, for a man can never be certain a jibe will be treated as a joke by the recipient. The insults and provocations are both a cause and a symbol of power.

One of the most talented jokers among the chemical workers was acutely aware of the connection between power and status and his ability to exercise his talent. At one point he was about to take the tests that men must pass before becoming apprentice mechanics. He was nervous about the effect that failing the tests might have on his reputation:

I don't want to look stupid. I call these guys retards all the time . . .
and then they'll call me a retard. You don't want to give 'em anything
to get on top of you.

Conclusion

Joking relations operate on three levels and summarize the nature of interpersonal
relations among Imperium workers.[10] First, they are symbolic statements of men's
values. This is the most important level, for every joking relation is a ritual statement
of a value. Among Imperium workers they express above all the values of friendship
and solidarity in general, and masculinity and friendship among men in particular.
This reflects a real solidarity among the work force that results from the coexistence
of a number of factors, at least three of which are commonly found in blue-collar
settings: the cooperative nature of most of the work, the common danger, the limited
prospects for upward mobility, a common incentive to create a joint social life at
work, and the shared experience of subordination to management and supervision.
Second, joking relations diminish the impact of the disputes that inevitably occur
within any social group. Third, joking relations reflect and constitute a jockeying for
power and status.

Conclusion to Part 3

Having examined a variety of blue-collar jobs, including those that characterize automated plants, we can now compare them with upper- and lower-white-collar work. This account draws also on other studies.[1] Most blue-collar jobs contain several, though not necessarily all, of the following features:

1. Work that is often dirty and sometimes dangerous (though not usually as dangerous as being a chemical worker) and that requires light or heavy physical labor. Hence the need to wear special, protective clothes—the "blue collar." But there are exceptions. For instance, at Imperium "weighmen" work in a clean guardhouse, and the only physical labor they perform is recording the weights of trucks that enter and leave. (Still, to obtain such clean jobs it is usually necessary to work first in the other ones.)

2. Work that is repetitive and therefore dull. Exceptions include the job of mechanic or truck driver.

3. Work that is clearly connected to the creation of a tangible product. This includes factory and construction jobs. Exceptions include the work of train, bus, and truck drivers, who do however produce obvious services.

4. Work that offers little chance of upward mobility. Workers may rise to first-line supervision, but above that level lack of educational qualifications poses a serious barrier.

5. Work that is supervised, in an obtrusive or unobtrusive manner. There is human supervision, and there is the mechanical supervision of a time clock.

These features provide enough real basis for distinguishing blue-collar from upper-white-collar jobs and, to a lesser extent, from lower-white-collar jobs. And they are the source of a class consciousness revolving around the concept of the working man, as I will show in part 4. But these features also suggest some similarities that allow those who occupy blue-collar positions a certain latitude. Workers can stress differences or similarities, and this too is fundamental for class consciousness.

Consider the relation between blue-collar and lower-white-collar work. Lower-white-collar work is not typically dirty or dangerous and does not involve heavy physical labor. Yet clerical and secretarial work is often as obviously repetitive and therefore dull as blue-collar work. It usually involves close supervision and surveil-lance. And it may offer limited chances of upward mobility, though probably not always as limited as most blue-collar jobs offer.[2]

Upper-white-collar work differs in a number of ways from blue-collar work and, though less so, from lower-white-collar work. But these distinctions should not be exaggerated. Upper-white-collar work is not usually as repetitive and dull as the assembly line or the process operator's job or much clerical work (however, the work of lawyers, schoolteachers, and doctors in general practice can become repetitive and dull). Upper-white-collar work is not usually "supervised" in the way factory work or secretarial work may be (but bureacracies do provide a "supervised" context, if less obtrusively, for upper-white-collar workers). Upper-white-collar workers usually have a promotional ladder (though most eventually "get stuck" too, for their ladder is a pyramid, and pyramids narrow as one climbs).[3] In sum, there are real differences between this situation and those of most blue-collar and lower-white-collar workers, even if some of those differences should not be pushed too far.

Thus the distinctions between these three sectors—the blue-collar working class and the upper- and lower-white-collar sectors—are in part based on real features and are in part a matter of the perceptions of those who occupy these jobs. Workers can stress differences or similarities. This raises the topic of politics and class conscious-ness.

Part 4

Politics and Class Consciousness

The attitude of Americans, including the working class, toward politics and the political system presents a paradox. On the one hand is widespread disdain and contempt for politicians, who are seen as untrustworthy and corrupt. This view does fluctuate somewhat over time (for instance, it is commoner now than it was in the mid-1950s), but it has a long history. In the nineteenth century the Knights of Labor opened their ranks to all except a small number of occupations considered beyond the pale of decency. Such barred occupations included professional gamblers, lawyers, liquor dealers, and politicians. In the 1930s Robert and Helen Lynd wrote in their classic study of Middletown: "In the minds of many citizens politics is identified with fraud . . . this political corruption is taken for granted by most citizens and by both parties."[1] And in 1980 the University of Michigan's National Election Study asked people's views about the honesty of those "running the government." The largest group of respondents believed that "quite a few" of those running the government were "crooked," and 70 percent believed that the government "is pretty much run by a few big interests looking out for themselves," rather than "for the benefit of all the people."[2]

Given such views, wide support could be expected for movements that offer alternative political systems. One writer put this expectation as follows: "A democratic political system cannot survive for long without the support of a majority of its citizens. When such support wanes, underlying discontent is the necessary result, and the potential for revolutionary alterations of the political and social system is enhanced."[3] Yet most Americans, including most of the working class, appear attached to the political institutions of the republic, providing little encouragement for radical movements such as socialist or communist parties that would overthrow or transform the political regime.[4]

This paradox—contempt for politicians yet apparent support for the political system—is not resolved by a look at writings on class consciousness in America. Few topics are more important yet more controversial. Marx predicted that the working class in advanced capitalism would become increasingly aware that its position in the system of production was as an exploited group, with common interests and concerns in opposition to those of capital. In this tradition of Marx, some writers argue that

American workers approach, though they have not reached, such a class outlook. For instance, in 1949 Richard Centers (one of the earliest survey researchers to take this view) commented:

> A man's way of getting his livelihood dominates much of his waking life, and it is out of the forces acting upon him in this economic sphere that class consciousness has been seen to emerge. . . . Americans have become class conscious, and a part of them, calling themselves the working class, have begun to have attitudes and beliefs at variance with traditional acceptances and practices.

There are a number of theories concerned to challenge or modify this picture of a class-conscious proletariat. Some writers argue that the working class sees society as split not into "workers" versus "capitalists" but, in populist terms, into "the rich" or "the haves" versus "the poor" or "the have-nots." Others argue that racial or ethnic consciousness is more important than class consciousness, so that for the working class society consists of whites and blacks, or of ethnic groups such as Poles, Italians, and Irish, rather than of separate social classes. Some writers stress national consciousness, maintaining that workers see a society and world composed above all of "Americans" versus foreigners. Finally, there is the claim that for the working class society is a collection of atomized individuals, not groups at all, in a competitive struggle to rise up and achieve the "American dream."[5]

These issues—class consciousness and attitude toward politics and the political system—are the topics of part 4. They are central to the question of alienation and integration, and to the question of how far the beliefs of blue- and white-collar workers overlap.

9

Politics and the Structure of Power: Democracy and Freedom

Democracy and Elections

In societies like the United States political legitimacy rests heavily on the electoral process. It is above all the existence of free elections that is said to distinguish such societies from authoritarian and dictatorial regimes. Universal suffrage is the central political ritual of liberal democracies.

But how do elections produce "democracy"? There are two "official" theories that explain this connection. According to one theory, the voters choose that candidate who is best qualified to lead—who is likely to make the best decisions while in office. This is often called the *leadership theory* of elections. According to the second theory voters choose a program rather than a leader. During the election campaign politicians present their policies, and the voters make their choice on this basis. The victorious candidate then carries out the program the electorate has selected. This is often called the *mandate theory* of elections.[1]

Yet few Imperium workers consider either theory an accurate account of politics, for almost all of them view politicians as typically duplicitous and corrupt. This in their eyes, is one of the most obvious truths about life in America. The people's elected representatives are a venal facade behind which real power operates.

There are two main senses in which workers consider politicians corrupt.[2] First, they are liars. They make electoral promises solely to obtain votes, with no intention of keeping them. Consider these typical comments:

A mechanic in his mid-fifties:

The politicians are all liars.

A batch worker in his late forties:

Politicians! They'll tell you anything. They piss on your leg and tell you it's raining!

A mechanic in his early forties:

Governor Byrne promised heaven and earth not to introduce a [state] income tax and then he did! But then with politicians that's par for the course.

A process worker in his early fifties:

I don't vote. Both parties are the same. The politicians promise to do one thing and then they do the opposite.

The second sense in which politicians are seen as corrupt is that they take bribes. A candidate who has not sold himself before the election will succumb to temptation soon after. This process by which graft operates is often viewed in very personal terms. A powerful interest hands a politician money or stocks or other material goods. Consider these representative comments:
A process worker in his early fifties:

You show me a politician and I'll show you a crook. They're all on the take.

A laboratory technician in his late thirties:

I hate politicians, especially lawyers. Big money buys them all.

A process worker in his late fifties:

They've [politicians] all got their hands in the till. The only honest politicians are those dead for two years. Then everyone eulogizes them!

A batch worker in his mid-forties:

Yes, Proposition 13 is a good idea. It'll stop the politicians spending our money. It's the hoods, the Mafia, who get all the money. That's who the politicians give it to.

A batch worker in his late twenties:

They [politicians] all take $10,000 off the top here and $10,000 there.

Sixty-four percent of these workers think *all* politicians are dishonest and entirely untrustworthy and routinely take graft. Another 16 percent think *most* politicians are corrupt, and 12 percent waver between these two positions. Thus 92 percent think all or most politicians are corrupt and deceivers.[3]
These views are clearly inconsistent with the two main official theories of the meaning of political elections. Elections are not a real choice between competing leaders (the leadership theory), because most or all the candidates are viewed as

similar in character—dishonest and corrupt. Nor are elections a time to choose from competing policies or programs (the mandate theory), because few politicians are seen as keeping their promises after gaining office.

Asked about politics, workers often dismiss the subject with disgust, but it is quite wrong to infer that they lack interest. Their interest is just of a special kind. They do not, for example, follow the details of relations between Congress and the president, or the overall shape of foreign policy. But many are immersed in, almost obsessed with, the intricacies of each piece of infamy as it comes to light. A new disclosure is likely to be avidly and angrily discussed. Many workers display an impressive knowledge of the details of a case. They will recount the exact quantity of cash and bonds a congressman had hidden in his house, the precise way American grain companies "laundered" payoffs to politicians and Korean agents, the exact price a Carter aide paid for a house that men are convinced he could not afford from legally earned income. Often men will read each other the minutiae of a particular transaction as it is reported in publications like the *Daily News*. Typical of this interest in detail is the following, in 1974, from a batch worker in his mid-thirties:

> Politics, it's terrible. They're all the same. This guy's [Ford] a real dodo. He pardons Nixon, the chief criminal. As far as I'm concerned, Nixon should be hung. Instead, we're paying him a $60,000 pension plus expenses. And the mayor of Newark. He talks about the city's budgetary crisis and then goes and gives himself a $25,000 raise, and he's already getting $40,000.
> Now this dodo, Ford. He likes to swim. So he builds a swimming pool at the White House. Now, that's all right because it doesn't come from my money, it's from private donations. But they've got to maintain it, and pay for that. And Ford says we've got to save energy! But the pumps and lights for the pool use energy [the speaker had just installed a pool in his backyard and so was sensitive to these issues], and we've got to cut back on energy for Christmas because this dodo likes to swim!

There is no shortage of local material to feed these beliefs. Consider one month, chosen at random from the period of fieldwork. In this time a local newspaper read by most workers reported twenty separate items concerning alleged or proved political corruption.[4] These included four accounts of graft in local police departments; a lengthy discussion of whether permitting casinos in Atlantic City would weaken or strengthen the network, which everyone agreed was extensive, of Mafia-run illegal lottery and gambling operations in the state; and discussion of various alleged or proved kickback schemes involving, in turn, a Rahway assemblyman, a member of Governor Byrne's cabinet, and the entire Newark city council.

The national level also provides abundant material to feed men's beliefs. Among the most notable cases during the research period were Watergate in the Nixon administration; banking scandals involving Bert Lance, Carter's budget director; and the FBI's "Abscam" investigation into graft among congressmen and senators, which was national news during the Carter and Reagan administrations.

The Power Structure

If elected representatives constitute a venal facade, then who really runs America? This question is a source of endless debate and discussion. Apart from sports, there are few topics most men find so engrossing. When groups of workers sit around talking, for instance during lunch or coffee breaks or after work, the question of who runs America is one of the commonest items of conversation. And each major political or economic development—a scandal, a strike, an important new legislative proposal—is likely to provoke further discussion.

Big Business

The overwhelming majority (90 percent) of those who believe politicians are hopelessly corrupt believe that major corporations, "big business," really run America. Remarks like "it's business that runs the country" or "big money is behind everything" are commonplace. Sometimes workers claim particular sectors of the corporate structure are the most influential, controlling the other corporations as well as the rest of society. In this context the oil companies and "Rockefeller" are most likely to be mentioned. But the auto industry, especially General Motors, is often singled out for special mention too, as, more recently, is Japanese industry. Typical are these comments.

A mechanic in his late fifties:

> I reckon Carter's got the Georgia Mafia in there. I think he's honest, but the guys around him. . . . There's that Hamilton Jordan. He just bought a $135,000 ranch, and before then he had nothing. It's all the same, just like it was with Ford. The oil companies are running everything. They always have done.

A warehouse worker in his late fifties (complaining about inflation and rising property taxes):

> Rockefeller runs the country. The working man hasn't got a chance. Rockefeller and Nixon were behind most things that happened. And David Rockefeller, he's the manager. Did you ever read a book *The Rockefeller File*? You should. It tells you exactly what's going on.

A batch worker in his mid-thirties:

> Politics! You can't change anything. It's big business that runs things. You can't fight money. There ain't a person that can't be bought, not all with money, but there's always something someone wants. You know, a guy may be a big coin collector and need a particular coin for a set.

There is a variety of kinds and sources of evidence to which workers appeal in support of these views. Sometimes they cite their experience as consumers, watching business raise and raise again the prices of the goods and services they buy. Sometimes they mention their own experience as producers, citing such instances of corporate power as a company's ability to bribe OSHA inspectors or to close an entire plant and move it to a more favorable location, especially the South.

But in explaining their belief that business runs America men cite, above all, the idea that big business is the source of most of the funds with which politicians are bribed. Since business supplies the graft, it is obvious that business reaps the benefits. In this way the view that corporations run America is linked with the belief that most politicians are irredeemably venal and corrupt.

Unions

Yet fewer than a quarter of those who think business runs the country think it does so alone. The rest believe that business and some other group compose the power structure. Thus, of those workers who think business runs the country, at least 32 percent at some point said the unions do too. Sometimes a worker will state that business and the union hierarchy collaborate to benefit each other. Consider this process worker in his mid-forties:

> Politics? It's all money! Big business pays out money to get what it
> wants, and the unions . . . they all play golf together. So the union
> leader passes around the word that this guy he plays golf with is "pro-
> labor." It's getting worse.

Sometimes a worker will say on one occasion that big business runs the country and on another occasion that the unions do; or he may even make both statements in the same conversation. An example is a batch worker in his late thirties:

> Who runs the country? Well, I suppose the president does. He makes
> the decisions. Of course business is behind him. They make the real de-
> cisions. Politicians are all on the take. Just look at Nixon. They're all
> like that.
>   And the unions, now they really control everything. The big un-
> ions—steel, autos, construction. You can't do anything without asking a
> union. And the construction workers, they get ten, eleven, twelve dol-
> lars an hour [in 1977].

The Jews

Another 25 percent of those who think business runs the country at some point claimed that the Jews do so too, for they think Jews control the top echelons of big business and finance. These workers superimpose beliefs about the economic power of Jews on the more widely held belief in the economic dominance of business. An example is a worker in his mid-fifties:

You know they say the Jews work for two months before Christmas and
then go to Florida to count their money. Big money runs this country,
and the Jews own most of the money.

Often workers give only a part of their view at one time. A man who on one occasion
states that business runs America may say on some other occasion that the Jews do.
For instance, a laboratory technician was complaining about the state income tax
Governor Byrne had recently introduced. On this occasion (1977) he argued that
business ("big money") ran the country:

I hate Byrne, he's a phony. He lied to us. I hate politicians, especially
lawyers. Big money buys them all.

A month later, in a discussion of politics and economics, this same worker volun-
teered the view that the Jews run America:

The Jews are intelligent. The Jews were the first hit men. They worked
for the Mafia. Then they got to figure they were smarter than the Italians [the speaker is of Italian origin], so they kicked them out. It's your
Jews who run business. I don't care where you look, you'll find a Jew at
the top.

Usually these beliefs are asserted without supporting evidence. But sometimes
men cite Jewish ownership of the stores and small businesses in the areas where they
live as evidence that Jews run the major business and financial corporations in
America. Occasionally men make wild claims, such as that "Rockefeller is really
Jewish."

The figures presented above on the numbers who believe that big business,
unions, or Jews run America are the result of several years I spent listening to
workers discuss these issues among themselves, as well as of numerous individual
conversations with them. These figures are useful as a general indication of the main
directions of men's views, but they should not be taken too literally. For one thing,
workers may be less certain than they maintain about some of these questions. As I
pointed out, a man who may have insisted on numerous occasions that business runs
America might suddenly say the unions or the Jews do. Asked about this apparent
contradiction, he will usually say that the sectors collaborate (especially unions and
big business) or that one is the same as another (notably the Jews and big business.[5]
But in many cases these appear to be post-factum explanations. Most workers are
sure big business dominates the power structure, but they are often somewhat
undecided about other aspects of these questions. And their views may change as
new information comes to light. For instance, a television program about the power
of the Teamsters Union in Alaska, or a lengthy miners' strike, might, at least for a
while, convince a man that unions are part of the power structure. The following is
typical of the debates that occur all the time over the composition of the power
structure. A group of mechanics were talking in the maintenance shop a few days

before their contract with the company was due to expire (May 1976). They were anxious and apprehensive about the problems of negotiating a new contract during such a severe economic recession. They had given the union an almost unanimous strike vote, but many were afraid the company might close down the plant. The conversation turned to the question of who was ruining the country and, as usual, to the related question of who was running it. Everyone had an answer to both questions.

> **First mechanic:** The unions are ruining the country. Big unions like the Teamsters. See, they can strike and the whole place closes down [a reference, not without envy, to the recent truckers' strike in which Teamsters blocked major highways to protest the price of gasoline]. They already run Alaska.
>
> **Second mechanic:** No, it's business that runs the country. You only have to look around you.
>
> **First mechanic:** No, it's the unions.
>
> **Third mechanic** [suggesting a way out of the difficulty]: Well, the unions are run by big business.
>
> **Fourth mechanic** [anxious that politicians not be forgotten]: And the politicians—did you ever see an honest politician? Now tell me, is Ford a poor man? Of course not—he gets 1 percent off every contract that's negotiated. One percent goes to the politicians, 1 percent to the union, and 1 percent to the company [the rest nod gloomy agreement].

Other events may induce a worker to add new groups—for instance the judiciary—to the power structure. A process worker was angry because the New Jersey supreme court had recently ruled that financing local education solely from property taxes was unconstitutional. As a result the state income tax had been introduced.

> I don't like Byrne [the Democratic governor]. He's a judge, and the judges are running everything in this country. They said there had to be an income tax.

I commented that last month this man had insisted business ran the country:

> Oh yes! Business runs the country, period! There's no doubt about that.

Democracy and the Working Class

Almost all these workers criticize the American political system from the point of view of an extreme democrat. Most adhere to the "mandate theory" of what elections *ought* to be about, for they believe politicians have an obligation to carry out their programs if elected. They are angry because they think venal politicians are subverting the promise of liberal democracy. During the entire research period only one man, a supporter of George Wallace of Alabama, ever suggested a dictatorship as the solution to the problems he perceived in America, and he made this proposal in private. Those workers who voted for Nixon in 1968 or 1972 often remark— angrily as they reflect on their mistake—that Nixon fooled them, for he really wanted to "set up a dictatorship."

This is important, for some writers have argued that the working class is only loosely attached to democratic institutions and practices—that their attachment is of the unthinking, surface kind. The real bulwark of the democratic system is said to be those at higher socioeconomic levels—the wealthier, the more educated, the better informed.

This entire argument confuses democracy—popular control of government— with a certain strand of liberalism. The evidence produced in support of the claim that the working class is not firmly attached to democracy has almost entirely to do with liberalism. Thus it is maintained that the working class is more likely to be racially prejudiced, religiously bigoted, and generally intolerant of social differences than are wealthier, better-educated groups. Whatever the empirical merits of these claims (and they have recently been seriously questioned), they are not basically about belief in popular control of government. The evidence of this study suggests that, on the contrary, the American working class has a classic democratic vision by which it measures the current political scene and finds it seriously wanting.[6]

Freedom

Yet among Imperium workers this severely critical view of political power and practice coexists with a notable lack of approval for alternatives to the current political system. There is a general acceptance of the American Constitution, ranging from enthusiasm ("It's the best in the world") to the lukewarm ("I complain a lot, but it isn't any better anywhere else").

This needs explaining. In part it is based on a distinction between the system and those who operate it, between politicians and the Constitution. The political system is sound, but it is in the hands of scoundrels.

In part lack of support for alternative political systems results from a perception that radical change in the United States is impractical. The country is too large, and potential leaders are too prone to sell out. As a process worker in his mid-twenties put it after lamenting corruption in government:

It's very hard to change anything in this county. The government is so big. It's hard to move it. You can have a revolution and you find nothing has changed.

But in part the widespread acceptance of the Constitution and the political system is based on a key distinction most workers make, either explicitly or implicitly, between freedom and democracy. The United States does offer freedom and liberties, which are very valuable. Consider these typical comments, all made by workers who believe venal politicians subvert the electoral process.

A man in his mid-thirties:

> In America you have freedom. That's important. I can say Reagan is a jerk and no one is going to put me in jail.

A worker in his late fifties:

> You know what I like about America? You're free. No one bothers you. If I want to take a piss over there [points to a corner of the tavern] I can.

This view often emerges when men are contrasting the United States with the Soviet Union or China or Cuba. A worker in his mid-forties (discussing the Soviet presence in Afghanistan and what the United States should do about it):

> We should invade [Afghanistan]. If we don't, they'll [the Russians] be coming over here. I like this country. There's all kinds of freedom that we'd lose if they invaded.

A worker in his late fifties (discussing his recent visit to China):

> They brainwash them over there. They all wear the same clothes, and they line up the children and make them all recite the same words. They're not free like we are here.

Socialism and communism are ruled out in almost everyone's eyes, for they are seen as synonymous with dictatorship. They are political systems that permit neither popular control of government (democracy) nor individual freedom and liberties. Indeed, the term "dictatorship," used to refer to systems that are neither democratic nor free, is the commonest category for classifying undesirable political systems. Typical of this use of the term is the following interchange between three workers:

> **First worker** [In his early twenties. He was discussing, with approval, President Reagan's support for the government of El Salvador. The conversation occurred in 1981]: We should send arms to the government there. If we don't, the communists will take over. China and Russia and Cuba have been sending them [the oppostion] arms. If we don't send arms, the communists will take over, and all they'll do is have a dictatorship.
>
> **Second worker** [in his late twenties]: Yes, look at Afghanistan. The Russians just went in there, and we didn't do nothing to stop them. And

Poland. . . . The Russian armies are just sitting outside ready to crush them and still the Poles are so desperate they're willing to risk it for freedom. Communism is no fucking good. They're dictators.

Third worker: Yes, look at Iran. This Khomeini has set them back five-hundred years. They're in the Middle Ages now.

This equation of communism and socialism with the current political system of the Soviet Union and thus with dictatorship (absence of both freedom and democracy), cuts across the political spectrum. Consider one of the most liberal workers, discussing the high levels of unemployment (during the 1974 recession) with a more conservative worker:

Liberal worker: I'll tell you, in the spring there's going to be riots. It'll begin in Detroit. There's 30 percent unemployent there. And then it'll spread to all the cities. And it won't be the blacks. It'll be guys like you and me . . . well, and a lot younger [the speaker is in his mid-fifties]. Guys in their mid-twenties paying $300 a month mortgages, who suddenly go to $85 a week.

Conservative worker: Yes, but you know this kind of talk is just what the guys in Moscow want to hear. We're a capitalist system.We don't want Socialism.

Liberal worker [agreeing]: No but if something isn't done we'll have fucking communism. That'll be much worse.

The view that the United States offers freedom, though not democracy, is somewhat obscured by the fact that a minority of workers sometimes use "democracy" as a synonym for freedom. They apply the term to current American politics, but in a context where they clearly men "freedom" or "liberty" rather than popular control. Consider this example, a worker in his late twenties. He believes all politicians are corrupt, "taking $10,000 off the top here, and $10,000 there." Still, it is important to vote:

That's what a democracy is all about, isn't it? There's your fredom of speech and your freedom of religion.[7]

Survey data suggest that, like mistrust of government, this attitude toward freedom is widespread among blue- and white-collar Americans. The vast majority both value freedom and consider it an important feature of contemporary America. For example, Herbert McClosky, in an article intended to stress the wide disagreements among Americans that national survey data revealed, commented that the question of freedom was an exception. All sections of the electorate "respond so overwhelmingly to abstract statements about freedom that one is tempted to conclude that for these values, at least, a far-reaching consensus has been achieved."[8]

Conclusion

There is a common claim about the political outlook of the American working class. According to this view, as a result of America's early adoption of liberal democracy the working class is imbued with a staunch republicanism, a firm attachment to the political status quo.[9]

My research suggests that such a view needs modifying. Most of these workers believe that the American political system in theory confers both democracy and freedom but in practice delivers only freedom. As a result, though staunch republicans and staunch democrats, they are far from attached to the political status quo. Most believe the promise of liberal democracy is, in most cases always has been, and will continue to be subverted by corrupt politicians. American workers fully subscribe to the ideals of a democratic society while firmly believing that current politics falls hopelessly short of these ideals. They are strongly allegiant to the democratic-republican vision yet strongly critical of its current political practice.

There are several reasons why this does not usually translate into support for radical transformation of the political structure. There is the belief that the system delivers freedom, even if not democracy. There is the belief that venal politicians, not the system, are to blame for what is wrong. There is the belief that some of the main alternative systems, especially socialism and communism, represent the loss of freedom *as well as* the absence of democracy. And there is the belief that the United States is too large for radical change to be feasible.

There is a further reason for the lack of support for alternative political systems. This raises the question of class identity—of how workers see their own position within the class structure—the subject of the three chapters that follow.

10

Position in the System of Production: The Concept of the Working Man

I have pointed to the range of theories of class consciousness in America—theories that variously stress class, racial, ethnic, national, and individual identity. In part this proliferation of theories results from the scarcity of studies that examine the way workers actually think and talk about *all* these topics—about class, race, ethnicity, religion, and nationalism. And in part it results from difficulties with the two main approaches to conducting systematic research into perceptions of the class structure. The difference between these two approaches rests on the form of the question they pose to respondents. The first relies heavily on a question in the following basic form:

What social class do you think of yourself as belonging to? (select one of the following responses)

Upper class
Middle class
Working class
Lower class

This is known as the "class identification" question with fixed responses.[1] It has two major problems. First, as chapter 10 will argue, the possible response "working class" is fraught with difficulties. Blue-collar and lower-white-collar Americans typically think of themselves as "working men" or "working women," but not as "working class." Further, in the United States the term "working class" is hopelessly ambiguous. As a result, the class identification question with fixed responses overlooks the meaningful categories "working man" and "working woman" in favor of a category, "working class," that is problematic.

Another difficulty is the presumed neutrality of the approach. The central assumption behind this method is that the basic class identification question is neutral. It offers a range of possible choices, of class identities, without predisposing respondents toward a particular one. Yet researchers have long been aware that this assumption is invalid, for they know that the wording of the question has important effects on the answers obtained. For example, if respondents are offered the four fixed choices referred to above, then about half of a cross section of the population tends to choose "working class." But if "working class" is excluded from the choices offered, then the largest number of respondents place themselves in the "middle class." Yet no researcher has explained why this is so or made a particularly convincing case for offering one set of choices over the other.[2]

An alternative way of investigating perceptions of position in the class structure has seemed to some researchers to solve the neutrality problem, for the main question it uses avoids offering respondents a choice of fixed categories (this approach is heavily influenced by W. Lloyd Warner). Instead, it asks an open-ended question such as What does the phrase "social class" mean to you? (In answering this question few respondents classify themselves as "working class.") Yet this question is not neutral either, for, as chapter 11 will argue, the term "class" suggests to American workers a particular image of society based on factors outside work, above all on income level.[3]

The method adopted here assumes that the attempt to find neutral questions is a mistake, for they do not exist. There are no questions that allow a researcher to investigate perceptions of the class structure in America without suggesting to respondents a particular image of that structure.

During more than four years' observation of workers discussing politics and society, it became clear to me that the image they have of their position in the class structure is based on three distinct identities, all of which presuppose the existence of the power structure outlined in chapter 9. This book investigates these three identities separately by asking workers about the key term or terms around which each identity revolves.

There is an identity that refers to workers' lives *at work*—to their position in the system of production. This centers on the concept of the "working man." (For women the pertinent identity is the "working woman." The way women use this concept differs, in interesting ways that I will briefly explore later, from men's use of the term working man.) The concept of the working man implies that blue-collar workers as an occupational group have distinct experiences that set them apart from other segments of society. This reflects the reality of workers' position in the system of production, where there is a division between blue-collar workers and the rest of the class structure.

A second identity refers to workers' lives *outside work*, above all to their income level and the standard of living it makes possible. This identity centers on concepts such as being "middle class" and "lower middle class." It implies a set of links with people at a certain income range and standard of living. This identity ignores differences based on occupation, and is held, with modifications, by many Americans. It reflects the reality of men's lives outside work, where the distinction between these blue-collar workers and the rest of the class structure, especially the white-collar sectors, is somewhat blurred.

The third identity centers on the related concepts of "Americans," "the American people," and "the people." It refers to workers' lives as inhabitants of the United States. This identity is the broadest and most inclusive of all, for it implies a common bond between all Americans.

In my research I presented respondents with a term that, as fieldwork has shown, enables people to accept and discuss a particular identity in the class structure. What validates the responses is that workers assent to such an identity and talk fluently about it. This is not to foist on them views they do not hold, for most have no hesitation about rejecting a political or social view they do not believe in. The willingness of workers to accept and to talk with conviction about a particular identity is what shows they believe in it—not, as in the approaches just discussed, their formal choice of one image over another in response to a question that aims for an unachievable neutrality.

The Concept of the Working Man

A close reading of formal and informal interviews reported by a variety of researchers suggests that blue-collar workers in America commonly refer to themselves as "working men," but rarely as "working class." This can be seen from interviews with voters during the 1968 and 1972 presidential election campaigns,[4] from the views of working-class residents of a new suburban township about their preferred political candidate,[5] from a group of skilled workers in Providence, Rhode Island, from a group of white working-class males in an East Coast city,[6] from workers in Milwaukee, Chicago, and Pennsylvania,[7] and from auto workers in Detroit.[8] The concept of the "working man" has also been central in the history of the American labor movement. For example, when trade and craft workers before the Civil War founded political parties they called them "Workingmen's Political Parties," and the *Workingman's Advocate* was the name of one of the most important newspapers of the nineteenth century.

Imperium workers also continually refer to themselves as working men. No one ever disputed the appropriateness of the term as a description of himself. Almost everyone at some point during the research period used the term, and most men do so regularly. (Sometimes, as an alternative, they talk about the "working guy," occasionally the "working slob" or "working stiff.") Consider these examples.

A worker in his late thirties:

> No, I don't like Byrne [the governor of New Jersey]. He doesn't care about the working man. He's just for business and the middle class.

A worker in his late fifties (discussing the power structure in America):

> Rockefeller runs the country. The working man hasn't got a chance.

A worker in his mid-forties:

> Unions are a good thing. You know they [politicians and the media] always blame the working man for inflation, but it's not his fault. Without unions they'd [employers] really squeeze you.

A warehouse worker in his mid-fifties (commenting with relief on the easing of the recession in mid-1978):

We're working seven days a week now. You see what I told you [the researcher] about the Democrats being for the working man. When the Democrats are in power it's better for the working man.

This suggests that blue-collar workers who choose the option "working class" in response to the class identification question do so, at least in part, because they think of themselves as working men (or, if female, working women). Yet researchers seldom investigate the meaning of these terms.

The concept of the working man expresses both class and gender consciousness for Imperium workers. As a form of class consciousness, its central idea is that blue-collar work takes a distinctive form and is productive in a way that the work of other classes is not. As a form of gender consciousness it implies such work is for men, not women. Both these motifs reflect the historical context in which the concept of the working man developed.

Class Consciousness

The class consciousness part of the concept has two central components. First, it refers to features of the job. Being a working man involves one or more of the following cluster of related ideas:

a. Physical work. Working men do manual work, physical work, laboring work. ("It's hard physical work," "It's working with your hands.")

b. Dangerous or dirty work. They are often exposed to physical discomfort and even danger on the job. ("We get our hands dirty," "We breathe in chemical fumes.")

c. Boring and routine work. Their work is repetitive and monotonous. ("We do the same thing over and again.")

d. Factory work. They work in factories as opposed to offices.

e. Closely supervised work. They work under the close direction of supervisors. ("We have to punch in and out," "We're told what to do.")

This set of ideas will be referred to as the "job features" aspect of the concept of the working man. Clearly these features resemble those popularly and, as parts 2 and 3 showed, often actually associated with blue-collar work, though *c* and *e* are also associated with lower-white-collar work.

The second central component of the concept of the working man links it to a moral and empirical theory about who really works in America. It implies, in one or more of the following ways, that those who are not working men are not really productive, do not really work. Those who are not working men:

a. Literally do not work. They really do nothing. ("Big business don't work, they just hire people who do," "People on welfare aren't working men, they don't want to work.")

b. Perform no productive work. Their particular activities in the labor market are viewed as not useful. ("Teacher aren't teaching the kids anything," White-collar office workers "just sit on their butts all day.")

c. Are overpaid. Though their work may be productive, they are seen as being paid more than their labor is worth. ("Doctors earn huge fees." "Lawyers charge whatever they want.")

This set of ideas will be referred to as the "productive labor" aspect of the concept of the working man. The combination of the "job features" and the "productive labor" aspects of the concept logically entails the idea that only those whose labor involves such job features are productive. As a result, blue-collar work is generally seen as productive. But those whose work lacks many or all such job features, definitely big business and in general the upper- and lower-white-collar sectors, are not. Consider these examples of workers asked to discuss the concept of the working man and illustrating in their responses the two central ideas—first, that the labor of working men involves one or more of the set of related job features, and second, that, unlike the rest of the class structure, working men perform labor that is productive.

A batch worker in his mid-forties:

Researcher: What do you mean when you talk about the working man?

Worker [begins by stressing job feature *a*—physical work]: The working man really refers to laboring work, hard physical work.

Researcher: Are big business working men?

Worker [derisively]: Of course not. They don't do nothing all day [productive labor *a*—literally do not work].

Researcher: Am I [professor] a working man?

Worker: Well, you have a job, but you're not really a working man. [Returning to job feature *a*—physical work] It really refers to physical work. Everyone here [in the plant] is a working man. [Shifts from job features back to productive labor *a*—literally do not work] But not above a certain plateau. You know, Kennedy and his family. They inherited their money from liquor.

Researcher: Are lawyers working men?

Worker [continuing to stress productive labor *a*]: No! They don't really work. They just sit there and hire people who do the work.

Researcher: How about secretaries?

Worker [continuing with productive labor *a*]: No! They often spend half the afternoon reading magazines. I've seen them through the window.

A Process worker in his early fifties, talking with other workers:

Worker: The working man is the nub of the whole thing. We do all the work. [Stressing productive labor *a*—literally do not work] We produce everything. If we stopped work here [the conversation was taking place in the control room] would Henry Imperium [the company president] come down and work? No! He'd send in some guys like us. The working man is the nub of the whole thing. We do all the labor.

Researcher: Are big business working men?

Worker: Of course not. They just sit on their butts all day.

Researcher: Am I [professor] a working man?

Worker [bitterly]: No! You're not a working man. [Stressing job feature *b*—dangerous or dirty work] You don't breathe in all these fumes, all these chemicals and shit.

Researcher: How about secretaries?

Worker [stressing job feature *d*—factory work]: No, they work in an office. [Moving to productive labor *b*—perform no productive work] They just answer the phone and type letters.

A mechanic in his late forties. This discussion took place outside, in freezing weather, while the mechanic was wrapping insulation around one of the storage tanks.

Worker: Am I a working man. You bet! [Stressing job feature *b*—dangerous or dirty work] I'm standing here freezing and breathing in all these fumes [a reference to the fumes crowding out of vents in the ground].

Researcher: Are big business working men?

Worker: No. They don't have to stand out here in the cold.

Researcher: How about lawyers and doctors?

Worker: No, they're not working men. They don't have to breathe in this shit [the fumes]. You're not a working man if you work in an office [job feature *d*—factory work]. [Resentfully] Let them [office workers] try to do this kind of work!

Researcher: How about secretaries?

Worker: No. [Switching to job feature *a*—physical work] To be a working man you have to do hard physical work. They [secretaries] don't come home exhausted.

Contradiction 1: The Upper-White-Collar Sector

The view that all those without certain job features (mostly found in the blue-collar sector) are unproductive is the view implicit in workers' everyday use of the concept of the working man. And it is the view all workers are prepared to make explicit if asked about big business. But when it comes to the upper- and lower-white-collar sectors there are, for some workers, interesting contradictions between their implicit view and the view they are prepared to defend explicitly. And these contradictions reflect some of the real difficulties in separating the blue-collar from the upper- and lower-white-collar sectors, difficulties discussed at the conclusion of part 3.

Consider the case of the upper-white-collar sector. Many of-the job features of this sector can be distinguished from those of the blue-collar sector (though those distinctions should not be pushed too far). But it is not always easy to maintain that all upper-white-collar workers are unproductive.

The professions are illustrative. The three professions workers mention most often are lawyer, doctor, and teacher. The dominant attitude toward all these groups is mistrust and often hostility, rooted in a belief that part or all of their activity is in some way unproductive.[9] This hostility is clearest in the case of lawyers, in large part because lawyers are commonly equated with politicians. In addition, men's individual need for lawyers is usually connected with periods of personal unhappiness and even danger—an injury compensation claim, a car accident, an arbitration hearing arising from a contract dispute, a divorce (a common euphemism among these workers for starting divorce proceedings is "getting a lawyer"). Resentment against doctors takes a familiar form. Often doctors are said to charge excessive fees, abuse privileges such as free parking, make careless diagnoses, bungle treatments, and, if they can, conceal their incompetence by claiming the adverse results were "natural" and "unavoidable." Hostility toward teachers has a variety of sources. First, most workers' own experiences at school were generally unhappy. It was teachers who classified them as nonacademic, as intellectually inferior. Second, men see their own children progressing through the educational system, and if—as often happens—that progress is not smooth, there is a tendency to blame the teachers. Further, workers often see themselves as paying the teachers' salaries through property taxes that finance local education. This exacerbates their resentment, especially if teachers' earnings and benefits are better than their own.[10]

On the other hand, such hostilities may be offset in various ways. Many workers have seen law and lawyers work to their advantage, especially in injury compensation claims and the arbitration of disputes with the company. The union lawyer usually handles such cases, and he is generally well liked and respected, both because he is seen as very competent and because he charges a low retainer fee ($10 a month). With his help men can, and do, regain their jobs after being fired, win overtime, back pay, and extra holidays in disputes with the company over the interpretation of the contract, and obtain compensation for injuries received at work. Further, most workers have shopped around to find a personal doctor in whom they have some confidence. And they may have a friend, neighbor, wife, or adult child who is a teacher. Nor do everyone's children do badly at school. Some have used the educational system to obtain good jobs. All these factors operate to diminish the general ill feeling toward these professionals.

As a result some workers, if asked, are prepared to include certain lawyers, doctors, and teachers as working men because they consider them to perform productive labor in at least one of the senses discussed. But their implicit view that the entire upper-white-collar sector is unproductive appears when they begin by explaining that being a working man involves certain job features—for instance, hard physical labor—that such professions lack. However, the following cases show workers, on reflection or questioning, modifying this implicit view.

A worker in his mid-forties:

Researcher: What does the working man mean?

Worker [begins by stressing job feature *a*—physical work]: Well, it means laborers like us [looks around at the other members of the crew in the process plant control room where the conversation is taking place].

Researcher: Are doctors and lawyers working men?

Worker [acknowledging that most doctors and lawyers perform productive labor and ignoring his earlier emphasis on physical labor as a defining characteristic of working men]: Sure, most of them work for a living. I mean the oil companies and big business. They're not "working men" [implying productive labor *a*—literally do not work].

A batch worker in his late forties:

Worker: All the guys here are working men.

Researcher: What does that mean?

Worker [stressing job feature *e*—closely supervised work]: Well, they work, and under the direction of someone else.

Researcher: Are doctors working men?

Worker [realizes the concept of the working man implies that those who are not working men are not productive and is unwilling to make this assumption explicit for all professions; he therefore classifies some doctors, the honest ones, as working men, though they do not meet his earlier characterization of working men in terms of job feature *e*—closely supervised work]: Some of them are and some aren't. You know, some are honest and some are crooks. [Honest doctors perform productive labor *c*—they are not overpaid; they deliver the services they are paid for.]

Nevertheless, these cases are a minority. Most workers, on explicit questioning, are sure that those in big business are not working men and reasonably sure those in the upper-white-collar sector are not either.

Contradiction 2: The Lower-White-Collar Sector

Consider now the lower-white-collar sector. The dominant attitude of these blue-collar workers toward this sector is that its labor is mostly unproductive. This attitude is shown by the men already quoted. Indeed, it is noticeable that in their general conversations Imperium workers rarely refer to this sector or the categories that compose it. A man will say his wife works as a secretary in a school or sells in a particular store. But men hardly ever talk about secretaries or salesworkers as a group. For their view of the class structure this sector hardly exists.

This implies what interviewing reveals, that they mostly consider lower-white-collar work unimportant. In part this is because of the kind of nonproductive work this sector is seen as performing—office work that is easy and somewhat trivial. In part this is because this sector is dominated by female labor, whose significance men tend to dismiss. Further, the lower-white-collar sector lacks a number of the job features such as physical work and danger associated with the labor of working men. As a result, men's general use of the concept of the working man implies that those in the lower-white-collar sector are not working men.

Yet not all workers are prepared to explicitly defend their implicit assumptions about the lower-white-collar sector. They may believe most lower-white-collar work is unproductive, but many perceive that it shares one or two of the job features of the labor of working men. Above all, it is obvious that lower-white-collar workers are often in the same position of subordination as blue-collar workers. Their tasks are directed by "authority." Further, their work is often routine. This reflects a truth about the class structure, a real overlap between blue-collar and lower-white-collar work (as pointed out in the conclusion to part 3), and a real difficulty in defining the two spheres so as to distinguish them. This is why a minority of workers, when discussing the concept of the "working man," include the lower-white-collar sector. Consider the following cases.

A batch worker in his early twenties:

Worker: Oh yes, I'm definitely a working man. What does it mean? Well [stressing job feature a—physical work], it's when you work with your hands rather than your brain. It's physical work, it's not mental work.

Researcher: How about the women in the office, the secretaries?

Worker [conceding that secretaries, like blue-collar workers, follow orders under close supervision and therefore are working men, though in his first definition of a working man he has emphasized physical, manual work]. Well yes, they're like us. Someone gives them letters and files to do. They just do what they're told to do. they're working men [job feature e—closely supervised work].

A batch worker in his mid-fifties:

Worker: Am I a working man? Yes, I work, I have a job.

Researcher: How about clerical and secretarial workers?

Worker [picking up on the similarity between the repetitive nature of blue-collar and clerical work—job feature c]: Yes, they're working men. Their work is boring, it's repetitive. I'd say they're working men.

As when workers discuss the upper-white-collar sector, what shows that these men are modifying their implicit, everyday use of the term is that they usually begin explaining the concept of the working men by referring to a job feature such as physical labor. Logically, secretarial and clerical workers cannot then be working men.

Discussion of the attitude of workers toward the lower-white-collar sector raises a central point about the concept of the working man. The term expresses both class and gender consciousness. It expresses class consciousness in that it implies that blue-collar work is especially productive. But it also implies that blue-collar work is for men (working *man*) rather than women, which is a form of gender consciousness. This reflects the history of American labor. In the early stages of industrial growth women (and children) were the first factory workers, for then such jobs were seen as less desirable than agricultural work. As the status and pay of factory work and other blue-collar jobs rose, women were pushed out of most except the least desirable. The blue-collar working class is now composed primarily of men. The same is true of management and the higher-status professions. But the lower-white-collar sector, consisting of jobs that are often poorly paid and carry low status, is filled mostly by females.

The idea that blue-collar work is for men is a form of sexism most workers are prepared to explicitly support in discussing their *own* jobs. For example, they will maintain, sometimes in argument with those of their wives who are feminists, that women cannot be chemical workers because they are too weak to move heavy chemical drums.

But such sex stereotyping of occupations is under increasing attack in the United States. As a result few workers are prepared to explicitly defend this implicit view for the entire spectrum of blue-collar jobs. Consider the following cases of workers responding, usually with some surprise, to a question that probes the tacit sexism underlying the concept of the working man.

A mechanic in his early fifties:

Researcher: Can a woman be a working man?

Worker: Yes, that girl over in California just proved it [a reference to a recent court case in which a female employed as a firefighter was permitted to breastfeed her baby at work].

A warehouse worker in his early sixties:

Can a woman be a working man? Women? Well . . . it's happening now. They're hiring women for these jobs. They're working women.

A mechanic in his early sixties:

Can a woman be a working man? [Pauses, trying out the sound of the phrase "working woman"] . . . a working woman . . . ? I guess if she works in a factory, but not if she works in an office.

This willingness of most workers, when questioned, to modify the implication that blue-collar work is for males, not females, reflects a broader change in social attitudes toward women in the labor force. As this change takes root a concept such as the "working person," or the phrase "working men and women," is likely to become a more popular, non-sexist alternative to the concept of the working man.

The Working Man and the Unemployed

Most workers are clear that the bulk of the unemployed poor are not working men, for in their eyes the majority do not work and do not *want* to work. They are unwilling to be productive.

The lack of sympathy with which many workers view the poor—the long-term unemployed and those on welfare—is striking. A number of studies have noted a similar attitude among Americans of all social classes.[11] Often Imperium workers become angry, bitter, and abusive when they consider the poor. They speak of them as living an easy life off government-financed welfare programs that, indirectly, are paid for by the taxes of working men. Time and again the poor are criticized as scroungers, idlers, and parasites who, in contrast to the working man, do not work and do not want to work.

These men divide into three groups distinguished by the extent of their belief that the poor are unwilling to perform productive labor. The two largest groups, together about three-quarters of Imperium workers, believe that all or many of those on welfare do not want to work. A third group, the smallest, are sympathetic to those on welfare and believe most would rather work if they could.

Consider the most extreme group, who believe all or almost all the poor are malingerers. For these workers it is axiomatic that those on welfare are not working men.

A mechanic in his late fifties:

People on welfare? No! They're not working men. They don't want to work.

A batch worker in his mid-forties, talking about the welfare population:

Worker: And now with welfare. If you come over here and get a job that's all right, but we've got these Cubans and Mexicans and Puerto Ricans and they come over and go straight on welfare and their children go on welfare and their children's children.

Researcher: Are they working men?

Worker [looking disgusted]: No! They don't want to work. All they want to do is collect their [welfare] checks.

A second group is less extreme, but they still believe an important proportion of those on welfare, probably half or more, are malingerers. The following comments are illustrative.

A worker in his early thirties:

Researcher: Are those on welfare working men?

Worker: Well, some of them are, and some of them ain't. But I'll tell you, the people who shouldn't be getting it [welfare] are getting it, and the ones who should be getting it can't.

A warehouse worker in his mid-fifties, discussing the difference between blacks who worked and blacks who did not:

Worker: There have always been blacks up here [in the Northeast, around Elizabeth]. They're good people. We always get along. But these ones from Africa and the South, they're no good. They don't want to work.

Researcher: Are they working men?

Worker: Well, the ones who want to work, but not the ones who don't.

There are two main reasons for the widespread hostility toward the poor. First, a number of workers equate them with the black and Hispanic population. As a result their attitudes toward the poor are flavored with any racial or ethnic stereotypes they have. For example, they may see blacks as lazy and dishonest, inclined to support themselves by cheating and stealing. The second source of hostility toward the poor is the widespread belief in the American dream, referred to in part 3. If success in America is possible for anyone prepared to work hard, then the ranks of the poor must be composed mostly of idlers who prefer not to work. Men often point to the help wanted section of their local newspaper in support of the claim that there are plenty of jobs, unskilled and skilled, for those who want them. These two motifs—the belief in upward mobility and the belief that the poor consist largely of blacks and Hispanics—reinforce each other. Unemployed blacks and Hispanics are seen as mostly lazy operators, parasitic on the employed blue-collar labor force.

Still, about 25 percent of these workers believe most of those on welfare would rather have paid jobs. Consider examples of these workers discussing the welfare population.

A worker in his early forties:

Worker: Welfare? No, I wouldn't like to say it's being abused. I don't have any figures.

Researcher: Are those on welfare working men?

Worker: Yes, I'd say so. I reckon they'd like to work if they could.

A worker in his mid-fifties:

Worker: Thirty-five years ago I was on relief in Scranton, Pennsylvania, and I never want to be on it again. It is degrading and humiliating. Anyone who

wants to be on relief must be crazy. I feel very sorry for people who have to
be on it. It strips your dignity away and leaves you naked. As for welfare
cheaters, I don't know any figures, but cheaters are hurting everyone.

Researcher: Are those on welfare working men?

Worker: Yes, I think everyone except a few want to work.

Interviewing among the small number of upper-white-collar males at Imperium,
and among upper-white-collar males in other work settings, underlines the difference between the way blue-collar and upper-white-collar men see their position in
the system of production. Thus, asked if they are working men, most, though not all,
upper-white-collar males tend to distinguish themselves in some way from blue-
collar workers. They may, for example, reply that they work, but not with their
hands. In this way they display an understanding that the concept of the working man
tends to apply to blue-collar workers. At the same time most upper-white-collar
males, in stressing that they work, indicate that they too perform productive labor.
They are reluctant to accept the idea that blue-collar workers have a special claim in
this area.

The Working Woman

The concept of the "working woman" is central to the way many females see their
position in the system of production. The account that follows focuses on women in
lower- and upper-white-collar occupations. It is less systematic than the previous
section but is intended to throw further light on what is distinctive (as well as what is
r.ot) about the concept of the working man among male blue-collar workers. The
discussion is based on data from just under half the wives of Imperium workers,
supplemented by more general fieldwork.

The current and past experience of women in the American labor market
includes both class and gender discrimination. I pointed out earlier that as factory
and blue-collar jobs increased in status and pay women were pushed out of most
except the least desirable. Since World War II they have worked mainly in the home
(housewives) or in poorly paid and low-status sales, clerical, and secretarial jobs
(though of course a minority are in professional or managerial positions).

The Working Woman: Class Consciousness

The concept of the working woman reflects this experience. On the one hand it is a
form of class consciousness, reflecting an occupational solidarity. It conveys the view
of a number of females in lower-white-collar occupations that their work is more
productive than that of the upper-white-collar sector and of big business. For
instance, there is the view that secretaries perform much of the work that is really
part of the boss's job, and for which the boss gets credit. Secretaries may proofread
and improve written material, organize a disorganized boss, and provide creative

ideas. This reflects a view that lower-white-collar work is especially important in the chain of production. About a third of the women I interviewed in lower-white-collar occupations use the concept of the working woman in this way. Consider these examples. An Imperium wife who is secretary for a corporate executive:

Researcher: Are you a working woman?

Secretary: Oh yes, I have a job.

Researcher: Are managers working women?

Secretary: Well, they're not really like us. Like, I do a lot of my boss's job. I screen visitors, I know who he'll want to see and who he won't. And I do a lot of his writing for him, I write a lot of his memos. He doesn't tell anyone else, but he says I write better than he does, so he often tells me what he wants and I write it out.

Or there is the view that lower-white-collar work is particularly unpleasant, in contrast with that of the upper-white-collar sector. Consider this example of an Imperium wife who works as a cashier in a university cafeteria:

Researcher: Are you a working woman?

Cashier: Sure I am, I've been working for twelve years.

Researcher: Are professors working women?

Cashier: Well in a way, but not really. Like we [the cafeteria staff] have to be here at 9:00 and we stay until 4:00. But a lot of the professors don't come in until 11:00 or 12:00, and then they leave at 3:00. And on a lot of days they don't come in at all. And our job is boring. It's very routine.

Or there is the view that lower-white-collar workers are exploited, since they are particularly poorly paid. Consider the wife of an Imperium worker who is a saleswoman in a department store:

Researcher: Are you a working woman?

Saleswoman: Oh yes, I work at Abraham and Strauss.

Researcher: Are the managers working women?

Saleswoman: Not really. We [the salespeople] do all the work, *they* just stand around. And yet we get paid much less than them.

Another group of females in lower-white-collar occupations also use the concept of the working woman in a way that reflects class consciousness, but in a weak or mixed form. They will refer, like the group just discussed, to ideas about their work as especially important in the chain of production or expecially unpleasant or exploited. But they will offset these views by also referring to the particularly productive features of upper-white-collar work. Among these features are the fact that upper-white-collar work is seen as involving responsibility, knowledge, and qualifications that require lengthy training and education. This attitude reflects the well-known tendency for some of those in lower-white-collar jobs to feel a certain identification with their superiors, the common bond conferred by the "office." Even if their work is dull and closely supervised, at least they work in an office rather than a factory and come into regular contact with managers and professionals. Further, not all office work is organized "factory style." The private secretary, for instance, has a very personal relation with a superior, a relation Kanter refers to as "wife style." This may permit the secretary to enjoy some of the status reflected from her boss.

Consider this example of an Imperium wife in a lower-white-collar job expressing such mixed feelings toward the professional and managerial sector. In her early thirties, she works as a secretary in a corporation and has a female boss, a middle-level manager:

> **Secretary:** Am I a working woman? Yes, me and the rest of the girls [the other secretaries in the office] are working women.
>
> **Researcher:** Is your boss a working woman?
>
> **Secretary:** She works, but no, she's not the same. [Starting with the productive aspects of upper-white-collar work] She's got more responsibility, she's accountable for more, and she's got more education. [Switching to the theme of the exploitation of the lower-white-collar sector] And then we're [secretaries] treated differently. We get less respect, and we don't get the perks. We don't have expense accounts to take people out to lunch. And they [managerial women] keep their distance. There isn't much contact between the secretaries and the professional women.

The Working Woman: Gender Consciousness

Yet for about half of the women interviewed in lower-white-collar occupations the concept of the working woman implies gender rather than class consciousness. It reflects a solidarity with other women in a society that discriminates against females. Class or occupational differences are less important than the fact that they are all women in the labor market. In this form the concept of the working woman leads some females in lower-white-collar occupations to perceive a solidarity between themselves and women in the upper-white-collar sector. "Working women" are *all* females in paid employment rather then in unpaid "housework."

Consider the wife and married daughter of an Imperium worker. The wife has been keypunching at a bank on Wall Street for ten years. She went to work after her youngest child turned sixteen. Her daughter has always worked as a keypuncher. She continued working after her children were born, switching to the midnight shift in order to combine raising children with work. Are they working women?

Wife: Yes, now I am. I wasn't when I stayed at home.

Daughter: Yes, I always have been.

Researcher: Are female lawyers and doctors working women?

Wife: Yes, they don't stay at home. they support themselves [daughter agrees].

Or consider the wife of a batch worker at Imperium. She had been married before and between marriages had been sole economic support for her two children. She has had a variety of jobs, including her own business, working as a traveling salesperson, and working in a store that sells submarine sandwiches. She has also known periods when she was unable to find work:

Woman: Working woman? Well, in my opinion anyone who is working outside the home earning money is a working woman.

Researcher: How about a female lawyer?

Woman: Sure, she's a working woman. [Starts to talk about the problems of combining employment outside the home and raising children] You wouldn't imagine the responsibility, the tension, the fear raising kids and working. You worry about how involved you're getting in your job, are you neglecting the kids. It's a highly emotional thing. Your kids need you, but you have to go out to work. Yes, if you're working outside the home earning money you're a working woman. A working woman is anyone who has to go out to work. Not that staying home and looking after kids isn't hard work, it is, it's very hard, I know. But I wouldn't say she's a working woman.

Other females go further. They use the concept of the working woman to include not only all women in paid employment, but also those who do housework. In this way they stress that housework, so often demeaned as unimportant and easy, is valid and legitimate work. Again gender consciousness supersedes class consciousness, but for this group it includes all women. And their use of the concept of the working woman bridges the world of paid employment and the world of the home. They perceive a solidarity between women in the labor market and unpaid housewives. Consider the wife of an Imperium worker who is employed in a school cafeteria:

Researcher: Are you a working woman?

Cafeteria worker: Yes, well I do the same thing more or less every day. It's really like working at home.

Researcher: Are female lawyers and doctors working women?

Cafeteria worker: Yes, they have to work hard.

Researcher: Are housewives working women?

Cafeteria worker: Oh yes, what they do is work.

This current of sympathy for housewives somewhat moderates the tendency to feel hostility toward the unemployed and the poor. Like many blue-collar workers, many of these women believe large numbers of the poor are lazy, unwilling to work. But this attitude is less common among those who extend the concept working woman to include women who do unpaid housework.

So far we have considered women in lower-white-collar occupations. How about women in the upper-white-collar sector?

I pointed out that most men in upper-white-collar occupations are fairly clear that they are not working men. They work, but they tend to emphasize a distinction between this and the occupations of blue-collar workers. Some women in upper-white-collar occupations take a similar view, wishing to distinguish themselves from females in clerical and secretarial positions and in blue-collar jobs. Consider this example of a woman in management:

> **Manager:** Working woman? Well, I'm employed, but I'd never use the term to describe myself. People might ask what I do, and I'd say what I do for a living. But I wouldn't describe myself as a working woman. I might say I'm [describes her job level].
>
> **Researcher:** Would you say a secretary is a working woman?
>
> **Manager:** Well, I wouldn't necessarily use the term, but if you're asking if I see a distinction between a secretary's job and mine, yes, I see an enormous distinction. I have a secretary working for me. She doesn't carry with her the responsibility, the headaches, she doesn't have to take work home.

But as many women in upper-white-collar occupations do not emphasize this distinction. In this way too gender consciousness supersedes class consciousness. Just as a number of females in lower-white-collar occupations do not stress the difference upward between themselves and females in upper-white-collar occupations, so about half of the latter do not stress the difference downward. Consider this example of an Imperium wife, a teacher in her late forties:

> Yes, I'm a working woman. All women in paying jobs are working women. And women who do housework are working women too. The only women who're not working women are those who hire other women to do the housework.

Conclusion

Blue-collar workers at Imperium have a class identity that distinguishes them from big business and from the upper- and lower-white-collar sectors. It is true that the distinction between their position and that of the white-collar sectors is not rigid. Some workers will concede that parts of the upper-white-collar sector are productive and that the work situation of the lower-white-collar sector may share some of the job features of blue-collar work. Nevertheless, in their everyday conversations the concept of the working man implies an important distinction between blue-collar workers and the rest of the occupational world. Only by ignoring this concept can one argue that male blue-collar workers lack class consciousness.

Further, this class consciousness is more pervasive than is often thought. Most researchers who maintain that class consciousness is important among the American working class base their argument on responses to the class identification question posed in the form: "Are you upper class, middle class, working class, or lower class?" They typically find that over half of blue-collar respondents classify themselves as working class. Yet this ignores the concept of the working man, a concept held by almost all Imperium workers. Indeed, what is striking is that the concept is so widely held.[12] Further, if this is true for workers in better-paid blue-collar jobs, then it is likely to be true for much of the blue-collar working class. In addition, among Imperium workers the concept of the working man is associated with a politics surrounding the workplace, work-related issues, and the union.

Yet a consideration of the concept of the working man suggests that, if class consciousness is widespread, it remains limited in a number of other ways. First, for an important group of Imperium workers this concept implies as much hostility toward the poor as toward big business and the power structure. And one current underlying this hostility is a tacit racism, an implication that the poor consist mostly of blacks and Hispanics, and that many are unwilling to work. This perception hinders the formation of alliances between blue-collar workers and the unemployed.

Second, the concept of the working man contains a tacit sexism, an implication that blue-collar work is for men, not women, and a related implication that lower-white-collar work is less than productive. This perception clearly hinders the formation of industrial and political alliances between blue-collar workers and the lower-white-collar labor force. At the same time, such perceptions are not rigid. Few workers are prepared to explicitly defend the view that the world of occupations is broadly divided into those appropriate for men and those appropriate for women, though they retain this view for particular jobs—for instance, those seen as requiring heavy physical labor. And some workers will freely acknowledge that much lower-white-collar work, like blue-collar work, has been heavily rationalized and routinized.

A third, and crucial, way the concept of the working man reflects a limited form of class consciousness is that it is not connected in workers' minds with belief in an alternative economic and political system. It implies serious moral criticisms of the system of production under capitalism. Those who perform the really productive work do not receive a fair reward compared with the reward of those who are related to production indirectly or not at all. But this is not accompanied by a view that capitalism itself should be replaced. Indeed, few workers talk about "capitalism," a clear indication they are not thinking of the economic system of the United States in relation to alternative systems.

This discussion of class consciousness in incomplete. Almost all Imperium workers have at the same time another, different image of their place in the class structure. The next chapter analyzes this second image.

11

Position outside Work: Income Level, Standard of Living, and Residential Situation

A cardinal division in contemporary society is between home and work. Once, people typically lived within walking distance of their jobs or even worked at home, on the ground floor of the house or on the farm. But the streetcar, bus, subway, and auto mean that now place of residence and place of employment usually are geographically separated.

This division is reflected in a second image these blue-collar workers have of their position in the class structure. Unlike the concept of the "working man," this second image refers to life away from work rather than on the job. It implies a class structure composed of a hierarchy of groups distinguished above all by income level, but also by standard of living and residential situation. Income level, life-style, consumer goods, and neighborhood constitute the material framework of men's lives outside work (it is true that income originates from their employment, but its effect on their lives is outside, where almost all income is spent).[1]

This image of their position in the class structure increases the range of persons with whom workers consider they have common interests. Thus, though most see a clear gap between their situation and that of the upper and lower extremes (for instance, "the rich" and "the poor"), the categories in between almost all are ones to which they consider they do or could belong. As a result, according to this second image, the class structure has a sizable middle range that displays some fluidity, permits individual movement, and takes no account of a person's occupation. This reflects the actual ability of workers, in their life outside the factory, to enjoy a certain mobility through their choice of house, neighborhood, possessions, and life-style.

It should be noted that, like the identity that revolves around the concept of the working man, this second identity assumes the existence of a power structure on top. For many, but not all, workers it also assumes a parasitic poor below.

During the fieldwork it became apparent that to most workers the term "class" suggests this second image of the class structure. This is not surprising since, in public discussion by American government agencies and social scientists, that is the meaning usually attached to the term. For this reason I investigated workers' second image of class by asking men if they were "middle class." What is important is not so much whether they say they are or are not, since the question is clearly and deliberately not neutral. The difficulty of posing neutral questions was explained in the introduction to part 4. On the contrary, this question is designed to permit workers to discuss their second image of class, but it specifies minimal form or content to that image. (Indeed, in the image it triggers the question is equivalent to the open-ended question, "What does class mean to you?") What is important are the follow-up questions exploring the image of the class structure that underlies men's responses. In this way their second image of class can be considered separately from their first image organized around the concept of the working man and their position in the system of production.

The precise form of this second identity varies in a number of ways from worker to worker. Despite such variations, every worker does have such an identity and an image of his position within the class structure based upon it.

Income Level

Income level is the most important of the factors underlying this second image of class. Almost everyone has at least a rough idea of the income distribution in America and his place within it. Workers read government statistics in newspapers and magazines on the average income of an American family, and they are aware of estimates of the income level needed to maintain a minimum, a comfortable, and an affluent standard of living. The federal and state income tax systems both entail a picture of the class structure based on income, and most workers follow with keen interest the relation between their weekly earnings and the taxes deducted from their paychecks.

The commonest example of this image of the class hierarchy distinguishes three levels. At the top are "the rich" or "the millionaires" or "the upper class." Beneath are "the middle class," and at the bottom are "the poor," "peons," "people who can't make it." Most of these workers place themselves in the middle class. Consider these examples. (Most of the interviews reported in this chapter took place in 1978, which should be borne in mind when reading the income figures workers cite.)

> **Worker:** Yes, I'm middle class. All these guys [in the plant] are middle class.
>
> **Researcher:** What does that mean?
>
> **Worker:** Well, take Frank Leiter [the plant manager]. Let's say he makes fifty g's, and I make twenty-five g's. I'm not the same as him and then I'm not *poor*. Down below is the poor.

A batch worker in his mid-twenties, complaining about the level of taxes:

> **Worker:** I'm going to look into the Social Security tax to see whether we have to pay. You know, congressmen and civil servants have their own fund,

so why can't we? Our fund [Social Security] is going bankrupt. It's the
middle class who're getting screwed in this country. The tax system is unfair.
The rich all have loopholes, and the poor don't pay.

Researcher: So you'd say you're middle class?

Worker: Yes, my income level makes me middle class. And it's still hard [to
survive financially]. I made $17,000 last year, and it isn't enough. I'm
struggling.

Researcher: At what income level does the middle class begin?

Worker: Well, you have to make at least $10,000 in this country else you
can't survive.

Life-Style and Material Possessions

Income level is not the only criterion underlying this image of class based on the
setting outside work. Life-style, material possessions, and the quality of residence
and neighborhood are other criteria men often use. Usually they also include
income, for income is so obviously the source of these other aspects of their lives
outside work. Consider these examples of workers stressing possessions, notably a
reasonable house and a car, as well as income.
    A worker in his mid-fifties had a threefold classification:

> Am I middle class? Yes. Well [thinks] . . . It's if you have to work and
> you have a house and a car and a couple of bucks, and every so often
> you blow $30 or $50 and take your family out to eat or to the movies,
> and now and then you take a vacation.
>   Now above is the upper class. That's if you don't need to work . . .
> you're living on some kind of inheritance or dividends. The upper class
> are the ones who know everything beforehand. Like they didn't tell *us*
> when they had plans to build the Turnpike or the Garden State Park-
> way, but big business, they knew. So they could buy up land in the path
> of the highway for maybe $100 an acre and sell it two years later for
> $1,000 an acre; then you've got a lot of money to pass on to your chil-
> dren and your children's children.
>   Below the middle class is the lower class. They're the ones who if
> they lose their job are on the balls of their feet. They don't have noth-
> ing . [Long pause: then equates the lower class with blacks] You know,
> a lot of black people, they spend everything all at once. So one week
> they'll have champagne and whiskey, and the next day wine. There's
> some guys in here like that too.

A worker in his late thirties:

> **Worker** [complaining about taxes]: The middle class is getting screwed in
> this country.

Researcher: What is middle class?

Worker: Well, I'd say middle class is if you earn at least $30,000 a year and you own a shack of some kind—a halfway decent house—and a car.

Researcher: What is below middle class?

Worker: Well, the poor and then the paupers.

Researcher: And above middle class?

Worker: Well, the rich. Like take Henry Imperium [as an example of "the rich"]. A few years ago in the company reports they published his income. Well, he only got $50,000, but he had a $30,000 expense account, and that was several years ago. Well, that means he was putting $50,000 a year in the bank. After a few years of that, that's a lot of money. Yes, it's all money. Money's the name of the game.

A worker in his mid-forties considered that being middle class involved having a certain quantity of assets that could be converted at short notice into cash:

Worker: Am I middle class? I'd say yes. It's if you can lay your hands on around $30,000 quickly. Like, my wife has $11,000 in Manufacturers Hanover stock, and I have some Imperium stock of my own. And we have some money in the bank.

Researcher: Who is above the middle class?

Worker: The rich.

Researcher: And below?

Worker: Those who'll take anything from you, towels, food, sheets, anything they can get.

Number of Levels in the Hierarchy

Workers vary in the numbers of levels they include in the hierarchy. For instance, some insert a level, usually referred to as the "upper middle class," between the top and the middle. Or they insert a level, usually referred to as the "lower middle class," between the middle and bottom.

Consider this example of a worker in his mid-twenties. He implicitly includes a fourth level between the middle and the top and a fifth between the middle and the bottom.

Worker [discussing Reagan's budget cuts]: I don't really like them. They're going to hit the average person.

Researcher: Who is the average person?

Worker: They're the ones in the middle. Like, I'd say they're between $18,000 and $30,000. I'm in the average. I make $18,000.

Researcher: Who's above the average?

Worker: Well, they're the rich, over $100,000 [implying an intermediate group between "the rich"—over $100,000—and "the average"—$18,000–$30,000]. They have stocks, and the dividends on the stocks keep going up, so they're not hurt by inflation like me.

Researcher: Who's below the average?

Worker: They're the poor, the one's who're struggling. Nowadays if you earn less than $15,000 you're struggling [implying an intermediate level between the average—$18,000–$30,000—and the poor—less than $15,000].

Position in the Hierarchy

Not all workers place themselves in the middle of the hierarchy. Most do, but some identify with a category between the poor and the middle class. This view is commoner among younger workers. They may have a mortgage, young children, and a wife who stays home to look after the children. For these men being middle class implies the ability to live a certain life-style without economic pressure. Their own situation is below the middle class because they cannot live such a life-style, at least without a serious strain on their resources. Their income level, material possessions, and life-style make them better off than the poor, but not comfortable or free from major economic worries (the middle class). For instance, a batch worker in his early thirties, who pays rent:

Worker: Am I middle class? No, you're not middle class if you're struggling with a mortgage and to pay your bills and buy your food. If my wife wasn't working we wouldn't be able to travel, go out to eat every week, buy a car. [Anxious to point out he is better off than some] But then I'm not poor. I've got something.

Researcher: Who are the middle class?

Worker: Well, homeowners, the rich.

Researcher: Who's above the middle class?

Worker: They're the ones that don't have to worry about prices and property taxes. They can live where they want, and the property tax doesn't bother them at all, they don't even have to think about it.

Or a mechanic in his late forties:

Am I middle class? Well, I don't have nothing. I'm not at the bottom. I have something. Like, if you earn less than $10,000 then you're struggling. But then I'm not middle class. I don't have enough money to go out more than once every two or three weeks to movies or dinner with the wife and children.

The Power Structure and the Poor

Like the identity that revolves around the concept of the working man, this second identity presupposes the existence of an exploiting power structure in America. For almost all these workers "the rich" are synonymous with whomever they consider to compose the power structure.

Yet when discussing this second conception of their position in the power structure workers tend to stress a somewhat different aspect of that structure. Most commonly, they point to the ability of the "wealthy," "the rich," to find loopholes in the fiscal system that enable them to pay little or no tax. They also refer to the way those at the top, "the rich," use power and influence illegitimately to enrich themselves. The top of the power structure is conceptualized here not so much as "big business" or "the union" as "the rich" and "the wealthy." And what is emphasized is less the ability of the power structure to run America and more its ability to avoid taxes or to increase their wealth in other morally or legally dubious ways.

For many, but not all, of these workers the second identity, like the identity revolving around the concept of the working man, presupposes the existence of a corrupt and idle poor. Yet the bottom of the social structure is also conceptualized a little differently. More stress is placed on the free or heavily subsidized items that the poor receive and that, in these men's eyes, are financed by the taxes workers pay than on the fact that the recipients do not have jobs (are not working men). These free or subsidized items include low-income housing, food stamps, and various "welfare" programs.

The Politics of Neighborhood and the Politics of Homeownership

Associated with Imperium workers' first image of class, the concept of the working man, is a politics centering on work and the union, described in parts 2 and 3. Associated with their second image of class is another politics that centers on life outside work. This takes a number of forms and focuses on various issues, both for renters and for homeowners. But homeownership sharpens people's interest, for many issues are seen as affecting the value of their houses and the level of property taxes they pay.

There is a general concern among workers about the quality of life in their townships or neighborhoods. This can center on a number of issues. How much industry, if any, should be allowed into the area? Industry pays local taxes and therefore lowers a homeowner's property tax. But industry can pollute, may detract from the environment, and might require the township to build costly services such as roads.[2]

There is a plethora of issues concerned with what kind of school system there should be and how much money should be spent on it. Among these issues are busing for racial integration (a controversial issue throughout the region—most Imperium workers are strongly against busing); bilingual education (which usually requires hiring extra teachers and therefore leads to higher school taxes); and drugs and discipline in the schools (a serious problem in schools all through the region).

Another issue is apartments, especially high-rise buildings. On the one hand there is a growing local demand for rental units, for as homeowners age they may prefer to live in apartments, and the rising divorce rate creates a demand for apartments for the newly single. On the other hand homeowners (including many Imperium workers) often view apartment dwellers with suspicion. They are seen as contributing less than their fair share to property taxes while benefiting from the services these taxes finance. They are seen as potentially unruly. And there is also often a fear that renters will include large numbers of blacks and Hispanics.[3]

The possible influx of blacks and Hispanics into an area is a major issue, above all for homeowners. Since an important part of the satisfaction workers derive from homeownership comes from possessing an asset whose value over the long run shows a marked rise, anything that threatens to check or reverse this is unwelcome. Most workers who live close to expanding inner-city ghettos are angry and resentful about the movement of blacks and Hispanics into the area. This is a very common topic of conversation and one about which workers become very heated. A desire to protect the value of their property combines with a belief that minorities lower the quality of residential life. These comments are typical.

An older worker, an Irish Protestant who had lived in Elizabeth all his life:

> This town [Elizabeth] is going downhill. Of course there are all kinds of blacks. We've had blacks in Elizabeth for years. They were respectable and clean, and they worked. But this garbage, they don't work, and they knock down old people. It's not safe anymore.
>   [A few months later] Fucking Cubans! You believe this? I saw a kid on Delancy Street breaking bottles in the middle of the street. He said, "My mother said I'm an American and I have a right to do this." We talk about the shines, but they're angels compared to some of these.

A worker giving the standard complaint about blacks reducing property values:

> I guess everyone's told you the problem. I hear you've got the same trouble in England—the Pakistanis, you know. Those do-gooders have been buying up houses on behalf of Pakistanis and then they sell them [block busting]. Well, you know you've put a lot of money into your house and then you see the value fall like that. It's understandable you'd get angry.

The property tax is itself the arena for a ferocious politics. There is considerable concern about the level of this tax, and of the local government expenditure it finances. Such concern is widespread among homeowners in the United States, and in this respect, as with many of the other issues outside work, blue-collar homeowners are little different from white-collar workers. In addition, the work force at Imperium, like the rest of the industrial work force in the northeastern United States, is mostly Catholic. Often workers make only limited use of the public school system, preferring to send their children to parochial school.[4] For this reason local taxation, much of which goes to finance public education, may seem especially irksome. And sometimes workers perceive a clear connection between, for instance, the new swimming pool at the local public school and the pool they would like to build or improve in the backyard if property taxes were lower. Consider these examples of the politics of the property tax.

A group of older workers, most of whom live in Elizabeth or Linden, angrily discussing the recent upward assessment of their homes:

> **First worker:** It's ridiculous. You know, forty-eight cents of every tax dollar to the city goes for education, then there's another five cents for interest on building for the schools. So that's fifty-three cents. It's ridiculous. It isn't worth it. And they just hired twenty bilingual teachers. Why shouldn't they [the students] learn English like we had to?

> **Second worker:** Yes, and they're coming out illiterate. And my taxes went up $600 to $1,600 a year. I was so angry. I could understand if it was a large piece of property, but it isn't. And I've got old fixtures in there—a bath with legs. I haven't modernized yet. I said to the wife, "Let's wait to modernize until they've done the new assessment." And then they slap me with this!

> **Third worker:** Tell me, is it right that I send my children to parochial schools and have to pay school taxes when I don't use the schools?

> **Fourth worker:** Now I'm paying $1,600 a year in property tax. It went up from $1,200. They say the cost of living has risen, but when I bought my house I was earning $5,000 a year and my taxes were $300. So if I'm paying $1,600 in taxes I should be earning $26,000.

A worker in his late twenties had just bought a house down by the Jersey shore. He explained the fiscal angle:

> Lots of younger guys move out there. Is it cheaper down on the shore? Well it depends on the property taxes. You can get a cheap house, but that isn't any good if the taxes are high. The thing is to find a place that's just beginning, with no expenses. You can send your kids to the school in Linden or something.

An older man preferred another strategy:

> You have to pick a stable, well-established township where they've already got a police force and school system so the taxes don't rise too high. With new townships sooner or later they'll start to spend a lot of money on schools or police.

Many of the concerns discussed here are shared by all homeowners and a number by renters too, regardless of occupation. Being a blue-collar worker may add a distinctive flavor, as Gans pointed out for Levittown.[5] The sources of this flavor, a modest level of education and an orientation toward friendships and enjoying leisure rather than a career, are the same as some of the sources of a distinctive flavor in the leisure and marital lives of these workers. For instance, some blue-collar workers— but by no means all and not necessarily even a majority—may be less concerned about an elite, highly competitive public school system or an expensive library and more concerned about such possible sources of leisure activity as a volunteer fire department.

Nevertheless, this flavor is also part of a general context outside work that in other ways cuts across collar color. It creates a politics of consumer issues and local, neighborhood, and house issues that affects most of those in the area with limited regard for occupation.

Some writers deny the existence of such a politics. In particular they argue that homeownership has no effect on political outlook. Such is the conclusion of Berger's study of auto workers in California and Goldthorpe's study of industrial workers in Luton, England. This claim is based on the observation that as workers move to outlying areas ("suburbs") and become homeowners their political party affiliation remains largely unchanged. Most continue to be Democrats (or in England to support the Labor party). This observation about political party affiliation is also true of Imperium workers (see conclusion to part 4), though with modifications (a growing number of mostly younger workers are classifying themselves as "independents"). But what it demonstrates is not that there is no politics of homeownership, but that political party affiliation is a very incomplete indicator of political outlook. A worker may be involved in all kinds of local political issues related to his house and property taxes while continuing to view himself as a Democrat. Further, the meaning of that affiliation can vary over time. For example, what has happened in heavily Democratic towns such as Linden and Elizabeth is not that "Democratic" homeowners have switched to Republican party affiliation, but that the Democratic party has on some issues adopted "Republican" politics. Thus many local (and, of course, national) Democratic politicians have now also become identified with the move to lower government expenditure.[6]

Two Images of Class, or One?

Imperium workers have two separate images of their place in the class structure, one referring to life at work (the "working man"), and one referring to life outside work (being "middle class" or "lower middle class"). To what extent is this true of the other main occupational groupings? We lack the data needed for a confident answer, but I can sketch out a suggestion.

Most of the lower-white-collar women in this study, when asked if they are middle class, tend to refer to their life outside work, like the blue-collar men. But a few mention occupation too (for instance, they are middle class because they work in a hospital or an office). In this way they combine aspects of the two images. And upper-white-collar men and women, in response to the same question, are quite likely to combine features of their occupation with features of their life outside work.[7] It seems that the separation between images of their position at and outside work is clearest in the minds of male blue-collar workers and somewhat less clear for female lower-white-collar workers and for male and female upper-white-collar workers.

The 1978 study by Rainwater and Coleman supports such a view.[8] They investigated the meaning of the term "class" for a sample of Americans in a variety of occupations and found that for most people income level and standard of living (the house they lived in, the car they drove, the recreations and vacations they could afford) were the dominant considerations in placing themselves on a status ladder. Thus this status image is based on items that constitute life outside work. Nevertheless, some people also add, as secondary factors, their occupation and level of education. But they tend to do this only if such items raise rather than lower their status. Thus white-collar workers may point to the higher status of their jobs (or the autonomy they permit), or they may point to their superior level of education. In mentioning their jobs, white-collar workers are combining in one image factors that relate to their work (their occupation) and factors that relate to life outside work (their material standard of living).

But, according to Rainwater and Coleman, blue-collar workers rarely point to factors such as job status or level of education, for neither of these items adds to their status. In this way they tend to clearly separate their picture of themselves at work from their second picture based on life outside work.

Conclusion

The two images of class discussed in this chapter and in chapter 10 correspond to the position of workers in the class structure and reflect the clear difference between experience at work and experience in the residential setting. The concept of the working man implies, as its central idea, a moral and empirical distinction between blue-collar workers and the rest of the class structure. This reflects the fact that in men's work setting there is a distinction between their situation and that of the white-collar sectors (though that distinction cannot be pushed too far).

The second image of class clearly expresses the material framework of men's life outside work. And the various forms in which this second image exists among these blue-collar workers all have in common a blurring of the middle ranges of the class structure. Workers usually believe there is a top and a bottom, but the area in between is vastly increased, and within it blue and white-collar differences of occupation are muted and of minor importance. This reflects the reality of men's residential, leisure, and family situation, where such differences in some ways *are* blurred.

Method

Given that almost all these blue-collar workers have these two images of the class structure, it is now clear why attempts to investigate class identity by formulating neutral questions cannot succeed. There are no neutral questions. In a society where the federal government, as well as many sociologists, uses "class" to refer to income level or life-style, a question containing the term suggests, at least to blue-collar respondents, an image of the class structure based on their life outside work—on income level, life-style, or residential neighborhood. It is no surprise then that Rainwater and Coleman, who asked respondents, "What does the phrase 'social class' mean to you?" should conclude that Americans (blue- and white-collar) perceive the class structure as a hierarchy, with income level as the most important criterion. This is precisely the image of class triggered by the question.

Americans do perceive the class structure in this way.[9] But such studies are one-sided, for at least blue-collar and lower-white-collar Americans also perceive the class structure in another way, based on the notions of the "working man" and "working woman." This image, for male blue-collar workers and, though to a lesser degree, for female lower-white-collar workers, refers to their position in the system of production and implies boundaries between "working men" and "working women" on the one hand and the rest of the class structure on the other. What is more, it is used as often as the first image to understand the operation of political and economic power. As a result, investigations of the class structure based primarily on the open-ended question, "What does the phrase 'social class' mean to you?" omit an essential part of the picture.

On the other hand, the class identification question with fixed responses, the second main way of investigating class consciousness, is also flawed. Asked if they are upper class, middle class, working class, or lower class, male blue-collar workers tend to classify themselves as working class. But researchers rarely investigate in detail the meaning respondents attach to this or to the other categories they select.

The problem is that the fixed responses trigger *both* images of the class structure. Thus "class" and "middle class" suggest the image outside work, while "working" suggests the image based on the idea of the "working man"—the idea of productive labor.

As a result—and research trying various approaches among Imperium workers confirms this—some workers classify themselves as working class because they are thinking of themselves as working men. Others classify themselves as working class because, like the group of mostly younger Imperium workers considered earlier, they are thinking of their position in the class structure outside work and believe their income level or life-style is not high enough to place them in the middle class. Either way, the two images of the class structure are hopelessly jumbled in the term working class, making it impossible to interpret. This is why working class is not a usable research category in the United States (unless carefully defined to respondents).[10]

12

Nationalism and Populism

Nationalism is one of the most powerful movements in the world today. It was a primary force behind World Wars I and II, and it underpins the current nuclear arms race between the United States and the Soviet Union that threatens the entire world.

Yet nationalism was for a long time underestimated as a force in advanced industrial society. Many social thinkers in nineteenth- and early-twentieth-century Europe regarded it as a passing phase, to be replaced by more expansive visions of the unity of men and women across national frontiers.[1] As a result, popular support for World War I and, in the United States, McCarthyism and Cold War ideology, and even the recent wave of sympathy for American hostages in Iran, came as surprises.

The third main aspect of the picture these workers have of their position in American society reflects a national identity. This revolves around a set of related terms—"an American," "the American people," and "America." But contained in the use of these terms is also a third class identity—populism.

The study of nationalism raises a number of problems. First, How does it coexist, in the minds and lives of blue-collar workers, with the two concepts of class outlined earlier? What is its relation to class consciousness?

Other questions concern nationalism among all social classes, not just blue-collar workers. It is not a constant sentiment. It can lie fairly dormant for long periods and then flare up. The Iranian seizure of American hostages in 1979 triggered a burst of nationalism within the United States that culminated in the "yellow ribbon" movement heralding their return. Until recently Britain had gradually retreated from its role as an imperial power and avoided major outbreaks at home of the virulent nationalism that often accompanies "vanished glory" in fading empires.[2] Yet the Argentine seizure of the Falkland Islands in 1982 triggered just such a nationalism in Britain. Conversely, national sentiment can be quickly dampened. The classic instance is among soldiers at war. Whatever national sentiment underlay the decision to enlist rapidly disappears as soldiers encounter the reality of military engagement. The authors of *The American Soldier* document this for United States troops during World War II, and in his classic novel *All Quiet on the Western Front* Erich Remarque describes a similar shift in the attitudes of German soldiers during

World War I: "While they [civilians in authority back home] continued to write and talk, we [soldiers at the front] saw the wounded and dying. While they taught that duty to one's country is the greatest thing, we already knew that death-throes are stronger."[3]

Nationalism also raises a historical problem. It did not exist, in its current form, in the Middle Ages. As the historian E. H. Carr put it, "nations in the modern sense are the product of the disruption of the international—or rather pre-international—order of medieval Christendom." Moreover, in the United States nationalism was relatively weak up to the end of the nineteenth century. Inhabitants were often more likely to identify with their state than with the nation. They were as inclined to see themselves as from Massachusetts or Pennsylvania or Virginia as to consider themselves Americans.[4] This poses the question of how modern nationalism differs from ethnic or local consciousness.

Central to all these questions is the problem of defining nationalism. Many writers discuss "nationalism" without defining it at all. This makes it hard to properly understand, let alone evaluate, what is being said.[5] Other writers offer a definition that is unsatisfactory. Isaiah Berlin, for instance, maintains that nationalism consists of four related beliefs:

1. Men belong to particular and distinct human groups with distinct cultures.
2. Such groups or societies are like biological organisms with their own needs and goals.
3. To be fully complete, the lives of individuals and families must be directed to the maintenance of the society (nation). The most compelling reason for living in a certain way and holding certain beliefs is not because this leads to happiness or justice or liberty, but because this is how the "nation" lives and thinks.
4. In case of conflict between the aims and goals of individuals or individual groups and the aims and goals of the nation, the latter always have priority.

The problem with such a definition is that it does not accurately describe the beliefs of many ordinary citizens. For example, there is little evidence that most Americans experience the United States as a biological organism, or believe that their lives should be directed toward living as the "nation" prescribes, or consider that, in a conflict between their goals and those of the federal government, the latter should have priority. On the contrary, such beliefs conflict with a common view of Americans as displaying a characteristic individualism.[6]

This chapter adopts a different approach to the study and definition of nationalism. Within each nation there are certain central concepts around which nationalism revolves. For the United States these are the concepts of "an American," "the American people," and "America." Social scientists have paid little attention to the way Americans actually use these terms. Yet such terms constitute the arena of nationalism, and the key to understanding nationalism lies in understanding their use. Only when this is done can we address the definitional question.

This chapter, then, considers the meaning these blue-collar workers attach to the concepts of an American, the American people, and America.[7]

The Concept of an American

The Modern Nation-State

Imperium workers use the related concepts of an American, the American people, and Americans in three ways. The first, and central, way involves the view that Americans are all those persons born within the boundaries of the United States or admitted to citizenship by the government. Consider these examples of workers asked about the concept of an American.

> Who is an American? Well, if you're born here. Everyone who is born here is an American.

> I'm an American. I was born in this country. My father was born in Russia, but they [the United States government] made him an American because he fought for them in World War I.

> My parents were Polish, but I'm an American. I was born in America.

> My father was Irish. He was born in Ireland, although he became American when he came over here. They [the United States government] made him a citizen. But I was born here. I'm an American.

This concept of an American implies and constitutes the modern idea of nationality, for it presupposes a central government that sets the boundaries of the nation-state and defines its citizens. Such central governments, which administer a defined territory, emerged in Europe beginning in the feudal period. In their early history they assigned nationality less generously, for the nation was identified with the monarch or the aristocracy. Even as late as the nineteenth century, in much of Eastern Europe the restriction of the nation to the upper classes still held. As one study put it: "It was said of a Croat landowner that he would sooner have regarded his horse than his peasants as a member of the Croat nation."[8]

Despite such survivals, from the French Revolution onward and with the development of the modern nation-state, the idea grew steadily that members of the nation are *all* those born within the territory of the nation-state or admitted to citizenship by the central government. This characteristically modern idea of nationality is reflected in the comments of these blue-collar workers, all of whom use the concept of an American in this sense.

Populism

Almost all these blue-collar workers also routinely use the concepts of the American people and the people in a second, populist sense. This involves the idea of a clear opposition between the power structure, especially big business and politicians, and the rest of the population. According to this view the American people no longer consist of all those defined as citizens by the federal government. Instead, they consist of all those excluded from the heights of political and economic power.

Consider these workers, all of whom also subscribe to the modern nation-state version of nationalism, expressing this populism.

Discussing corruption in politics:

> Take Johnson, for example. When he entered the White House he had $20,000 and then he bought all those estates with the American people's money.

Discussing the energy crisis:

> Gas shortage? No, there ain't no shortage. We're getting fucked over. The American people are getting stuck up the ass by the oil companies.

Discussing the recent election for governor of New Jersey:

> No, Byrne [the incumbent] didn't get my vote or any of my family. He gave a referendum on the income tax and the people said No! And what do you do with a guy when the people say No! and he does it anyway?

Discussing whether newly elected President Reagan would involve America in a war:

> No, the American people won't stand for a war right now, not after Vietnam. We lost that one.

This populism is clearly visible when those workers who fought in the armed forces talk about their experiences. There is a widespread belief that most wars have been fought for the benefit of big business (American and foreign) and at the expense of American citizens.

There are major divisions among veterans, especially over the question of the obligation to fight for one's country. One group argues that this obligation remains regardless of the nature or conduct of the war. Another group either began with this idea and then changed their minds after a period in the military or, right from the start, fought only because they were drafted. Yet in almost all cases these two groups concur in their belief that big business is behind most wars, exploiting "the people" or "the American people." Consider these examples, all instances of workers who also believe in a citizen's obligation to fight for country regardless of the justice of the war or the motives of those directing it.

> Why did I fight [in World War II]? It was my country. My parents came over here, and this was my country. I'm an American, and if you're an American you have to fight for your country.
>   Still, you know FDR had a deal with Churchill. He wanted to get

into World War II because business wanted it and so he kind of forced the Japanese, provoked them. Wall Street is behind all wars. They're making money off the American people.

Yes, I fought in World War II, and I was in the D-Day invasion on Omaha Beach. I was so scared I couldn't eat. I felt sick.

Why did I fight? Well, it's your country. I would have fought in Vietnam too. [Returns to the topic of World War II] Of course, the politicians were all dumb asses. Churchill, Roosevelt, they didn't care. But it was really business, business was behind the whole thing. Once, we were in [an area in Germany], and they ordered us to level everything in the area except the Leica factory. American and German business had an agreement. You know all those German plants and factories that were producing those weapons that were killing us Americans, and we were ordered to leave them alone!

Almost all these workers routinely use the concepts of an American and the American people in this populist sense.

This populist current is very important. It is the third major aspect of the class consciousness of these workers. The concept of the working man refers to their position in the system of production. The concept of being middle class or lower middle class refers to their position outside work—to their life-style and standard of living. The concept of the people or the American people, in its populist sense, refers to the division between *all* ordinary citizens and those with political and economic power.

This populist current suggests at least one reason why nationalism, in its American version, is fragile. It has a tendency to dissolve into populism. This is in part why whatever national sentiment may accompany the decision to enlist rapidly dissipates as soldiers experience actual life in the army, especially combat. It gives way to a pervasive cynicism about the motives of leaders and politicians.

An interesting example during the research period was the case of the Americans held hostage in Iran. During their captivity there was strong support for them among these blue-collar workers, as among most Americans. But this disappeared with remarkable speed when the hostages returned to the United States, for there was a perception that politicians were exploiting them. As one worker commented:

I think they're [the politicians] going too far. Now why can't they just let them [the hostages] go home? Instead, they're having these parades in Washington and New York, and it's all for the politicians. And who is paying? We are! The American people. And there's only one hostage who has signed up for the New York parade, and that's the one who lives in Brooklyn!

Nativism

Many of these blue-collar workers also, at least from time to time, use the concepts of an American and the American people in a cultural sense. Being American, according to this view, involves the idea of an indigenous culture to which certain racial, religious, or political groups are inimical ("foreign"), regardless of how long they have lived in the country. This view is usually called "nativism." Thus the main historian of nativism in the United States defined it as "intense opposition to an internal minority on the grounds of its foreign (i.e. "un-American") connections."[9]

In the history of the United States three themes stand out as major nativistic currents. The oldest is religious—Protestant hatred of Catholics and Catholicism. The second is political—fear of radicalism. The third is racism—the notion that the United States belongs to the white, Anglo-Saxon "race." As a result Catholics, or political radicals, or blacks are viewed as "non-Americans" whether they have lived in the country one year or several generations.[10]

Since most of these workers are Catholics, they are not inclined to the anti-Catholic version of nativism. But about a third are attached to the racist version. Its characteristic form is the view that blacks, and sometime Hispanics, are not really "American." Consider these examples.

A worker was complaining about the recent increases in property taxes in his township. He considered excessive school expenditures to be the major problem:

> We're up to here in taxes [places his hand above his chin]. There's too much padding in the school system. Take that bilingual program. They want to hire all those Spanish teachers. But when my grandparents came here [from Germany] they had to learn English. There were no bilingual programs. The Spanish and niggers, they shouldn't have been let in. What are we Americans going to do who've been here all the time?

A worker in his late fifties:

> You know, they used to say about the Negro he couldn't go back home because he had no country to go to. But he could go back to Africa, and some of them would.

Nativism rests on the idea there is an "American culture" to which certain people and ideas whose origin is abroad are alien. For these workers, mostly themselves the children or grandchildren of immigrants, such a view is hard to maintain without logical contradiction. Few succeed. Thus, of the group inclined to the racist version of nativism, most go back and forth between two notions of what constitutes being an American—the "modern nation-state" view (Americans are those born in the United States or admitted to citizenship by the government) and the nativist view (Americans are those possessing certain cultural traits). Workers apply whichever version is more convenient for making their point. When discussing their own immigrant ancestors they tend to use the modern nation-state view, for as new immigrants their ancestors clearly lacked many of the cultural attributes of "Americans." But when discussing groups to whose presence in the United States they object, they use more restrictive, nativistic criteria. Consider a second-generation Italian worker (discussing his father and applying a formal, modern nation-state concept of an American):

He never managed to learn English properly, but he was very attached to America. You know, it's like the Catholic church. Often the ones who're not born but converted are better Catholics. It's like that with Americans.

Later, in a different context, discussing first-generation immigrants from Cuba now living in Elizabeth and Miami, he switched to a nativist definition of an American, involving fluency in English:

No, they're not Americans. They don't speak the language. They still speak Spanish.

From time to time some Imperium workers will also adopt the version of nativism that sees political radicalism as "un-American," especially in the form (discussed in chap. 9) that implies that socialism and communism are foreign, usually Russian or Cuban, imports.

The Concept of America

Nation-State

As with the concept of an American and its cognates, the concept of America is used in a central sense that revolves around the idea of the modern nation-state. America (or the American government or the country) then refers to the territory controlled by the central government, or to the central government itself, or to both. This use of "America" is commonplace among these blue-collar workers.

America as Image or Fantasy

But the concept of "America" also triggers images or fantasies concerning life within the United States and relations between the United States and other nation-states. In *Tropic of Cancer* Henry Miller describes one particular image that he and his friends, living in Paris, had about the United States:

The three of us were Americans. We came from different places, each of us, but we had something in common—a whole lot, I might say. We were getting sentimental as Americans do when it comes time to part. We were getting quite foolish about the cows and sheep and the big open spaces where men are men and all that crap. . . . It's best to keep America just like that, always in the background, a sort of picture post-card which you always look at in a weak moment. Like that, you imagine it's always there waiting for you, unchanged, unspoiled, a big patriotic open space with cows and sheep and tenderhearted men ready to bugger everything in sight, man, woman or beast. It doesn't exist, America. It's a name you give to an abstract idea.[11]

Few workers have such a rural image of America, not surprisingly since most of them live in cities or suburbs. Most, when asked what "America" means, talk about a set of related themes. America connotes a place that is a "melting pot," that permits "opportunity," and that allows political and economic "freedom."

Workers vary in which one of these ideas they stress. Consider these examples.

America? It's freedom to go from job to job and do what you want. Like, I was in Red China last year [on vacation], and there are only forty-five lawyers in the main city. That means there's no freedom, no fair trials.

America? Well, it's a melting pot. You know, anyone can come here.

America? It's opportunity. Like, when my parents came here they didn't have nothing.

Workers for whom the concept of America triggers only positive associations are a minority. For most it triggers both the themes they view positively and also a series of grievances concerning the way these positive themes are being curtailed or limited, or the way they coexist with negative features. Such grievances focus on topics such as inflation and unemployment, corrupt and incompetent politicians, high crime and excessive immigration. Consider these examples.

America? [Approvingly] It's a melting pot. Everyone can come here. [Switching to a negative feature of this unlimited immigration] Like, it's the asshole of the world. We take in too many people.
    And there's freedom. I can get up and call Reagan an asshole and it doesn't matter. You try doing that in Russia. [Switching again to a negative feature] Mind you, communism is not all bad. Like in Russia you have free medical care. That's how it should be here.

America? America is free. That's what I like about it. There's all kinds of freedoms. [Switching to a negative feature] But it's not as free as it used to be. The politicians are always poking their nose in people's business.

A minority of workers will mention only negative features. Consider these examples.

Stressing a government biased toward the rich:

America? I'll tell you, right now under Reagan America is for the rich. The poor are hurting, and the middle class are paying all the taxes.

Stressing high crime:

America? America is stupid! They don't enforce the laws enough. I came here in 1947, and it was quite different. You could walk down the

street then with no problems at all. Now you get mugged and everything.

Stressing economic problems:

America? It's a mess! There's so much unemployment. And prices keep
going up all the time.

America in Relation to Other Nations

When these blue-collar workers consider the United States in relation to other
nations a number of images come to mind. There is an image of America policing the
world, preserving it for freedom. There is a related, though much less confident,
image of America in danger of being overrun from outside by communism. These are
examples:

A worker in his mid-forties (discussing the United States–led boycott of the 1980
Moscow Olympics, in retaliation for the Soviet invasion of Afghanistan):

We should have stopped them [the Russians] in World War II. We
should never have let them take Germany and Poland. The Russians
want to take over the world. That's what they're all about.

A man in his early thirties (discussing the Reagan administration's support for the
government of El Salvador):

If we don't support the government the communists will take over there.
China and Cuba and Russia.

Offsetting such views is a large minority of workers who, at least when there is no
"foreign crisis" in which the president insists the country is involved, believe America should behave as a medium-size power and curtail its presence on the international scene:

A worker in his late twenties:

America should not be concerned with all these other countries. We
should leave everyone alone. We try to do too many things abroad.

A worker in his mid-fifties:

I don't think we should be in the Middle East [a reference to Henry Kissinger's
diplomatic efforts]. Let them [Israel and its enemies] fight it out themselves.

Yet even many of these moderates tend to share with most other workers the
view that America merits a certain amount of respect and honor and may need to

retaliate in a vigorous manner against perceived insults if that respect and honor are to remain undiminished. Consider the two cases just cited:

Discussing the hostages in Iran:

> I'm a thoughtful guy. I don't know what I would have done [if he had been president]. But I do know the way it's happening now those guys over there [the Iranians] look like heroes and we Americans look like jerks.

Discussing the same event:

> We should go right in there [Iran] and zap it to them. Stick it up this Khomeini's ass! He's making us seem like idiots. Now any country thinks it can treat America like shit.[12]

The Field of Nationalism—Few Symbols, Many Meanings

We can now take up the questions about nationalism, above all the definitional question, raised at the start of this chapter. The key terms—an "American," "the American people," and "America" convey a variety of meanings to these blue-collar workers. Without studies of the meanings other social groups attach to these terms, it is hard to make detailed comparisons. But some overlaps are obvious (as are certain differences). The pivotal set of senses centering on the idea of the *modern nation-state*—"America" as the territory of the nation-state and "Americans" as those born within this territory or admitted to citizenship by the federal government—are clearly shared by most Americans. Given the important history of populism in the United States and the broad current mistrust of government that national survey data reveal, it is likely that the populist current too is widespread. Nativism is clearly a presence among some other Americans, as among some Imperium workers, but it is likely to take varying forms. For instance, non-Catholics are more likely than these blue-collar workers to espouse an anti-Catholic nativism. Finally, the concept of America may trigger certain ideas in most Americans, notably freedom and opportunity. But it certainly triggers other ideas less widely shared.

Thus nationalism revolves around a small number of terms and symbols that convey a large number of meanings and thus are enormously ambiguous. The central symbol is the flag of the United States, and the central song is the national anthem. It is the heterogeneous field of meanings these few terms and symbols convey that should define the area of nationalism, for this explains why nationalism can be so powerful and explosive a force. It explains why survey data show that the popularity of an American president typically rises dramatically among all social classes at the start of a foreign crisis, and it explains why such popularity is often short-lived.[13]

The flag (and references to America and Americans) can trigger each person's image of life and society in the United States, and of the United States in relation to other nation-states. For immigrants it can symbolize the chance for a new and better life. For the third generation and beyond it can symbolize the life they and their families have achieved. For those in rural areas it can symbolize wide open spaces, agricultural land, and beautiful scenery. For those in the cities and suburbs it can symbolize blue- and white-collar jobs and the chance to own a house. For the nativist it can symbolize a people threatened by the influx of Catholics or Jews or blacks or Hispanics or political radicals. For the latter groups it can symbolize a society committed, at least in part, to the principle of equal opportunity and the outlawing of discrimination. And for everyone it can symbolize the defense of these objects from other nations, or their extension abroad.

If the appeal of nationalism results from the breadth and ambiguity of its central terms, this is also the cause of its fragility. Over time it often fades and dissolves into its original diverse components.

First, as a situation becomes more concrete ambiguity decreases. For example, the support for some foreign policy stance of those who see America as a land of freedom and opportunity may diminish as it becomes clear that the stance involves allying with a dictatorial regime (as in South Vietnam or El Salvador).

Second, nationalism is inherently fragile because embedded in it, using the same key terms and concepts, is a class identity, a populism. As a result those who united with "America" against a perceived external threat may become disaffected if they see their loyalties exploited by their own government, believed to be composed of corrupt and unresponsive politicians.

Third, as a situation becomes more concrete the question of personal sacrifice emerges. Those who support the general idea that America merits respect in the world may be less enthusiastic if maintaining that respect means buying a domestic auto rather than a preferred foreign import, paying higher taxes, or even losing relatives or friends in war. This is clearly an essential part of the reason why soldiers in combat, who are risking their lives, tend to shun nationalistic rhetoric.

The identity with America and as an American supports a politics, just as do the other two identities, as working men and as middle class or lower middle class. But among these workers the politics associated with the identity with America and as an American can vary broadly. Some workers are willing to volunteer to fight for their country, others would acquiesce in a draft. Some workers favored an aggressively massive reaction to Iran's seizure of American hostages; a few went so far as to advocate the use of nuclear weapons. Others were more moderate. Many workers support the idea of a large defense budget, others consider the current budget too large. And many workers think the present level of immigration into the United States is too high and favor curbing it. Finally, for the reasons I have pointed out, in a "foreign crisis" most workers will support the policy of the president, though such support will typically fade, sometimes rapidly, to reveal wide disagreements among workers (as among the electorate) and deep mistrust of most political leaders.

Conclusion to Part 4

For the purposes of analysis and presentation the preceding chapters have discussed separately workers' views of the power structure and each of their three main social identities. But in practice these views are linked, forming a coherent and comprehensive picture of politics and the class structure of America. They constitute a structure of beliefs that explains for workers the political and social world and their place within it. These views permit room for considerable individual variation. Yet this remains variation around a constant set of identities and themes. To see this whole picture, consider just one set of scenarios from among those that occur all the time.

Scenario

A group of workers in the warehouse were discussing an article in *New York Magazine* (1978) about Carter's financial connections. The article, which one man had brought to work, was read by everyone with great interest, since it provided a firm basis for a suspicion that most already held. On this occasion their discussion turned on the first image of class, based on the concept of the "working man."

> **First worker:** Carter, he's in with international finance—big business is behind Carter. There was a long article about it in the *New York Magazine*. The Rockefellers and Fords and those cliques, they're all behind him. We all read that article [the others concur].

> **Second Worker:** And that Lance thing [a reference to the controversy surounding President Carter's budget director Bert Lance's mixing of his own financial affairs with those of the National Bank of Georgia, of which he had been a director], it's getting worse and worse. Watergate and Lance, it's all the same thing. The working man doesn't stand a chance.

> **Third worker:** Agh! Business runs the country. It always has. Roselle [where he lives] is all white, but Roselle Park [next door] is half black. They [the government] want to bus the kids in Roselle Park [for racial integra-

tion]. It's a General Motors conspiracy. The company that makes the buses is owned by General Motors.

What we need is a parliament that is representative. There are too many lawyers. There are about six doctors in Congress, but how many welders are there? We need a Congress with people who will represent the working man.

A few months earlier the same group of workers had had a conversation in which the second image of class, based on life outside work, was most apparent. They were angrily discussing the recent citywide reassessment of property values in Elizabeth, as a result of which many of them were now paying considerably higher property taxes:

Fourth worker: Dunn [the mayor of Elizabeth] is a two-faced scumbag.

Third worker [introduces the second image of class based on the setting outside work. This version of it emphasizes the common interests of homeowners, who pay property taxes]: Yes! He talks out of all sides of his mouth. The middle class is being squeezed, and we're the ones who are paying the taxes. The taxes on my house went up $100 last year.

Second worker: There's no need for more taxes. We're up to here in taxes [places his hand above his chin]. There's too much padding in the school system, and the teachers just got a big raise.

Finally, here are the same group of workers in 1981 discussing President Reagan's foreign policy and the draft, illustrating a variety of uses of the identities "American" and "America."

First worker: No, Reagan doesn't scare me. The main thing is to do something about inflation. That's the biggest problem right now.

Second worker: Well Reagan scares me. He wants to get us into a war.

First worker [slipping into populism]: No, the American people won't tolerate a war. You saw when they [the government] tried the draft again how they were all out demonstrating and protesting. I'm not even sure America could fight a war. There's a lot of drugs in the army.

Fifth worker: Yes, patriotism isn't what it used to be. There's too much protesting in this country. [Slipping into an image of America] We have things no other countries have. The standard of living is the highest in the world, and there's the freedom.

Second worker [like the first worker, he is a veteran of World War II]: Well, we weren't fighting for America in World War II. We were fighting for ourselves, to stay alive. I wouldn't have gone if they hadn't drafted me. And now the politicians want to draft my son. It's not right.

It is not suprising that each of these three identities should play so major a role in workers' outlooks, for each reflects an important facet of their lives. The identity that revolves around the concept of the working man reflects the importance of work and the distinction at work between blue-collar workers and the rest of the class structure. The identity that revolves around the concept of being middle class or lower middle class, an identity shared by many Americans, reflects the importance of life outside work and the somewhat more fluid class structure that is present there. And the identity that revolves around the concepts of America and Americans, an identity shared by almost all inhabitants of the United States, reflects the fact that the federal government does play an important role in people's lives.

The presence of these three main identities explains much that seems paradoxical about the reaction of these blue-collar workers to politics on the level of the federal government. The clear tendency for blue-collar workers to favor the Democratic party was formed during the depression and New Deal, when Franklin Roosevelt's Democratic administration became associated with legislation that helped the formation and survival of unions and with economic policies that reduced unemployment. Such policies affected many blue-collar Americans directly at their places of work. This is how the Democratic party acquired its reputation as the party of the working man.

Most workers at Imperium who vote still identify themselves as Democrats (see table 28). Workers in the older, industrial suburbs of Linden and Elizabeth who vote in party primaries do so overwhelmingly as Democrats, and those living farther out favor the Democratic Party, though not as decisively. (The main social characteristic of the few workers who identify with the Republican party is that they are more likely than others to be Protestant rather than Catholic.)[1]

Table 28   Voting and Party Registration (1945–78) by Distance from Imperium

Registration and Voting	Percentage			
	Less Than Two Miles ($n = 42$)	Two to Four Miles ($n = 24$)	More Than Four Miles ($n = 56$)	All ($N = 122$)
Never voted	31	33	34	33
Constant Democratic registration[a]	50	29	32	38
Constant Republican registration	2	12	4	5
Changed registration[b]	—	4	2	2
Voted but never registered in primary	10	4	14	11
No information	7	17	14	12

Source: Voting records for Union, Middlesex, Monmouth, and Ocean counties.

[a]Refers to registration to vote in party primary.

[b]Refers to a worker's entire voting history.

Indeed, party identification is remarkably constant. Registration records make it possible to trace the voting history of these workers back to their first vote. Only two men have ever changed their registration from Democratic to Republican, or vice versa. Men often fail to vote in a particular election, but they rarely switch party allegiance.[2]

However, party identification increasingly does not guarantee voting the party ticket. Only about a third of those workers who identify themselves as Democrats can be relied on to vote for the Democratic presidential candidate, and most of these Democratic stalwarts are older men. They tend to explain that: "I couldn't ever bring myself to vote for a Republican." "I've never voted Republican and never will." "The Democrats are for the working man. "They'll learn (a reference to workers considering voting for Reagan in 1980)." By contrast, when the other workers who tend to register as Democrats discuss their voting behavior, they often stress their independence; they consider the merits of each candidate rather than automatically voting the party ticket. "My family were all Democrats, but I prefer to think about it." "I'm a Democrat, but I don't vote the party line, I vote the man." "I used to be a Democrat, but now I'm more independent."[3]

Their identity as working men does provide a clear base for the support of certain policies. For example, almost all workers at Imperium favor policies to reduce unemployment and increase economic growth. There is also very strong support for measures to make the workplace safer, provided these will not jeopardize workers' jobs. And most men favor legislation to limit the ability of companies to move their plants to another region or country. On the other hand, policies aimed at helping those in the labor force who are more disadvantaged, for instance minorities or women, are less strongly supported.

Further, workers have a whole set of interests based on their conception of their position outside the workplace. Here they tend to respond in other ways, as I have shown. For example, as taxpayers most want to see lower taxes, especially on their property. As residents of a neighborhood, and in most cases as homeowners, they are often concerned about the environment or about questions of schooling (for example, the debate over busing to achieve racially integrated schools.). Finally, workers will respond to some issues as "Americans" concerned about "America."

Thus, on the level of their attitude toward the federal government, their blue-collar occupation is an important potential basis for politics, but it coexists with other bases. That is why occupation is sometimes salient in explaining the political views and voting behavior of blue-collar workers, but so are other forces such as race, gender, age, region, and income level, as various studies have pointed out.[4]

The attitude of most workers toward the 1976, 1980, and 1984 presidential elections conveys some of the flavor of this situation. In 1976 a majority of Imperium workers voted for Carter. The two main issues that concerned them were integrity in government and the state of the economy. The incumbent, President Ford, was tainted because of his connection with the corrupt Nixon regime, especially because of his pardon of the former president. And high levels of inflation and unemployment troubled most workers. Carter promised a new integrity and an improved economy. Most workers were cautiously skeptical about Carter's ability to deliver in either area. Some were also wary of his southern background, and a few suspected that a man who smiled all the time might be a homosexual. Still, many workers preferred Carter to Ford.

By 1980 Carter had lost much ground. His claims to be able to reduce unemployment and inflation were patently ill-founded. Trust in his personal integrity had been damaged by his taking so long to request the resignation of Bert Lance, his budget director, after Lance was charged with financial wrongdoing. It was clear that Ronald Reagan was no partisan of working men as unionized employees, but his promise to reduce the federal budget appealed to some workers as taxpayers. Further, Reagan claimed to have the answer to the problem of unemployment and inflation, and unlike Carter's, his claim had not yet been undermined by events. And Reagan's promises to reduce malingering by those on welfare, and his opposition to school busing for racial integration, appealed to some workers (while angering many of the staunch Democrats). Finally, Carter had projected an image of himself as weak and indecisive, and had failed to secure the release of the American hostages held in Iran. Reagan promised an improvement in this area. As a result, a majority of workers voted for Reagan in 1980.

However, by spring 1984 most Imperium workers saw Reagan as fiercely anti-union and a danger to their interests as working men. His administration broke the Air Traffic Controllers union when its members went on strike and appeared to condone employers' declaring bankruptcy to rid themselves of a union, then reopening with nonunion labor. These events were seen by almost all Imperium workers as the key parts of a nationwide antilabor offensive by employers. At Imperium this offensive took the form of a management demand that workers give up their job classifications; management wanted a general labor pool it could assign to tasks in the plant as it wished, and it threatened dire consequences if workers refused. At a crowded union meeting workers did refuse, mostly convinced that if they gave in management would demand still further concessions. The company's new militancy was widely seen as made possible by the climate Reagan had created, and it aroused general anger among workers. Thus by June 1984 it looked as if this time a majority of workers would vote for the Democratic candidate (probably Mondale). Yet two main factors limited this support. First, between 1980 and 1983 the inflation rate of consumer prices fell from 13.5 percent to 3.8 percent, and most men gave Reagan credit for this. He jeopardized their interests as working men, but he appeared to have helped them outside the workplace as consumers. Second, the United States was involved in a number of areas on the international scene, any one of which could flare into a "crisis" that could produce a (temporary) surge in Reagan's domestic support. These areas included El Salvador, Nicaragua, the Persian Gulf, and Israel and her neighbors. Interesting here was the Soviet boycott, announced in May 1984, of the Olympic Games to be held that summer in Los Angeles. Some commentators suggested the Soviet decision was made, in part, to damage Reagan's reelection chances. But among Imperium workers the commonest reaction to the boycott announcement was defiance, as in remarks like "Who needs the Russians anyway?" or "Let them not come. We're better off without them." And while some workers saw Reagan as dangerously trigger happy, others associated Mondale with Carter's perceived weak foreign policy, especially his inability to rescue the American hostages held in Iran. As a result, Mondale was unlikely to win by a landslide among Imperium workers.

Theories of Class Consciousness

It is now apparent that many of the theories of class consciousness in America are flawed because they focus on only part of the picture. The view that workers lack any kind of class consciousness, viewing themselves as isolated individuals competing to attain the American dream, contains an important truth, but at the same time it is seriously misleading. It is true that workers tend to consider their own, and other people's positions in the class structure to be the result of individual effort. In the occupational structure, for instance, they believe they are blue-collar workers rather than upper-white-collar employees mostly because they lacked the talent, desire, or willingness to work to advance through the educational system. And outside work the material possessions they have acquired and the standard of living they enjoy are also, in their eyes, a result of individual and family effort. Finally, their very presence in the United States is clearly the result of a huge initiative taken by their forebears who immigrated.

Yet this view that position in the class structure is largely a result of a person's own efforts coexists with the view that there *is* a class structure, composed in the system of production of working men and working women, and outside work of groups such as the upper, middle, and lower classes, or of the people in opposition to the government.[5]

A number of other theories are flawed because they stress only part of the picture. Writers who point to a working class whose consciousness of itself is organized around production are correct, but they overlook the second image of class based on criteria outside work such as income level, neighborhood, and possessions. And both these currents overlook nationalism and populism, so that periodic outbursts such as the widespread support for the American hostages in Iran come as a surprise, as hard to explain as is their sudden demise.[6]

Class, Race, and Gender

Every serious observer of the American working class has been struck by the importance of racial and ethnic divisions. Such divisions are, for instance, probably the commonest explanation offered for socialism's failure to make deep inroads into the American working class.

Yet a fundamental question remains: How do class and racial/ethnic categories coexist in people's minds—how do workers combine these outlooks? If this question is not usually asked, it may be because the answer is often taken for granted. For the dominant model implies that the self-conception of the American worker varies. At times a person thinks of himself in racial terms, as white or black (or in ethnic terms, as Irish or Polish or Italian). At other times that same person thinks of himself in class terms, as a working man or as middle class, or as part of the people. Consciousness wavers between class and racial/ethnic categories, depending on the context. This model of the *variability of self-conception* is certainly one way class and racial/ethnic categories coexist in workers' minds. Consider, for example, a worker of Polish origin complaining about affirmative action programs that favored blacks and Hispanics. On this occasion he stressed a self-identity based on race.

It's not fair. What about us whites who've been here all the time?

On other occasions he stressed self-identities based on class—for example, beginning with the second image of class, based on life outside work.

It's the middle class in this country who are getting screwed. The rich don't pay taxes. In five years there won't be any middle class, just the rich and the poor, [Now moves, via the theme of corrupt politicians, into the first image of class] Politicians are to blame. What I don't see is all these government handouts to bums who don't want to work. They should have to work like we do. It's not fair to the working man.

But this is not the commonest way racial/ethnic and class identities coexist in thought. The preceding chapters on class consciousness analyzed the way many workers see *other* groups in racial/ethnic, rather than class, terms. Many view the poor and unemployed as consisting largely of blacks and Hispanics, rather than as working men and women or as poor.

Thus the Irish, Polish, or Italian blue-collar worker does not *typically* react to the incursion of blacks or Hispanics into his residential area or workplace by shelving his self-conception as middle class or as a working man and moving to the fore a conception of himself as white (or Irish or Polish or Italian). It is not his self-conception that varies. He questions not his own class identity but that of the perceived intruders. *They* are seen as blacks or Puerto Ricans or Cubans rather than as working men or as middle class or, for some, as Americans. Racial/ethnic categories operate to conceptualize the "intruders" rather than himself, to cast doubt on *their* class standing but not on his own. Racial/ethnic consciousness primarily functions not as an alternative to class consciousness but to limit the range of groups with whom people feel a class solidarity.

The relation between class and gender is also fundamental. There are a number of studies of the way certain occupations are typed as mostly for women or mostly for men, but we know very little about the way workers combine class and gender identities in their minds.

I suggest that, when blue-collar workers consider their position in the system of production, class identity and gender identity are intimately connected. The very concept of the working man is *both* a class and a gender identity. It is a class identity because it implies that blue-collar work is productive in a way that big business and upper- and lower-white-collar work is not. And it is a gender identity because it implies that such work is for men, not women.

At the same time, the sexism implicit in this concept is increasingly under attack in the United States, and this is reflected in the willingness of many workers to concede, on questioning, that women can perform many blue-collar jobs once reserved for men. The concept of the "working person" or of "working men and women," offers a nonsexist class identity in the occupational sphere.

Finally, the intimate connection between class and gender identities applies only to the way workers conceive their position at work. Their identities outside work, as middle or lower middle class and as Americans, are not gender specific.[7]

Part 4 began with a paradox—the coexistence in America of widespread mistrust of politics and widespread support for the political system. Chapter 9 offered a number of explanations for it: the belief that the political system is sound but subverted by corrupt politicians; the belief that America offers freedom, if not democracy; the belief that America is too large to change.

But the preceding discussion of class consciousness has introduced a further set of considerations. Many better-paid employed workers do not see themselves as being at the bottom of the class structure. Each of the three main forms of class identity that Imperium workers possess implies considerable hostility toward politicians and the power structure, but each in its own way may imply hostility or indifference toward groups seen as lowest in society. The concept of the working man may imply hostility toward the unemployed poor as well as toward big business, the power structure, and many white-collar employees. The concept of being middle class or lower middle class may imply wariness of those with little or no wealth or possessions as well as of the rich. Finally, American nationalism contains a populism—a strong mistrust of those in political power—but for some workers it can also slide into the nativistic view that certain groups such as Hispanics, blacks, or radicals are "un-American."

This hostility or indifference toward those at the bottom of the class structure should not be exaggerated. Some workers, though a minority, are entirely free of it, and others lapse into this perspective only from time to time. Yet it is a force that makes for some reluctance to subscribe to radical ideologies that imply a common bond and interest with the poor and the most downtrodden in society.

Part 5

A Sociology of the Mediocre: Religion, Ethnicity, and National Rituals

There is in America a public culture of national rituals. This involves an annual series of occasions such as Independence Day, Thanksgiving, Memorial Day, Christmas, New Year's Eve and New Year's Day, Election Day, the Super Bowl, the World Series, and the whole range of nationally televised sporting events. This culture touches almost all Americans as well as Imperium workers. In this respect blue-collar workers and their families are not a class apart but belong to the mainstream of society. They live out its successes, but also its conflicts and contradictions.

Analysis of this public culture is essential for understanding life in contemporary America, especially since some writers have mistakenly seen this culture as integrated, as reflecting consensus over basic values and goals, and as a major source of political and social cohesion in America. For example, in a famous account W. Lloyd Warner wrote that Memorial Day, Christmas, Thanksgiving, and Independence Day, "function to draw all people together to emphasize their similarities and common heritage; to minimize their differences, and to contribute to their thinking, feeling and acting alike."[1]

This is too simple and one dimensional. For instance, most Americans ignore the ceremonial aspect of Memorial Day altogether, using it as an occasion for leisure—for going to the beach or the park, barbecuing in the backyard, or shopping.[2] And an important part of the ceremonial focus of Christmas, the most extended holiday, is Santa Claus, an idea widely considered both false and so trivial as to be reserved for the smallest of children. Above all, analyses like Warner's fail to distinguish between a public culture that is shared (as this is) and one that is integrated and reflects a consensus over basic values and goals (as in the main this does not).

Durkheim provides a starting point for analyzing this public culture. In his classic study of religion he argued that every society has a tendency to celebrate at regular intervals the main values and institutions that compose it. At these times participants indicate their respect and appreciation for certain common objects of thought and feeling. In Durkheim's words:

There can be no society which does not feel the need of upholding and reaffirming at regular intervals the collective sentiments and the collective ideas which make its unity and its personality. Now this moral re-making cannot be achieved except by the means of reunions, assemblies and meetings where the individuals, being closely united to one another, reaffirm in common their common sentiments.[3]

For instance, life among the Australian aborigines alternated between two phases. Sometimes the population was dispersed into small groups, which wandered alone procuring food. During such periods life was uniform and dull. But at other times the population gathered for ceremonies that lasted several days to several months. Such occasions were characterized by considerable collective excitement, joy, and energy and marked the celebration of certain basic, shared values. In similar fashion, Jews traditionally gathered on Passover to remember the exodus from Egypt, and French citizens annually commemorated the 1789 Revolution.

Yet contemporary societies, Durkheim believed, lack consensus over values and ideals. As a result their public rituals and cults have a mediocre quality. Indeed, beliefs that are seen as of uncertain truth or minor relevance, and rituals that are flat and fail to inspire, are widespread in modern society. As Durkheim put it:

> We are going through a stage of transition and moral mediocrity. The great things of the past which filled our fathers with enthusiasm do not excite the same ardor in us. . . . We can longer impassionate ourselves for the principles in the name of which Christianity recommended to masters that they treat their slaves humanely, and on the other hand the idea which it has formed of human equality and fraternity seems to us today to leave too large a place for unjust inequalities. . . . In a word, the old gods are growing old or already dead and others are not yet born.[4]

This implies the need for a systematic analysis, which so far does not exist, of the ways public rituals and beliefs in advanced industrial society fall short of an ideal. We need a sociology of the mediocre. The chapters that follow develop such a sociology. I begin with an analysis of "religion," of the ways "the old gods" have grown feeble, then discuss the deficiencies of the newer public rituals such as Memorial Day, Thanksgiving, the Super Bowl and World Series, and Election Day.

Only in this context can we understand the attitude of Imperium workers, as well as most Americans, toward the public culture in which they live. And only in this context can we analyze the difference between a national culture that is shared and one that is integrated.

13
Religion

Studying religion among Imperium workers provides a perfect opportunity to construct a sociology of the mediocre.[1] Their religious beliefs are fragmented and full of doubt and avoid many of the important issues in their lives. Their attitude toward the church and clergy falls far short of the respect often associated with religion, and their attitude toward God cannot be described in terms of awe and the sacred. As a result their religious rituals lack color and life. But how is this flatness to be analyzed?

Religion is a combination of beliefs and rituals. As Durkeim put it, "every religion is made up of intellectual conceptions and ritual practices"[2] Thus it is essential to begin with definitions of "ritual" and "belief." These will provide a measure against which to assess particular systems of beliefs and actions.

A cursory look at religion among these workers underlines the importance of starting with such definitions. At first sight Christianity might appear very important in their lives. Almost all believe in God. Explicit atheism is unusual. Further, like most Americans, almost all these workers acknowledge a religious identity, as Catholic, Protestant, Jewish or some combination. Most classify themselves as Catholic, a minority as Protestant or as half Catholic and half Protestant, and there is one Jew (four workers say they are part Jewish).[3] In addition, church attendance is common. Most go at least once a month, and about half attend every week.

Citing such evidence, some writers have argued that religion is of primary, not secondary importance in America.[4] Yet this conclusion is too hasty. Consider, for example, attendance at church. This is an activity, but is it a ritual? To answer this we need a clear definition of ritual. Likewise, consider the idea of God. By itself "God" is just a proper name (and "Jesus" is just another one). We cannot assess the importance of these ideas without a clear notion of what constitutes "religious beliefs."

Thus I shall begin by defining ritual, then consider the religious activities and attitudes of Imperium workers in this light. I will go on to do the same for religious beliefs, focusing on Catholicism, the religion of most of these workers and also of most industrial workers in the northeastern United States.

Ritual

Most definitions of ritual include three components. First, and above all, rituals involve a particular attitude, for they draw people's attention to objects of thought and feeling considered very special, if not sacred. Second, rituals rely heavily on symbols. Third, they involve rule-governed behavior. I will, then, define a ritual as "rule-governed behavior of a symbolic character that draws the attention of its participants to objects of thought and feeling they hold to be sacred or of special significance."[5]

Rituals, then, involve an attitude that can be characterized as special or sacred. Yet the most striking feature of religion among these workers is the widespread disrespect for God's representatives on earth, the clergy. Conversations about theology or God are rare. Instead, mention of religion is likely to trigger a litany of complaints about the moral failings of priests and the church. These complaints focus on financial greed and sexual misbehavior, but excessive drinking and arrogance are also vices commonly attributed to the clergy.

Financial Greed

It is unusual for these workers to discuss religion without complaining about the church's greed. Consider these examples.

A warehouse worker in his mid-forties:

> I was an altar boy with Father——— [names a local priest]. When we did weddings and funerals we'd get money from the people, and he always took it and put it in his pocket. And at my church they're always having three and four collections. I don't know where the money goes.

A batch worker in his mid-thirties:

> My aunt went to the Vatican and she came back and said to me, "You should have seen how they treated the pope. They carried him in a gold chair, and there was so much gold and silver around!" That's the trouble. Every church has to send money each month to the Vatican.

A batch worker in his early forties:

> I believe in God and a lot of those things, but I got kind of turned off. They [the church] wanted me to give 10 percent of my income and attend all kinds of functions and affairs like bingo. But I've got seven kids of my own and there's all kinds of things connected with their school [public school] that I go to, and I don't have time for those church things.
>
> And then I don't like some of the ways the church gets money. Like they try to embarrass you at school. Tommy's [a friend of his] son went to parochial school and that's expensive. And if you're late with the fees they broadcast your name over the loudspeaker. That's not right.

It's all money with the church. Now I understand they need money, but still. . . . And the trouble is if you don't belong to a parish they can give you a lot of trouble when it comes to christenings and weddings. They look you up on their register and say you're not on it. And I'll tell you it's hard to get buried in America if you don't belong to a church. That's not right. Everyone has a right to a burial.

The routine activities of the church provide abundant material to feed such views. For instance, the commonest theme preached from the pulpit is the importance of disinterested generosity, the unselfish use of wealth. The next item in the church service is passing the collection basket, often twice or three times, with most

Plates 31 and 32. Church.

of the funds usually explicitly destined to support the clergy and the church. The timing escapes few Imperium workers, many of whom conclude that the church is less interested in generosity in general than in generosity toward the church. Further, almost every church is deeply and visibly involved with bingo, proclaiming its support with large signs (plate 32). Bingo is clearly designed to appeal to parishioners' pecuniary desires and fits badly with warnings against materialism, another common theme in sermons.

There are various other ironies. Among them are parishioners emerging from church after hearing a sermon on the importance of love and the spiritual life to see outside, obviously placed to attract their attention, a gleaming new car, first prize in a church raffle.[6]

Sexual Misbehavior

Sexual misbehavior is the second commonest moral failing attributed to the clergy. Stories about sexual relations between priests and nuns and between clergy and nonclergy are commonplace. And the intimate setting of the confessional, together with the tendency for women to attend church more often than men, create in the minds of many workers a deep suspicion that priests abuse their position in order to establish sexual relations with their female parishioners. Sometimes workers become angry about this. A batch worker in his mid-forties recounting his experiences as an altar boy:

> I was going to be a priest. Then when I was in eighth grade my mentor died. Celibacy! I saw those guys. We went camping and I used to clean out his [the priest's] ashtrays, and there was lipstick all over his cigarette butts.
> My mother, a sweet woman, said, "I know they're [priests] all rotten, but just go to church."
> My father used to say it was the Catholic church that fucked up Poland [the speaker is a second-generation Pole].

At least two workers believed the lechery of their local priests was responsible, at least in part, for the breakup of their marriages. For instance, a briquetter worker who lived in Elizabeth:

> [Bitterly] The priest heard her [his wife's] confession, and then he put the make on her. He had an affair with my wife. That's how my first marriage ended. My parents-in-law never went to church again they were so disgusted, but I still went. It's a question of faith.

The perceived sexual misbehavior of the clergy is the subject of ribaldry and humor as often as anger. A typical example is the following joke, told by one mechanic to another. The speaker attends church every week and believes in God.

> A nun goes to confession and says, "Father, last week I jerked off a man's penis with my hands. What shall I do?" The father said, "Don't

worry, go back to the convent and wash your hands in holy water." So she washed her hands in the morning and again in the afternoon and again in the evening, and next day she washed them too. The mother superior sees her and asks what she is doing. So the nun says, "I confessed to the father that last week I jerked off a man's penis with my hands, and the father told me to wash them in holy water." So the mother superior turns pale, grabs the holy water and gargles with it! [Both mechanics laugh heartily.]

The owner of Lesniak's tavern, where many workers drink, has a doll representing a monk. When the monk's head is pushed down a large penis protrudes from his robes. From time to time the doll is passed around, to the amusement of workers present.

Greed and sexual misbehavior are the main, but not the only, failings workers see in the clergy and the church. Other themes they complain about are heavy drinking and authoritarianism. A worker commenting on the greed and authoritarian disposition of his local priest:

One day my son came home from [parochial] school—he was six—and he had shit all over his pants. So I said to him, "Why didn't you use the bathroom?" And he said, "There's only one for seventy students." So I said, "No, I know there's more. I go there to play bingo." And he said, "They're locked." So I went in there, and seven of the [eight] bathrooms were locked. You know, they wanted to save water and cleaning. I said to the priest, "You should open them all," and he said to me, "I'm the guy in charge here. Don't you tell me what to do!"

Next time I was in Newark I stopped in to see the bishop, and I went in there and I told him. Next week in his sermon the priest said a communist had complained to the bishop! He said it in his sermon! Afterward I went up to him and said I'd sue, I had 700 witnesses!

Partly as a result of these perceived moral failings of the clergy and partly because of an egalitarian social outlook that makes them uncomfortable in a markedly deferential relationship with another human being, many workers prefer to establish their primary relationship directly with God. Thus some attend church but put their main energy into a direct personal relation with God.

A batch worker in his mid-forties:

I go to church every Sunday, but there are some things I don't agree with. I don't agree with the confession. I sit in church and I confess the things I want to to God, but I don't need the priest. I can do that [confessing] with anyone, just like you and me sitting here [in the tavern]. Just me and God, that way it's more direct.

A batch worker in his mid-fifties:

You know, nine times out of ten when a man goes to confess, which I do, he doesn't tell everything. You know he's ashamed to admit some things, like adultery or stealing. So I confess to God. Then you can tell everything. Anyway, like this Methodist minister once said to me, a lot of these priests are sons of bitches.

Other workers rely exclusively on this direct relation with God and no longer attend church. A mechanic in his late fifties:

I believe in God, but going to church and attending mass isn't important. It's how you live your life. That's what is important.

Other ethnographies suggest that the attitudes of Imperium workers toward the church are not unusual for blue-collar Catholics. Herbert Gans refers to the lack of respect for the clergy among inner-city first- and second-generation Italians in Boston. And Gerald Suttles refers to a similar attitude among Puerto Ricans, Mexicans, and Italians (as well as blacks) in Chicago.[7]

Rituals That Fall Short

We can now construct a classification of rituals, based on the extent to which attitudes of participants fall short of being sacred or special. Earlier I defined a ritual as "rule-governed activity of a symbolic character that draws the attention of its participants to objects of thought and feeling they hold to be sacred or of special significance." Rituals so defined can be called "primary rituals."

But the preceding discussion of working-class Catholicism suggests that few of the men's attitudes measure up to those that characterize "primary rituals." There are no workers whose attitude to religion can be described as sacred. Almost all of them, for instance, enjoy hearing jokes about the sexual misbehavior of the clergy even if they do not tell such jokes themselves. Nor does much of their attitude toward religion even count as special. The general view most of these workers have of God and Jesus can at best be described as positive rather than special. Rituals that elicit such positive, but not special or sacred, attitudes should be distinguished from primary rituals. They will be called "secondary rituals."

Further, toward a number of items many workers feel neutral or indifferent, or almost so. An example is the notion of the Sabbath, Sunday as the Lord's Day, on which certain activities such as drinking in the tavern, shopping in large department stores, and working should not be permitted. Hardly anyone at Imperium takes such a view seriously. And these prohibitions are widely seen as anachronistic and without meaning, as is clear from the tendency of state legislatures to repeal Sabbath legislation. For instance, New Jersey recently repealed a law forbidding large department stores to open on Sunday. Such rituals that draw, or attempt to draw, attention to objects people view as of minor importance can be called "tertiary rituals." And rituals that attempt to draw attention to objects viewed as of no importance can be called "empty rituals."

There are other rituals whose effect, though unintended and regretted, is to draw people's attention to objects they view negatively. For example, collection in

RELIGION 259

church tends to remind these workers of the pecuniary interest the clergy have in their parishioners. As a result the collection often stirs negative feelings, and sometimes even stronger feelings of disgust. (In an obvious, but largely unsuccessful, attempt to dissociate the clergy from monetary motives, the collection is one of the few church rituals performed by laymen rather than priests.) Rituals that in fact evoke unfavorable attitudes can be called "negative rituals," and those that evoke feelings of extreme disapproval and disgust can be called "black rituals." Table 29 summarizes these various types of rituals.[8]

As this discussion suggests, there is often a difference between the intentions of those who conduct rites and the attitude of those toward whom the rites are directed—the potential participants. The clergy who conduct rites that turn out to be negative or black are usually attempting to present certain objects in a positive, very favorable, or sacred light. Unfortunately some of these objects, for instance themselves and the church, may be seen negatively; and a rite designed to draw attention to an object people do view positively may actually draw attention to another object they view negatively. Thus, given the unfavorable view most workers have of the church, the bulk of the rites the clergy perform have a dark or negative component; for it is hard to avoid drawing people's attention to the clergy, and some rituals, such as the collection, are suffused with blackness or negativity.

Two further points about rites. First, many are mixed, evoking more than one attitude at the same time. Thus even the ritual of collection occurs within the context of the church, which contains a number of religious symbols—especially the cross and Jesus—toward which many workers have a positive attitude. The preceding distinctions between different types of rituals are based on the dominant attitude the ritual evokes (such as respect, indifference or disgust), but it should not be forgotten that a ritual may simultaneously evoke more than one attitude in the same person.

Second, attitudes can fluctuate, from positive on entering the church to negative (the collection) and back to positive (the mass that follows the collection).

It is now clear how one-dimensional a concept of ritual (and how inadequate an ethnography) underlies the view that because workers perform certain religious activities, such as attending church, religion is of considerable importance to them.

Table 29   Varieties of Rituals

Actual Attitude Produced among Participants	Type of Ritual
Special or sacred	Primary
Positive	Secondary
Minor importance	Tertiary
Indifference	Empty
Moderately negative	Moderately negative
Negative	Negative
Extreme disapproval and disgust	Black

Most of these religious rituals are at best secondary, and many are tertiary, empty, negative, or black.

In the two chapters that follow I will use these distinctions between types of rituals to analyze other central national rituals in America. Voting, for instance, is in many ways an empty, negative, or black ritual. It is supposed to draw attention to the democratic process in operation, yet it reminds many workers of the opposite—of the lack of popular control over government in America. And it often evokes disgust instead of enthusiasm. Yet before extending the analysis of ritual it is important to consider the beliefs that accompany rituals.

Beliefs

As with ritual, it is essential to begin with a clear definition of beliefs. The point about religious beliefs is that they explain the world, or at least an important part of it. In this sense they are no different from other explanatory beliefs. Durkheim put this cognitive aspect of religion as follows: "[Religion] is not merely a system of practices, but also a system of ideas whose object is to explain the world; . . . even the humblest [religions] have their cosmology." I will, then, define religious beliefs as "beliefs that explain a part of the world that is important to those who hold the beliefs."[9] I will refer to such beliefs as a "cosmology."

The Old and New Testaments together, or even separately, once came close to constituting an entire account of the world, which in part explains their attraction. But nowadays no single set of beliefs is sufficient to explain to people their entire world. As a result we have a number of cosmologies, corresponding to different areas of our world. Imperium workers implicitly divide the world into five areas. First, there is *politics and the class structure of America*. Second, there is *interpersonal relations*, including relations with family, friends, and work associates. Third, there is that part of the *natural-physical world* that people need to understand in their everyday lives. This includes, for example, enough knowledge of physics, chemistry, and engineering to enable them to handle the electrical circuits and plumbing in their homes, their automobiles, and, for these workers, the chemical equipment and machinery at their place of employment. Fourth, there is the world of *bodily and mental health*. Finally, there is the (possible) *world after death*.

Imperium workers have beliefs that provide them with an understanding of each of these areas. What role do the categories of Christianity play in these beliefs? How far for these workers is Christianity a cosmology?

The World after Death

If religious ideas are important, it is in dealing with death and its aftermath that they can be expected to play a major part. For at the heart of Catholicism is the quest for salvation of the soul after the death of the body. It is around this quest that religious life on earth is organized.

Yet only a minority of workers (35 percent) are sure there is life after death. The largest number (40 percent) are unsure about this central question. Consider these examples of workers, all of whom believe in God, asked whether they believe in life after death.

A warehouse worker in his mid-fifties:

I'm too busy to worry about that shit. I don't have time to think about it. That garbage is the kind of thing you do when you're in a wheelchair.

A mechanic in his early thirties:

I'm not sure. I know what the church says, but I'm not sure.

A mechanic in his late fifties:

Worker: We buried Walter Banasiak [a worker who died of leukemia] this morning.

Researcher: Do you think there's anything afterward?

Worker [smiles]: Well, I know what our religion tells us. Like the priest said to me this morning that Walter had gone to the world above. But I don't know. There ain't no one ever come back to tell us about it.

A mechanic in his early fifties who, a year earlier, had survived a serious heart attack:

[Quietly] I really don't know. I got close myself, but I don't know.

Another group of workers (about 25 percent) go further. They are sure, or fairly sure, there is no life after death. These comments were made by workers who all say they believe in God.

A batch worker in his mid-fifties:

No, I don't think there's anything after death. When you're gone you're gone. As far as I'm concerned they can give me flowers or piss on my grave—it isn't going to make any difference.

A batch worker in his mid-twenties:

An afterlife? No, I've never seen anyone come back to tell about it! There's no evidence there's anything after death.

A warehouse worker in his early sixties [besides believing in God, this man attends three church services each weekend]:

Do I believe in life after death? No! I believe in living for the present. I've had a good life, and if I go tomorrow I'll be satisfied. I said to the priest once, "The only difference between you and me is that when I die I'll be a little deeper in the earth than you [the speaker is a heavy man]." He said I didn't take things seriously enough!

This leaves a third group (35 percent) who are sure life exists after death. Yet it would be a mistake to assume that even this group views life after death in classic Christian fashion. Neither the orthodox Catholic view that after the body dies most souls either go to hell or spend a lengthy period in purgatory and then enter heaven, nor the mainstream Protestant variant that eliminates purgatory and focuses on heaven and hell, is frequent. Instead, most of the workers who believe in life after death discuss it in distinctly non-Christian terms.[10] One group, for instance, talks about spirits and ghosts. The following comment was made by a batch worker in his early forties who believes in God and attends church regularly:

Researcher: Do you believe in life after death?

Worker: Yes, yes I do. Like there was a movie on television about this woman. Her husband died and the spirit wouldn't leave. It haunted the house.

Another group believe in some form of continual human reincarnation. And some combine belief in spirits with belief in human reincarnation. Consider this example of a worker in his mid-fifties (discussing death and when it happens).

Worker: I think whatever happens is written in the Lord's book. I just hope when I go it's fast.

Researcher: Do you think there's anything afterward?

Worker: Oh yes, definitely. There has to be. I have this feeling inside me that tells me there is. And you hear about those guys who've had four or five lives. They've come back four or five times. [Switching from human reincarnation to spirits and ghosts] And haunted houses and spirits. You know, there's this one haunted house in New Jersey. You know where all those haunted houses come from? From England. They're all in England and Scotland and Ireland.

Some workers make forays into other realms, such as the world of extraterrestrial beings. A worker in his mid-twenties:

Life after death? Yes, well I believe in extraterrestrial beings. Like, there has to be life on some of those planets, not Mars or Jupiter, but some of the others. I'd give my whole life for just a week with one of those extraterrestrial beings, just to see what they're like.

The Sociopolitical World

Christian beliefs and categories play almost no part in workers' explanations of the sociopolitical world. The previous chapters outlined men's beliefs about who holds power in America and about their three main identities as working men, as middle class or lower middle class, and as Americans. This is a coherent set of views, a sociopolitical cosmology, in which God and Jesus have no role. To inject theology here is to invite ridicule. Only one worker, who is a lay preacher, ever introduces biblical references into his discussions of politics and society. He is a general object of fun among other workers, ridiculed precisely because he lets religion and theology out of the narrow confines the others place them in. During the entire period of research no one else cited theology to explain current American politics and society. No one ever mentioned, or even hinted at, classic Catholic social and political theories such as that work is God's punishment to man for Adam's original sin, or that political legitimacy derives from God.

This view that questions of politics, economics, and society are not the domain of God and religion was illustrated by the derision and disapproval with which most workers greeted the news that President Carter had summoned religious leaders as well as experts on economics and politics to confer with him at Camp David on the "energy crisis" triggered by the latest round of price increases from OPEC. Consider these two workers.

> **First worker** [A mechanic in his mid-forties. He is one of the very few men who speak well of their local priests]: Well [satirically], we're all waiting to hear what the priests and rabbis are going to tell him [Carter] to do! Yes, they can send all of them to Camp David!

> **Second worker** [Also a mechanic, in his early forties. This man shares the more general view of the clergy. As a result he rarely attends church though he is "religious" and believes in God]: Those people [the clergy] shouldn't be involved in politics. [With disgust] It's not their business. What do they know about it?

Bodily and Mental Health: God and Luck

Occasionally a man will refer to God where most people would refer to personal luck. The commonest area for such explanation is the sphere of physical and mental health, though workers from time to time apply it to any area of the world they seek to explain. In accounting for physical and mental health, they clearly subordinate religious explanations to explanations from the realm of medical science, but there is an opening for religion in areas that medicine deliberately vacates. Why, for instance, does one person become sick while another, in the same condition and context, does not? Or why does one person recover from an illness while another, in similar circumstances, dies? These are areas medicine cedes to luck or chance. Most workers generally do so too, but occasionally they invoke theology.

A worker has a friend who is a doctor. One day this doctor noticed a lump on his friend's cheek. He investigated and discovered a tumor in the process of spreading. A speedy operation removed the hazard. The worker commented on his double good fortune, having a doctor friend and a nonmalignant tumor.

I guess the guy up there, God, was looking out for me.

Consider another example of this view that the question of who becomes sick and who does not may be the sphere of divine intervention. A warehouse worker in his early sixties was voicing his disappointment. Despite regular attendance at church he has arthritis, an ailment from which other, less religious people, are free. Why hadn't God protected him?

I have arthritis in my legs. I ask myself all the time why someone like me who goes to church every week should have arthritis while other people who never go to church don't have nothing wrong with them. But they [the priests] tell us we can't ask those kinds of questions.

Yet even in such cases God is invoked infrequently, far less often than luck or chance, and often without conviction but with an implication that God is more a synonym for luck than an independent explanatory principle.

The way these workers sometimes combine explanations involving God with explanations involving empirical-medical science is, from one viewpoint, similar to Evans-Pritchard's analysis of the role of witchcraft beliefs among the Azande in Africa. In their accounts of unfortunate events the Azande combine, without illogic, natural-empirical explanations with explanations based on notions of witchcraft. For instance, they are aware that a man who is trampled to death by an elephant died because he was crushed by the elephant (the natural-empirical explanation). But they go on to ask why *this* man was killed while his companions, who could just as easily have been killed, were not. Here Azande tend to resort to witchcraft as an explanation, just as workers occasionally resort to God to explain why one person becomes sick when another does not.

Yet the comparison with witchcraft beliefs among the Azande underlines the relatively minor role Christianity plays in explaining personal fortune and misfortune for these workers. Whereas the Azande very often use witchcraft to explain misfortune, these workers use religion only occasionally, and luck (good or bad) very commonly.[11]

Bodily and Mental Health and the Natural-Physical
   World: The Meaning of God

If belief in God is the criterion that distinguishes those who are religious from those who are atheists, then it makes sense to investigate the meaning of the idea. What meaning do workers attach to the idea of God?

Systematic investigation of this question uncovers two further areas in which theology is present. One has to do with the origin of life, the other with the origin of the world. These topics are often related in men's minds, for both concern the question of "first origin." They touch on men's view of the natural-physical world and of the world of bodily and mental health. Neither is a topic workers speak about often, but they emerge when men's perceptions of God are investigated.

It should be noted that for most workers the question of what God means, what God does, is difficult and somewhat perplexing and tends to provoke considerable thought. In a way this is no surprise, for the question is difficult for many theologians too. Yet, given the very sketchy role of the categories of Christianity in workers' beliefs, their uncertain view of God is one more indicator of the minor place religious beliefs have in their outlook. Consider these examples of workers explaining their view that God is the creator of life and the world.

A laboratory technician in his mid-forties:

Researcher: Do you believe in God?

Worker: Well, I'm not a regular churchgoer if that's what you mean. But I guess I believe in God.

Researcher: What does God do?

Worker [looking slightly irritated at the question]: I don't know, it's very hard to say. [Thinks] I guess God creates life . . . well, someone has to . . . [Pause] But I don't know about those things in the Bible, I don't know if they ever happened.

A batch worker in his late fifties:

Researcher: Do you believe in God?

Worker [thinks]: Well, yes, you have to believe in something.

Researcher: What does God do?

Worker [pauses, thinks]: Gee! It's tricky business! [Thinks] God is why there's night and day and light and summer and winter. [Pause] God creates life. [Pause] Well, there's no other way to explain those things, is there? [Pause, thinks] Yes, there has to be something to explain all this.

A worker in his early thirties:

Yes [describing his conception of God], I think there's something like a basic force. Like they say the world was originally made of helium and oxygen, but who put the helium and oxygen there? I believe in extrasensory perception and poltergeists. That has to do with the power of the mind. Some people can do amazing things with their minds. I think maybe God was some fellow who was just like us but had amazingly strong thought control, so strong he could create things with his mind.

These two main functions attributed to God, the origin of the world and of life, are based mostly on metaphysical speculation. They are a residual category, the domains that physics and biology have not yet entered. In a sense they are the key questions, but in another more obvious sense they remain in the realm of metaphysics so long as workers perceive little or no way of drawing on God's power for their personal benefit.

Interpersonal Life

There is one additional area in which Christian beliefs play some role. This is the sphere of interpersonal life. Interpersonal life covers relations within the family, among friends, and among work associates. Chapters 2 and 3 discussed the interplay and tensions in the lives of these workers between the principle of the nuclear family and other principles of how to live interpersonal life—the principles of male friendships, of extramarital sexual relations, and of work.

In this context the moral ideas and precepts of Catholicism play some, though a limited, role in supporting a conservative version of the principle of the nuclear family. There are three areas that may be relevant here. First, there is the church's prohibition against birth control. In fact this is widely disregarded. Consider these examples.

An Imperium wife in her mid-fifties who attends church each week:

Yes, I used birth control. I used to go to confession every year and confess, and the priest would say you shouldn't [use birth control], but I went on using it.

A mechanic who considers himself religious but no longer goes to church:

Sure I use birth control. I have four kids already. If the pope wants more kids let him pay for mine!

Despite these views some workers clearly have not used birth control, and there is some presumption that the attitude of the church has been an important influence.

Second, there is the church's prohibition against abortion. A number of these workers agree with the church and cite it in support of their view that abortion is murder.

Third, there is the attitude of the church toward divorce. No one ever mentioned the church as a reason for not obtaining a divorce, in contrast to the large numbers who mentioned a fear of losing their property.

In sum, the church's attitude toward abortion finds some support among Imperium workers, but its attitude toward birth control, and probably divorce, is widely, but not entirely, disregarded.

Cosmologies That Fall Short

It is now clear that to understand cosmologies as they actually operate we need a classification based on the extent to which beliefs as explanations fall short of "cosmologies." Chapter 3, on marriage and family life, distinguished one way this may happen, for it pointed out that the beliefs of many Imperium workers, and many Americans, about how to live interpersonal life are contradictory and confused. I called such a set of beliefs a "contradictory cosmology."

The present discussion suggests two further ways beliefs that aspire to constitute a cosmology may fall short. First, they may explain aspects of the world that are not centrally relevant to people's lives. For instance, the belief that God created the world is in itself of little relevance to workers' lives, and the belief that God creates life, including human life, is not of much greater relevance so long as it is not accompanied by a belief that people can tap God's creativity for their own purposes.

Second, beliefs that resemble a cosmology may fall short because, though they concern an area of central relevance, people may lack confidence in their truth. People may be undecided about the beliefs or even sure they are false. For example, life after death is of central relevance to workers, but many are uncertain if the church's view is correct, and some are sure it is not. Likewise, physical and mental health is of central relevance, but most workers are at best uncertain whether God has anything to do with why one person becomes seriously ill while another, in similar circumstances, does not.

Beliefs and belief systems may, then, be arranged in a hierarchy based on two criteria: on how far they concern an area of the world that is of central relevance, and on how far they are seen as true. On this basis it is possible to distinguish "primary" and "secondary" cosmologies and "tertiary" beliefs (see table 30).

A primary cosmology is a set of beliefs that a person considers true and that explain an aspect of the world that is of central relevance to that person. Workers have a primary cosmology for three of the five main areas of the world that they consider of central relevance. First, the beliefs they have about who runs America and their own position within society constitute a primary cosmology about the sociopolitical world. Second, medical science in popular form encompasses their central beliefs about the causes of health and sickness and as such constitutes a primary cosmology about the area of physical and mental health. Third, the body of practical knowledge they have about electricity, plumbing, car maintenance, and such topics constitutes a primary cosmology about the natural-physical world.

Table 30   Belief Systems Classified by the Perceived Relevance of the Area They Explain and by Their Degree of Perceived Truth

Perceived Relevance of Area Explained	Degree of Perceived Truth		
	True	Probably or Possibly True	Probably or Definitely False
Centrally relevant	Primary cosmology	Secondary cosmology	Tertiary belief
Somewhat or partially relevant	Secondary cosmology	Secondary cosmology	Tertiary belief
Largely or wholly irrelevant	Tertiary belief	Tertiary belief	Tertiary belief

By contrast, for almost no workers are the beliefs of Christianity a primary cosmology, whether such beliefs deal with life after death, physical and mental health, the natural-physical world, the sociopolitical system, or interpersonal relations.

A "secondary cosmology" concerns an aspect of the world that is of some relevance but not central, or it is of central relevance but embodies beliefs about which a person has serious doubts. Thus Christian beliefs about life after death are of central relevance but for most workers are uncertain or untrue, and Judeo-Christian beliefs about God's creating life are viewed by many workers as true but of less than central relevance, since few believe they can tap God's creativity for their own benefit.

"Tertiary beliefs" refer to all the remaining possibilities. They are beliefs that explain an aspect of the world that is of little or no relevance to an individual, regardless of whether those beliefs are seen as true. And they are beliefs a person has no confidence are true, regardless of how relevant they may be. Thus ideas about Santa Claus are tertiary beliefs, since they are widely seen as neither true nor relevant. And the set of beliefs about the birth and life of Jesus are tertiary beliefs, since, though workers may consider them true, they have little or no relevance to their current lives. (Tertiary beliefs as beliefs in whose truth people have little or no confidence include most of the ideas often referred to as myths, fairy tales or ideologies. And tertiary beliefs as beliefs that explain an aspect of the world of little or no relevance to most people include large parts of many academic disciplines such as history, philosophy, and anthropology as well as most of the Old and New Testaments.)[12]

These distinctions underline the problem involved in concluding that Judeo-Christian beliefs are important simply because people say they believe in God. It is essential to set such beliefs in the context of people's other ideas about the world. When this is done for Imperium workers it is clear that Judeo-Christian ideas and beliefs occupy a very limited and defensive terrain—excluded on pain of ridicule from workers' views about politics, class, and American society; occupying a small fraction of the domain medical science cedes to chance and luck in the area of physical health; uncertainly located in the area concerning life and the origin of the world that biology and physics have not yet occupied; in a losing competition with popular beliefs about spirits and reincarnation for the minority who feel sure there is life after death; and supporting an extreme and increasingly unpalatable version of the nuclear family.

In summary, the categories and beliefs of Christianity aim to be of some relevance to most aspects of the world that concern these workers. But in the context of workers' actual beliefs they end up as a structure of "secondary cosmologies" and "tertiary beliefs." Such a set of beliefs, which purports to explain more than one area of the world but falls short in all areas, can be called a "set of mediocre cosmologies."

Conclusion

As a set of beliefs or cosmologies and as a set of rituals, Christianity is at best of secondary importance for almost all these workers. This is not to deny that religion performs other functions. For many workers it is a "way of sociability or belonging." This function of religion in America is widespread, as Will Herberg has pointed out.[13] The United States was first settled by God-fearing Christians escaping religious intolerance in Europe. As a result, for later immigrants to acknowledge an identity as Protestant, Catholic, or Jew is part of assimilating into America and making contact with a particular social network.

Religion does offer several social advantages to Imperium workers—access to wedding and burial rights, to parochial schools for their children, and to leisure activities such as Bingo (more popular among women than men). Likewise, Gans pointed out that Catholics who moved to suburban Levittown set up a church primarily to provide a parochial school to give their children what they saw as a better *secular* education than the public schools offered; and Jews set up a temple mainly to provide a social network that would discourage their children from intermarrying.[14]

Further, beliefs that are seen as of uncertain truth can still influence actions. Thus asked why, given their skepticism about the moral character of the clergy and about many aspects of Christian theology, workers still attend church, the commonest explanation is insurance. Many are doubtful about the official view of heaven and hell, but why take a chance? A couple of hours a week and a couple of dollars for the collection are a small price to pay should the church's account of life after death prove correct.

This chapter has focused on Catholicism among working-class men. It could not claim to be about religion in America. Variation by region (especially the North versus the South and the West Coast), by time ("religious revivals"), and by gender should not be ignored. But my findings are consistent with much of what Herberg has to say in his classic study of religion in America. According to Herberg, the Protestant, Catholic, and Jewish churches have generally allowed their beliefs and rituals to change so as to conform with American life and ideals. As a result, and despite widespread church attendance:

> the religiousness characteristic of America today is very often a religiousness without religion, a religiousness with almost any kind of content or none, a way of sociability or "belonging" rather than a way of reorienting life to God. It is thus frequently a religiousness without serious commitment, without real inner conviction, without genuine existential decision. What should reach down to the core of existence, shattering and renewing, merely skims the surface of life.[15]

14
Ethnicity

Ethnicity throws further light on actions that fall short of rituals and on beliefs that fall short of cosmologies. More than any other advanced industrial society, the United States has incorporated waves of immigrants from a variety of countries. The effect of this immigration has been the subject of much debate. One of the best-known theories concerning ethnicity is that of the "melting pot." This argues that, in general, the influence of the immigrant culture fades in the second and third generations.

The theory can be stated in a number of ways, but the most convincing version contains two caveats. First, it is essential to distinguish between ethnicity and race. Ethnicity refers to a foreign culture. Thus an ethnic is defined as "any individual who considers himself, or is considered to be, a member of a group with a foreign culture and who participates in the activities of the group."[1] By contrast, race refers to certain physical traits that are inherited. The distinction between race and ethnicity is cardinal, for in the United States ethnicity melts whereas race, in one aspect at least, does not. Foreign cultures fade in importance with the second and third generations, but a particular physical distinction, especially dark skin, persists, accounting for the caste or castelike position of most blacks.

The second caveat concerns the relation of ethnicity and class. Ethnic distinctions based on immigrant cultures fade, but the class structure of America persists. Indeed, the former melts into the latter. The fading of ethnicity reveals not a society without distinctions but a society in which the major distinctions are those of class and race, not ethnicity.[2]

My findings are consistent with such a version of the melting pot theory (though with a third caveat, to be added later, concerning "symbolic ethnicity"). That is why ethnicity in America cannot be analyzed without a set of categories, a sociology of the mediocre, designed to capture a phenomenon of secondary and fading importance.

Ethnic Beliefs

There are two major respects in which ethnicity is secondary for these workers, mostly second-, third-, or fourth-generation immigrants. First, as a set of beliefs it is, like religion, a set of mediocre cosmologies. In the two areas of the world to which it purports to be relevant, the sociopolitical and interpersonal, it is at best a secondary cosmology, playing a limited and uncertain role.

Consider the role of ethnic beliefs in workers' sociopolitical outlook. Workers rarely use ethnic categories to understand and explain their own position in contemporary America. They see a large part of economic and political life happening to them as working men or as the middle class or as Americans. But very little happens because they are Italians or Poles or Irish or Germans. Occasionally a worker may complain about ethnic stereotypes, like this second-generation Italian in his early thirties:

> Everyone thinks if you're Italian you've got to be part of the Mafia. It's not fair. The first hit men were Jews, not Italians at all.

But even for this man being Italian explains little about what happens to him now in America, far less than does being a working man or being middle class or American.

There are no organizations comparable with the local union or with the local or the federal government that actively represent workers' political and economic interests as Italians or Irish or Germans. And it is hard to envisage what such an organization might do, for workers rarely have "ethnic" interests. Certainly they have an interest in not being discriminated against, but this amounts to saying they have an interest in being treated equally, as Americans. When discrimination in this negative sense ceases to exist, then so in most cases do the cohesive economic and political interests of the ethnic group.[3] Thus, on the political and economic level the category of being an American largely supersedes ethnic categories.

Ethnic beliefs concern the area of interpersonal relations as well as the sociopolitical world. Thus in some forms they contain the idea that those of similar ethnic origin should spend their social life together and should intermarry. Here too such beliefs are of secondary or tertiary importance. There was a time, among the first generation, when exogamy, if not taboo, was viewed with disapproval. People were expected to marry within their ethnic groups. But among the second and third generations such norms are widely disregarded. Assimilation, intermarriage between ethnic groups, is common (though across racial lines it is rare). As a third-generation worker of Irish origin explained:

> You know, years ago in the 1930s if you wanted to marry an Italian or a Pole your family would give you all kinds of trouble. They didn't want it. Now things have changed. It doesn't matter anymore.[4]

Beliefs that those of similar ethnic origin should spend their social life together are even weaker. No one, younger or older, first or third generation, ever expressed such a view.

This is why ethnicity as a set of beliefs about politics and the class structure and about interpersonal life consists of mediocre cosmologies.

Ethnic Rituals

Ethnic rituals reflect this attitude. They typically have a less than serious tone. They attach themselves to symbols chosen partly because they are easily expressed and require minimal interference with other aspects of life. Consumer goods, especially "ethnic" food, are an obvious source of such symbols. So are sporadic festivals and parades like Saint Patrick's Day, Columbus Day, and Pulaski Day. For most workers these are at best secondary rituals—more likely tertiary—or, especially in regard to ethnic food, empty rituals drawing attention to items viewed as of minor and fading importance or of no importance at all. Consider these examples.

A second-generation Polish worker, in his late fifties, discussing the monthly dances he attends with his wife at a Polish social club:

> No, the Polish thing is just habit. It doesn't really matter. I have a lot of friends there, but it [being Polish] isn't really important.

A third-generation Italian worker, discussing food:

> I like Italian food. We eat it at home a lot. But that's just taste. It's what I grew up with.

An indicator of the secondary importance attached to ethnicity is the extent to which it is commonly accompanied by joking. The election of a Polish pope in 1978 was interesting in this context. It was certainly viewed with pride by most workers of Polish origin. At the same time a barrage of jokes reflected the idea that the ethnic origin of the pontiff was really of minor significance (the discussion of joking relations in chap. 8 pointed out how ethnic jokes reflect ethnicity's relative unimportance).

A worker of German origin:

> Do you know why the new Polish pope raised all the urinals in the Vatican a foot? To keep the Guineas [Italians] on their toes!

A worker of Polish origin:

> They'll be serving kielbasa and sauerkraut in church instead of wine and wafers.

A worker of Irish origin:

> Hey, it's open gates in heaven for the Polacks!

A worker of Polish origin:

> Well, the Polacks are on top now. We've got our guy in the Vatican.

When workers are asked about ethnicity in general, their comments usually illustrate its secondary role. Some attach almost no importance to their ethnic background. Others view it as having some, though limited, significance. But either way, ethnicity is usually secondary to being an American. These are examples of workers who dismiss ethnicity almost entirely.

A second-generation worker of Ukrainian origin:

> Ethnic? No, that's dead, that's long past! I'm Ukrainian and so is my wife, but that's old history. I'm an American.

A third-generation worker of Italian origin:

> **Researcher:** How important is being Italian?
>
> **Worker:** No, it's not important. It doesn't make any difference. That's the great thing about this country. There are Italians and Irish and Spanish and Jews, and it doesn't matter. Everyone can get ahead.
>
> **Researcher:** Do you belong to any Italian organizations?
>
> **Worker:** No, why should I? I don't need it. Italians aren't discriminated against. Just look at all the well-known ones.

A second-generation worker of Polish origin:

> Yes, I'm Polish. But I'm American first. I was born in this country, and I don't really give a shit about Poland. I've never been there and I don't know anyone there. Maybe with someone like John [a worker who came to the United States from Poland as a young boy] it's different. He was born there, and he still has relatives there, but this [America] is my country.

A second-generation worker of Irish origin:

> **Researcher:** What do you think about Bobby Sands [the first of a group of Irish Catholics imprisoned by the British to die on a hunger strike]?
>
> **Worker:** Well, we've got our own problems over here in America. There's too many problems over here to worry about what's going on over there [begins discussing, as an example, the recent assassination attempt on President Reagan and the problem of violence in America].
>
> **Researcher:** How important is being Irish?
>
> **Worker:** It's not really important. I don't really follow that stuff. Now my father was different. He was born there, in Dublin [as was his mother]. He used to hate the English. They did all kinds of bad things to him, like torture. Still, even with him at his club he had all kinds of Limey friends. Some

people take that stuff seriously but I don't. There's too many problems over here to worry about, like drugs [spends several minutes discussing the problem of heroin addiction among young people].

There are some workers who take ethnicity more seriously, but ethnic origin remains firmly subordinate to the category of being American. Consider these examples.

A worker in his early sixties:

Worker: Ethnic? Oh yes, it's important. The more you mix the stronger the result [he means genetically]. I'm German and WASP and Indian and Irish and Jewish! It's [ethnicity] important.

Researcher: But what are you?

Worker: Oh, I'm an American.

A worker in his late forties whose parents were born in Italy:

The ethnic thing? You know, it's mostly these young kids. They're third generation and they say they're Italian or Polish or Irish but they don't know anything [ethnic identity was not, however, especially pronounced among the younger workers at Imperium]. They don't know the history or anything. They don't know what they're talking about, and they never will.

With *us*, we were really first generation. My parents were born in Italy. We wanted to become American—"Americanization," you know. We had Italian organizations, but they were always called "Italian-American," and there was always a picture of Roosevelt.

Symbolic Ethnicity

Yet this account needs modifying. Certain events can temporarily raise ethnicity from a matter of indifference or minor importance to a more important plane. Usually these events concern the role of workers' countries of origin on the international scene. An example during my research was the possibility of a Soviet invasion of Poland. This triggered strong feelings among workers of Polish origin.

A second-generation worker in his early fifties:

Researcher: How important is being Polish?

Worker: Oh, it's important. If I was younger I'd be over there right now with my M15 [rifle] to fight the Russians. Sure I mean it. I'd fight for them [the Poles] against the Russians.

Researcher: So it's really important being Polish?

Worker: Sure, I learned Polish and Polish history at school [a parochial school in an ethnic parish].

Researcher: Do you belong to any Polish organizations?

Worker: Well, I used to. I was a member of the YPSO [Young Polish Social Organization].

Researcher: Which is more important, being Polish or American?

Worker: They're both important.

Researcher: And if there was a war between Poland and America who would you fight for?

Worker: Oh, America. Well, this is my country, this is where I was born. Anyway, I'd have to. They'd draft me.

A worker in his early fifties:

Researcher: You're Polish?

Worker: Yes, and I'm not half-Polish, I'm full Polish! Both my parents were born there. [Moves on to the topic of Solidarity and the upheavals in Poland] We have a song [recites in Polish, then translates], "There'll always be a Poland, Poland will be free."

Researcher: Which is more important, being Polish or being American?

Worker: Oh, being American. That's where you're born. That's why we always say "Polish-American," not "American-Polish."

Another example of the ability of a particular event to stir ethnic identity was, for Irish Catholics, the election of John F. Kennedy as president. Recall the worker of Irish origin quoted earlier, who saw his ethnicity as "not very important" and the fate of Bobby Sands and the Irish Catholic hunger strikers as of minor significance compared with what was going on in America. He was asked if it made any difference to him that the governor of New Jersey [Brendan Byrne] was Irish:

No, it doesn't. Now Kennedy made a difference because he was the president. That was a question of pride. But that was an exception. Otherwise it's the policies that are important.

For American Jews the equivalent subject that stirs ethnic identity is clearly the State of Israel and its perceived insecure position.

Herbert Gans has coined the term "symbolic ethnicity" to refer to such a situation. Once, ethnicity suffused the primary relations of new immigrants. They lived in ethnic communities, married within their ethnic groups, and worked in ethnic settings. But in later generations these primary relations have dwindled. As a result, ethnic activities are increasingly confined to rituals that are of secondary importance or trivial. And ethnic beliefs are no more than secondary or tertiary cosmologies, often limited to an *identification* as a particular ethnic. This identification (for instance, as Italian or Irish or Polish) has only minor consequences for behavior or beliefs, *except in special circumstances*. Examples of such special circumstances are Jews in relation to the politics of Israel, Poles in relation to the military presence of the USSR in Poland, and Irish in relation to the struggles of Catholics in the North of Ireland. This situation—a fairly accurate description of most Imperium workers— is what Gans calls "symbolic ethnicity." It is, he argues, generally characteristic of the third generation and beyond in America and is consistent with the melting pot theory.[5]

Recently some writers have taken issue with the melting pot theory of ethnicity. The argue that, albeit in new forms, ethnicity plays a vigorous and important role in the lives of second-, third-, and fourth-generation Americans.[6]

Clearly, my findings do not support such a view. There are two main explanations for this. First, most proponents of the "new ethnicity" cite a jumble of manifestations of ethnicity without seriously analyzing their meaning and significance or even separating rituals from beliefs. In this way they often present as major what is really of minor or trivial importance. Second, they tend to define ethnicity much more broadly than I do. Some define it so broadly that it becomes synonymous with "group identity" or "social diversity."[7] Not surprisingly, when ethnicity is defined this broadly it is "discovered" almost everywhere. But then the point of the debate in the United States becomes lost. For no one denies that America, like any complex society, is composed of numerous different groups. The important debate concerns the extent to which new immigrants and their cultures will be absorbed into American society. That is why I have defined "ethnicity" as attachment to a *foreign* culture. Such a definition captures what is distinctive about American history—the continual influx of immigrant (foreign) groups—and it bears centrally on the debate over the melting pot. Ethnicity in this sense is generally of secondary importance as a set of beliefs and a set of rituals.

15

National Holidays and Cults

The preceding discussion has laid the basis for analyzing national holidays and ceremonies. There are a number of such occasions. These include Independence Day, Thanksgiving, Memorial Day, Halloween, Christmas, Easter, New Year's Day, Election Day, the Super Bowl, the World Series, and the round of nationally televised sporting events. Some of these are marked by public holidays or parades, and some involve events broadcast on nationwide television. The main national occasions are:

January
New Year's Day
Rose Bowl
Super Bowl

February
Lincoln's Birthday
Washington's Birthday

March/April
Good Friday
Easter Sunday

May
Mother's Day
Memorial Day

June
Father's Day

July
Independence Day

September
Labor Day

October
Columbus Day
World Series
Halloween

November
Election Day
Veterans Day
Thanksgiving

December
Christmas

As I pointed out earlier, Durkheim argued that in many societies public events and ceremonies function to express and strengthen social solidarity—to celebrate and recreate common values and ideals. In such societies these reunions and ceremonies can be called "cults," for a cult is "A system of diverse rites, festivals and ceremonies which reappear periodically."[1]

Yet contemporary societies, as Durkheim saw them, lack consensus over values and ideals: "The old gods are growing old or already dead, and others are not yet born." The previous chapters explored the way that for Imperium workers the beliefs and actions associated with the old gods—religion and ethnicity—fall short of cosmologies and rituals. This chapter explores the way national occasions and ceremonies in America, drawing on the possible new gods as well as some of the old ones, fall short of cults.[2]

Almost all of these national occasions operate on two levels at the same time. There is the interpersonal setting in which participants experience them, and there is their public meaning. For instance, the public meaning of Thanksgiving concerns the first harvest of the Pilgrim settlers in America, and the public meaning of Christmas concerns the birth of Jesus and the arrival of Santa Claus. Their interpersonal settings are relations with family and sometimes with friends.

The Interpersonal Aspect of National Occasions

Consider first the interpersonal aspect of events such as Mother's Day and Father's Day, Thanksgiving, Christmas, and Halloween and the Super Bowl and World Series. These reflect four principles of how to live interpersonal life.

There is the principle of the nuclear family—husband, wife, and children as a cohesive emotional unit. This is a central component of most such occasions.

However, almost all also include kin relations beyond the nuclear group. Even Mother's Day and Father's Day involve grandparents as well as parents. And the chief ritelike activity of Thanksgiving, the ceremonial dinner centering on the turkey, usually includes a range of kin in addition to the nuclear group. The same is true of the Christmas meal. Thus the second principle sometimes represented on these occasions is the family in broader form, including older generations and more extended relations (such as in-laws and cousins).

Third, there is the principle of friends and friendship. For example, the Christmas ceremonial dinner focusing on relatives is preceded by celebrations that extend over a number a days and involve interaction with, and gift exchange between, friends as well as kin. And interaction with friends is an important part of New Year's Eve. Likewise, though the focus of Halloween is the nuclear family—especially the children—friends and neighbors also participate by giving small gifts, usually candy.

The fourth interpersonal principle often present on these occasions is a particular kind of friendship consisting of bonding on the basis of gender, men with men and women with women. For instance, masculinity and male bonding are reflected in the prominent role that spectator sports play in many of these events. An important part of Thanksgiving, Christmas, and New Year's Day is the televised football game, which thrusts male bonding into the heart of the interpersonal gathering. Indeed, via televised sport, masculinity intrudes on the nuclear family regularly, not just on special occasions.

An obvious problem now arises in considering these public ceremonies, in their interpersonal aspect, as cults. A cult is a dense set of rituals. A ritual draws people's attention to "objects of thought and feeling that are special, if not sacred." What then are the "objects of thought and feeling" to which these public occasions draw people's attention?

The difficulty is that such occasions involve a number of principles of how to live interpersonal life that are often, though not always, in conflict. This is the set of principles I earlier called a "contradictory cosmology." There is the conflict between the modern ideal of the nuclear family (husband, wife, and children as each other's closest friends) and competing principles—for the husband the principles of masculinity and male friendship (for instance, will husbands spend most of an extended holiday with the nuclear family or with male friends?), and for the children the principles of peer friendships (for instance, will adolescent children spend the holiday with the family group or with their peers?).

The addition of such gatherings of broader kin introduces another set of possible conflicts, between generations. There are the well-known disputes between parents and their adult children and children-in-law. In part the presence of an older generation at such gatherings reflects a younger generation's respect and concern for their forebears. But it is as likely to reflect unconcern or limited concern, or concern that is one-sided, not mutual. For these gatherings are often a device by which those who feel they should see more of their kin and perhaps even live with them, but who have no desire to do so, fulfill an obligation. They reflect a concern that is fictional, or rather they substitute a minor and circumscribed expenditure of time and effort for a major and continuous expenditure that the development of pensions and Social Security has often made less than mandatory.[3] (Kin relations tend to be fairly dense among Imperium workers, as among blue-collar workers in general, but that does not preclude conflict.)

Not only do these four principles of interpersonal life commonly conflict, the main ideas underlying the nuclear family—the dominant interpersonal principle on many of these occasions—are themselves confused and uncertain. The principle of sexual faithfulness within marriage is violated widely, if usually secretly. Marriage "until death us do part" is so commonly broken by divorce that it is unclear for how many people it remains a principle. The principle of patriarchy has been under increasing attack for a long time, more recently from a feminist movement that has nothing but scorn for two of its central dogmas, the idea that a woman's place is in the home and the idea that authority in the family should lie with the husband. And the principle of parental authority over children is subverted above all by the school system, but also by an array of government agencies that "police the family."[4]

Thus even national occasions whose interpersonal base is primarily the nuclear family may produce attitudes that are troubled and problematic. I cited a number of examples in discussing the married life of these workers (chap. 3). Larger occasions, such as Thanksgiving and Christmas, are nodal points for conflicts between these various models of interpersonal life, including that of the nuclear unit. As a result, many of their intended heroes are challenged, derided, or disregarded. Who, for instance, are the heroes of Thanksgiving. Is it the Pilgrims, the Indians, older

kin—especially grandparents—parents with young children, the children themselves, those who cook the meal (usually the women), those who finance it, or the
football players on the nationally televised game?

Because of such conflicts and unclarities, these occasions among Imperium
workers often trigger not only joy but also disputes, anger, frustration, indifference,
and boredom. They may bring together for celebration kin and friends who, during
most of the year, lead their separate lives. But the common sentiment such occasions
generate is in many cases thin and volatile, prone to lapse into dispute and medioc-
rity, then to reappear. Consider these examples of workers discussing their holiday,
illustrating some of the more frequent disputes.

A worker in his mid-twenties complained about conflicts between parents and
their adult children:

> How was my Thanksgiving? Don't ask! My father's parents are nuts.
> They don't like my mother's parents. Of course *they* think *we're* nuts,
> but really it's the other way around! Thank goodness it's only twice a
> year [he includes Christmas here].

A worker in his early fifties complained about the unwillingness of his siblings and
siblings-in-law to share equitably in the entertaining associated with Christmas:

> How was my Christmas? Well, we had it at our place again. So my wife
> had to do all the cooking, and that's not fair. The year before last we
> had it at our place, so this year I expected one of my sisters or sisters-
> in-law to offer, but they didn't. It got to halfway through December and
> no one had said anything, so finally my mother said she'd have it at her
> place, but she's old and it's too much work for her. So we said we'd
> have it at our place again, but it's not fair, it's a lot of work for my
> wife.

A worker in his mid-forties complained about the unruliness and untidiness of his
children:

> Thanksgiving? Well, I got very angry with my son and daughter. I came
> home in the morning [after working the night shift], and there were
> newspapers all over the house. The place was a terrible mess. I yelled at
> them. I've told them before but they don't listen. Then I was upset all
> day.

Another worker complained that his children used the house to entertain friends but
made little financial contribution:

> Christmas? Well, my house was like a hotel! The kids had their friends
> in and out all the time. I'm feeding half the kids in the neighborhood.
> And then they don't contribute nothing. Peter [his seventeen-year-old
> son] just quit his job [as a security guard]. And he says he doesn't want
> to work for a while. But I'm feeding him and his friends.

These occasions—the regular gatherings of the nuclear family during the week and over the weekend and the more extended gatherings on special days like Christmas and Thanksgiving—are clearly less than cults, for they often draw attention to interpersonal principles that are confused and mutually contradictory, a "contradictory cosmology." Events that for these reasons fall short of being cults can be called "contradictory cults."

One area of interpersonal life does contain a highly developed system of cultlike activities—sporting events. These recur regularly, and pinnacle occasions such as the World Series and the Super Bowl arouse high levels of enthusiasm and excitement. Sporting events constitute a highly developed series of activities.

Yet these are activities that celebrate above all masculinity and male friendship and competition, which are only one part of a fractured and contradictory cosmology composed of competing principles of how to live interpersonal life. (This changes when sporting events are between nations. See below.) This is why attempts to argue that sports is the "new religion" are unconvincing. A highly developed set of activities that are attached to one part only of a fractured cosmology can be called a "partial cult."[5]

Thus an important part of interpersonal life revolves around cults that are contradictory or partial.

The Public Meaning of National Occasions

Consider now the *public meaning* of these occasions. For Durkheim successful national rituals and cults draw people's attention to those values and institutions they share as members of a society. In that case the public meaning of these national occasions in America could be expected to bear centrally on people's view of American politics and their position in the class structure. For it is through such views that people understand their relation to other Americans. Moreover, national survey data suggest that interest in politics and political issues remains high and widespread in America. Despite strong mistrust of politicians and the current political process, most Americans maintain a keen interest in politics. Finally, in the West there is a long tradition of viewing politics as the arena in which members of a society can express the values and goals they share. As Sheldon Wolin put it:

> Throughout the long development of the Western tradition of political thought, there has been a recurrent tendency to identify what is political with what is general to a society. The inclusiveness of political society, for example, has always been contrasted with the parochialisms of family, class, local community, and sect. Again, the general responsibility for the welfare of the whole society has been consistently regarded as the special function of the political order. . . . Finally, political authority has been defined as the authority representing the generality of society and speaking in its name.[6]

Yet, on the contrary, one of the most striking features of these national occasions in America is the extent to which they skirt beliefs about politics and the class structure of America. They do this in two main ways. Some move away from or avoid the sociopolitical and refer to other areas such as interpersonal relations or life after death. This process can be called "apoliticization." Others focus on sociopolitical beliefs, but on ones like ethnicity or a distant nationalism that are secondary and tertiary, not primary. This movement from primary beliefs to secondary and tertiary beliefs is a movement from the more to the less important. As such it can be called a tendency to "trivialize." These two processes, apoliticization and trivialization, are often combined. For example, a movement away from politics into other areas in many cases goes along with a tendency to treat these other areas in a trivial manner.

Consider Halloween as a prime example of an occasion whose public meaning is apolitical and trivial. This is a night when witches, goblins, and spirits are supposedly at large. Children, dressed in costumes that often represent ghouls of various kinds, go to houses and stores demanding small gifts, usually candy, and carrying out, or threatening, minor vandalism against the property of those who do not comply.

The public meaning of Halloween is based on beliefs that hardly anyone accepts as true or relevant. They are tertiary beliefs. Indeed, so vague and insubstantial are the beliefs about spirits that it is not even clear what area they refer to—the sociopolitical world, interpersonal relations, physical health, or life after death. What is clear is that these are beliefs to which little or no credence is attached, for otherwise no one would permit children outdoors at such a dangerous time. Halloween is an occasion whose public meaning is obviously trivial.

Halloween is, of course, a minor public event. Christmas is the pinnacle of the year, at least measured by the money people spend on it. Christmas obviously is not centrally about politics. In part it concerns Santa Claus, a trivial theme for very young children. Christmas also has a religious meaning, which divides into two components. There is the birth of Christ, an event that is much less important in Christian theology than his death and resurrection (Easter). And Christmas is also about certain unobjectionable themes concerning interpersonal behavior, or politics at the most abstract level, such as joy, fellowship, love, peace, and world brotherhood. These themes are very spongy and diffuse, as Katherine Richards, the main historian of Christmas in America, has pointed out.[7]

There is another group of national occasions, of great interest, that are less trivial. They center on the concepts of America and Americans. These events include Independence Day, Memorial Day, Veterans Day, Thanksgiving, and international sporting contests, especially the summer and winter Olympic Games. They are less trivial, for the identity as an American is one of the three main social identities to which workers adhere. It is for them and for most Americans a part of their primary sociopolitical cosmology.

Yet such rituals face two related problems. First, attached to the idea of America is much positive sentiment but attached to politicians, America's current leaders, is as much negative sentiment. Second, there are a number of issues over which Americans are deeply divided. Most obvious is the racial division between black and white that pervades the residential setting as well as other spheres. Also important is the sectional division between North and South, reflecting the bitterness and resentment that lingers from the Civil War. Thus, though almost all Americans have an affection for and allegiance to America, they are deeply divided in these and other ways over the kind of place they would like it to be.[8]

The problem for these rituals with a nationalistic component is how to tap the positive sentiment associated with the idea of America without also tapping, and being swamped by, the negative sentiment associated with America's leaders (politicians) and with diverse notions of what America should be like. How can one draw attention to the idea of America without also drawing attention to its current leaders and their policies?

Occasions such as Independence Day, Thanksgiving, and Memorial Day illustrate a number of solutions, based first on the principle of separating "America" from its current leaders (politicians) and second on the principle of not drawing attention to the issues over which Americans are divided. Such solutions can be called "separation devices."

Historical time is a common separation device. Thus the "public meaning" of Thanksgiving and Independence Day focuses on early events in American history. A worker in his mid-fifties explained the meaning of Thanksgiving. His explanation is typical of the way it is understood by other workers and most Americans. The main ingredients are the story of the Pilgrims and their relations with the Indians:

> What is Thanksgiving? It's giving thanks! The Indians helped the first settlers. They gave them turkey and fruits and taught them how to plant corn.

The truth about Thanksgiving is quite different. As an annual national holiday it dates from the Civil War and especially the desire of Presidents Lincoln and Andrew Johnson to publicly mark the victories of the Union, notably the battle of Gettysburg.[9] There is no study of the process by which Thanksgiving moved backward in time, from a celebration of Union victory to a celebration of the Pilgrims. But clearly the Civil War, in contrast to earlier American history, is enormously divisive and controversial. Thanksgiving, then, also illustrates a second separation device. Not only does it make use of historical time, shifting back from the Civil War to the earliest days of white colonization, but its meaning has been changed from a topic that is controversial and divisive (the Civil War) to a topic that is not (the Pilgrims). This second separation device can be called a *tendency to avoid the controversial*.

Now consider Memorial Day. This probably originated during the Civil War, with southern women placing flowers on the graves of their war dead. Nowadays, of those who attribute ritual significance to Memorial Day some see it as a time to show respect to Americans who have died in war in general rather than in the Civil War. And as many, if not more, of those who attribute ritual significance to Memorial Day some see it as a time to honor dead kin and friends regardless of whether they were killed in war. As one worker put it:

> Memorial Day? It's to honor the dead.

For these people Memorial Day has to do with any dead person for whom they had some concern.

Thus Memorial Day illustrates the second separation device whereby an event that is about a politically controversial topic (the Civil War) becomes an event about a politically less controversial topic (dying for one's country). But it also illustrates a third separation device whereby an event that concerns the political world becomes an event about *another area*, in this case death and its possible aftermath.

A fourth separation device is *abstraction*. The turkey symbolizes Thanksgiving (a giant turkey filled with helium floats at the head of the Macy's parade), and the American flag, commonest national symbol of all, stands for America.

The tendency to avoid serious sociopolitical issues and to trivialize on so many national occasions is clear from an analysis of parades. A number of occasions in America are marked by parades. On the local level, individual towns organize these. In the region I studied, most limit themselves to one or two a year, on a particular day and theme (such as Halloween or Christmas or Independence Day or Memorial Day.) Large older cities such as New York or Newark may have several parades a year. Two groups make up the heart of a typical parade, regardless of its ostensible theme. There are school marching bands, and there are representatives of the forces of safety and order, especially police, fire trucks, and volunteer ambulance groups in a celebratory rather than working capacity. In the audience children predominate, often with their parents.

It is the prominent, if not central, role that children play in most parades, both as participants and as spectators, that is so striking . For in modern society the presence of children signals a lack of seriousness, a lack of importance. The world of children has to do with less momentous events than the world of adults.[10] As a result, for many workers mentioning "parade" triggers the idea of entertainment for children.

A worker in his late forties:

> Parades? Yes, I went to parades when I was a kid. On Staten Island we had all kinds of parades. They still do, but I wouldn't go. They're for kids.
> Memorial Day parade? Yes, they have that [on Staten Island]. I loved those parades when I was a kid. I remember sitting on my brother's shoulder. Of course I hadn't the faintest idea what they meant. Who cares!
> I'll tell you, the best parade you'll ever see is in Disney World. They have an electric parade in the evening that goes all the way through Disney World. It's fantastic. They have all those animals in the parade, Mickey Mouse and Minnie Mouse and the elephant. I went last year and this year, and next year I'll probably go and take my nephew.

A worker in his mid-fifties:

> Parades? They're for kids. You know, my niece was in a Halloween parade a few years ago, and she was elected queen of the parade.
> Memorial Day parade? Well, it used to be taken seriously, but not now, unfortunately.

Plate 33. Mickey Mouse leads the annual nationally televised Macy's Thanksgiving Parade, accompanied by a turkey and a flying creature, reflecting the tendency of national rituals to move toward the trivial and the apolitical.

Television raises certain parades to the national level. These include, from New York City, the Macy's Thanksgiving Parade and the Saint Patrick's Day Parade and, from Pasadena, California, the New Year's Day Rose Parade that precedes the Rose Bowl football game.

The floats in these parades reflect the tendency toward triviality, toward themes that concern secondary cosmologies and, more often, tertiary beliefs. Thus the Macy's and Rose Parade floats are dominated by tertiary themes such as Walt Disney characters (for instance, Mickey Mouse and Donald Duck), figures from children's television (such as Kermit the frog, Popeye, and the Lone Ranger and Tonto), comic strip characters (such as Snoopy), themes and figures from fairy tales and mythology (such as Mother Goose, Merlin and a dragon, Snow White and the seven dwarfs, the Loch Ness monster), musical shows, topics from ancient history (for instance, Cleopatra or Roman gladiators), and animals (giraffes, lions, tigers, elephants, and real horses). In addition to such tertiary fragments there is a sprinkling of primary themes relating to the concept of America, carefully separated by devices such as time or abstractness from America's current leaders. These include the giant floating turkey that leads the Macy's parade, cowboys and Indians, George Washington, Pilgrims and "multiethnic" floats containing a variety of American ethnic and racial groups and illustrating the "melting pot" idea.

The various separation devices I have pointed out protect the positive sentiment associated with America from the negative sentiment associated with its leaders and with divisions over what kind of place America should be. But there is a price, for all these devices reduce the current relevance of a ritual and therefore the energy and enthusiasm it arouses. Consider the use of historical time. It is hard to generate much enthusiasm over an event such as Independence that happened so long ago and celebrates a victory over the country that in the twentieth century has been America's closest military ally. Thanksgiving is hardly more exciting, for it celebrates an act of kindness toward the Pilgrims by Indians, a group now viewed either with embarrassment (they were, after all, mostly wiped out by later Americans) or with lingering hostility.

As a result, many of these national rituals have a serious problem in generating enthusiasm. For instance, most Imperium workers attribute little or no ceremonial significance to Memorial Day, viewing it as the start of the summer season and a three-day weekend for extended recreation such as visits to family and friends or trips to the beach. Consider the attitude of one worker. He is a veteran of World War II and has a flagpole outside his house on which he sometimes displays the American flag. But his interest in the local (Piscataway) Memorial Day parade is slight. To the extent that it evokes his war years he feels it is an anachronism, for being a veteran is no longer of much value.

> I'm not a member of a veterans' organization. They don't do nothing for you. They're just drinking groups.

The part of Memorial Day that evokes the dead he views with skepticism:

> They [veterans' organizations] put a flag on your grave when you're gone. What do I need that for! When I'm gone they can put shit over me for all I care!

On Memorial Day he was planning a barbecue with his wife and son. The rest of the holiday weekend he intended to spend painting his house.

National rituals that are apoliticized and trivialized skirt serious views about politics and society at the cost of making themselves less pertinent to people's real concerns and interests. As a result they often have difficulty arousing enough enthusiasm to sustain them. Consider the lament of the organizer of the Linden Halloween parade. He was having trouble getting teachers and students to decorate enough floats to make the parade substantial. As he complained to a meeting of the Linden recreation board ten days before Halloween:

> I'm at the point where I'm having to beg. We all know the bottom line is how much pressure the teacher puts on the kids [to decorate floats]. I'm having to beg teachers, and we shouldn't have to. New York and the other cities have parades. The Halloween parade is the only thing we've got. It's what puts Linden on the map.

The presence of the forces of order and safety in most local parades also underlines the difficulty they face in sustaining enthusiasm and interest. For the point about the town's police and fire departments is that they are quasi-captive. Their participation is almost mandatory. In a way the same is true of school bands, for students' participation is less than totally free (usually it falls midway between voluntary and manadatory).

There is an important exception to the tendency of most public occasions to be trivialized and apoliticized and thus to generate little enthusiasm. Certain international sporting events, especially the Olympic Games, are notable for the excitement and energy they can trigger. This is due to their use of a fifth separation device. During such events the athletes temporarily replace politicians as the nation's leaders. They become, for the duration of the event, the representatives of America.

I pointed out earlier that normal sporting events arouse considerable energy, but that it is harnessed only indirectly or not at all to workers' sociopolitical cosmology via the emphasis on masculinity and competition. This changes when sporting encounters are between nation-states. The reason these trigger such emotion is that here the energy of sporting involvement and a positive attitude toward athletes are combined with an aspect of workers' primary belief system, nationalism. At the same time, the emotion of nationalism is not blunted by popular dislike of politicians, the nations actual leaders, for during the sporting event the leaders or symbols of the nation are the athletes themselves. Further, the event can become a symbolic encounter with real and current adversaries, most obviously the Soviet Union, rather than with anachronistic adversaries like Britain.

Sporting competition between nations does indicate the power of nationalism among ordinary citizens. As one writer on the Olympic Games commented: "The 'whole United States' understands itself to be taking on other whole nations. Our most consensual national symbols are arrayed on the playing fields of each 'New Olympia': flag, anthem, initials, uniforms."[11] Yet the heights of emotion such events can stimulate are possible in America only because they are sporting events, not real contests, in which national leaders are athletes, not politicians.

The tendency of most public rituals to avoid people's main beliefs about politics and society, their primary sociopolitical cosmology, is underlined by what happens when they fail to achieve this avoidance. To the extent that primary beliefs about politics and society stray into these rituals, they tend to be contaminants. They dampen, and even turn negative, what positive sentiment is attached to the rituals. For example, some of the positive sentiment associated with Thanksgiving and Christmas is diminished and reversed by the perception that these are occasions when big business "cleans up" at the expense of the consumer. Such is the meaning of complaints about the commercialization of Christmas and Thanksgiving. Consider a worker in his early fifties:

Oh yes, there are Thanksgiving parades. The stores get together, Macy's, Gimbels, Bamberger's, and organize parades. And at the end Father Christmas arrives. It's like the beginning of Christmas. [With disgust] And then the stores get together and raise the prices and everything costs twice as much as in April or May.

Or another worker, in his early forties. His wife was discussing her Christmas shopping. He cautioned her:

> Hey, let's not go crazy. The only people who gain from Christmas are the store owners. They get all the money!

In 1939 Franklin Roosevelt moved Thanksgiving forward to the third Thursday in November and announced that the next year he would move it to the second Thursday. His aim, openly stated, was to help business. If Thanksgiving came earlier people would have longer to save and therefore have more to spend at Christmas. This intrusion on Thanksgiving for business-related motives met a storm of protest at the time, and it failed. Several workers recall the episode with resentment. As one put it:

> [With disgust] Roosevelt tried to change Thanksgiving from the fourth to the third Thursday of the month so the stores could make more money at Christmas.

Voting

Voting is one of the most revealing national rituals of all, for unlike most of the others it does relate centrally to people's primary sociopolitical cosmology. It is about politics and power in America. Yet Imperium workers typically approach the act of voting with at best moderate expectations, and in many cases with indifference, skepticism, or disgust.

It is worth analyzing the meaning of voting in more detail, for it casts light on the texture of political life in America and on the nature of modern rituals. In his study of symbolism in politics Murray Edelman stressed the importance of elections as the central political ritual in contemporary society. Elections, he argued, "give people a chance to express discontents and enthusiasms, to enjoy a sense of involvement." And they draw attention to the "importance and apparent reasonableness of accepting the public policies that are adopted." But, he maintained, elections could not serve this vital social function if "the common belief in direct popular control over governmental policy through elections were to be widely questioned."[12]

Yet the views of Imperium workers cast doubt on the existence of any such "common belief in direct popular control over governmental policy through elections." Further, as I pointed out in chapter 9, most of the electorate are just as skeptical, believing the government is run for the benefit of special interests rather than for the people. Imperium workers do not believe that when they vote they are in a meaningful sense choosing leaders (the "leadership theory" of elections), for the candidates are almost all equally defective in character. Nor do they believe they are setting policy (the "mandate theory"), for most politicians in office disregard the programs on which they were elected.

Then why do they vote? A third of workers do not vote at all (see table 28). Of this group almost half abstain out of principle. They are boycotting a political process that they believe serves only to advance individual politicians and the power groups who control them. One of these principled nonvoters, a worker in his late twenties, explained why he was not taking part in the 1977 election for governor:

> I ain't interested in voting. I never voted. Those politicians are all on the take. I won't vote unless it [disaster] comes right up to my front door. Otherwise, screw'em.
>   I live across the road from the mayor. They came to ask me to vote last year. I told 'em to shove it up their ass. Bateman, Byrne [the main candidates for governor], they're all the same.[13]

But most of these workers both vote and believe that politicians typically take graft and break their election promises. Often they vote because, however skeptical they may be, they believe that occasionally the electorate has an impact. According to this theory, every so often among the many incumbents and contenders a worthy prospect can be found or an electoral promise is made good. This view, based on a slim hope that perhaps this time things will be different, is a major factor accounting for men's continuing to visit the polls. For them voting is like playing the lottery or giving up whiskey for Lent—it is unlikely to pay off, but you never know. A worker in his forties reconciled the paradox of both believing politicians to be hopelessly corrupt and continuing to vote in the following way:

> Occasionally there's an honest one, maybe one in a hundred.

A second reason for voting stems from the belief that the longer politicians are in office the more corrupt they become. Thus, turning out the incumbent is a way of limiting the degree and depth of damage. A process worker in his mid-forties explained why, despite his beliefs about politicians, he still voted:

> Well, let's say you're in there [political office] taking $100,000 graft a year, and there's another guy taking $600,000 graft, you have to vote to get the other guy out. I vote just to get the guy out, because they get corrupter and corrupter the longer they're in.

Sometimes voting is a form of revenge, of retaliating against a politician whose actions have caused special anger and exasperation. Usually little hope is seen of changing the disliked policy, but by helping to elect an incumbent's opponent a voter can at least make a modest contribution to his enemy's downfall. Consider, for example, a warehouse worker in his mid-fifties. He usually had voted in presidential elections, until now always for the Democrat. But just before the 1977 election for governor he was eagerly looking forward to casting his first-ever Republican vote:

> Who am I voting for? I'll tell you who I ain't voting for, that son-of-a-bitch Byrne, even though [like the speaker] he's an Irishman. I never

did like him. He lied to us [a reference to Byrne's introducing a state
income tax for which, in his first election campaign, he had said he fore-
saw no need]. I'm getting my wife and daughter and son, and the four
of us are going to vote for the Republican. I'll give him a try, even
though I'm a Democrat. If he turns out to be no good I can always
switch around next time. They're all the same, politicians.
　　[A few days after the election, which Byrne won] Agh! I'm not
going to vote anymore, fuck'em!

Sometimes workers believe the forces with which a particular candidate is allied
are beneficial to their interests. They do not expect honest politics, but they have an
idea that the brand of dishonesty likely to be practiced will be to their advantage. Or
they fear a newcomer might ally with forces from which they (the voters) have
something to lose. A mechanic in his mid-fifties, a registered Democrat, had voted
every year since 1945:

Sure, politicians are all corrupt. [Smiles] Well, some of them are honest,
just a few, not many. If I think a guy will help me, I vote for him.

Some workers vote because they feel that failure to do so will strengthen the
forces that wish to subvert the republican form of government. Politics in the United
States might be thoroughly corrupt, but a dictatorship would be worse, for it would
mean the demise of freedom as well as of even the possibility of democracy. For
instance, a batch worker in his mid-twenties:

Politicians are all the same. They're all on the take. You can't trust any
of them.
　　Yes, I voted in the election [the 1977 election for governor]. Why?
You have to vote, otherwise you lose your freedom. If you don't vote,
you'll soon have a dictatorship.

Voting, the central act in the legitimating process of Western democracies, does
not have for these workers the meaning officially assigned to it. Those who vote do so
for a number of reasons, but rarely with the view that they are "exercising direct,
popular control over governmental policy." And they typically approach voting with
low expectations or even distaste rather than with enthusiasm. For many of them,
voting is a ritual that is at best secondary, and more often empty, negative, or black.
　　Survey data suggest that, despite wide mistrust of government and skepticism
about the likelihood of politicians' responding to popular desires, many people have
not abandoned the belief that they ought to vote and that their vote has an impact.[14]
But the nature of the impact voters have in mind needs more investigation. In the
1940s and 1950s studies of voting behavior argued that, in terms of their knowledge
of political issues and attentiveness to the arguments of the candidates for office,
many members of the electorate fall far short of the expectations of democracy.[15] The
case of Imperium workers, and survey data, suggests that in the eyes of many voters
so do their elected leaders.

Conclusion

The basic shape of national holidays and cults in America is no accident, but the uneasy result of the nature of popular beliefs. There is widespread mistrust of politicians, and there are deep disagreements among citizens over social and political issues. The extent of such mistrust varies over time, as do many of the issues over which people disagree. Yet mistrust and lack of consensus are persistent features of the American scene.

In such a context national rituals that draw attention to current politics risk triggering strong negative feelings and degenerating into black rituals, as the case of voting illustrates. This is why most national rituals distance themselves from current political and social issues. The result is three main types of cults. There are the elaborate "partial cults" that revolve around sporting events such as football and baseball games and that celebrate above all masculinity and competition. There are "trivialized cults" such as Halloween and much of Christmas. And there are "politically anesthetized cults" such as Thanksgiving, Memorial Day, and Independence Day. The latter are about "America," but in a distant sense.

The extent to which these occasions fall short should not be exaggerated. On the personal level a holiday like Thanksgiving serves, to some degree, to reunite family members who may seldom meet during the year. International sporting events, above all the Olympic Games, do reinforce a sense of national identity.

Yet in general these national occasions form a public culture that is widely *shared* by Americans regardless of occupation, race, or income but that serves in only a minor way to *integrate*. The themes of these holidays tend to represent not the highest levels of social and political awareness among Americans, but rather the social and political lowest common denominator. It reflects the extent to which citizens disagree over social and political issues that the motifs they can agree to celebrate tend to be so trivial and devoid of current political import.

16

Conclusion: Class and Politics in America

In terms of method, the main implication of this book is the need to consider every aspect of blue-collar life. Much of the confusion over the nature of the working class, and over whether it is middle class, results from viewing a part of the picture as the whole.

Watching many blue-collar workers (like many other Americans) become aroused by the spectacle of American hostages held in Iran or American athletes competing in the Olympic Games, it is easy to stress an image of a nationalist worker while forgetting how quickly nationalism can turn into populism and how easily the ardor that fueled support of American hostages or athletes can change to anger at politicians who exploit the "American people." It is easy to stress this populism while overlooking the existence of another widespread class consciousness based on position in the system of production and revolving around the concept of the working man. And it is easy to stress this concept of the working man without noticing that workers have a third class identity that refers to life outside the workplace and implies that, in choice of where and how to live and in leisure pursuits and marital relations, the class structure has some fluidity. Finally, it is easy to notice that most blue-collar workers consider their position in the class structure a result of their own individual efforts and talents, without also noticing that they do have a clear idea of that class structure, based on the identities I have outlined.

Still, viewing a part of the picture as the whole is not the only reason for the coexistence of so many images of the working class. There are real differences between certain populations of blue-collar workers. Thus it is important to remember the specific features of the workers who formed the basis of this study. They are not in poorly paid blue-collar jobs, nor are they unemployed. They are almost all white, they are all male, and for the most part they are second and third generation. And they live in the Northeast, not the South or West. Care should be taken when generalizing from workers at Imperium to others who differ along these dimensions.

A final reason for the coexistence of so many images of the working class is confusion over the meaning of the claim that blue-collar workers are middle class, around which so much of the debate over the modern working class has revolved. This claim contains two main questions, which should be separated. First, how far do the lives and beliefs of blue-collar workers overlap with those of the upper- and lower-white-collar sectors (the "middle class")? Second, how far are blue-collar workers integrated into, or alienated from, American society? In this concluding chapter I will draw together the main answers I have suggested to these two questions and discuss their implications.

Consider the first question. It is *at work* that the clearest differences exist between blue- and white-collar occupations. Jobs classified as blue collar tend to manifest several of a cluster of features. Even in automated plants, they often involve work that is physical and that may be dirty and dangerous. That is why workers usually wear special protective clothing (sometimes "blue," sometimes gray or green or brown). Blue-collar jobs often have other features. They tend to be closely supervised, to offer limited chances of upward mobility at work, to be mostly repetitive, and to be associated with the production or maintenance of a product.

These points should all be qualified. Some blue-collar jobs are neither physical, dirty, nor dangerous (such as, at Imperium, the job of recording the weight of tank cars), though such clean jobs often can be obtained only by first spending time in other jobs. Some blue-collar employees are hard to supervise (for instance, truckers). Some blue-collar workers produce services, not products (such as drivers of trains, trucks, or buses). And some blue-collar jobs are neither repetitive nor uninteresting (such as much maintenance work).

Further, lower-white-collar jobs tend to resemble blue-collar jobs in some respects. They are often routine and closely supervised and may offer limited chances for upward mobility. There are also overlaps between upper- and lower-white-collar employees (for instance, both tend to work in "clean" officelike settings), but not blue-collar employees. Finally, there are certain broad similarities between all these groups. Few control the means of production, and most are formally subject to the rules of the organizations that employ them. And the degree to which even many upper-white-collar jobs are interesting or offer chances for upward mobility should not be exaggerated.

Nevertheless, most of the jobs classified as blue collar do tend to have several of a cluster of features that are distinctive. This is underlined by the fact that in work settings that have a variety of employees, management mostly has little difficulty deciding which workers should be classified as blue collar, be assigned to distinct work areas, and wear special work clothes, though some groups on the margin may be hard to classify. The result is that males who occupy such jobs tend to have a specific form of class consciousness based on the concept of the working man. This class consciousness takes account both of what is distinctive about blue-collar jobs and of some of the ways they may overlap with lower- and upper-white collar positions. And among Imperium workers this class consciousness is more widespread than has been realized even by survey researchers eager to find class consciousness, for the concept of the working man is understood and used by almost all these blue-collar workers. And if this is true of workers in the better-paid and more highly automated jobs found at Imperium, then it is likely to be true of many blue-collar workers in less favorable circumstances. Thus the concept of the working man suggests an important caveat to the view that the "significance of class in America is declining."

It is *outside work* that the distinctions between these occupational groups are less clear. Differences coexist with important similarities. Let us consider first the differences.

Blue-collar workers typically have less education than upper-white-collar employees, and they typically have jobs, not careers. This may affect their leisure lives and marital relations. Having a job rather than a career means that blue-collar workers are less likely than some upper-white-collar workers to blur the distinction between work and leisure or to subordinate friendships and other personal relations to the quest for upward mobility. A modest level of education is associated with little interest in "high culture" (for instance, classical music, ballet, serious literature), although the interest of most educated people in these pursuits should not be exaggerated. And a modest level of education may produce unease in the company of highly educated people, marital tension if men's wives have white-collar jobs—especially good ones—some difficulty in following the education of children, and a tendency to encourage children to obey instructions at home and in school rather than to be "self-directed."

Further, the class structure has some tendency to reproduce and reinforce itself. By comparison with upper-white-collar workers, blue-collar workers are more likely to have blue-collar friends and blue-collar fathers, and their sons are more likely to enter blue-collar jobs. Finally, workers in pre–World War II industrial suburbs still live in occupational communities, often with large numbers of fellow workers (though highways and the growth of government and company welfare and insurance programs have undermined an important part of the solidarity such communities once manifested).

If there is a working-class culture outside the workplace, then these are its ingredients. Yet some of them, such as a modest level of education or an uninteresting job, extend in a systematic way to lower-white-collar workers and may also be present among some upper-white-collar employees.

Further, there are various ways the residential situation, marital relations, and leisure lives of blue-collar workers clearly overlap with those of many of the upper-white-collar sector. There is the income overlap, which makes it possible for better-paid blue-collar workers to compete with many white-collar employees in the housing market, to purchase similar consumer goods, and to enjoy a comparable leisure life. In modern America there are no "working-class" cars, washing machines, video recorders, or even, with some exceptions concentrated on the young, styles of dress. In an urban department store or suburban shopping mall it is hard to know if a customer has a blue- or white-collar occupation.

Further, forces besides occupation and income affect life outside work. Consider gender differences. Certain sports such as football, baseball, and boxing clearly attract more men than women (though other sports such as jogging or tennis are less dominated by males). And most married women, rather than their husbands, remain responsible for the bulk of the housework and child care. Or consider age and the life cycle. The central place of rock music in the lives of many young people is at least as striking as are variations in musical taste by social class. So is the fact that children consume large amounts of their parents' spare time. Finally, there is race. Much of residential America is clearly divided into areas for blacks and areas for whites.

This is a complex picture. Outside the workplace, forces that could be said to constitute a "working-class" culture interpenetrate with forces that make for important overlaps between blue-collar workers and the upper-white-collar sector. However, the case of Imperium suggests that many blue-collar workers do not see themselves as basically part of a working-class culture when away from their jobs. They are aware of their modest level of education and somewhat low-status jobs. But they do not consider their leisure, family, or residential lives distinctly working class. On the contrary, most see life outside work as an arena where they can escape the humiliations and constraints of the factory. This attitude is reflected in a class identity, based on the concepts of being "middle class" or "lower middle class," that refers to life outside the workplace and implies overlaps between themselves and others of comparable income, life-style, and material possessions.

Above all, it is apparent to almost all Imperium workers that differences between collar colors are far more blurred outside the workplace. Life away from the job certainly has constraints, but it does not systematically separate blue-collar workers into an occupational group. There is nothing in their leisure or marital lives comparable to the obligation to wear distinct work clothes, to engage in distinct tasks, in a distinct area, under a distinct supervisor.

The different impact of education in the two spheres of workers' lives underlines this. To an outsider, most blue-collar workers simply lack education. But to Imperium workers there is an important distinction between the way this affects their lives at and outside the workplace. There is nothing but their inclination to stop them from listening to classical music, attending the ballet, or purchasing serious literature. By contrast, their modest education presents an impassable barrier between blue-collar and most upper-white-collar jobs.

The distinction between how workers see their lives away from their jobs and how others see them is crucial. Outsiders may stress that the houses of workers in post–World War II suburbs were built by developers on a quarter or a fifth of an acre. Imperium workers also notice that these are the houses in which live many of the less-well-paid upper-white-collar sector. Outsiders may stress the difficulties some men have communicating with their wives. Imperium workers also notice they are not the only ones who may have troubles in the quest for the "modern intimate marriage." Outsiders may stress that many men drink in taverns with other workers. Imperium workers also know that when they go for an evening out the restaurant customers are often an occupational mixture.

People who stress the distinct nature of working-class life often argue that similar activities can have different meanings. Thus blue-collar workers may see the same movie as a lawyer or an engineer but, because of differences in education or occupation, not necessarily interpret it in the same way. They may eat in the same restaurant but talk about different topics over dinner. In this sense, what appear to be the same activities are really different.

This may be partially true, but the case of Imperium workers suggests the same argument operates in reverse. If blue-collar workers do not see these activities as different, then for the purposes of class consciousness they are not different. Without understanding this, as well as the importance better-paid blue-collar workers attach to their income level, it is not possible to see why they often view their lives outside the workplace as at least approaching middle class.

American society operates on a third level—that of the *public political and national culture*. The framework for this national culture consists of two components. There are the activities and main institutions of the federal government—Congress, the executive branch, and the Supreme Court. And there are the mostly festive national events such as Thanksgiving, Memorial Day, Independence Day, the Super Bowl, and the World Series. In their attitude toward this third level too there is much overlap (though also some differences) between blue- and white-collar employees. This level gives rise to a third image blue-collar workers have of their position in the class structure—an image based on nationalism and populism.

Consider, for instance, presidential elections. There are issues to which, as I have argued, Imperium workers will respond as "working men." These include the level of unemployment, questions of occupational safety, measures to restrict employers' ability to move plants to other locations, and measures to limit foreign competition for the products workers make. However, for many other issues that currently occupy the national political scene, racial, gender, age, income, or regional differences among the electorate are more important than differences of occupation. And to many issues Imperium workers respond as "middle class" (or one level below middle class), or as "Americans," rather than as working men (they may, of course, respond with a combination of these identities).

Or consider national holidays. Attitudes toward these are widely shared. Differences of occupation (or even education) are not prominent when Americans celebrate holidays such as Thanksgiving or Christmas and observe (actually mostly ignore) the ceremonial significance of occasions such as Memorial Day or Independence Day. And such differences as exist concern other items, for instance age or gender, as much as social class. Thus sporting occasions such as football, which increasingly penetrates Thanksgiving, Christmas, and New Year's Day, clearly interest men more often than women.

The importance of these three levels—the workplace, life outside (place of residence, leisure and marital relations), and the federal and national level—and the existence of a powerful social identity associated with each level—the concept of the working man, of being middle or lower middle class, and of being an American—solves one of the most puzzling problems raised by studies of the American working class. It explains why those researchers who have found a class-conscious proletariat, and those who have found a working class sufficiently mobile to see themselves as middle class and sufficiently attached to America to respond to certain national symbols and appeals, have both been able to produce enough evidence to sustain their models. Each theory contains part of the truth, but each needs the other for a fully accurate picture.

Sociologists like to discover and explain variance. I found plenty of variance in this study, but none when it came to the *holding* of these three identities. Many workers insisted that ethnicity or religion was unimportant to them, but I could not discover any who lacked a meaningful concept of themselves as working men, as middle class (or somewhat lower), and as Americans. There is variation in the content workers give to each identity, which I have described, but no case of a worker who did not subscribe to each identity. Aware that this lack of variance is unusual, if not a sociological scandal, I tried hard to find counter instances, but without success. In the chapters where I outlined my findings on these identities I tended to refer to "almost all" or "the overwhelming majority." This was not because I found workers who did not hold each identity, but because I could not claim to have talked to every worker about these questions. I usually stopped when I had talked with 75 percent, for my method of research was laborious and time consuming.

Still, there is outside support for my findings. First, sociologists who ask blue-collar workers about the meaning of "class" discover, as I did, that almost all produce an image based on income level and material standard of living. Second, it is obvious that the concept of an "American" is widely held, though I have suggested that its sociological and political significance has not been paid the attention it deserves. Third, there is much scattered evidence that points to the importance of the concept of the working man among male blue-collar workers (though not necessarily confined to them).

It is not surprising that these three identities are so widely held among the workers I studied, for each reflects an essential facet of their lives. This points to the relevance of a certain kind of "materialist" approach to ideology in advanced capitalism. The reluctance in certain circles to acknowledge that life outside the workplace can allow better-paid blue-collar workers some fluidity in the class struc-ture, and can generate a class identity that reflects this, has led to the popularity of Gramsci's concept of the "hegemony of ruling-class ideas" as an alternative to materialism. After all, if life at work is the sole source of "real" consciousness, then other forms must result from the imposition on workers of alien or "ruling-class" ideas.[1] But the case of Imperium workers suggests that Marxists may have aban-doned materialism too easily, or at least not applied it in as thorough a manner as they should have. Position at work is only *one* of the material spheres that influence ideology. The other spheres are life outside the workplace and life as a "citizen" of a nation-state.[2]

This is not to say that the views of Imperium workers on politics and social class are simply determined by the material base of their lives. Important parts of their outlook cannot be explained in this way. But it is to suggest that the work setting, the setting outside the workplace, and the federal government each provides a separate framework for their attitude toward the social structure.

We can now turn to the second question with which this book is concerned. How far is the blue-collar working class in America integrated into society or alienated from it?

Two opposing, and extreme, images have dominated discussion of this question. There is the classic Marxist model of the totally alienated and oppressed proletariat.

And there is the model of contented employees, socially and politically quiescent. It is obvious that the blue-collar workers studied here fit neither image. When most workers (and most of the population) believe their Constitution confers a political system that is equal or superior to any, a society is not on the verge of revolution. Yet when most workers (and most of the population) believe corrupt politicians are subverting the democratic promise of the Constitution, and are likely to continue to do so, a society can scarcely be said to be integrated.[3]

The question of integration and alienation can be clarified by considering, in the light of my findings, some of the better-known statements on the subject. There is, for instance, a group of writers who stress the "integrating" and even "narcotizing" tendencies of life outside work. The modern nuclear family and the goods and services it consumes have, they claim, defused social discontent and overridden any concern with class-based activity. This view can be stated in various forms, by those who welcome as well as those who lament the tendencies they outline. Consider three of the strongest versions, those of Marcuse, Alt, and Zweig. These authors claim that one of the major transformations of the twentieth century has been a shift from the primacy of labor to the primacy of consumption. Employees are no longer concerned about work-related issues, for "consumerism has become the major form of domination and reification."[4] Further, even outside work, interests have narrowed to those of the private, nuclear family. This contrasts with the past when social relations included a broad range of kin, friends, and institutions such as the local tavern. As Alt put it: "Modern employees, concerned primarily with the immediate gratifications of familial intimacy and consumerism, come to tolerate the exploitation of labor and even political authoritarianism so long as the system sustains a rising standard of living." Or, in Marcuse's words: "The people recognize themselves in their commodities; they find their soul in their automobile, hi-fi set, split-level home, kitchen equipment. . . . Mass production and mass distribution claim the entire individual . . . there is only one dimension, and it is everywhere."[5]

This view is based on certain truths, but it goes too far. It is true Imperium workers derive considerable pleasure from the consumer goods they buy—car(s), house, color television(s), stereo, fishing and hunting equipment, perhaps a swimming pool, vacations in Florida or Las Vegas or abroad. And "overtime," when workers are paid time and a half or double time, is eagerly sought by many. They commonly pick up an extra $350 or so by putting in twenty hours overtime. This money can be immediately translated into purchases and, in an obvious sense, compensates at least partly for the boredom or hardship of work.

Further, the realm of consumer goods is one in which workers can advance in both an absolute and a relative manner. They can advance absolutely by accumulating possessions, of which a house is usually the most prized, that take them further and further from poverty. And they can advance relatively by outstripping other blue- and white-collar workers in material goods and in this way move a certain distance up the class structure outside work. As a result workers do see this class structure outside the workplace as somewhat fluid and as permitting considerably more mobility than their work setting. In this sense they are not stuck, nor do they perceive themselves to be.

Certainly when economic times become brutal, when jobs are lost and new ones cannot be found, then many workers become downcast and frightened. But enough have attained, or have seen friends and relatives attain, material benefits under capitalism to make it obvious to them that economic advance is possible, if not for them then for people like them, and if not for them now then perhaps for them in the future. And when economic times are hard those who do have jobs are as likely to feel themselves lucky compared with the unemployed as they are to lose faith in capitalism.[6] Many do not believe the allocation of rewards under capitalism is just (neither did Keynes, the main economist of modern capitalism).[7] Indeed, the concept of the working man implies a moral critique of the distribution of income. But that is not the same as losing a belief in the possibility of attaining material benefits within the system.

Yet Marcuse and Alt are making a stronger statement about the role of income, consumer goods, and the nuclear family, which they see as acting almost literally as narcotics, erasing discontent at and outside work and in the realm of politics. This is an inaccurate picture. Residential, family, and leisure life is not unambiguously integrated. Residential America remains largely and blatantly segregated by race into black and white sections in city and suburb. And the nuclear family is hardly a model of an integrated institution. Consider Zweig's version: "As he [the modern worker] sits by the fire and watches t.v. he feels free and happy. The wife doesn't snap at him as she used to: the children are no longer seen crawling about on the floor, shouting and screaming."[8]

This is a one-dimensional view of modern marriage. On the contrary, both spouses, whether blue- or white-collar, often face serious difficulties in combining the principle of the modern nuclear family with alternative principles and relationships, especially with life at work. The modern family, as chapter 3 argued, is a "contradictory cult." It may soothe discontent at work, but it is as likely to contribute additional discontent. And while for some people relations in the nuclear family compensate for a mediocre life at work, for others social relations with co-workers, or the intrinsic pleasure of their work, compensate for mediocre relations in the nuclear family.

Further, Imperium workers do *not* lack class consciousness outside work. They have an image of their position in the class structure outside work based on income level, consumer items, and residence. And while they perceive the *middle* of this class structure as a graduated hierarchy, most perceive the top as a system of economic power that in many ways subverts and dominates political power.

Above all, theories like those of Marcuse and Alt present an inaccurate picture of life *at the workplace*. The idea that life at work has in some sense been superseded by life outside (the shift from the "primacy of labor" to the "primacy of consumption") is a serious error. On the contrary, life at and life outside the workplace coexist as usually separate spheres, sometimes in harmony, more often in various degrees of tension. And life at work remains an important source of class conflict that can take several forms.[9] In one form it separates blue-collar from upper- and lower-white-collar workers and, in the United States, generates a class consciousness based on the concept of the "working man" that reflects this separation. And this class consciousness implies clearly felt dissatisfaction with relations of production and with the work setting. There is the view blue-collar work is often routine, possibly dangerous, uncomfortable, and dirty, and closely supervised (and therefore in an important sense unfree). And there is the view that blue-collar work is productive in a way that lower- and upper-white collar work often, and "big business" almost always, is not.

Life at work can generate class conflict and alliances in other forms. There are ways the situation of blue-collar workers overlaps, and is seen by them to overlap, that of lower-white-collar workers. Both groups tend to be subject to close supervision, in theory if not always in fact, and to have limited prospects for upward mobility at work. This creates the possibility of antiemployer alliances between blue-collar and lower-white-collar workers. (There are also barriers to such alliances. For instance, sexism hinders some blue-collar workers from seeing, and acting upon, the similarities between their situation and that of lower-white-collar workers, seen as "women." And status considerations based on a view of themselves as "office workers" hinder some lower-white-collar employees from seeing, and acting upon, the similarities between their position and that of blue-collar workers, seen as manual workers in physically dirty jobs.)

There is even the possibility, though less likely, of alliances between blue-collar, lower-white-collar, *and* upper-white-collar workers, acting together against employers. For example, most of these three groups are employees, subject to regulations in the workplace and without control of their means of production.

Some writers have argued not, like Marcuse and others, that divisions at work have been suppressed and narcotized, but that nowadays in the workplace divisions based on race or gender have supplanted divisions based on class. But this is inaccurate. It is true the workplace produces, in fact and in consciousness, divisions based on gender and race. But these coexist with, rather than supersede, divisions in fact and in consciousness based on class.

Certainly the extent of class conflict at the workplace should not be exaggerated. The idea that contradictions at work will produce a revolutionary proletariat is an unlikely scenario for today's America. In this sense there is, in modern capitalism, a certain containment of class conflict.[10] Nevertheless, the mode of production remains an important source of class conflict, albeit of a more limited kind than some people once expected.

These are criticisms of those who exaggerate the influence of consumer goods and the modern nuclear family or who claim an absence of class conflict in the workplace. There is another problem facing such theories, and this problem also faces a group of writers who point to the influence of ideas or ideology on working-class and popular politics. Among the latter are those who, on the right wing of the political spectrum, claim the existence of "value consensus" or those who, on the left wing, point to a "hegemony of ruling-class ideas" (Gramsci's concept). Above all, such theories are intended to account for a perceived popular quiescence in the area of national politics. Yet to characterize the attitude of most workers at Imperium to national politics as "quiescent" or "integrated" is misleading.

It is true that much of the American working class (and the American populace in general) is firmly attached to the Constitution and the structure of government it specifies and at best is unimpressed with or hostile toward the various forms of "socialist" regimes that have emerged as the main alternatives in the twentieth century. On the other hand, most of that same working class believe their own government is in the hands of corrupt and dishonest politicians who have subverted its democratic promise, though not its freedoms. And though most reject existing socialist regimes as viable alternatives, they do so in part on the grounds that they too are undemocratic. Their main alternative to the current political status quo in America is not socialism Soviet or Cuban or Yugoslavian style, but democracy American Constitution style.

The public themes of most American holidays illustrate the limitations of theories of the dominance of "consumer goods," or of "value consensus," or of "the hegemony of ruling-class ideas." These public themes do tend toward the trivial and childish (Santa Claus, Mickey Mouse, Kermit the frog, Halloween witches), toward motifs that are apolitical or distant from current politics (Thanksgiving, Independence Day, and Memorial Day), and toward interpersonal themes based on the nuclear or extended family (Christmas, Thanksgiving, Mother's Day) or on male bonding (sporting events). But it is a mistake to suppose this is because in their social and political outlook most Americans are too besotted with consumer-related fantasies and concern for family and friends to rise above Mickey Mouse or the New York Yankees; or that such motifs summarize their deeply held social values; or that they have been duped or, more subtly, "educated" at school to accept these ruling-class motifs while forgetting, or never acquiring, more critical views.

On the contrary, it is because of keen and widespread critical attitudes toward the current political and social scene that public holidays skirt it. The themes of these holidays represent the minimum Americans can agree to "celebrate" without excessive conflict and dispute. It is because they disagree over so many social and political issues that the motifs they can agree to jointly mark are often so banal and without current political relevance.

This book has clear implications for those who favor values such as democracy, equality, and respect for the individual. It suggests that in almost every area there coexist the potential for progress and the potential for reversal. At each level of Imperium workers' lives—at their workplace, in their places of residence, and on the national level, there is an identity that contains the seeds of both a progressive and a reactionary response, and which one is dominant will depend on the possibilities people are presented with. That is why the main political implication of this book is the importance of political activity itself.

Thus, the situation I have presented makes possible a variety of politics based on issues at work, in the residential setting, and in relation to the nation-state. At work blue-collar workers may be prepared as working men (or working people) to form unions and strike, at the same time as they may criticize the perceived indifference or self-serving attitude of the union's leaders. (In this context a change that would transform the image of the AFL–CIO in the eyes of the rank-and-file worker would be if the head of the AFL–CIO were elected directly by *all* affiliated union members in the United States.) They may perceive and affirm links with lower-white-collar unions, though such links are hampered by a pervasive sexism and a view such workers are unproductive. And they may perceive and affirm links with upper-white-collar workers such as teachers and social workers, though such links are hampered by a pervasive suspicion that their jobs are both easy and in some ways unproductive. They will support a national economic policy to reduce unemployment and increase the number of jobs, but many may be suspicious of "job creation" programs aimed at the poor and at blacks and Hispanics.

Outside work, blue-collar homeowners, like most American homeowners, will become involved in a "politics of homeownership" centering on an identity as middle or lower middle class, and on issues such as the level of property taxes, the quality of the items these taxes fund (the school system, local police and fire services), and the quality of the neighborhood and township, especially insofar as this affects the value of their houses. But the widespread division of residential America by race into white and black or Hispanic areas and the importance workers attach to maintaining the monetary value of their houses mean that concern about the neighborhood may lapse into support for a politics of racial segregation and exclusiveness. The local politics of renters will differ in that their concerns will center less on maintaining the value of their homes.

On the national level also blue-collar workers, like almost all Americans, will support a variety of politics. They will support a national defense effort, though in varying degrees of lavishness. And in certain circumstances they can be whipped into a nationalistic fervor. But populism and time make this fervor fragile and prone to dissolve rapidly into anger at America's leaders. Finally, some blue-collar workers, like some Americans, who are susceptible to nativism in its various currents may support a politics that turns against new immigrants or blacks or that represses political radicals.

This situation contains both opportunities and dangers, both hope and pessimism. There is the opportunity for a politics of progress based on the struggle for full democracy, for full employment, for the dignity of the worker, for fair and safe working conditions, for a vigorous trade union movement, for equal treatment of working men and working women and whites and blacks, and for a moderate and balanced foreign policy. Yet there is also the danger of a domestic politics that draws on hostility toward blacks and Hispanics, women and the poor, and of a foreign policy based on grandiose and reckless images of America's role in the world—the kind that fed support for the Vietnam War and that continue to fuel a nuclear arms race that could easily destroy the world.

Appendix
Supplementary Tables

Table A1   Ethnic or Racial Origin of Imperium Workers

Ethnic or Racial Origin	Percentage ($N = 126$)
Eastern European[a]	58
German	13
Irish	9
Italian	8
English	5
Scottish	2
Hispanic	2
Black	2
Jewish	1

Source: Fieldwork.

[a]Includes Polish (numerically the largest group of Eastern Europeans at Imperium), Austrian, Hungarian, Czechoslovakian, Rumanian, and Russian.

Table A2   Place of Birth of Imperium Workers

Place of Birth	Percentage ($N = 93$)
Within two miles of Imperium	65
Elsewhere in New Jersey or Staten Island	5
Elsewhere in United States	24
Abroad	6

Source: Voting records and fieldwork.

Table A3   Size of Lots on Which Imperium Workers' Houses Stand, by Distance from Imperium

Distance from Imperium	Average Width of Lot (feet)	Average Length of Lot (feet)
Within two miles[a]	41 (30–50)[c]	112 (100–125)[c]
Two to four miles	43 (35–50)	120 (100–150)
Over four miles[b]	68 (50–100)	122 (100–150)

Sources: Company directory of addresses; property atlases for Union, Middlesex, Monmouth, and Ocean counties.

[a]Mostly the pre–World War II industrial suburbs of Elizabeth and Linden.

[b]Mostly areas developed by the automobile after World War II. (The figures for workers living more than four miles from Imperium exclude one worker, an exceptional case, who owns a five-acre farm in Piscataway.)

[c]The range within which at least three-quarters of the cases fall.

Table A4   Residence of Homeowners by Average Value of Their Homes and Average Age of Owners, 1980

Distance from Imperium	Average Value of Homes (dollars)	Average Age of Owners
Less than two miles	51,738	51
Two to four miles	51,995	46
More than four miles	68,368	39

Sources: Company directory of addresses; property atlases for Union, Middlesex, Monmouth, and Ocean counties; seniority and age list in Appendix C of contract between Imperium and Local — of the Oil, Chemical and Atomic Workers Union.

Table A5   Businesses Entered by Workers Who Quit

Type of Business	Number
Tavern or fast-food	3
Auto-connected (repair, gas station, racing)	3
Retail store	3
Welding business	1
Total	10

Source: Informants.

Notes

Introduction

1. A pseudonym. Elsewhere I have changed minor details that might reveal the identity of the plant. For instance, the location of Imperium, as it appears on maps 1, 2, and 5, is slightly altered.

2. For instance, Ferdynand Zweig, *The Worker in an Affluent Society* (New York: Free Press, 1961).

3. Rubin, *Worlds of Pain: Life in the Working-Class Family* (New York: Basic Books, 1976).

4. William H. Whyte, *The Organization Man* (New York: Simon and Schuster, 1965), 298–300.

5. Bennett Berger, *Working-Class Suburb* (Berkeley: University of California Press, 1968), 93.

6. Zweig, *Worker in an Affluent Society*, 207.

7. Rubin, *Worlds of Pain*, passim.

8. Robert Blauner, *Alienation and Freedom* (Chicago: University of Chicago Press, 1964), 142 ff.

9. Harry Braverman, *Labor and Monopoly Capital* (New York: Monthly Review Press, 1974), 183–233.

10. See, for instance, Richard Coleman and Lee Rainwater, *Social Standing in America* (New York: Basic Books, 1978).

11. For example, Richard Hamilton, *Class and Politics in the United States* (New York: John Wiley, 1972).

12. See, for instance, Arthur Miller, "Political Issues and Trust in Government: 1964–1970," *American Political Science Review* 68 (September 1974):951–72; Jack Citrin, "Comment: The Political Relevance of Trust in Government," ibid., 973–88; Arthur Miller, "Rejoiner to 'Comment' by Jack Citrin: Political Discontent or Ritualism?" ibid., 989–1001. The debate between Miller, who stresses the seriousness of political mistrust, and Citrin, who downplays it, concerns the electorate as a whole, not just the working class.

Other statements of the view that the working class is, or is becoming, "middle class" include (on the United States) Werner Sombart, *Warum gibt es in den Vereinigten Staaten keinen Sozialismus?* (Tübingen, 1906), trans. P. Hocking and C. Husbands as *Why Is There No Socialism in the United States?* (New York: International Arts and Sciences Press, 1976), 106,109–10; Kurt Mayer, "The Changing Shape of the American Class Structure," *Social Research* 30 (Winter 1963):458–69; (on Western Europe) Raymond Aron, *Dix-huit leçons sur la société industrielle* (Paris: Gallimard, 1962); (on England) George Orwell, "England Your England," in *A Collection of Essays by George Orwell* (New York: Doubleday, 1954).

Other critics of this idea are Anthony Giddens, *The Class Structure of the Advanced Societies* (New York: Harper and Row, 1973), and Gavin Mackenzie, *The Aristocracy of Labor: The Position of Skilled Craftsmen in the American Class Structure* (Cambridge: Cambridge University Press, 1973).

13. A first-rate study that does consider life both at and outside work is William Kornblum, *Blue-Collar Community* (Chicago: University of Chicago Press, 1974). Kornblum analyzes the effect of work setting and of union and local politics on ethnic and racial divisions among a community of steelworkers.

Examples of studies of the working-class that focus on couples with young children are Lillian Rubin, *Worlds of Pain*, and Goldthorpe et al.'s three-volume *The Affluent Worker* (Cambridge: Cambridge University Press, 1968–69). This concentration on a life-cycle stage at which financial problems are likely to be severe weakens one of Goldthorpe's central conclusions, that modern workers are concerned, above almost all other goals, with earning money. For more discussion of *The Affluent Worker*, see chapter 16, note 9.

14. Norbert Elias and Eric Dunning, "The Quest for Excitement in Unexciting Societies" (paper presented at the annual conference of the British Sociological Association, London, 1967).

15. The historical questions revolve around this issue: *If* there is overlap between the modern working class and the modern middle class, is that because the former is coming to resemble the latter (often also called "embourgeoisement") or vice versa (often called "proletarianization")? Such questions are important but are beyond the scope of this study. Anyway, most people are interested in the historical questions less because of their intrinsic interest than because they want to know whether, in the *present*, the working class is integrated or alienated. This *is* one of the two central questions I deal with here.

16. C. Wright Mills, *White Collar* (New York: Oxford University Press, 1951), 291.

17. In table 1, "upper white collar" consists of the census groups "managerial and professional specialty occupations." "Lower white collar" consists of "administrative support occupations, including clerical," and "sales workers" (retail and personal services). "Blue collar" consists of "precision production, craft, and repair occupations," and "operators, fabricators, and laborers." The data refer to the "experienced" labor force and are reported in United States Department of Commerce, Bureau of the Census, *Detailed Occupation of the Experienced Civilian Labor Force by Sex for the United States and Regions: 1980 and 1970* (Washington, D.C.: Government Printing Office, 1984).

A large majority of clerical workers are women, though men and women are about equally represented in sales work. See Valerie Kincade Oppenheimer, *The Female Labor Force in the United States: Demographic and Economic Factors Governing Its Growth and Changing Composition* (Berkeley, Calif.: Institute of International Studies, 1970); and Donald Treiman and Kermit Terrell, "Women, Work and Wages: Trends in the Female Occupational Structure since 1940," in *Social Indicator Models*, ed. Kenneth Land and Seymour Spilerman (New York: Russell Sage Foundation, 1974).

The figures in table 1 give only a rough indication of the distribution of the employed population between the three main occupational groups defined in this study—blue collar, upper white collar, and lower white collar. However, a rough indication is all we need here. There are two main reasons why the figures can only be rough. First, the census classifications on which the figures are based do not correspond exactly with the definitions I use. Second, it is hard to decide whether certain occupations are blue collar or upper or lower white collar. For example, the figures in table 1 exclude "service workers" (13 percent of employed workers) because the census category "service workers" is a ragbag including, for example, "waiters," who are hard to classify (blue collar or lower white collar?), "cleaners" and "janitors," who should probably be classified as blue collar, and "head cooks," who should probably be classified as professionals. (That it is hard to decide whether certain occupations are blue collar or upper or lower white collar is of importance for class consciousness in America, as chapter 10 will argue.)

The division of the occupational force into a "blue-collar working class" and "upper-white-collar" and "lower-white-collar" sectors provides the most useful distinctions for my purposes. Above all, these distinctions do not depart too far from the way workers themselves view the class structure in the workplace, as chapter 10 will show. But these distinctions are not sacrosanct. For interesting discussions of the issues connected with defining the "working class" see Mills, *White Collar*; Nicos Poulantzas, *Classes in Contemporary Capitalism* (London: New Left Books, 1975), part 3; Erik Olin Wright, *Class, Crisis and the State* (London: New Left Books, 1978), chap. 2; and Giddens, *Class Structure of the Advanced Societies*.

18. For a clear statement of this view by one of the coauthors of *The Affluent Worker*, see David Lockwood, "Sources of Variation in Working Class Images of Society," *Sociological Review* 14 (November 1966):249–67.

19. For example, Serge Mallet, *La nouvelle classe ouvrière* (Paris: Editions du Seuil, 1969).

20. Data from New Jersey Department of Labor and Industry (Trenton).

21. Men are concentrated in blue-collar craft and laboring jobs, while both sexes are about equally represented in blue-collar operative work. See Treiman and Terrell, "Women, Work and Wages."

22. Compare Alain Touraine's comment on the automated workshops of the Renault auto workers: "In ordinary times they [the workers] seem unoccupied, bored, before the measuring and control apparatus." *L'évolution du travail ouvrier aux usines Renault* (Paris: Centre National de la Recherche Scientifique, 1955), 123.

23. Several months after starting research I began distributing to workers a survey containing many of the questions that social scientists commonly ask concerning attitudes toward work, class, and politics. I stopped after a 40 percent response rate, for the survey was jeopardizing my ties with several workers. Some were offended that a relationship they had considered personal should suddenly become impersonal—that they should be subjects of a questionnaire. Others were suspicious, especially about a question that asked their annual incomes. I continued to collect data through long conversations with workers, in order to ascertain the views of those who had not completed my questionnaire, to supplement my knowledge of those who had, and to study the numerous topics I had never thought to ask about when starting the research.

Chapter 1

1. Werner Sombart, *Why Is There No Socialism in the United States?* 76. The 1975 figures are from an AFL-CIO survey of its members and are cited in Dolores Hayden, "What Would a Non-Sexist City Be Like? Speculations on Housing, Urban Design, and Human Work," *Signs* 5 (Spring 1980):170–87. See also Gwendolyn Wright, *Building the Dream* (New York: Pantheon, 1980).

2. Hamilton, *Class and Politics in the United States*, 163; Berger, *Working-Class Suburb*.

3. In 1982 the chemical industry in New Jersey employed 124,000 persons, making it the largest manufacturing sector. See Economic Policy Council and Office of Economic Policy, *Fifteenth Annual Report* (Trenton, N.J.: State of New Jersey, 1981).

4. For this quotation and the history of the oil industry in New Jersey, see Ralph Hidy and Muriel Hidy, *History of the Standard Oil Company*, vol. 1, *Pioneering in Big Business, 1882–1911* (New York: Harper, 1955); see also I. Tarbell, *The History of the Standard Oil Company* (New York: Harper and Row, 1966; originally published 1904); and Herbert Gutman, "La politique ouvrière de la grande entreprise américaine de 'l'âge du clinquant': Le cas de la Standard Oil Company," *Mouvement Social* 102 (January–March 1978):67–99.

5. The job categories in figure 1 are explained in chapter 4. In their study of occupational mobility, Duncan and Blau point to the relative infrequency with which sons of white-collar workers enter blue-collar jobs. A look at the occupations of fathers of Imperium workers is certainly consistent with this finding. Duncan and Blau suggest that, for status reasons, sons of white-collar workers would prefer to take poorer-paid white-collar jobs rather than better-paid blue-collar jobs. There is surely much in this, but it should not be forgotten that sons of white-collar workers are less likely than sons of blue-collar workers to have the close kin ties so important for obtaining better-paid blue-collar jobs, even if they want them. See Peter M. Blau and Otis Dudley Duncan, *The American Occupational Structure* (New York: John Wiley, 1967), chap. 2.

6. This discussion of the old port area and of areas developed by the railroad, streetcar, and automobile draws on various sources. These include A. Van Doren Honeyman, ed., *History of Union County New Jersey, 1664–1923* (New York: Lewis, 1923), various maps and documents in the possession of the relevant townships, and the "Residential Security Maps" for the region—maps developed in the 1930s as part of the Home Owners Loan Corporation's systematic survey of residential areas throughout America and available in the National Archives, Washington, D.C. For a discussion of these surveys, which offer an unusual snapshot of residential America in the 1930s, see Kenneth T. Jackson, "Race, Ethnicity, and Real Estate Appraisal: The Home Owners Loan Corporation and the Federal Housing Administration," *Journal of Urban History* 6 (August 1980): 419–52.

Above all the account that follows is based on extensive travel around the region and interviews with older residents. For a discussion of the importance of viewing a region for reconstructing its residential, industrial, and transportation history see Sam Bass Warner, *Streetcar Suburbs: The Process of Growth in Boston, 1870–1900* (Cambridge: Harvard University Press, 1962), appendix.

For a discussion of boarding and lodging as common practice in colonial American families as well as in nineteenth and early twentieth century urban America see John Modell and Tamara Hareven, "Urbanization and the Malleable Household: an Examination of Boarding and Lodging in American Families," in *Family and Kin in Urban Communities, 1700–1930*, ed. Tamara K. Hareven (New York: New Viewpoints, 1977). For a discussion of boardinghouses in the late nineteenth century in Elizabeth's larger neighbor, Newark, see Ronald A. Foresta, "The Evolution of the Modern Urban Core: The Implications of Newark's Late Nineteenth-Century Housing and Population Patterns," in *New Jersey's Ethnic Heritage,* ed. Paul A. Stellhorn (Trenton: New Jersey Historical Commission, 1978). Foresta stresses the numerical importance of blue-collar boarders.

7. Most tracts are subdivisions of townships, but some constitute entire townships, since many towns in New Jersey are small in area and population.

The relation between census occupational categories and the categories "blue-collar working class," "lower-white-collar sector," and "upper-white-collar sector" used in this book is discussed in note 17 of the Introduction.

There is a debate among sociologists using census data over how far residential America is divided by occupation. An early statement that stresses division is Otis Duncan and Beverly Duncan, "Residential Distribution and Occupational Stratification," *American Journal of Sociology* 60 (1955):493–503. For a later analysis suggesting that division by occupation is much less prominent, see Reynolds Farley, "Residential Segregation in Urbanized Areas of the United States in 1970: An Analysis of Social Class and Racial Differences," *Demography* 14 (November 1977):497–518. Farley's analysis is based on census data for the twenty-five largest urban regions in America and includes both the inner city and suburban rings.

8. The term "suburb" is difficult, for it is commonly used in a number of senses. In this book it refers to land recently converted from disuse or agricultural use to residential or industrial use. "Recent" means either the present or, in discussing earlier development, the earlier period being referred to.

Some writers use "suburb" to refer to an area that is totally residential rather than industrial. This use can be misleading, for it conceals the fact that important sections of newly developed land, now and in the past, contain industry as well as housing. "Suburban" also sometimes refers to a particular way of life, contrasted with a typically "urban" style. This is also misleading, for there is no such distinct "suburban" way of life (on this see Herbert Gans, *The Levittowners* (New York: Vintage Books, 1967). For discussions of the various uses and complexities of the term "suburb" see Herbert Gans, "Urbanism and Suburbanism as Ways of Life: A Re-evaluation of Some Definitions," in *Human Behavior and Social Processes*, ed. Arnold M. Rose (Boston: Houghton Mifflin, 1962), 625–48, and Kenneth T. Jackson, "Urban Deconcentration in the Nineteenth Century: A Statistical Inquiry," in *The New Urban History*, ed. Leo Schnore (Princeton: Princeton University Press, 1975).

Examples of classic industrial suburbs developed during the last part of the nineteenth century and the start of the twentieth are Pullman and Gary on the outskirts of Chicago, and Homestead on the fringe of Pittsburgh. The oil refining industry in the New York Metropolitan area, in the period 1870–1910, was located in urban fringes such as Brooklyn and Linden. Much of the auto industry also was developed in outer regions. The first auto plants in Detroit were located in what were the outskirts of the city. See David Katzman, *Before the Ghetto* (Chicago: University of Illinois, 1973), 58.

For a contemporary study of such industrial suburbs see Graham Taylor, *Satellite Cities: A Study of Industrial Suburbs* (New York: Appleton, 1915). For more recent analyses see Sam Bass Warner, *The Urban Wilderness: A History of the American City* (New York: Harper and Row, 1972), chap. 4, and Allen Pred, "The Intrametropolitan Location of American Manufacturing," in *Internal Structure of the City*, ed. Larry Bourne (New York: Oxford University Press, 1971).

For evidence of homeownership as an important phenomenon among blue-collar workers before World War II see John Dean, "The Ghosts of Home-Ownership," *Journal of Social Issues* 7 (1951):59–68.

9. For studies in the 1950s and 1960s that discuss the drive among blue-collar workers for homeownership see Ely Chinoy, *Automobile Workers and the American Dream* (Boston: Beacon Press, 1955), Berger, *Working-Class Suburb*, Komarovsky, *Blue-Collar Marriage*, and Gerald Handel and Lee Rainwater, "Persistence and Change in Working-Class Life Style," in *Blue-Collar World*, ed. A. Shostak and W. Gomberg (Englewood Cliffs, N.J.: Prentice-Hall, 1964), 36–41.

Gavin Mackenzie argued that homeownership had a distinct meaning for the skilled blue-collar workers he studied, for they valued it more because it conferred freedom from a landlord's control than because of its economic advantages (the "middle-class" view). But the attitude of Imperium workers toward homeownership suggests that this distinction is less clear-cut. It is true that when many of the older workers bought homes, in the years after World War II, they did not expect to make large amounts of money from their purchases. However, they certainly enjoy the sharp increase in the value of their homes, and in retrospect they see them as an excellent investment. For Mackenzie's view, which is an important part of his case against the idea that there is much overlap outside work between the blue- and white-collar sectors, see *The Aristocracy of Labor*, 74–77.

10. See chapter 2 for a discussion of the time workers spend improving their houses.

11. On the growth of town houses (row houses) in new suburbs see J. Dingemans, "Urbanization of Suburbia: Renaissance of the Row House," *Landscape* 20 (1975):19–31.

12. For a study based on 1970 census data that emphasizes the way a working wife can boost a family's income to the level of a much higher-paying occupational group see Valerie Kincade Oppenheimer, "The Sociology of Women's Economic Role in the Family," *American Sociological Review* 42 (June 1977):387–406.

13. However, some sections of land in these townships, usually farthest from transportation stops, remained undeveloped until after World War II when the widespread use of the automobile made them easily accessible.

14. See John Bebout and Ronald Grele, *Where Cities Meet* (Princeton: Van Nostrand, 1964).

15. Most of the figures in table 7 are from United States Bureau of the Census, "Money Income of Households, Families, and Persons in the United States: 1980," *Current Population Reports* (July 1982). The figures exclude self-employed persons. Figures on the earnings of miners and auto and refinery workers are from United States Bureau of Labor Statistics, *Employment and Earnings* 25 (March 1981). The 1981 figures for Imperium workers are an estimate. They are based on figures from management for average wages in 1976 ($16,400), raised by 58 percent, which is the average increase in the hourly wage rate at Imperium between 1976 and 1981, then reduced by 20 percent to allow for the fact that in 1981, as a result of the recession, Imperium workers averaged less than a five-day week, with limited overtime.

For a detailed account of weekly earnings for 247 blue- and white-collar occupations see Peter Ward, "Occupational Earnings from Top to Bottom," in United States Department of Labor, Bureau of Labor Statistics, *Occupational Outlook Quarterly* 26 (Winter 1982). Ward's data make clear the numerous income overlaps between blue- and white-collar jobs. For other studies that stress, in various ways, the income overlaps between better-paid blue-collar workers and certain categories of white-collar workers see Gavin Mackenzie, "The Economic Dimensions of Embourgeoisement," *British Journal of Sociology* 18 (March 1967):29–44; and Blau and Duncan, *The American Occupational Structure*. For a dissenting view see Richard Hamilton, "The Income Difference between Skilled and White Collar Workers," *British Journal of Sociology* 14 (December 1963):363–73.

It might be argued that banks discriminate against blue-collar workers when giving mortgages. But not a single worker ever suggested that this occurs, and it is unclear why banks should behave in this way.

16. Even in the small number of areas that are notoriously wealthy and expensive, such as Colts Neck, Westfield, Rumson, and sections of Scotch Plains, the proportion of upper white collar rarely rises above 55 percent and the proportion of blue collar rarely falls below 7 percent.

17. Census figures suggest there is something very unusual about the California suburb on which Berger based his view that post–World War II suburban America was divided into "working-class" and "middle-class" suburbs. Berger claimed that the suburb he studied was typical of the experience of blue-collar workers who moved to the suburbs after World War II (a typical "working-class suburb"). Yet a massive 70 percent of those living in Berger's suburb were blue-collar workers (foremen and skilled and semiskilled workers and laborers), while only 7.5 percent were professionals or managers. In the region to which Imperium workers have access the only tracts with such a high proportion of blue-collar workers and such a low proportion of professionals and managers are inner-city black (or Hispanic) areas. How, then, can we explain the strikingly high density of blue-collar workers in Berger's suburban tracts?

The auto workers he studied originally lived and worked in the industrial town of Richmond. In 1955 Ford relocated its plant to Milpitas, a "semirural community" about fifty miles from Richmond. Many of the workers who relocated moved into "new tract suburbs which had been built not far from the plant." As a result these tracts, the object of Berger's study, contained "large concentrations of workers." Indeed, almost a third of those interviewed reported that their two closest neighbors were also Ford workers.

This suggests that the unusual concentration of blue-collar workers resulted from the special circumstances of the plant relocation, for a large number of Ford workers happened to be looking for houses at the same time in the same area. In this situation, if there was new tract housing available for sale close to the relocated plant it would be natural for many workers to purchase houses there (as opposed to being scattered around various occupationally mixed residential areas as would have happened had they not all been forced to move at the same time). Thus the relatively high proportion of blue-collar workers in the California suburb is not, as Berger argues, typical of working-class suburban experience, but is more plausibly viewed as a special situation resulting from the mechanics of that particular plant relocation. See Berger, *Working-Class Suburb*, v–vii, 117.

Richard Hamilton's argument that suburban America is separated by occupation into working-class and middle-class suburbs rests on two startlingly misleading uses of census data. First, he classifies all areas with a working-class majority as working class (rather than occupationally mixed), regardless of how slender the majority may be. Second, Hamilton classifies wives and dependent children of blue-collar workers as blue-collar workers even if those wives and children are in middle-class occupations or do not work. This definitional move is, as he admits, highly questionable. For further criticisms of such definitional moves, especially ignoring the wife's occupation when considering the class character of a marriage, see chapter 3. For Hamilton's argument see *Class and Politics in the United States*, 152–87.

18. Asked if such areas are working class or middle class, some workers will say middle class (almost never working class), but what they usually have in mind is a classification based on income level, not occupation. These questions are considered in detail in part 4.

19. For example, to explain what he saw as the division of late nineteenth and early twentieth century Boston into working-class and middle-class areas, Sam Bass Warner pointed to the different transportation needs of each class. He argued that skilled blue-collar workers, whose income level could be as high as that of sections of the middle class, tended to buy houses in the more cramped inner suburbs, while the middle class lived in the outer suburbs where, for the same price, they could buy larger houses. This was because skilled blue-collar workers changed jobs frequently and sometimes held several at the same time and thus needed to live close to a variety of streetcar commuting routes, which meant the inner suburbs with their easy access to "crosstown" routes. By contrast the middle class people such as lawyers, schoolteachers, and large contractors tended to work at a single, stable location. They thus could purchase houses in the outer suburbs along a single streetcar route leading from home to work (the "linear" routes) without needing to worry about easy access to crosstown routes. See Warner, *Streetcar Suburbs*.

20. The various Levittowns in the region are often viewed as synonymous with "working-class" suburban housing. This is a serious mistake. For example, the inhabitants of Levittown, New Jersey, the subject of Gans's classic study, constitute a mix of occupations. In 1960, 26 percent of the males were blue-collar workers and 31 percent were managers, minor officials, or professionals (Gans, *Levittowners*, 22–23). Nor is Levittown characterized by the type of housing it contains, for with minor variations in size and style this type of housing is typical of medium and large tract housing built throughout the region. The only unusual feature of Levittown is its scale—the number of such houses built in one area by the same developer.

It is interesting to note that Gans began his study with the idea that the Levitt type of housing *was* purchased mainly by the working class, for his original intention was to study a working-class suburb. On arrival he found that Levittown was occupationally mixed, and he changed the focus of his study. See *Levittowners*, xxviii–xxix.

21. The following discussion of racial separation in the residential setting uses census data but is based on detailed observation of the region. Census data alone underestimate the degree of racial separation, for a single census tract may contain both part of a heavily white area *and* part of an adjoining heavily black area. This combination of a distinct white area and a distinct black area in the same tract gives the false appearance of racial mixing. For discussion of this point see Otis Duncan and Beverly Duncan, "A Methodological Analysis of Segregation Indexes," *American Sociological Review* 20 (1955):210–24; and John K. Wright, "Some Measures of Distribution," *Annals of the Association of American Geographers* 27 (December 1937):177–211. Still, census data reveal deep racial divisions in urban and suburban America. For an analysis of census data that takes a position similar to that taken in this chapter (that urban and suburban American is segregated by race much more clearly than by class), see Reynolds Farley, "Residential Segregation in Urbanized Areas of the United States in 1970: An Analysis of Social Class and Racial Differences," *Demography* 14 (November 1977):497–518.

The discussion in this chapter also focuses on blacks rather than Hispanics. From the point of view of most Imperium workers and most white inhabitants of the region, in general the darker their skin color the more Hispanics are seen as black. Of course the way blacks and Hispanics see themselves is more complex. For an account of the perceptions that Puerto Ricans in America, especially in the New York region, have of their racial and ethnic identity see Clara Rodriguez, "Puerto Ricans: Between Black and White," *Journal of New York Affairs* 1 (1974):92–101. From 1933 until at least the late 1960s federal mortgage policies encouraged racial discrimination in the private housing market by favoring all-white areas and discriminating against black or mixed areas. For an analysis of the policies of the Home Owners Loan Corporation and the Federal Housing Administration see Jackson, "Race, Ethnicity and Real Estate Appraisal."

There was, of course, a time when certain residential areas were difficult for Catholics and Jews to penetrate. Such discrimination is now muted, being individual and sporadic where it exists rather than systematic as in the case of blacks. The residential strongholds of anti-Catholicism or anti-Semitism have almost all fallen. Rumson, for example, a wealthy residential community, had a reputation as a Protestant township that excluded Catholics and Jews. But in the 1950s and 1960s a large number of wealthy Catholics moved in, and more recently so have some wealthy Jews.

22. The residential development of the surrounding white areas may cause serious economic problems for the black residents, especially the older and poorer ones, who can be displaced by rising property taxes they cannot afford to pay. Property taxes may rise because as the surrounding areas grow the township's expenses, especially for education, increase. Further, as the areas adjoining the black sections are developed from wasteland into white residential sectors, there may be pressure from the surrounding white homeowners to use property taxes to displace blacks, whose proximity is seen as preventing the value of their own property from rising as high as it otherwise might.

For an excellent historical and demographic account of black suburbs see Reynolds Farley, "The Changing Distribution of Negroes within Metropolitan Areas: The Emergence of Black Suburbs," *American Journal of Sociology* 75 (1970):512–29.

23. Census data suggest that post–World War II suburbs are, if anything, more segregated by race than urban areas. See Farley, "Changing Distribution of Negroes."

White areas with a few blacks sprinkled around them can hardly be called integrated. A number of sections on the edge of expanding inner-city black and Hispanic ghettos contain a mix of blacks and whites, but only because they are in transition, as whites leave, from all white to all or predominantly black. These sections can hardly be called integrated either. Only two areas in the region might reasonably be said to be integrated. These are the southern part of Plainfield (the Watchung Avenue area) and Levittown, New Jersey (which, not far from Philadelphia, is actually just outside the region). Yet whether even these areas are integrated rather than in transition to predominantly black is unclear. The southern part of Plainfield was predominantly white until the black riots in the central part of the city in 1967. As a result of the riots whites began to leave southern Plainfield, and blacks took their place. The current crisis in the housing market halted or slowed this process of white flight, for high mortgage rates made it hard for whites to find comparable housing elsewhere. Levittown, originally segregated, attracted the attention of prointegration groups, since it was the largest new suburb in New Jersey. Under the pressure of lawsuits, Levitt agreed to sell to blacks. (For an account of desegregation in Levittown see Gans, *Levittowners*, 371–85.) At this time Levittown is integrated, but whether it will remain so in the face of other pressures is unclear. For instance, in the late 1970s a number of residents came to suspect that federal mortgage money was harder for Levittowners to obtain than for homeowners in white residential areas of the state. A trip to Washington by the town clerk corrected the problem, at least for the moment.

24. Other examples of large expanses of water are the Raritan River, which separates blacks and Hispanics in Perth Amboy from whites in South Amboy, and Wesley Lake, between blacks in Asbury Park and whites in Ocean Grove. Route 22, running through North Plainfield, also separates black apartment dwellers from white homeowners to the south.

Examples of wasteland are the area between the black section of southeastern Piscataway and the housing a short distance to the west and also the area that completely surrounds the black section of Edison. An example of agricultural land as a barrier is the farmland that isolates pockets of blacks in South Brunswick.

The following are additional examples of minor barriers operating alone or in combination. A brook separates whites in North Plainfield from blacks in Plainfield. The white inner-city enclave in northeastern New Brunswick is separated from New Brunswick blacks to the east by the Pennsylvania Railroad and from Franklin blacks to the west by a large park. A well-used railroad in combination with a large commercial center separates black sections of Elizabeth to the east of the railroad from white sections to the west.

25. Within both markets, the white and the black, income level (and wealth) is the major determinant of the allocation of housing.

26. Berger, *Working-Class Suburb*, 25. For Reisman's quotation see Chinoy, *Automobile Workers and the American Dream*, xx.

27. The Jersey shore has a long history since the nineteenth century as a vacation and resort area, especially for urban inhabitants of New York City, Newark, and Philadelphia. For studies of the shore, all of which emphasize the variety of social classes and income levels it catered to, see Charles E. Funnell, "Atlantic City: Washbasin of the Great Democracy," in *Urban New Jersey since 1870*, ed. William C. Wright (Trenton: New Jersey Historical Commission, 1975), 96–116; Writers Project, *Entertaining a Nation: The Career of Long Branch* (Bayonne: Jersey Printing Company, 1940); and Harold F. Wilson, *The Story of the Jersey Shore* (Princeton: D. Van Nostrand, 1964). Although the two main resorts, Long Branch and Atlantic City, attracted some of the wealthiest and most fashionable Americans in the second half of the nineteenth century (for example, from 1869 President Grant regularly vacationed at Long Branch), numerically the bulk of the vacationers were of moderate means, staying in cheap, not fashionable, hotels and in boardinghouses.

28. The problem of deciding if retirement communities are divided by (former) occupation into working-class and middle-class residents is similar to that of deciding whether the rest of residential America is mixed or divided by occupation. It is important to consider not only residents' former occupations but also their current perceptions of the class composition of the communities where they now live.

To start with the question of the former occupation of residents: a large proportion of New Jersey's retirement villages are in Ocean County (see the inset to map 1). One study of these villages, which includes only those whose occupants own detached or attached houses and excludes trailer parks, found that the former occupation of about 23 percent of the retired residents was blue collar. See Katherine McMillan Heinz, *Retirement Communities* (New Brunswick, N.J.: Center for Urban Policy Research, 1976), 16, 35. A study of a retirement village (in "the West," probably California) composed entirely of detached houses found that about 18 percent of the residents had been blue-collar workers. See Jerry Jacobs, *Fun City: An Ethnographic Study of a Retirement Community* (New York: Holt, Rinehart, and Winston, 1974), 46–47. Such villages of detached and attached houses represent the middle and upper end of the spectrum of housing for the retired. The percentage of former blue-collar workers is much higher in retirement communities of mobile homes.

The question arises whether such retirement communities are "working class," "middle class," or occupationally mixed. For example, are somewhat expensive villages of detached or attached houses, about a fifth or a quarter of whose occupants were once in blue-collar occupations, middle class or occupationally mixed?

This question cannot be answered without considering the perceptions of those who live in these communities. Studies rarely do this. Actually, Imperium workers about to move into such communities, of whatever type, hardly ever refer to the former occupations of the residents. They certainly do not see them as divided along occupational lines. Instead, they discuss the price and type of housing and the location and character of the community. This unconcern with (former) occupation makes obvious sense for communities of people who have retired, or are about to retire, from the labor market. Fieldwork inside such communities in New Jersey confirms the relative unimportance to residents of former occupation. The question of what kind of occupation residents had usually meets a response that they had "all kinds" and, further, that this is not important. What is important, residents tend to emphasize, is a person's effort at sociability, at getting along with other residents.

29. Philippe Ariès, *The Hour of Our Death*, trans. Helen Weaver (New York: Alfred Knopf, 1981).

Chapter 2

1. The quotation is from United States Department of Labor, *How American Buying Habits Change* (Washington, D.C.: Government Printing Office, 1959), 6. For writers who argue that blue-collar leisure is clearly distinct from middle-class leisure see Berger, *Working-Class Suburb*, and Rubin, *Worlds of Pain*. For more moderate accounts that point to overlaps as well as differences between the leisure of better paid blue-collar workers and that of the middle class see Gans, *Levittowners*, Kornblum, *Blue-Collar Community*, Mackenzie, *Aristocracy of Labor*, and Handel and Rainwater, "Persistence and Change in Working-Class Life Style."

2. For a summary of the literature on the history of the tavern, including the "saloon period" in the United States, see Robert Popham, "The Social History of the Tavern," in *Research Advances in Alcohol and Drug Problems*, vol. 4, ed. Yedy Israel (New York: Plenum Press, 1978), 225–302.

3. For distinctions between different types of tavern see Kornblum, *Blue-Collar Community*, 75–81. In addition to the types mentioned in this chapter, Kornblum discusses the "ethnic" tavern, which is the meeting place for a particular ethnic group, and bars that cater to alcoholics—men and women who have lost control of their drinking and can no longer patronize the more "reputable" taverns. First-line supervisors tend to select different bars from those favored by the workers they supervise.

4. Another source of this interest in cuisine is men's experience in the army. This was often where these chemical workers learned to cook. Compare Remarque's comment that food is one of the two main topics of conversation in the army. See Erich Maria Remarque, *All Quiet on the Western Front* (Greenwich, Conn.: Fawcett, 1958; orginally published 1929).

5. See the discussion in chapter 6 of men's leisure activities at work.

6. Robinson found that activities such as attending and participating in sports events, outdoor activities such as fishing and hiking, and frequenting nightclubs and bars were engaged in predominantly by men, regardless of social class. See John Robinson, *How Americans Use Time* (New York: Praeger, 1977), 159. Robinson's data are from a survey conducted between 1965 and 1966 that excludes respondents living in areas with populations under 50,000.

7. For an account of the tendency of workers with young children to choose those jobs within the plant that enable them to earn as much overtime pay as possible, see part 2.

8. In a fascinating study, Mihaly Csikszentmihalyi and Eugene Rochberg-Halton investigated the meaning people of various social classes (but not the rich or poor) in Chicago attributed to the objects in their homes. Education does make some difference, for instance in attitude toward books (professionals tend to value books highly) and art (upper-middle-class people value paintings and drawings more, especially originals). But in general there were "surprisingly few social class differences." On the other hand, differences resulting from age were great. See *The Meaning of Things: Domestic Symbols and the Self* (Cambridge: Cambridge University Press, 1981).

9. Compare Kornblum's observation about the tavern in south Chicago: "Although a large number of men . . . continue to 'stop in' after work, television, better housing and the auto, which can take the family away for a weekend or an evening, all claim their share of a man's time." Kornblum, *Blue-Collar Community*, 76.

10. It is true that the earnings of blue-collar workers tend to peak sooner than those of many white-collar employees. But for the reasons I have stated, the expenses of most Imperium workers decline about the same time. And blue-collar workers are less likely than upper-white-collar people to feel the need to finance an expensive private college education for their children. Many workers are eager for their children to attend college, but they see little wrong with an inexpensive public college. As their expenses decline, workers tend to bid into lower-paying but more comfortable jobs within the plant. See part 2.

11. For a historical account of relations of social solidarity based on economic interdependence see Michael Anderson, *Family Structure in Nineteenth-Century Lancashire* (Cambridge: Cambridge University Press, 1971). For a survey of the growth of fringe benefits such as pensions and unemployment compensation since the 1930s see George Ruben, "Major Collective Bargaining Developments—A Quarter Century Review," *Current Wage Developments* 26 (February 1974):42–54.

12. See part 2 for an account of the work setting and its dangers.

13. Harold Wilensky, "Mass Society and Mass Culture," *American Sociological Review* 29 (April 1964):173–97. Wilensky studied the cultural interests and activities of men in a variety of occupations in

Detroit. He found that educational level was the main determinant of interest in "high culture." Especially important was the difference between those with and those without a college degree and the quality of the university attended. However, he found that most people at all educational and occupational levels spent a great deal more time absorbing popular culture than high culture. For educational level as the main determinant of interest in "high culture" see also Herbert Gans, *Popular Culture and High Culture: An Analysis and Evaluation of Taste* (New York: Basic Books, 1971), 70. "Culture" (defined as going to movies, concerts, and the theater and attending adult education classes) was one of the very few sets of leisure activities that Robinson found to be clearly more popular among those of higher social class. Yet, as in Wilensky's study, the actual time spent on "culture" was small. See Robinson, *How Americans Use Time*, 159.

14. For other studies that point to the effect on blue-collar workers of their relatively modest level of education see Handel and Rainwater, "Persistence and Change in Working-Class Life Style"; A. Shostak, *Blue-Collar Life* (New York: Random House, 1969), chap. 1; and Melvin Kohn, *Class and Conformity* (Chicago: University of Chicago Press, 1977; orginally published 1969).

15. For a discussion of the tendency of the working class to be "person oriented" see Herbert Gans, *The Urban Villagers* (New York: Free Press, 1962). Likewise, Mackenzie found that skilled blue-collar workers and clerical workers were more likely than managers to be involved in considerable informal social interaction with kin and friends. See *Aristocracy of Labor*, chap. 4.

Some people argue that having a dull job with limited promotion prospects produces a depressed worker with little energy or inclination for vigorous leisure activities and friendships. Such is the position taken by Lillian Rubin in her study of working-class families and, in a more moderate form, by Bennett Berger in his study of California auto workers. This view is too simple. Certainly few of these workers are pleased to be stuck in dull jobs. And some, especially the heaviest drinkers, are clearly depressed. But the evidence of this chapter does not support the idea that as a group their leisure life is noticeably dull or restrained.

Studies that argue to the contrary suffer from a number of problems. First, they tend to concentrate on married couples with young children, precisely the group whose leisure life is likely to be severely curtailed. (This is certainly true of Rubin's study, *Worlds of Pain*. Although 21 percent of the auto workers in Berger's study are over forty five, only 8 percent are older than forty-nine. See Berger, *Working-Class Suburb*, x.) Second, they ignore men's leisure life at work. Third, some of the more lively leisure activities in which workers engage are of a clandestine or semiclandestine nature, as I pointed out in the Introduction. They may be of doubtful legal or moral status, or the men's wives may disapprove of them. It is no surprise if such activities are glossed over as men in their homes recount that leisure life to an interviewer.

Elias and Dunning present a more general version of the argument of this chapter, that dull activities in one sphere lead to a quest for excitement in other spheres. They maintain that the increasingly routinized and restrained nature of ordinary life in advanced industrial societies, at and outside work, produces a drive for excitement in leisure. See Elias and Dunning, "Quest for Excitement in Leisure."

16. Not all blue-collar workers are in jobs that permit an active social life at work, and not all engage in such a social life when it is possible. But a number of studies besides this one point to a tendency for workers in dull jobs with limited or blocked mobility to focus on friendships and leisure at work. See Noel Tichy, "An Analysis of Clique Formation and Structure in Organizations," *Administrative Science Quarterly* 18 (June 1973):194–207; Rosabeth Moss Kanter, *Men and Women of the Corporation* (New York: Harper, 1977), chap. 6, and J. M. Pennings, "Work Value Systems of White Collar Workers," *Administrative Science Quarterly* 15 (1970):397–405. The suggestion that because their jobs are usually dull and routine blue-collar workers may attach greater importance to friendships is also made by Constantina Safilios-Rothschild, "Family and Stratification," *Journal of Marriage and the Family* 37 (November 1975):855–60.

On the other hand, two studies of British workers suggest a caveat. Both Michael Mann, who analyzed workers in a coffee processing plant, and Goldthorpe, who analyzed workers in various plants, report hearing a general maxim that "workmates are not friends." This view seems to be a characteristic of the English scene, for such an idea is alien to Imperium workers and is not reported in studies of American workers. See Goldthorpe et al., *Affluent Worker*, and Michael Mann, *Workers on the Move* (Cambridge: Cambridge University Press, 1973).

17. This quotation and the one above are from Young and Willmott, *Symmetrical Family*. 166, 117.

18. Lynda L. Holmstrom, *The Two-Career Family* (Cambridge, Mass.: Schenkman, 1972), 14.

19. For the point that many upper-white-collar employees whose careers have advanced as far as they are able, or willing, to take them become more "person oriented" see Gans, *Urban Villagers*, and Kanter, *Men and Women of the Corporation*.

20. Robinson, *How Americans Use Time*. Robinson found that gender was a much more important predictor than occupation of how people spend time outside their paid jobs. Above all, wives rather than husbands are responsible for most of the housework and child rearing, and this does not change even if the wives have full-time jobs. Robinson's study is now twenty years old, but in their recent replication of the Lynds' study of Middletown, Caplow and his colleagues found that wives are still basically responsible for these tasks. See Theodore Caplow, Howard Bahr, Bruce Chadwick, Reuben Hill, and Margaret Williamson, *Middletown Families: Fifty Years of Change and Continuity* (Minneapolis: University of Minneapolis Press, 1982), chap. 5.

Age too has an important effect on leisure pursuits, as I have argued. On this see also Frith's analysis of the concentration among the young of interest in rock music. Class differences do exist, but they are not as striking as differences of age. Simon Frith, *Sound Effects* (New York: Pantheon, 1981).

Like Robinson, Caplow concluded that class differences in how people spend leisure were not major. For the limited impact of occupation on leisure in the English family see Michael Young and Peter Willmott, *The Symmetrical Family* (New York: Pantheon, 1973). For a summary of the literature on leisure that emphasizes the secondary importance of occupation, see John Wilson, "Sociology of Leisure," *Annual Review of Sociology* 6 (1980):21–40.

Chapter 3

1. Morton Hunt, *Her Infinite Variety: The American Woman as Lover, Mate and Rival* (New York: Harper and Row, 1962), quoted in Komarovsky, *Blue-Collar Marriage*, 112. This modern ideal has been given a number of names—for instance, the "symmetrical family" or the "companionate marriage."

2. For historical accounts of the development of the modern ideal of the "companionate marriage" see Philippe Ariès, "The Family and the City," in *The Family*, ed. Alice S. Rossi (New York: Norton, 1978), and idem, *Centuries of Childhood: A Social History of Family Life* (New York: Vintage Books, 1965); Ernest Burgess, Harvey Locke, and Mary Thomas, *The Family* (New York: American Book Company, 1963); Young and Willmott, *Symmetrical Family*; Lawrence Stone, *The Family, Sex and Marriage in England, 1500–1800* (New York: Harper and Row, 1977). The quotations in the text are from Ariès, "Family and the City."

3. For accounts of the way the American family has lost many of its material functions see Kenneth Keniston, *All Our Children: The American Family under Pressure* (New York: Harcourt Brace Jovanovich, 1977); Eli Zaretsky, *Capitalism, the Family and Personal Life* (New York: Harper and Row, 1976); Susan Strasser, *Never Done: A History of American Housework* (New York: Pantheon, 1982). For a dissenting view see Caplow et al, *Middletown Families*, chap. 13.

4. For a discussion of the emotional overload that the modern "companionate family," with its pull to separate members from the community, places on spouses and children see Ariès, "Family and the City"; Stone, *Family, Sex and Marriage in England, 1500–1800*, 682–87; and Zaretsky, *Capitalism, the Family and Personal Life*.

5. See Lee Rainwater, Richard Coleman, and Gerald Handel, *Workingman's Wife* (New York: Oceana Publications, 1959), 25, and Rubin, *Worlds of Pain*, 215 and passim. For Komarovsky's concern with similarities as well as differences see *Blue-Collar Marriage*, especially 22 and 355. For families in Middletown today see Caplow et al., *Middletown Families*. In later writings on the same topic Rainwater and Handel present a picture more like Komarovsky's. See, for instance, Handel and Rainwater, "Persistence and Change in Working-Class Life Style" and "Changing Family Roles in the Working Class," in *Blue-Collar World*, ed. Shostak and Gomberg.

6. Komarovsky also concentrated on couples with these characteristics, which would explain most of the differences, not striking in any case, between her findings and mine.

For the concentration on one stage in the marital cycle, couples with young children, see Rubin, p. 9, Komarovsky, p. 9, and Rainwater, p. 19. Rubin specifies at least one child under twelve and still in the home as well as a wife under forty. Komarovsky aimed to include only couples under forty-one years of age and with at least one child. Rainwater concentrates on young housewives with children.

For the exclusion of couples where either spouse has more than a high-school education see Rubin, p. 9, and Komarovsky, p. 9. Rainwater et al. do not insist on wives with no more than a high-school education, but they imply that all, or almost all, of their sample are in this position (see, for instance, pp. 26 and 99–101).

For the definition of a blue-collar or working-class marriage as one where the husband is a blue-collar worker regardless of the wife's occupation see Rubin, p. 9, Komarovsky, pp. 9 and 65, and Rainwater, p. 16. In fact, these authors do not always stick to this definition. Thus toward the end of her study Komarovsky added a small number (10 percent) of white-collar husbands (pp. 9 and 356). And not all the wives Rainwater studied turned out to have husbands in blue-collar occupations (19 percent of the husbands were not—p. 219). In general there is an awkwardness when these authors discuss the occupations of their "blue-collar" or "working-class" couples. This reflects the difficulty of ignoring the wife's occupation when defining the social class of the marriage.

7. As the Introduction pointed out, from a variety of social occasions I knew the wives of most men and came to know very well about a third, who were representative of the range of occupations of the wives in general.

Anyone who has conducted sociological research into marital relations is likely to consider his own work, and other people's, with some humility. The inner life of a marriage, often personal and delicate, is not something most people are eager to reveal to a researcher. This chapter is not intended as a complete analysis of marriage. Rather, it aims to consider the light their marriages throw on these chemical workers' position in the class structure. For that reason it discusses a more limited range of themes than existing studies of "blue-collar marriage."

Yet compared with the data from those studies, the information I gathered has a major strength. Much of it comes from men speaking in as natural a setting as a researcher is likely to find. By contrast, until recently the vast majority of research into the family (blue collar and white collar) was based on interviews with the wives. This provoked the comment that "family sociology" is really "wives' sociology" (Constantina Safilios-Rothschild, "Family Sociology or Wives' Family Sociology?" *Journal of Marriage and the Family* 31 (1969):290–301). And when husbands were interviewed too, albeit separately from their wives, it was sometimes in a context where they could not feel entirely free to be candid. This might have been because they knew the interviewer was also speaking to their wives. Or it might have been because such interviews usually occurred in the home, where men are often more restrained and subdued than outside among male friends. For instance, Komarovsky's classic study, in which husbands and wives were interviewed in their homes, together and separately, was conducted under conditions where men clearly did not feel entirely comfortable. As she wrote: "The husbands talked easily enough about their jobs, but when the interviewer turned to the marriage relation many became obviously uncomfortable. They squirmed, perspired or got up and moved about the room" (*Blue-Collar Marriage*, 14). By contrast, the bulk of the discussions reported here occurred outside men's homes, at work or in a setting such as the tavern.

8. Thus what most workers are reporting here is not quite the same as whether they have a psychological sense of well-being ("happiness") with their wife and children. At the same time, when workers ask themselves if they are glad or sorry to be married, the question whether the time they spend with wife and children brings about such a psychological state is a major consideration, for increasingly in America "happiness" in this sense is seen as the goal of marriage.

Measuring "happiness" as a psychological state of well-being, akin to pleasure, is fraught with difficulties, as has often been pointed out. See, for instance, Edwin Lively, "Toward Concept Clarification," *Journal of Marriage and the Family* 31 (February 1969): 108–14. For an example of a study that does attempt to measure marital happiness as a psychological state see Susan Orden and Norman Bradburn, "Dimensions of Marriage Happiness," *American Journal of Sociology* 73 (May 1968):715–31. Such studies typically find the vast majority of respondents reporting themselves as "very happy" or "happy." These are higher proportions than I found among Imperium workers talking either about "happiness' in marriage as a psychological state or about whether they were glad or sorry to be married. However, in the light of the high and rising divorce rate in America the main effect of such widespread reports of psychological well-being in marriage is to cast doubt on the measurement instrument itself. As one study put it: "The fact that persons tend to rate their marriage as 'very happy,' 'happy,' or 'average in happiness,' and rarely as 'unhappy' or 'very unhappy' is the major weakness of self-rating of happiness as a criterion of marital success" (Burgess et al., *Family*, 292).

9. This is also a major theme in Komarovsky's study. A number of works have discussed the struggle between the blue-collar husband and his wife, most intense at the start of the marriage, over whether the husband will continue to spend most of his leisure time with his friends or will now spend it with his wife. See Gans, *Urban Villagers*, 70–71, and Komarovsky, *Blue-Collar Marriage*, 28–32.

10. Young and Willmott, *Symmetrical Family*, 252–53.

11. Kanter, *Men and Women of the Corporation*, 116–17. Kanter argues that the ways a manager's job intrudes on his wife's life and leisure change as he moves up the career ladder. See her discussion of the "corporate wife's career progression," pp. 112 ff.

12. For this point see also Komarovsky, *Blue-Collar Marriage*, 332.

13. The classic statement of the view that if a wife's occupation approaches (or worse, equals or exceeds) her husband's a destructively competitive element is likely to be injected into the marriage is made by Talcott Parsons. See, for instance, "The Kinship System of the United States," *American Anthropologist* 45 (January–March 1943):22–38, and "The Social Structure of the Family," in *The Family: Its Function and Destiny*, ed. Ruth Anshen (New York: Harper and Brothers, 1949), 173–201.

A more recent theory also predicts marital trouble if the status of the wife's occupation, especially as measured in income, considerably exceeds that of the husband's. However, this theory suggests that a wife's occupation may approach, equal, or even moderately exceed that of her husband without causing marital problems so long as her occupation enhances rather than detracts from the status of the *family as a whole*. Thus a wife whose *earnings* equal those of her husband may, by raising the joint family income, enhance the status of the family. Yet if her *occupation* considerably exceeds that of her husband in status then it is likely to cause problems (i.e., detract from the family's status) by casting doubt on the husband's role as breadwinner. For this view see Oppenheimer, "Sociology of Women's Economic Role in the Family."

Komarovsky stresses the difference education makes in marital satisfaction and communication. See *Blue-Collar Marriage*, passim. For a recent study, based on a national survey, arguing that education (rather than occupation) is salient for people's ability to handle and resolve marital conflict effectively, see Anne Locksley, "Social Class and Marital Attitudes and Behavior," *Journal of Marriage and the Family* 44 (May 1982):427-40.

14. This couple illustrates another way existing studies that concentrate on families with young children overlook or underestimate those wives of blue-collar workers in professional or semi-professional occupations. One reason this wife was able to pursue a college education was that she is childless. Women in such marriages could be expected to be more likely to have careers than any other group of blue-collar workers' wives.

15. See chapter 7.

16. For the studies of Cahalan and associates see Don Cahalan, Ira Cisin, and Helen Crossley, *American Drinking Practices: A National Study of Drinking Behavior and Attitudes* (New Brunswick, N.J.: Rutgers Center of Alcohol Studies, 1969); Don Cahalan, *Problem Drinkers* (San Francisco: Jossey-Bass, 1970); Don Cahalan and Robin Room, *Problem Drinking among American Men* (New Brunswick, N.J.: Rutgers Center of Alcohol Studies, 1974). The literature on drinking and problem drinking is enormous. For a useful summary of the sociological, psychological, medical, and biological literature see Julian Roebuck and Raymond Kessler, *The Etiology of Alcoholism* (Springfield, Ill.: Charles C. Thomas, 1972).

17. For a summary of this data see Eli Ginzberg, "The Job Problem," *Scientific American* 237 (November 1977):43–52.

18. The data are reported in Oppenheimer, "Sociology of Women's Economic Role in the Family." They are based on a sample of white couples drawn from the 1970 census.

19. For data on the extent to which most of the new jobs created in America since 1950 have been low-paying clerical and secretarial jobs filled largely by married women see Ginzberg, "The Job Problem." For data on the disproportionate concentration, amounting in some cases to segregation, of women

into certain occupations see Valerie Kincade Oppenheimer, *The Female Labor Force in the United States*, and Treiman and Terrell, "Women, Work and Wages." Women are concentrated in clerical and service jobs and in certain professions, notably teaching, nursing, and social work.

20. Drawing on national survey data, Glenn and his co-workers stress this point. See Norval Glenn, Adreain Ross, and Judy Corder Tully, "Patterns of Intergenerational Mobility through Marriage," *American Sociological Review* 39 (October 1974):683–700. The number of women from upper-white-collar families who marry blue-collar workers contrasts with the infrequency with which sons of upper-white-collar fathers take blue-collar jobs. In explaining this finding Glenn comments that sons of white-collar workers may be deterred from taking blue-collar jobs by the dirty conditions and physical labor often associated with such work. However, the wife of a blue-collar worker does not directly experience these conditions and "may typically be more concerned about the size of the family income than about symbols of white-collar status."

21. On the tendency for people to marry persons of similar social and educational background see Blau and Duncan, *American Occupational Structure*. For the strain toward status consistency within marriage see Oppenheimer, "Sociology of Women's Economic Role in the Family."

22. For the observation that if wives work this is important to them see Komarovsky, chap. 3, and Rubin, chap. 9. For a general protest about the tendency for studies of stratification to ignore women see Joan Acker, "Women and Social Stratification: A Case of Intellectual Sexism," *American Journal of Sociology* 78 (January 1973):936–45.

A number of studies have challenged the idea that a wife's conception of her social status is derived exclusively from her husband's occupation and not at all from her own. See, for example, Dana Hiller and William Philliber, "The Derivation of Status Benefits from Occupational Attainments of Working Wives," *Journal of Marriage and the Family* 40 (1978): 63–69; and Kathleen Ritter and Lowell Hargens, "Occupational Positions and Class Identifications of Married Working Women: A Test of the Asymmetry Hypothesis," *American Journal of Sociology* 80 (January 1975): 934–48.

For other writers who suggest that if the occupations of wives are taken seriously then the distinction between "blue-collar" and "middle-class" marriage becomes blurred, see Ernest Barth and Walter Watson, "Social Stratification and the Family in Mass Society," *Social Forces* 47 (March 1967):392–402, and Marie Haig, "Social Class Measurement and Women's Occupational Roles," *Social Forces* 52 (September 1973):86–98.

The view that wives of blue-collar workers are a type distinct from wives of upper-white-collar workers rests only in part on the notion that they have a distinct position in the labor market. In part it also depends on the idea that they have a characteristic personality or psychology. This book cannot seriously examine questions involving personality. Yet there are reasons to question the view that there is a distinct personality associated with women married to blue-collar workers, at least when applied to wives of better-paid workers.

First, few of the classic psychoanalysts argue that personality varies systematically with social class. Even those strongly influenced by Marxism rarely make a distinction between a "working-class" and a "middle-class" personality. Wilhelm Reich explicitly rejected this idea, arguing that "there are no 'class distinctions' when it comes to character." See Wilhelm Reich, *The Mass Psychology of Fascism*, 3d ed. (New York: Simon and Schuster, 1970).

Likewise, a recent attempt to combine sociology and psychoanalysis focuses almost entirely on differences of gender, not social class. See Nancy Chodorow, *The Reproduction of Mothering: Psychoanalysis and the Sociology of Gender* (Berkeley: University of California Press, 1978).

Second, there are the selection criteria of the two main sociological studies that do make this claim. The notion that nowadays wives of blue-collar workers, in contrast to wives of upper-white-collar workers, are "psychologically passive," characterized by "loneliness," "shyness and retreat," "a marked sense of inferiority to the male," and an "unwillingness to be assertive around men" lacks conviction if based on studies that disregard those wives of blue-collar workers least likely to conform to such an image—the women without young children and with more than a high-school education. (The two main sociological studies that posit a major difference between the personalities of working-class and middle-class women are Rainwater et al., *Workingman's Wife*, and Rubin, *Worlds of Pain*. The quotations above are from Rainwater. However, this portrait may have been more accurate before women seriously entered the labor market in large numbers, and it may be more accurate for wives of poorly paid blue-collar workers.)

Some wives of Imperium workers do correspond to such an image. Many do not. They are assertive and are unwilling to be treated in demeaning or sexist ways. Consider this woman in her late forties, with three sons in college or high school. She was recounting her reaction, hardly passive, to an insulting job interview:

> They guy [interviewer] asked me all kinds of questions like was I serious about the job, and did I plan to stay fifteen years. I got very angry. I said, "I don't know. I might be dead! Where are *you* going to be in fifteen years?" He got very red. Of course I didn't get the job. What they really want is some young girl who will think they're God and they can pat and pinch, and she won't know enough to say anything.

Another wife, a social worker with two years of college who worked for a Head Start program, successfully resisted her supervisor's attempts to fire her. For a year she mobilized the support of the parents of the children she worked with. Her husband also exerted pressure on her behalf through his union friends. Four years later, she still has her job.

The view that blue-collar men have a distinct personality is also difficult. This chapter and the previous one argue that a relatively low level of education and the absence of a job that is a central interest add a flavor and tone to men's lives. In his classic study of child-rearing Melvin Kohn argued that, as a result of these same forces, working-class parents tend to place more emphasis on their children's conforming to external standards, for this is what the parents are required to do at work. By contrast, middle-class parents are more likely to encourage their children toward self-direction, for this is a requirement of their own jobs. But Kohn is careful to stress that such child-rearing practices do not constitute a distinct personality. Further, in some areas of their lives, for instance their generally critical attitude toward politicians, most Imperium workers are far from conformist (and much of their conformity to rules in the workplace is cosmetic, more apparent than real, as will become clear in parts 2 and 3).

In this light it is not surprising that attempts to specify a basic working-class male personality are very few and are hedged with caveats. (Consider, for instance, Lipset's well-known claim that working-class men and women have "psychological predispositions" that are "authoritarian." This sounds like a statement about the personality of the working class; as such it has aroused much controvesy. Yet Lipset turns out to be unwilling to defend such a view. Instead he defends the much weaker, even banal view that "neither class, middle or working . . . is authoritarian but both classes have values which could be turned in the direction of authoritarianism under certain conditions.") For Lipset's original statement of his theory, and his later statement, see Seymour Martin Lipset, *Political Man: The Social Bases of Politics* (Baltimore: Johns Hopkins University Press, 1981), 87–126 and 476–88. The two critics referred to above are S. M. Miller and Frank Riessman, "Working-Class Authoritarianism: A Critique of Lipset," *British Journal of Sociology* 12 (September 1961):263–76. For Kohn's caution about going from statements about parental values and child-rearing practices to more general statements about personality, see *Class and Conformity*, xxxiii, and also 202, where he explicitly dissociates himself from Lipset's theory of a working-class "authoritarian personality structure."

23. See chapter 7 for discussion of how workers have the same belief about their own occupational attainments, and see chapter 7, note 13 for studies that point out how widespread this belief is in America.

24. Clifford Sager, *Marriage Contracts and Couple Therapy: Hidden Forces in Intimate Relationships* (New York: Brunner-Mazel, 1976), chap. 6.

25. For an analysis of the way most workers become locked into their jobs see part 3.

Chapter 4

1. This is the general view of Blauner, *Alienation and Freedom*; Alain Touraine, *Workers' Attitudes to Technical Change* (Paris: Organization for Economic Cooperation and Development, 1965); Joan Woodward, *Industrial Organization: Behaviour and Control* (London: Oxford University Press, 1970);

Serge Mallet, *La nouvelle classe ouvrière*; United States Department of Health, Education, and Welfare, *Work in America* (Cambridge: MIT Press, 1973).

2. For this picture see Braverman, *Labor and Monopoly Capital*, and Theo Nichols and Huw Beynon, *Living with Capitalism* (London: Routledge and Kegan Paul, 1977).

3. The case of the English miners is cited in Huw Beynon, *Working for Ford* (London: Penguin, 1973). Frederick Taylor considered these two worlds at work to be rampant during his time; "scientific management" was designed to break down the barrier between them. How far it has been successful is one of the topics of this book. For Taylor's view of the labor force see Frederick Taylor, *Scientific Management* (New York: Harper and Row, 1911), especially chap. 1. The informal organization of work was, of course, the main focus of the "human relations" school of industrial sociology. For notable examples of this approach see F.H. Roethlisberger and J. Dickson, *Management and the Worker* (Cambridge: Harvard University Press, 1939), and Alexander Horsfall and Conrad Arensberg, "Teamwork and Productivity in a Shoe Factory," *Human Organization* 8 (Winter 1949): 13–25.

In addition, there are questions about some of the survey data that has been used to support the more optimistic view of work in automated plants. For instance, some of Blauner's evidence, as he presents it, does not support his conclusions. See especially the data in his tables 36, 37, 39, 41, and 48.

On the other hand, an alarmingly large number of the case studies cited in support of the argument in *Work in America* rely entirely on the assessments of "plant managers," "project managers," and even a "vice-president." These are hardly independent sources. See *Work in America*, appendix.

Another important study that posits the more optimistic view is based almost entirely on discussion with French Communist party militants outside the plant. This hardly gets at the perspective of the ordinary worker. See Mallet, *La nouvelle classe ouvrière*.

4. Two outstanding studies are James Bright, *Automation and Management* (Boston: Harvard University Press, 1958), and Kornblum, *Blue-Collar Community*. Bright's analysis is, as he emphasizes, based on interviews with management. Kornblum's study of steelworkers deals mostly with a different, though related, set of issues than those discussed in parts 2 and 3 of this book. An excellent recent account of work in British and French oil refineries is Duncan Gallie, *In Search of the New Working Class* (Cambridge: Cambridge University Press, 1978).

5. "Fasic" is substituted for the real chemical name to avoid identifying the plant, as are "PVT" and "tryamine" in the following paragraphs.

6. Bright, *Automation and Management*, 41.

7. This method of ranking will underestimate the popularity of jobs in maintenance, since in order to enter maintenance a worker needs more seniority than other applicants and also must pass tests in mathematics and general intelligence. Some workers who would like to become mechanics and have enough seniority cannot pass these tests. This should be borne in mind when interpreting the data in tables 13 and 14.

8. This discussion of "automation" follows Bright, *Automation and Management*, and A. P. Usher, *A History of Mechanical Inventions* (Boston: Beacon Press, 1959), 117–20.

9. Usher, *History of Mechanical Inventions*, 117–20.

10. The concept of a "mechanization profile" was explained earlier in this chapter.

11. Bright shows, for a large number of automated plants, the variety of mechanization levels involved in the production process as a whole and in the jobs of individual workers. More than half the workers in the steel mill Kornblum studied did mostly manual, laboring work. Mallet mentions, but discounts the importance of, a sizable group of laboring jobs in the Caltex refinery in France. And most jobs in the English chemical plant Nichols and Beynon studied actually involved packing fertilizer into bags.

Chapter 5

1. Examples of employees who work alone are the boiler operators in this study, the operators in the chemical complex in the south of England studied by Nichols and Beynon, and some of the process workers in the Luton plant studied by Goldthorpe. Examples of settings that have several workers in a crew are the three other types of monitoring in this study, the coffee plant in Birmingham studied by

Mann, the chemical plant in the south of England studied by Woodward, and the American chemical plant studied by Blauner.

2. Compare the comment of a projectionist in a motion-picture theater: "The two-man operation has another sort of mental hazard. You just have to be compatible with your partner—it's just like being married to him. You live with him alone in a small booth for a good part of your time. . . . You must have read in the papers about the operator who killed his partner with the fire extinguisher in the booth, or the other case where the operator knifed his partner with a screw driver." Quoted in Eli Ginzberg and H. Berman, *The American Worker in the Twentieth Century* (New York: Free Press, 1963).

3. Ralph Landau, ed., *The Chemical Plant from Process Selection to Commercial Operation* (New York: Reinhold, 1960).

4. See Blauner and Mallet. In contrast, Gallie notes that, in the British and French refineries he studied, workers saw the dangerous nature of the job as a major drawback. See *In Search of the New Working Class*, chap. 4.

5. An example of this standard complaint is the following comment about his job from an auto worker: "Any junior high school kid could do it," quoted in Charles Walker and Robert Guest, *The Man on the Assembly Line* (Cambridge: Harvard University Press, 1952).

6. For other studies of shift work as a source of employee discontent see Paul Mott and F. Mann, *Shift Work* (Ann Arbor: University of Michigan Press, 1965); Zweig, *The Worker in an Affluent Society*, part 3; Gallie, *In Search of the New Working Class*, chap. 4; and John Dunlop, *Industrial Relations Systems* (New York: Holt, 1958), chap. 2.

7. For instance, Nedra Belloc and Lester Breslow, "Relationship of Physical Health Status and Health Practices," *Preventive Medicine* 1 (August 1972):409–21.

8. P. Pigors and F. Pigors, *Human Aspects of Multiple Shift Operations (Cambridge, Mass.: Addison-Wesley, 1944), chap. 4.*

9. Peter Doeringer and Michael Piore, *Internal Labor Markets and Manpower Analysis* (Lexington, Mass.: Heath, 1971), chap. 6.

10. This special knowledge is an important part of the reason why operators in such plants are "trained on the job." Management often cannot train them because there are aspects of the job supervisors do not know. This point is also made by Doeringer and Piore, *Internal Labor Markets and Manpower Analysis*.

11. As I explained earlier, because of differences in the strength of raw materials there is a certain unpredictability in the time a batch takes to cook. But twenty-four hours far exceeds this normal variation.

12. Mann, *Workers on the Move*.

13. The tendency to exaggerate the degree of "Taylorization" of the labor force in advanced industrial societies is further discussed in the conclusion to part 2. Chapter 6 provides more evidence of the extent to which these men have gained control over their work situation.

Reviewing the historical evidence, Richard Edwards commented: "the extent and incidence of scientific management has always been something of a mystery, but the available evidence suggests that Taylorism was largely confined to smaller, usually nonunionized enterprises." See Richard Edwards, *Contested Terrain: The Transformation of the Workplace in the Twentieth Century* (New York: Basic Books, 1979), 100–101.

Chapter 6

1. See chapter 7 for a full discussion of this point.

2. On the way engineers view their work see R. Ritti, *The Engineer in the Industrial Corporation* (New York: Columbia University Press, 1971), and Robert Zussman, *Mechanics of the Middle Class: Work and Politics among Engineers* (Berkeley: University of California Press, forthcoming).

3. The machinery on the second and third floors is operated by one worker, the briquetter leader. It is highly automated—the cooling system needs only occasional monitoring (mechanization level 11), and the briquetter machine makes briquette after briquette without human intervention (mechanization level 12). The leader's job is routine, though he is not as closely tied to the machinery as the helpers. Like

process and batch operators who monitor instruments, he can move around and spend time on other pursuits that interest him.

4. For general accounts of the often ambiguous and weak position of the modern foreman see Theodore Caplow, *Principles of Organization* (New York: Harcourt, Brace and World, 1964); Delbert Miller and William Form, *Industrial Sociology* (New York: Harper and Row, 1964); and Richard Hall, *Occupations and the Social Structure* (Englewood Cliffs, N.J.: Prentice-Hall, 1975).

5. Except for "tank car handlers" and "weighmen." See the following paragraphs.

Conclusion to Part 2

1. There are, of course, exceptions. A few men even say assembly work is interesting. See Walker and Guest, *Man on the Assembly Line*.

2. This is the problem with most "job enrichment" proposals. The changes suggested come nowhere near providing this kind of variety and freedom and often involve extra work. For a strong and optimistic statement of the benefits of job enrichment see the Report of a Special Task Force to the Secretary of Health, Education, and Welfare, *Work in America* (Cambridge: MIT Press, 1974).

3. As one study of privates in the American army put it: "the enlisted culture is to a large degree a working-class culture in the elementary sense that, to begin with, most enlisted men come from working-class origins." See Charles Moskos, *The American Enlisted Man* (New York: Russell Sage, 1970), 64.

It is, of course, just as hard to study army life as *it really is* as it is to discover what blue-collar workers actually do. And for the same reasons. If our image of army life is more realistic than that of industrial life the reason is probably that considerably more of the intellectuals who wrote about these areas had experience of the army (albeit through being drafted) than of work in the factory.

4. For a protest against the tendency to view assembly workers in the auto industry as automatons see B. J. Widick, ed., *Auto Work and Its Discontents* (Baltimore: Johns Hopkins University Press, 1976). A case study of the way auto workers in a Ford factory in England seized control of the line is contained in Beynon, *Working for Ford*,

5. Widick, *Auto Work and Its Discontents*, chap. 1.

6. For historical studies of workers in England and America that are compatible with this perspective see Andrew Friedman, *Industry and Labor* (London: Macmillan, 1977); and David Mongomery, *Workers' Control in America* (London: Cambridge University Press, 1979).

Introduction to Part 3

1. For this view see Blauner, *Alienation and Freedom*, and Touraine, *Workers' Attitudes to Technical Change*.

2. Chinoy, *Automobile Workers and the American Dream*, chap. 5.

Chapter 7

1. For an account of how management introduced such job hierarchies into the steel industry around the turn of the twentieth century in order to weaken solidarity among the work force see Katherine Stone, "The Origins of Job Structures in the Steel Industry," *Review of Radical Political Economics* 6 (Summer 1974):113–73.

2. A batch is worth from $40,000 to $100,000. Promotion up the blue-collar hierarchy is strictly by seniority unless the company can demonstrate that a worker is incompetent. Ruining three batches in a short space of time would be convincing evidence of incompetence.

3. Men in production, who work shifts, are less likely to take the job of chief or leader than are support workers, most of whom do not work shifts. Among production workers 57 percent declined the top job, while only 38 percent of support workers did so (table 19). This is because on the afternoon and midnight shifts, when most management and supervision have gone home, the opportunities for social activities are greater than during the day, and so a production worker is losing more than a support worker if he becomes a chief or leader.

4. See Kanter, *Men and Women of the Corporation*, chaps. 2, 6, and 7. Another study that notes the reluctance of many blue-collar workers (steelworkers in this case) to become supervisors, mostly because the extra money is seen as not worth the extra worry and responsibility, is Charles Walker, *Steeltown* (New York: Harper, 1950), chap. 4. See also Richard Hall, *Occupations and the Social structure* (Englewood Cliffs, N.J.: Prentice-Hall, 1975), chap. 7.

5. Gallie points out that blue-collar workers in the French and British refineries he studied rarely move into even the lowest levels of management, for companies are increasingly recruiting highly qualified engineers for such positions. See *In Search of the New Working Class*, chap. 9. On the limited chances blue-collar workers have for upward mobility see also Ginzberg and Berman, *American Worker in the Twentieth Century*, chap. 11, and Goldthorpe et al., *Affluent Worker*, vol. 1, chap. 6.

6. For this view see Blauner, *Alienation and Freedom*, Touraine, *Workers' Attitudes to Technical Change*, and Mallet, *La nouvelle classe ouvrière*.

7. Compare the remark of Aronowitz: "Even the Paperworkers Union, representing the highly dangerous asbestos-producing plants of Johns-Manville, is fearful that a serious effort to eliminate dangerous conditions would cause the company to run away from its New Jersey locations to more hospitable environments." See Stanley Aronowitz, *False Promises: The Shaping of American Working-Class Consciousness* (New York: McGraw-Hill, 1973), chap. 8.

8. M. Rothbaum, *The Government of the Oil, Chemical and Atomic Workers Union* (New York: John Wiley, 1962), chap. 2, discusses this development, and Gallie, *In Search of the New Working Class*, chap. 4, points to a similar tendency for management in French and British refineries to reduce the number of mechanics.

9. United State Department of Labor, *Employment and Earnings* (December 1974); United States Bureau of Mines, *Annual Petroleum Statement and Monthly Petroleum Statements* (1974); United States Department of Commerce, *Survey of Current Business* (May 1957 and May 1968).

10. On the tendency of blue-collar workers to stay in their jobs because they have built up seniority and because they probably cannot do much better elsewhere see Ginzberg and Berman, *American Worker in the Twentieth Century*, chap. 11.

11. Mann, *Workers on the Move*, chap. 7, emphasizes the extent to which mechanics are less dependent on the company than are other workers in the plant.

12. The kinds of jobs chemical workers consider ideal are very similar to the jobs auto workers fantasize about. See Chinoy, chap.7, and Beynon, chap. 5. The Berger quotation is from *Working-Class Suburb*, 88.

13. For an account of this belief among a group of white working-class men see Robert Lane, *Political Ideology; Why the American Common Man Believes What He Does*, (New York, Free Press, 1967), chap 4. A more recent study that finds the belief that America is an "effortocracy" to be widespread among all sectors of the population is Coleman and Rainwater, *Social Standing in America*, especially chap. 12. However, Coleman and Rainwater report much doubt among respondents whether America will *continue* to be an "effortocracy" in view of, for instance, the perceived oversupply of educated people.

The *actual* extent of upward mobility in America, both now and in the past, has been widely debated. See, for example, Stephan Thernstrom, *The Other Bostonians* (Cambridge: Harvard University Press, 1973); Seymour Martin Lipset and Reinhard Bendix, *Social Mobility in Industrial Society* (Berkeley: University of California Press, 1960); S. M. Miller, "Comparative Social Mobility," *Current Sociology* 9 (1960):1–89; Blau and Duncan, *The American Occupational Structure*; and Otis Dudley Duncan, David Featherman, and Beverly Duncan, *Socioeconomic Background and Achievement* (New York: Seminar Press, 1972).

14. For examples of this view see Goldthorpe et al., *Affluent Worker*, and Hamilton, *Class and Politics in the United States*.

Chapter 8

1. An account, albeit fictional, of a Welsh mining community—a classic site of working-class solidarity—that does not ignore the existence of conflict and disputes between workers is Richard Llewellyn, *How Green Was My Valley* (New York: Macmillan, 1940).

Many, but not all, of the disputes at Imperium are the direct or indirect result of management policies that structure disputes in this manner, converting management-worker conflicts into conflicts between individual workers or groups of workers. For an interesting discussion of the "translation of hierarchical domination into lateral antagonisms" in industry see Michael Burawoy, *Manufacturing Consent* (Chicago: University of Chicago Press, 1979), chap. 4.

2. See Leonard Sayles and George Strauss, *The Local Union* (New York: Harper and Row, 1953), chap. 3. However, attendance is higher at smaller locals, which probably explains the case of Imperium.

3. Ibid.

4. Radcliffe-Brown, "On Joking Relationships," in *Structure and Function in Primitive Society* (New York: Free Press, 1965).

5. "Ritual" here means "rule-governed activity of a symbolic character that draws the attention of its participants to objects of thought and feeling they hold to be of special significance." For a justification of this definition see Steven Lukes, "Political Ritual and Social Integration," *Sociology* 9 (May 1975):289–308. The whole question of ritual is discussed in detail in chapter 13.

6. Goosing is a common practice among the chemical workers. For a reference to it among construction workers see E. E. LeMasters, *Blue-Collar Aristocrats* (Madison: University of Wisconsin Press, 1975). A more explicit version of the same kind of ritual is the practice among Teamsters (long-distance truckers) of symbolically mounting each other. For other studies that suggest joking relations among blue-collar workers reflect friendship and solidarity, see Herbert Applebaum, *Royal Blue: The Culture of Construction Workers* (New York: Holt, Rinehart and Winston, 1981), and William Pilcher, *The Portland Longshoremen* (New York: Holt, Rinehart and Winston, 1972).

7. This is the aspect of joking relations emphasized by Radcliffe-Brown.

8. As this quotation implies, joking relations do not always succeed in mediating quarrels. If the issues are too serious men may fight. Compare Kornblum's statement that joking relations usually, but not always, blunt racial cleavages in the steel mill, where black workers are heavily concentrated among the laborers.

9. This was the aspect of joking relations that Marcel Mauss emphasized. See "Parentés à Plaisanteries," *L'Annuaire de L'Ecole des Hautes Etudes*, section des sciences religieuses, Paris, 1928; reprinted in Marcel Mauss, *Oeuvres*, 3:109–35. (Paris: Editions de Minuit, 1969).

For an account of the continuous competition for status and power that goes on among working-class Italians see Gans, *Urban Villagers*, 81–82.

The competitive aspect of joking relations can be clearly seen in, for example, "sounding." This is the practice, found among certain adolescent groups in America, of competing to offer the most colorful insults, especially about the opponent's mother. For examples of "sounding" see John Dollard, "The Dozens: Dialectic of Insult," *American Imago* 1:3–24; Roger Abrahams, "Playing the Dozens," *Journal of American Folklore* 75 (1962): 209–20; William Labov, "Rules for Ritual Insults," In *Studies in Social Interaction*, ed. David Sudnow (New York: Free Press, 1972).

The competitive aspect of joking relations is also very clear in the institution of the potlatch among the Kwakiutl Indians. At the height of the grease feast, during which a chief burns enormous quantities of fish oil to demonstrate his wealth and power, he launches into ritual insults against his rival. See Franz Boas, *The Social Organization of the Kwakiutl Indians* (Washington, D.C., 1897).

10. Joking relations operating on more than one level may be said to be "overdetermined" in Freud's sense of the term . See Sigmund Freud, *The Interpretation of Dreams*, trans. James Strachey (New York: Basic Books, 1959; orginally published in 1900).

Conclusion to Part 3

1. For other accounts of various blue-collar jobs, see the studies cited throughout parts 2 and 3. Being a chemical worker is not as dangerous as being a construction worker; see Applebaum, *Royal Blue*. For recent data showing the concentration among blue-collar workers of physical injuries incurred on the job and requiring amputation, see David McCaffrey, "Work Related Amputations by Type and Prevalence," *Monthly Labor Review* 104 (March 1981):35–40. The "Quality of Employment Surveys" conducted by the Institute for Social Research at the University of Michigan found the percentage of

production workers reporting at least one safety and health hazard in the workplace ranged from 38 percent in 1969 to 78 percent in 1977. See Richard L. Frenkel, W. Curtiss Priest, and Nicholas Ashford, "Occupational Safety and Health," *Monthly Labor Review* 103 (August 1980):11–40. See also Robert Quinn and Graham Staines, *The 1977 Quality of Employment Survey* (Ann Arbor: Institute for Social Research, University of Michigan, 1979).

2. For the repetitive and fairly closely supervised nature of much lower-white-collar work see Michel Crozier, *The Bureacratic Phenomenon* (Chicago: University of Chicago Press, 1964); Harry Braverman, *Labor and Monopoly Capital*; C. Wright Mills, *White Collar*; Erik Olin Wright, Cynthia Cosello, David Hachin, and Joey Sprague, "The American Class Structure," *American Sociological Review* 47 (December 1982):709–26; and Richard Hall, *Occupations and the Social Structure*. Recent studies suggesting that certain lower-white-collar workers have more chances for upward mobility than is sometimes thought are A. Stewart, K. Prandy, and R. M. Blackburn, *Social Stratification and Occupations* (London: Macmillan, 1980), and Thomas DiPrete and Whitman Soule, "Status Boundaries, Labor Markets and the Structure of Mobility: A Case Study in the U.S. Federal Government" (paper presented at the annual meeting of the American Sociological Association, Detroit, September 1983).

3. For professionals and managers see Kanter, *Men and Women of the Corporation*; Erwin Smigel, *The Wall Street Lawyer* (New York: Free Press, 1964); Dan Lortie, *Schoolteacher* (Chicago: University of Chicago Press, 1977); Eliot Freidson, *Profession of Medicine* (New York: Dodd, Mead, 1972); and "Professions and the Occupational Principle," in *Professions and Their Prospects*, ed. Eliot Freidson (Beverly Hills, Calif.: Sage Publications, 1974); William Goode, "Community within a Community: The Professions," *American Sociological Review* 22 (April 1957):194–200; and Robert Zussman, *Mechanics of the Middle Class: Work and Politics among American Engineers* (Berkeley: University of California Press, forthcoming). Some professionals clearly have more autonomy at work than many managers.

Introduction to Part 4

1. Robert S. Lynd and Helen M. Lynd. *Middletown* (New York: Harcourt, Brace and World, 1929), 420.

2. The data for the National Election Studies were originally collected by the Center for Political Studies of the Institute for Social Research, University of Michigan. The data used in this book were made available by the Inter-University Consortium for Political and Social Research.

A great deal of other evidence points to widespread current mistrust of government. For discussions of this evidence by writers of a variety of political persuasions, see Arthur Miller, "Political Issues and Trust in Government: 1964–1970"; Jack Citrin, "Comment: the Political Relevance of Trust in Government"; Morris Janowitz, *The Last Half-Century* (Chicago: University of Chicago Press, 1978), chap. 4; Seymour Lipset and William Schneider, *The Confidence Gap* (New York: Free Press, 1983); Samuel P. Huntington, *American Politics: The Promise of Disharmony* (Cambridge: Harvard University Press, 1981); and Angus Campbell, *The Sense of Well-Being in America* (New York: McGraw-Hill, 1981).

The most systematic source of evidence is a combination of five survey questions from the National Election Studies. These questions, combined to form a "trust in government index," concern respondents' attitudes toward the honesty, integrity, and competence of those people "running the government."

For the point that mistrust of government cuts across social class see Jack Citrin, "Political Disaffection in America: 1958–68," Ph.D diss., University of California, Berkeley, January 1972, and Jack Citrin, Herbert McClosky, J. Merrill Shanks, and Paul M. Sniderman, "Personal and Political Sources of Political Alienation," *British Journal of Political Science* 5 (January 1975).

3. Miller, "Political Issues and Trust in Government," 951.

4. For evidence on the comparatively weak support for socialist and communist parties in the United States as contrasted with, for instance, Italy and France see Michael Mann, *Consciousness and Action among the Western Working Class* (London: Macmillan, 1975), and Robert Dahl, ed., *Political Oppositions in Western Democracies* (New Haven: Yale University Press, 1968).

5. For writers who argue the class consciousness view see Richard Centers, *The Psychology of Social Classes: A Study of Class Consciousness* (Princeton: Princeton University Press, 1949), quotation from

chap. 12; Berger, *Working Class Suburb*, chap. 6; Hamilton, *Class and Politics in the United States*, 179–80; and Reeve Vanneman and Fred Pampel, "The American Perception of Class and Status," *American Sociological Review* 42 (June 1977):422–38.

For the view that consciousness is populist in form see Michael Mann, "The Social Cohesion of Liberal Democracy," *American Sociological Review* 35 (June 1970):423–39, and idem, *Consciousness and Action among the Western Working Class*, chap. 3.

For the view that working class people see society and each other as a collection of separate individuals competing to attain the American dream see Seymour Martin Lipset, *The First New Nation* (New York: Basic Books, 1963), chap. 3; Lane, *Political Ideology*; and Otto Kirchheimer, "Private Man and Society," *Political Science Quarterly* 71 (March 1966):1–24.

Ethnic consciousness is stressed by Andrew Greeley and William McCready, *Ethnicity in the United States* (New York: John Wiley, 1974). Nationalism is stressed by Mike Davis, "The Barren Marriage of American Labor and the Democratic Party," *New Left Review* 24 (November–December 1980):43–84.

Another important tradition maintains that members of the working class, and most Americans, see society as a status hierarchy based on groups distinguished from each other by factors such as income level, education, and social origin. For this view see W. Lloyd Warner, *Social Class in America: A Manual of Procedure for the Measurement of Social Status* (Chicago: Science Research Associates, 1949), and idem, *American Life* (Chicago: University of Chicago Press, 1953); Robert Dahl, *Pluralist Democracy in the United States* (Chicago: Rand McNally, 1967); and Coleman and Rainwater, *Social Standing in America*.

Chapter 9

1. For elections as the central political ritual of liberal democracies see Murray Edelman, *The Symbolic Uses of Politics* (Chicago: University of Illinois Press, 1976); see also Benjamin Ginsberg, *The Consequences of Consent* (Reading, Mass.: Addison-Wesley, 1982).

For the distinction between the "mandate" and "leadership" theories of politics see Joseph Schumpeter, *Capitalism, Socialism, and Democracy* (New York: Harper, 1950), and Graeme Duncan and Steven Lukes, "The New Democracy," *Political Studies* 11 (1963):156–77.

2. For a discussion of the various senses in which politicians are sometimes said to be corrupt see James Bryce, *The American Commonwealth* (New York: Macmillian, 1909), 2:155–56.

3. Most of the rest are younger workers, and there is some tendency for their opinions to change with time and the news. Consider, for instance, a process worker in his early twenties. In 1975 he maintained that most politicians were not crooked: "A few are, and they give the others a bad name. Anyway, I'm more interested in Eastern philosophies, Zen Buddhism, and in music, especially country music." Five years later his views on politicians had come to resemble those of the majority of workers. He was talking about a newspaper article he had read on a large road-building program President Carter had promised to support in Georgia. It turned out the roads were all to be built around Carter's house and peanut business: "Politics is all corrupt. You have to be corrupt to survive, not necessarily all graft, but giving favors. Someone does you a favor, so you do something in return."

4. *Daily Journal*, 1–30 November 1974.

5. In computing the figures cited earlier, such respondents are counted as believing that business *and* the Jews (or the unions) run America.

6. For examples of the view that the working class is less attached to democracy than are higher social classes see Philip Converse, "The Nature of Belief Systems in Mass Politics," in *Ideology and Discontent*, ed. David Apter (New York: Free Press, 1964); Lipset, *Political Man*, chap. 4; and Seymour Martin Lipset and Earl Raab, *The Politics of Unreason* (New York: Harper and Row, 1970).

As I mentioned, the evidence these authors usually cite in support of their claim that those of higher education and social class are more "democratic" tends to concern tolerance toward certain groups and support for certain individual rights, rather than a belief in popular control of government. These ideas should be separated, for belief in popular control of government (for example in majority rule) may well coexist with a certain intolerance toward minorities.

Anyway, recent research casts doubt on the view that those of higher education and social class are more tolerant. It all depends on whom people are asked to tolerate. More highly educated people are no more tolerant of groups they disapprove of, and that threaten them, than are other people. For these points see John J. Sullivan, George E. Marcus, Stanley Feldman, and James Piereson, "The Sources of Political Tolerance," *American Political Science Review* 75 (March 1981):92–106, and John J. Sullivan, James Piereson, and George E. Marcus, *Political Tolerance and American Democracy* (Chicago: University of Chicago Press, 1982).

On the other hand, belief in democracy, in the sense of popular control of government, so widespread among Imperium workers, is widespread among most Americans. Thus, of those respondents to the 1972 National Election Study who said they wanted a change in the *form* of government, the overwhelming majority wanted to see government become more democratic, more responsive to popular desires. See Miller, "Rejoinder to 'Comment' by Jack Citrin: Political Discontent or Ritualism?"

7. A second group of workers, the fewest of all, also conflate "freedom" and "democracy," but in a more complicated way. They sometimes point to the United States as a "democracy" and refer to the existence of free, universal elections in support of their view despite believing that corrupt politicians subvert the electoral process. In part this group, like the minority referred to above, are confusing "freedom" with "democracy." But in part they have in mind the view that elections are of some value, though this is strictly limited. For example, they may believe that occasionally a politician is honest or keeps a promise. This question of the limited and "unofficial" meanings most workers often ascribe to their act of voting is explored in detail in chapter 15.

8. Herbert McClosky, "Consensus and Ideology in American Politics," *American Political Science Review* 58 (June 1964):361–82.

9. See, for instance, Robert Dahl, *Pluralist Democracy in the United States* (Chicago: Rand McNally, 1967), and idem, *Political Oppositions in Western Democracies* (New Haven: Yale University Press, 1968).

Chapter 10

1. Among the many examples of this approach see Centers, *Psychology of Social Classes*; William Buchanan and Hadley Cantril, *How Nations See Each Other* (Urbana: University of Illinois Press, 1953); Center for Political Studies, *American National Election Studies*, 1956–80; Robert Hodge and Donald Treiman, "Class Indentification in the United States," *American Journal of Sociology* 73 (January 1968):535–47; and Hamilton, *Class and Politics in the United States*.

There is some minor variation in the choices these studies offer respondents. For instance, Buchanan and Cantril omit "lower class" and the Center for Political Studies omits "lower class" and "upper class," while Hodge and Treiman add "upper middle class." But what is important is that all these versions offer respondents at least the choice between "middle class" and "working class."

2. For examples of researchers who mention that the choice of which fixed responses to offer with the class identification question significantly affects the results see Hodge and Treiman, "Class Identification in the United States," and Hamilton, *Class and Politics in the United States*, 100.

3. For examples of the use of open-ended questions see Coleman and Rainwater, *Social Standing in America*, and Warner, *Social Class in America*. (Warner uses two methods to "measure social class." The one that is relevant here he calls "evaluated participation." It involves a researcher discussing in detail with respondents the way they see their own social class and that of other people. Much of this is done by asking about the terms "class" and "social class.")

For an argument that the open-ended question is more neutral than the class identification question with fixed responses see James Kluegel and Eliot Smith, "Beliefs about Stratification," in *Annual Review of Sociology*, vol. 7, ed. Ralph Turner and James Short (Palo Alto: Annual Reviews, 1981), 29–56.

It is striking how rarely partisans of the two main research methods discuss, or even acknowledge, each other's approaches. For example W. Lloyd Warner devoted an entire book to the problem of measuring social class, but this is no more than a manual for applying his particular method. He makes no mention of Centers's approach using the class identification question with fixed responses. More recently, Coleman and Rainwater also base their approach on the open-ended question, but they cite almost none of the literature and research based on the class identification question with fixed responses. See Warner, *Social Class in America*, and Coleman and Rainwater, *Social Standing in America*.

4. Samuel Lubell, *The Future While It Happened* (New York: Norton, 1973), 52, 95, 102, and "Man in the Street Looks to Nixon as the Middle Road Alternative," *Boston Sunday Globe*, 29 September 1968.

5. Gans, *Levittowners*, 105.

6. For workers in the East Coast city see Lane, *Political Ideology*, 66, 75, 357, 394. The workers Lane interviewed did sometimes refer to "class," but apparently only when Lane introduced the term into the conversation. For the workers in Providence see Mackenzie, *Aristocracy of Labor*, 101.

7. Studs Terkel, *Working* (New York: Pantheon, 1972), 189, 206–19, 552–58, and Walker, *Steeltown*, 230 ff.

8. John Leggett, *Working-Class Consciousness in Detroit* (New York: Oxford University Press, 1968), appendix A.

The Michigan National Election Studies contain several questions using the term "working man," but none that investigate its meaning.

9. Suspicion and mistrust of professionals is, of course, widespread in American society. William Goode has discussed one reason for this. Many people are unable to assess the quality of the services they receive from professionals because they lack the technical expertise. As a result they are, and feel themselves to be, open to exploitation. See William Goode, "Community within a Community: The Professions." See also Eliot Freidson, *Profession of Medicine* and "Professions and the Occupational Principle." For an account of the suspicion with which first- and second-generation urban Italians view professionals see Gans, *Urban Villagers*, chap. 6.

10. Chapter 3 gave an account of the unhappy school experiences of many workers. In addition to the sources of resentment against teachers just mentioned, teachers may be blamed for the current disorder in American public schools, (teachers "are not tough enough") and for a conflict between parental and school values.

11. For other studies that report widespread hostility toward the poor among blue- and white-collar Americans see J. R. Feagin, *Subordinating the Poor* (Englewood Cliffs, N.J.: Prentice-Hall, 1975); J. Huber and W. H. Form, *Income and Ideology* (New York: Free Press, 1973); Lane, *Political Ideology*, 71–72; LeMasters, *Blue-Collar Aristocrats*, 178–80; J. B. Williamson, "Beliefs about Motivation of Poor and Attitudes toward Poverty Policy," *Social Problems* 21 (1974):634–48; and idem, "Beliefs about Welfare Poor," *Sociology and Social Research* 58 (1974):163–75.

12. The following illustrates the view of one of the *least articulate* Imperium workers on the subject of the working man.

A young batch worker, in his mid-twenties, in the control room:

Worker: What does the working man mean? Well, you're looking at one [himself] right now.

Researcher: Yes, but what does it mean?

Worker: It's hard to explain.

Researcher: Are big business working men?

Worker [emphatically, demonstrating the productive-labor aspect of the term]: No, they just sit on their butts all day. They don't do nothing. They don't do the physical work.

Researcher: Are doctors and lawyers working men?

Worker [doubtfully]: Well . . . I suppose you might say they are, but I'd say they're more like professionals.

Researcher: Are people who work in an office, like the women who work in the office over there [the administration building in the plant] working men?

Worker: [definitely]: No!

Researcher: Why not?

Worker: Well . . . [thinks] you've got me there! I don't know. [Thinks] Well, there's a difference between the guys who sit in the office and write it all out on paper and us. They just sit on their butt and write it on paper [motions with his hand to indicate someone scribbling out instructions], but we're the ones who have to do the shit. [With a mixture of disdain and resentment] Let them [office workers] put on a uniform and come in here. Then they'll find out it's different.

It should be noted that this man, one of the very few who were not from the start articulate about the concept of the working man, after a few seconds of thought explained the term in the same basic way as everyone else.

Chapter 11

1. The distinction, in this and the previous chapter, between images of class based on life at work and on life outside work is preferred to Max Weber's distinction between "classes" and "status groups," for Weber's distinction is not always clear. Sometimes it refers, roughly, to the area of property ownership or production ("classes") in contrast to the area of consumption or life-styles ("status groups"). In this sense it does somewhat overlap with my distinction between work and outside work, though they are not identical. However, sometimes Weber bases the distinction between classes and status groups on the difference between the "objective" and the "subjective." In this sense "classes" are those persons who, while objectively in the same property or market position, do not necessarily view themselves as a group in common, whereas "status groups" are characterized by an awareness within and outside the group that it is a unit. For Weber's use of these terms see Max Weber, *Economy and Society*, ed. Guenther Roth and Claus Wittich (New York: Bedminster Press, 1968). For a discussion of the ambiguity in Weber's terminology see Giddens, *Class Structure of the Advanced Societies*, 78–80.

Ira Katznelson has recently drawn attention to the importance for class consciousness in the United States of the radical separation there of the workplace and of life outside the workplace (in the community). See Ira Katznelson, *City Trenches* (New York: Pantheon, 1981). For a discussion of the relation between Katznelson's view and my findings see the conclusion to part 4, note 6.

2. Imperium workers living in Linden tend to support the presence of Exxon's refinery. Partly this is because the refinery makes a huge contribution to property taxes; partly it is because the refinery was in Linden before these workers, and so its existence was considered in their decision to live there. On the other hand, Imperium workers in the post–World War II suburb of Piscataway are less clear that they want polluting industry there. Partly this is because most of the industry already in Piscataway is "clean"— offices and warehouses—so that a possible polluter such as a recently proposed new chemical plant risks changing the ecology of the town while lowering property taxes only a very little.

3. For a careful study that disputes the view that apartment dwellers contribute disproportionately less than homeowners to municipal revenue or constitute a disproportionate drain on revenue, see New Jersey County and Municipal Government Study Commission, *Housing and Suburbs: Fiscal and Social Impact of Multifamily Development* (Trenton: State of New Jersey, 1975).

4. Likewise, Gans observed that in Levittown most of the Catholics enrolled their children in the parochial school as soon as it opened. See Gans, *Levittowners*, 91.

5. Gans, *Levittowners*.

6. For Berger see *Working-Class Suburb*, chap. 3; for Goldthorpe see *Affluent Worker*, vol. 2, chap. 3. Actually, Goldthorpe found homeownership did make a difference even to political party affiliation but decided to discount the significance of this finding. For a study that shows the impact of homeownership (including among skilled blue-collar workers) on support for the movement in California in the late 1970s to reduce property taxes sharply and to restrict their future growth (the "Proposition 13" movement), see David Sears and Jack Citrin, *Tax Revolt* (Cambridge: Harvard University Press, 1982). For a strong statement of the view that the residential setting generates a politics of its own that is in many ways independent of residents' occupations see Janowitz, *Last Half-Century*, chap. 8. As Janowitz put it, "residential areas throughout metropolitan centers, regardless of their socio-economic status, have become more important as loci for political decisions and political participation" (269–70).

7. Likewise, a recent study stresses the way upper-white-collar men (engineers) have two distinct images of their class position, at and outside work. But these men tend to link their images with the description of themselves as the "working middle class." See Zussman, *Mechanics of the Middle Class*.

8. Coleman and Rainwater, *Social Standing in America*.

9. Mackenzie's study of skilled craftsmen stresses this aspect of class consciousness. However, when Mackenzie asked his sample why they supported the Democratic party, as most of them did, 40 percent of the "pure Democrats" spontaneously mentioned that they considered the Democratic party the party of the "working man."

Rainwater and Coleman suggest that for most Americans this image of class, based on income level and life-style, is perceived as an "almost infinitely graded hierarchy—a continuum, as it were—rather than as a series of discrete groups" (p. 24). Mackenzie makes the same point for the skilled craftsmen he studied. Most Imperium workers do perceive the *middle* of the class structure outside work as more or less a continuum; but, as I have pointed out, most perceive the top as a discrete group that exploits those below. The differences between my findings and those of these studies may have to do with different populations and periods of time. But neither Rainwater nor Mackenzie gave their respondents much chance to discuss their general views of politics and the power structure, which may also explain some of the difference.

10. In my original survey (see Introduction, note 23) I asked the class identification question with fixed responses. In talking to workers who did not respond, and in many further conversations with those who did, I came to realize how ambiguous was the category "working class."

In his 1949 study, Richard Centers was one of the first to argue that "working class" should be offered as one of the possible responses to the class identification question. In the light of the discussion in this chapter about the defects of the category "working class," it is interesting to reexamine Centers's statement of his case. He maintained that general observation had shown him that manual laborers "typically refer to themselves as the 'working class' or as the 'working people' or as the 'working class of people' and as 'labor' or the 'laboring class of people'" (p. 32). Yet if manual laborers typically refer to themselves in these various ways, what is the justification for offering respondents to the class identification question the category "working class" rather than any of the other categories? Centers never explains this.

Berger's study of blue-collar auto workers is interesting here. He uses a combination of the class identification question with fixed categories *and* in open-ended form. Of his respondents, 31 percent placed themselves in the "middle" or "average" class, and 48 percent placed themselves in the "working class." Berger discusses, briefly, what these blue-collar workers appear to mean when they classify themselves in these terms. He says that by working class they mostly seem to mean someone who works with his hands for an hourly wage, usually in a factory. This sounds like the image of class based on the concept of the "working man." By middle class, Berger argues, respondents mostly mean the attaining of a certain income level. This sounds like the image of class based on factors outside work. Yet Berger insists on squeezing the data into a single-image model based on the concept "working class." Thus he argues that the group of workers who say they are "middle" or "average" class really mean they are in the "middle of the working class." This is an ingenious but unconvincing attempt to explain what is much better accounted for by the view that workers have two class identities, referring respectively to life at work and life outside the workplace. For Berger's discussion see *Working-Class Suburb*, 80–90, especially 85–87.

Using data from the National Election Studies and focusing on the male, nonfarm labor force, Vanneman and Pampel found that the dichotomy "manual"/"nonmanual" has an important independent influence on the choice of "working class" or "middle class" in response to the class identification question. This is clearly consistent with the idea of the importance of the concept of the working man. See Vanneman and Pampel, "American Perception of Class and Status."

Chapter 12

1. On the tendency to underestimate nationalism see Isaiah Berlin, "Nationalism: Past Neglect and Present Power," *Partisan Review* 46 (1979):337–58, and Tom Nairn, *The Break-up of Britain* (London: New Left Books, 1977).

2. This phrase is from Karol Gess, "The Vanished Glory: A Problem in International Psychology," *Psychoanalytic Review* 37 (1950):345–50.

3. See S. A. Stouffer, *American Soldier*, vol. 2, *Combat and Its Aftermath* (Princeton: Princeton University Press, 1949), chap. 3, and Remarque, *All Quiet on the Western Front*, 16–17.

4. The quotation is from E. H. Carr, *Nationalism and After* (New York: Macmillan, 1945), 1. For the history of national identification in the United States see Merle Curti, *The Roots of American Loyalty* (New York: Columbia University Press, 1946).

5. For examples of writers who discuss the causes and effects of nationalism without defining it see Wilhelm Reich, *The Mass Psychology of Fascism*, 3d ed. (New York: Simon and Schuster, 1970), and Lewis Namier, "Pathological Nationalisms," *Manchester Guardian*, 26 April 1933.

6. For Berlin's definition see "Nationalism," 345–48. On American individualism see Emile Durkheim, "L'individualisme et les intellectuels," *Revue Bleue* 10 (1898):7–13, trans. S. and J. Lukes as "Individualism and the Intellectuals," *Political Studies* 17 (March 1969):14–30.

Consider another example of an author who defines nationalism in a broad manner. According to Louis Snyder "nationalism" is "that sentiment of a group or body of people within a compact or a noncontiguous territory, using a single language or related dialects as a vehicle for common thoughts and feelings, holding a common religious belief, possessing common institutions, traditions, and customs acquired and transmitted during the course of a common history, venerating national heroes, and cherishing a common will for social homogeneity." Again the problem is that this definition does not accurately describe many Americans. It is not clear what are the "common thoughts and feelings" supposed to exist in America, and the notion that Americans "cherish a common will for social homogeneity" is controversial. For Snyder's definition see Louis Snyder, *Varieties of Nationalism* (Illinois: Dryden Press, 1976), 25.

Other common definitions of nationalism also face problems. For example, nationalism is sometimes equated with "patriotism," defined as the willingness to die for one's country. Yet this definition is too narrow. Thus, the widespread support at home for the American hostages in Iran was clearly a form of nationalism with important consequences (arguably it was the main reason for the failure of Edward Kennedy's attempt to take the Democratic party's presidential nomination from Jimmy Carter in 1980). However, there is little reason to suppose that large numbers of Americans who were angered by the Iranian actions were willing to die for their country.

7. The studies I have referred to make many interesting points about nationalism. There is a huge literature on this topic. For two recent accounts see Ernest Gellner, *Nations and Nationalism* (Ithaca: Cornell University Press, 1983), and Anthony Smith, *Nationalism in the Twentieth Century* (New York: New York University Press, 1979).

8. Royal Institute of International Affairs, *Nationalism* (London: Oxford University Press, 1939), 96, cited in Carr, *Nationalism and After*, 3. For data on the restriction of nationality to the upper classes in the early history of the nation-state see Carr, pp. 2–6.

9. John Higham, *Strangers in the Land: Patterns of American Nativism, 1860–1925* (New York: Atheneum, 1963), 4.

10. Ibid.

11. Henry Miller, *Tropic of Cancer* (New York: Grove Press, 1961), 187.

12. For further examples of this idea of America as deserving a degree of respect and honor see, in the context of the 1972 election campaign and the Vietnam War, the cases in Lubell, *The Future While It Happened*, chap. 5.

13. For evidence of the tendency for a president's popularity to rise sharply at the start of a "foreign crisis" see John E. Mueller, *War, Presidents and Public Opinion* (New York: John Wiley, 1973); idem, "Presidential Popularity from Truman to Johnson," *American Political Science Review* 64 (March 1970):18–34; and Kathleen Frankovic, "Public Opinion Trends," in *The Election of 1980* ed. Marlene Pomper (Chatham, N.J.: Chatham House, 1981).

Conclusion to Part 4

1. The classic study of the social correlates of identification with the Democratic party during its heyday in the 1930s and 1940s points to the importance of religion (Catholic or Jewish rather than

Protestant), location (urban or suburban rather than rural), and socioeconomic status (lower rather than higher). See Paul Lazarsfeld, Bernard Berelson, and Helen Gaudet, *The People's Choice* (New York: Columbia University Press, 1948). No Imperium workers live in rural areas, and they are mostly about the same socioeconomic level, so it makes sense that religion would be the main factor distinguishing workers who are Democrats from workers who are Republicans.

2. This is true of the electorate in general. There is little evidence of a wholesale rejection of partisanship on the part of onetime party loyalists. Most of the increase in the proportion of the electorate viewing themselves as independents has come from generational changes—younger, less partisan voters replacing older, more partisan ones. For this point see Warren E. Miller, "Disinterest, Disaffection, and Participation in Presidential Politics," *Political Behavior* 2 (1980):7–32.

3. For studies that point to a rise in the tendency for presidential elections to be settled by the particular issues raised at each election rather than by loyalties resulting from party identification, see Miller, "Disinterest, Disaffection, and Participation"; Everett C. Ladd, "The Brittle Mandate: Electoral Dealignment and the 1980 Presidential Election," *Political Science Quarterly* 96 (Spring 1981):1–24; and Gerald Pomper, *Voters' Choice* (New York: Harper and Row, 1975).

4. For a thorough discussion of the relative importance for national electoral politics of social class (especially blue-collar versus varieties of white-collar) as compared with variables such as race, age, gender, and region, see Dennis Ippolito, Thomas Walker, and Kenneth Kolson, *Public Opinion and Responsible Democracy* (Englewood Cliffs, N.J.: Prentice-Hall, 1976). One of the best and most prescient discussions of the position of blue-collar workers in the coalition that Franklin Roosevelt put together to form the nucleus of electoral support for the Democratic party remains Samuel Lubell's *Future of American Politics*.

5. It often comes from the opposite end of the political spectrum, but the idea that workers are so beaten down, manipulated, or seduced by employers and the work context that they have little or no class consciousness faces the same problem as does the idea that consciousness is dominated by the quest for upward mobility. These ideas ignore the three forms of class identity I have discussed in these chapters, or imply they do not exist, but without systematically analyzing workers' views of politics and the class structure. Two such studies that nevertheless offer interesting accounts of the work process are Burawoy, *Manufacturing Consent*, and Richard Pfeffer, *Working for Capitalism* (New York: Columbia University Press, 1979).

6. Ira Katznelson argues that it is the radical separation between work and community in the United States that distinguishes class consciousness there from that in Western Europe. In the United States class consciousness is confined to the workplace; outside the workplace consciousness stresses not class but race, ethnicity, and territoriality. See Katznelson, *City Trenches*.

The case of Imperium workers certainly confirms the importance of the distinction between life at work and life outside the workplace. But it suggests that class consciousness does exist among blue-collar Americans outside work, though it is based on position in a hierarchy (which at the top merges into a power structure) involving income level and material possessions, not occupation. Further, blue-collar workers have a third form of class consciousness, based on populism, which also refers in many ways to life outside work. It is true, and important to notice, that these two forms of class consciousness are not based on occupational identity, but neither are they composed solely of racial, ethnic, or territorial considerations.

7. It is important to point out that many labor markets are segmented by race and gender as well as by class, and that this has an effect on class consciousness. On this see, for example, Richard Edwards, *Contested Terrain: The Transformation of the Workplace in the Twentieth Century* (New York: Basic Books, 1979). But this argument should not be taken too far. Thus, for blue-collar workers such as those I studied, class consciousness is not supplanted by racial and gender consciousness but coexists with it in various ways.

Introduction to Part 5

1. Warner, *American Life*, 7.

2. In the region I studied, Memorial Day parades were typically attended by a small fraction of a

township's population. Compare Williamson's comment about today's Middletown: "National holidays such as Washington's Birthday, Memorial Day, Independence Day, and Labor Day, pass almost unnoticed by Middletowners." See Caplow, *Middletown*, 225.

3. Emile Durkheim, *The Elementary Forms of the Religious Life*, trans. Joseph Swain (New York: George Allen & Unwin, 1915; reprint ed., New York: Free Press, 1965), 474–75.

4. Ibid.

Chapter 13

1. In this chapter I use "religion" in two senses. First, in a broad sense to refer to a combination of rituals and beliefs ("ritual" is defined in the next few pages, "beliefs" later in the chapter). This usage, continued in the chapters on ethnicity and public rituals, follows in outline that of Robertson Smith and Durkheim. I also use "religion" in a narrow sense to refer to the particular rituals and beliefs of Christianity.

Definitions of religion are, of course, an arena for enormous controversy. In the end, the test of a definition is whether it illuminates the material being studied; so the test of the main way "religion" is used throughout part 5 (the first, broad sense) is whether it throws light on Christianity, ethnicity, and national occasions in contemporary America.

See Robertson Smith, *Lectures on the Religion of the Semites* (Aberdeen University, 1888–89; reprint ed., New York: Meridian Books, 1959); Durkheim *Elementary Forms of the Religious Life*.

2. Durkheim, *Elementary Forms of the Religious Life*, 121.

3. The worker quoted here is one of the few explicit atheists among Imperium workers:

Researcher: Do you believe in God?

Worker [in his late forties]: No! I reckon if there was a God I wouldn't be here right now. I've done every sin there is—adultery, lust, murder [in the navy during wartime]—and I'm still here, so I reckon he [God] doesn't exist. And that stuff about a virgin birth! That's ridiculous. How can you have a virgin birth? Did God put his dick in Mary's mouth to get her pregnant if he didn't put it in her cunt?

As regards religious identity, the Catholics among Imperium workers usually specify whether they belong to the Eastern or Roman branch, for many of the Catholics from Poland and the Soviet Union belong to the Eastern church.

4. An example is Andrew Greeley, *Crisis in the Church: A Study of Religion in America* (Chicago: Thomas More Association, 1979), chap. 8. As indicators of the continuing importance of religion Greeley cites widespread praying, belief in life after death, and willingness to acknowledge having had a "religious experience." But the meaning of these actions and beliefs must be examined much more closely, and they must be placed in the context of people's other beliefs and rituals, before Greeley's conclusion can be justified.

5. This definition of ritual follows that of Steven Lukes except that it adds "sacred" alongside "special" to refer to the ritual attitude. For Lukes's definition, and for a discussion of alternative definitions of "ritual," see Lukes, "Political Ritual and Social Integration," 289–308.

6. For a year I went to Sunday mass at four of the Catholic churches most heavily attended by Imperium workers. These included two in the older industrial suburbs of Elizabeth and Linden, one in Woodbridge, and one in Piscataway. This research is the basis for observations about the general content of sermons and the form of the church service.

7. See Gans, *Urban Villagers*, 110–12, and Gerald Suttles, *The Social Construction of Communities* (Chicago: University of Chicago Press, 1972), 221.

8. Placing the attitudes of participants in rites along a continuum from "very special" (if not sacred) through "positive," "indifferent," "negative," and eliciting "extreme disapproval" or "disgust" involves modifying Durkheim's theory. He argued that rites divide society and the world into two distinct and clearly separate spheres, the sacred and the profane. According to Durkheim, these two spheres are mutually exclusive and jointly exhaustive.

But this dichotomy between the sacred and the profane is neither empirically nor logically sound. Empirically, attitudes do not always fall neatly into such a scheme, as Stanner has shown for the Australian aborigines and Leach for the Kachin. And the notion of the "sacred" is based on a naive psychology that ignores the difference between surface attitudes and deeper ones. For example, such a strongly positive attitude as "sacred" clearly raises the suspicion that it conceals an equally strongly negative attitude, as Freud pointed out in discussing the Australian totemism on which Durkheim based his views.

The dichotomy between sacred and profane is also logically flawed. As Stanner put it: "the 'profane' is a residual category which in fact includes a number of quite disparate classifications: namely, 'commonness' (work is 'an eminent form of profane activity'); minor sacredness (the less sacred is 'profane' in relation to the more sacred); non-sacredness (the two classes have 'nothing in common'); and anti-sacredness (profane things can 'destroy' sacredness)." For these and other criticisms of Durkheim's dichotomy see Edmund Leach, *Political systems of Highland Burma: A Study of Kachin Social Structure* (Boston: Beacon Press, 1954), 12–13; W. E. H. Stanner, "Reflections on Durkheim and Aboriginal Religion," in *Social Organization: Essays Presented to Raymond Firth*, ed. M. Freedman (Chicago: Aldine, 1967); E. E. Evans-Pritchard, *Theories of Primitive Religion* (Oxford: Clarendon Press, 1965), 64–65; and Steven Lukes, *Emile Durkheim: His Life and Work* (New York: Harper and Row, 1972), 24–28, 477–84. For Freud's discussion of totemism see Sigmund Freud, *Totem and Taboo: Resemblances between the Psychic Life of Savages and Neurotics*, trans. James Strachey (New York: Basic Books, 1959; originally published 1912–13).

9. For the Durkheim quotation see *Elementary Forms of the Religious Life*, 476. The definition of religious beliefs I offer in this chapter implies that there is no distinction between explanations of the world that are "religious" and those that are not. Nor do I distinguish between magic, religion, and science. Instead I classify explanations of the world into three main types (see the distinctions made later in this chapter between "primary cosmologies," "secondary cosmologies," and "tertiary beliefs"). For a critical discussion of many of the classic anthropological attempts, such as those of Frazer, Tylor, and Malinowski, to distinguish between magic, religion, and science see W. G. Runciman, "The Sociological Explanation of 'Religious' Beliefs," *Archives Européennes de Sociologie* 10 (1969):149–91, reprinted in W. G. Runciman, *Sociology in Its Place* (Cambridge: Cambridge University Press, 1970).

10. There are very few studies of the ideas of ordinary Catholics (or Protestants), in the past or now, that are open to exploring this distinctly unorthodox current of beliefs in phenomena such as spirits, ghosts, human and animal reincarnation, and extraterrestrial beings. Note 14 discusses this topic further in the context of the "secularization" debate.

11. For witchcraft among the Azande see E. E. Evans-Pritchard, *Witchcraft, Oracles and Magic among the Azande*, (Oxford: Clarendon Press, 1937), chap. 4.

12. For a discussion of the importance of distinguishing beliefs by their degree of perceived truth see Runciman, "Sociological Explanation of 'Religious' Beliefs."

13. Will Herberg, *Protestant—Catholic—Jew: An Essay in American Religious Sociology* (New York: Anchor Books, 1960).

14. See Gans, *Levittowners*, chap. 4. This chapter has argued that religion is of minor importance for these workers. It avoids the historical problem of whether this represents a long-run trend in America for religion to decline in importance—the "secularization" debate. This is a difficult question, for it is not clear how religious Americans were in the past. As one historian wrote:

Contrary to assumptions underlying much of the work in American religious history, American colonists had an ambivalent relationship with Christian congregations. After about 1650 even in New England only about one-third of all adults ever belonged to a church. The rate was lower in the Middle and Southern colonies, and on the eve of the American Revolution only about 15 percent of all of the colonists probably belonged to any church.

Colonists also proved surprisingly ignorant of elemental Christian beliefs and practices. Naturally, clergymen worried when settlers failed to join their own sects or denominations. But even secular observers wondered at the number of settlers who ignored organized religious activity altogether.

See Jon Butler, "Magic, Astrology, and the Early American Religious Heritage, 1600–1760,"*American Historical Review* 84, 2 (April 1979):317–46. Nor is it clear how religious immigrant Catholics were on first arriving in the United States. For instance, a study of Irish Catholic immigrants before the Civil War discovered widespread religious ignorance among the newcomers. As Jay Dolan wrote:

> Missionaries frequently bemoaned the low level of religious understanding among Catholics. People did not know if there was one God or three, and one priest recorded that "many young men were exceedingly ignorant with regard to religion, some of them not knowing the principal mysteries." Even such a simple ritual as the sign of the cross had to be taught to people for the first time. Many young adults and "not a few quite advanced in life" had never received communion and appeared to be Catholic in name and little more.

See Jay Dolan, *The Immigrant Church: New York's Irish and German Catholics, 1815–1865* (Baltimore: John Hopkins University Press, 1975), 57. Thus, though religion is of minor importance for these workers it is dangerous to conclude that this represents a long-run decline in religious fervor among the working class or among Americans in general, for the assumption that Americans were more religious in the past is controversial.

    15. Herberg, *Protestant—Catholic—Jew*, 260.

Chapter 14

    1. For this definition see W. Lloyd Warner and Leo Srole, *The Social System of American Ethnic Groups* (New Haven: Yale University Press, 1945), chap. 1. For a discussion of the various ways social scientists have defined "ethnicity" see Brian M. du Toit, *Ethnicity in Modern Africa* (Boulder, Colo.: Westview Press, 1978), introduction.

    2. Warner and Srole's study is a classic statement of this version of the melting pot theory. They argue that "the future of American ethnic groups seems to be limited; it is likely that they will be quickly absorbed." But they also argue that distinctions based on class and race are, and will continue to be, crucial in America. For a subtle account of the relation between race and ethnicity among Puerto Ricans in the New York region see Rodriguez, "Puerto Ricans: Between Black and White."

    3. Glazer and Moynihan pointed out that a major impetus behind the formation of ethnic organizations is the desire to overcome discrimination. See Nathan Glazer and Daniel Patrick Moynihan, *Beyond the Melting Pot* (Cambridge: MIT Press, 1963). Coleman and Rainwater also make this point. See *Social Standing in America*, chap. 6.

    4. For data on the frequency of interethnic marriage among American Catholics see Richard Alba, "Social Assimilation among American Catholic National-Origin Groups," *American Sociological Review* 41 (December 1976):1030–46.

    5. Herbert Gans, "Symbolic Ethnicity," *Ethnic and Racial Studies* 2 (January 1979):1–20. As Gans points out, the extent to which ethnicity as a way of living (a set of rituals) and as a set of beliefs that explain the world (a cosmology) was important even for the first generation should not be exaggerated. Indeed, for those early immigrants "national ethnic" categories such as Italian or Polish were from the start superimposed on more salient loyalties to particular towns and villages in the land from which people emigrated. On this point see also Herberg, *Protestant—Catholic—Jew*.

    6. For proponents of the "new ethnicity"" see Michael Novak, *The Rise of the Unmeltable Ethnics* (New York: Macmillan, 1971); Nathan Glazer and Daniel Patrick Moynihan, eds., *Ethnicity: Theory and Experience* (Cambridge: Harvard University Press, 1975); and Greeley and McCready, *Ethnicity in the United States*.

    For recent critics see Stephen Steinberg, *The Ethnic Myth: Race, Ethnicity and Class in America* (New York: Atheneum, 1981); and Coleman and Rainwater, *Social Standing*. Steinberg stresses the lack of institutional roots for ethnic identity beyond the second generation. Coleman and Rainwater report that, for most of their respondents, ethnicity was fairly unimportant unless they saw themselves as victims of ethnic discrimination.

7. Examples of studies that use very broad and loose notions of "ethnicity" are Glazer and Moynihan, *Beyond the Melting Pot*; Glazer and Moynihan, eds., *Ethnicity: Theory and Experience* Greeley and McCready, *Ethnicity in the United States*; George Hicks and Philip Leis, *Ethnic Encounters: Identities and Contexts*, (North Scituate, Mass.: Duxbury Press, 1977); and Horace Orlando Patterson, *Ethnic Chauvinism* (New York: Stein and Day, 1977).

Chapter 15

1. Durkheim, *Elementary Forms of the Religious Life*, 80.
2. The best-known analysis of public rituals in America is that of W. Lloyd Warner. This suffers from a one-dimensional approach to rituals and beliefs—an overemphasis on the concept of the "sacred" and on beliefs as primary cosmologies. Warner tends to cram all ritual attitudes into the dichotomy between "sacred" and "secular" (or "profane"), for instance arguing that Americans view the ceremonial aspect of Memorial Day as "sacred." This is a serious exaggeration, even allowing for a decline in popular interest in the ceremonial aspect of Memorial Day since the time Warner wrote. In general, Warner greatly overestimates the extent to which public rituals "succeed" and underestimates the extent to which they are mediocre. See W. Lloyd Warner, *American Life*, and idem, *The Living and the Dead* (New Haven: Yale University Press, 1959). For criticisms of Warner and of other one-dimensional accounts of public rituals (such as the British coronation) see Norman Birnbaum, "Monarchs and Sociologists," *Sociological Review* 3: (July 1955):5–23, and Lukes, "Political Ritual and Social Integration." For interesting recent discussions of some of these national rituals see John J. MacAloon, "Sociation and Sociability in Political Celebrations," in *Celebration: Studies in Festivity and Ritual*, ed. Victor Turner (Washington D.C.: Smithsonian Institution Press, 1982); and Caplow, *Middletown Families*, chap. 10. (The chapter on holidays in Middletown is by Margaret Williamson.) Unfortunately there is no adequate history of national holidays in America. In its absence, and given the scarcity of sociological studies on this subject, my analysis in this chapter can be only tentative. For a discussion of rituals in the Soviet Union that also makes some general comments about ritual in industrial society, see Christel Lane, *The Rites of Rulers: Ritual in Industrial Society—The Soviet Case* (Cambridge: Cambridge University Press, 1981).
3. Discussed in chapter 2.
4. For this phrase and a discussion of the growth of institutions that "police the family" see Jacques Donzelot, *The Policing of Families* (New York: Pantheon, 1979).
5. For an account of the relation between sports and masculinity in nineteenth-century America see Leonard Ellis, "Men among Men: An Exploration of All-Male Relationships in Victorian America" (Ph.D diss., Columbia University, 1982). An example of the view that sport is the new religion is Michael Novak, *The Joy of Sport* (New York: Basic Books, 1976).
Margaret Williamson analyzes the interpersonal aspect of national holidays in today's Middletown, stresses the focus on the family, and concludes this is because the family is the most *fragile* institution in Middletown. This analysis is clearly compatible with the one I have suggested. See Caplow, *Middletown*.
6. Sheldon Wolin, *Politics and Vision* (Boston: Little, Brown, 1960), 429–30. For the continued interest of most Americans in politics see Miller, "Disinterest, Disaffection, and Participation in Presidential Politics."
7. Katherine Lambert Richards, *How Christmas Came to the Sunday Schools* (New York: Dodd, Mead, 1934).
8. For a discussion of the serious divisions among the electorate in 1970 over attitudes toward poverty, over help to minority groups, over school busing for racial integration, and over the Vietnam War, see Miller, "Political Issues and Trust in Government: 1964–1970." Among the divisive issues revealed by the 1980 National Election Study (Pre- and Post-Election Surveys) are attitudes toward abortion, aid to minorities, and the ERA, and the question whether the United States government should try to get along with the Soviet Union. Americans are also deeply divided over which groups they wish to be tolerant toward. See Sullivan, *Political Tolerance and American Democracy*. On the lack of consensus in America see also Mann, "The Social Cohesion of Liberal Democracy."
Contrasting the richness and relevance of political ritual among the Swazi of southern Africa with the paucity of political ceremonies in England directed at *current* issues, Max Gluckman suggested that

English society contains too many serious divisions to support such a ceremonial life. See Max Gluckman, *Order and Rebellion in Tribal Africa* (London: Cohen and West, 1963). The same is clearly true of the United States. Notice how the 1983 Saint Patrick's Day parade in New York City began to disintegrate when the organizers selected a strong IRA supporter as grand marshal (making the parade relevant but also, inevitably, controversial). Many Catholic schools withdrew their bands, and after much pondering Cardinal Cooke decided to stay inside Saint Patrick's Cathedral until the grand marshal had passed. The following year the organizers selected from the leading candidates the one least identified with the IRA.

For a fascinating discussion of the change in America, from the construction of monuments that celebrated political figures to the designation of physical spaces that celebrate a vague vernacular past, see J. B. Jackson, *The Necessity for Ruins* (Amherst: University of Massachusetts Press, 1980). This movement away from the political occurred after the Civil War.

9. See H. S. J. Sickel, *Thanksgiving: Its Source, Philosophy and History* (Philadelphia: International Printing Company, 1940). Starting early in American history, the *season* of Thanksgiving gradually became observed each year throughout the New England colonies. And it was, of course, customary for Puritans and their families to offer thanks to God *whenever* any fortunate event occurred. In similar fashion, early American presidents would occasionally proclaim a particular day (but not to be repeated annually) for a national thanksgiving, often to request a military victory or show gratitude for one obtained. Yet the custom of presidents' proclaiming such national days lapsed for nearly fifty years after Madison. It was only the crisis of the approach, occurrence, and aftermath of the Civil War that stimulated the revival of Thanksgiving as a national day and its placement in the annual calendar on the last Thursday in November. Presidents Buchanan, Lincoln, Johnson, and Grant all had a hand in this process.

10. The classic account of the development of the concept of "childhood" in the West, and of the way being a "child" became associated with a certain triviality or lack of seriousness, is Ariès, *Centuries of Childhood*.

11. John MacAloon, "Sociation and Sociability in Political Celebrations," 268.

12. Murray Edelman, *The Symbolic Uses of Politics* (Urbana: University of Illinois Press, 1964), 2–3.

13. In his classic study of how voters make up their minds in a presidential campaign, Paul Lazarsfeld pointed out that most of those who do not vote have made a clear, strong, and long-standing decision not to do so. See Paul Lazarsfeld et al., *The People's Choice* chap. 5.

14. See Miller, "Disinterest, Disaffection, and Participation in Presidential Politics," and Paul Abramson and John Aldrich, "The Decline of Electoral Participation in America," *American Political Science Review* 76 (1982):502–21.

15. See Lazarsfeld, *People's Choice*, and Angus Campbell, Philip Converse, Warren Miller, and Donald Stokes, *The American Voter* (New York: John Wiley, 1960).

Chapter 16

1. There is, of course, a long tradition of Marxists who have acknowledged the ability of better-paid blue-collar workers to make absolute and relative economic advances. See, for instance, Wilhelm Reich, *The Mass Psychology of Fascism*, 3d ed. (New York: Simon and Schuster, 1970), and Poulantzas, *Classes in Contemporary Capitalism*.

2. Compare the broad materialism of Emile Durkheim and Marcel Mauss in *Primitive Classifications*, trans. Rodney Needham (Chicago: University of Chicago Press, 1963; orginally published 1903). For a critical discussion of the use of Gramsci's concept of the "hegemony of ruling class ideas" in advanced capitalism see N. Abercrombie, S. Hill, and B. Turner, "The Dominant Ideology Thesis," *British Journal of Sociology* 29 (June 1978):149–70.

3. The concept of "social integration," so central in sociology, is complex. The claim that a society is integrated really needs to examine the following factors: (1) The continued participation of a society's members in its institutions and practices. (2) Their conformity to its norms. (3) Their sharing of a common consciousness and their acting in concert. (4) The complementarity or reciprocity of their activities and roles. (5) The compatibility of their interests. (6) The degree of coherence of segments of parts of a society. (7) The functional compatibility or "degree of fit" between a society's core institutional order and

its natural base. (8) The persistence of structural features over time. For these distinction see Lukes, "Political Ritual and Social Integration."

4. See John Alt, "Beyond Class: The Decline of Industrial Labor and Leisure," *Telos* 28 (Summer 1976):55–80.

5. Herbert Marcuse, *One Dimensional Man* (Boston: Beacon Press, 1968). See also Zweig, *Worker in an Affluent Society*.

6. On this tendency see W. G. Runciman, *Relative Deprivation and Social Justice* (London: Routledge and Kegan Paul, 1980).

7. J. M. Keynes, *The General Theory of Employment, Interest and Money* (London: Macmillan, 1936). See especially chapter 24, where Keynes looks forward to the demise of the rentier.

8. Zweig, *Worker in an Affluent Society*.

9. Perhaps the most comprehensive attempt to understand the modern working class is the study of workers in Luton, England. In *The Affluent Worker* Goldthorpe et al. suggest that new industrial workers are distinguished from "traditional workers" in two ways. They are "privatized," and their orientation to work is "instrumental." I have not used these categories in my study. The view that workers are "privatized" rests on three related ideas. First, that relations of solidarity have eroded at work and in the community. Second, that the work setting is no longer an important source of men's class identity or their political outlook and interests. Third, that consumer goods and family life offset discontent arising from work. Among Imperium workers the first of these ideas contains important truths for the residential setting, but not for the workplace. The second idea does not fit at all, for the concept of the working man supports a lively class consciousness. The third idea is true, but only to a certain extent. The view that workers have an "instrumental" orientation to their jobs also contains three related ideas. First, that men work to earn money. Second, that they are prepared to subordinate all other goals to the goal of earning money. Third, that they are indifferent to friendships at work. The first idea is true but unexceptional and does not distinguish modern from "traditional" workers, which it is intended to do. The second and third ideas are not true for Imperium workers, as I have tried to show in parts 2 and 3 (though they are truer of workers with young families). Part of the difference between my findings and those of *The Affluent Worker* may result from differences between England and the United States. However, part may result from Goldthorpe's sample, consisting, as he points out, of workers particularly likely to subordinate all other goals to making money. The workers he studied were young men with families who had moved to Luton specifically in order to earn high wages. See *The Affluent Worker*.

10. See Giddens, *The Class Structure of the Advanced Societies*, and Mann, *Consciousness and Action among the Western Working Class*.

Bibliography

Abercrombie, N., S. Hill, and B. Turner. "The Dominant Ideology Thesis." *British Journal of Sociology* 29 (June 1978):149–70.

Abrahams, Robert. "Playing the Dozens." *Journal of American Folklore* 75 (1962):209–20.

Abramson, Paul, and John Aldrich. "The Decline of Electoral Participation in America." *American Political Science Review* 76 (1982):502–21.

Acker, Joan. "Women and Social Stratification: A Case of Intellectual Sexism." *American Journal of Sociology* 78 (January 1973):936–45.

Alba, Richard. "Social Assimilation among American Catholic National-Origin Groups." *American Sociological Review* 41 (December 1976):1030–46.

Alt, John. "Beyond Class: The Decline of Industrial Labor and Leisure." *Telos* 28 (Summer 1976):55–80.

Anderson, Michael. *Family Structure in Nineteenth-Century Lancashire*. Cambridge: Cambridge University Press, 1971.

Applebaum, Herbert. *Royal Blue: The Culture of Construction Workers*. New York: Holt, Rinehart and Winston, 1981.

Arensberg, Conrad. "The Community Study Method." *American Journal of Sociology* 60 (September 1954):109–24.

Ariès, Philippe. *Centuries of Childhood: A Social History of Family Life*, trans. Robert Baldick. New York: Vintage Books, 1965.

———. "The Family and the City." In *The Family*, ed. Alice S. Rossi. New York: Norton, 1978.

———. *The Hour of Our Death*, trans. Helen Weaver. New York: Alfred Knopf, 1981.

Aron, Raymond. *Dix-huit leçons sur la société industrielle*. Paris: Gallimard, 1962.

Aronowitz, Stanley. *False Promises: The Shaping of American Working-Class Consciousness*. New York: McGraw-Hill, 1973.

Barth, Ernest, and Walter Watson. "Social Stratification and the Family in Mass Society." *Social Forces* 47 (March 1967):392–402.

Bebout, John, and Ronald Grele. *Where Cities Meet*. Princeton: Van Nostrand, 1964.

Belloc, Nedra, and Lester Breslow. "The Relationship of Physical Health Status and Health Practices." *Preventive Medicine* 1 (August 1972):409–21.

Berenson, Conrad, ed. *The Chemical Industry*. New York: John Wiley, 1963.

Berger, Bennett. *Working-Class Suburb: A Study of Auto Workers in Suburbia*. Berkeley: University of California Press, 1968.

Berlin, Isaiah. "Nationalism: Past Neglect and Present Power." *Partisan Review* 46 (1979):337–58.

Beynon, Huw. *Working for Ford*. London: Penguin, 1973.

Birnbaum, Norman. "Monarchs and Sociologists." *Sociological Review* 3 (July 1955):5–23.

Blau, Peter, and Otis Dudley Duncan. *The American Occupational Structure*. New York: John Wiley, 1967.

Blauner, Robert. *Alienation and Freedom*. Chicago: University of Chicago Press, 1964.

Boas, Franz. *The Social Organization of the Kwakiutl Indians*. Washington, D.C., 1897.

Braverman, Harry. *Labor and Monopoly Capital: The Degradation of Work in the Twentieth Century*. New York: Monthly Review Press, 1974.

Bright, James. *Automation and Management*. Boston: Harvard University Press, 1958.

Bryce, James. *The American Commonwealth*. New York: Macmillan, 1911.

Buchanan, William, and Hadley Cantril. *How Nations See Each Other*. Urbana: University of Illinois Press, 1953.

Burawoy, Michael. *Manufacturing Consent: Changes in the Labor Process under Monopoly Capitalism*. Chicago: University of Chicago Press, 1979.

Burgess, Ernest, Harvey Locke, and Mary Thomas. *The Family*. New York: American Book Company, 1963.

Butler, Jon. "Magic, Astrology, and the Early American Religious Heritage, 1600–1760." *American Historical Review* 84, 2 (April 1979):317–46.

Cahalan, Don. *Problem Drinkers*. San Francisco: Jossey-Bass, 1970.

Cahalan, Don, Ira Cisin, and Helen Crossley. *American Drinking Practices: A National Study of Drinking Behavior and Attitudes*. New Brunswick, N.J.: Rutgers Center of Alcohol Studies, 1969.

Cahalan, Don, and Robin Room. *Problem Drinking among American Men*. New Brunswick: Rutgers Center of Alcohol Studies, 1974.

Campbell, Angus. *The Sense of Well-being in America*. New York: McGraw-Hill, 1981.

Campbell, Angus, Philip Converse, Warren Miller, and Donald Stokes. *The American Voter*. New York: John Wiley, 1960.

Caplow, Theodore. *Principles of Organization*. New York: Harcourt, Brace and World, 1964.

Caplow, Theodore, Howard Bahr, Bruce Chadwick, Reuben Hill, and Margaret Williamson. *Middletown Families: Fifty Years of Change and Continuity*. Minneapolis: University of Minneapolis Press, 1982.

Carr, E. H. *Nationalism and After*. New York: Macmillan, 1945.

Center for Political Studies. *American National Election Studies, 1956– 80*. Ann Arbor: University of Michigan, 1974–82.

Centers, Richard. *The Psychology of Social Classes: A Study of Class Consciousness*. Princeton: Princeton University Press, 1949.

Chinoy, Ely. *Automobile Workers and the American Dream*. Boston: Beacon Press, 1955.

Chodorow, Nancy. *The Reproduction of Mothering: Psychoanalysis and the Sociology of Gender*. Berkeley: University of California Press, 1978.

Citrin, Jack. "Comment: The Political Relevance of Trust in Government." *American Political Science Review* 68 (September 1974):973–88.

————. "Political Disaffection in America: 1958-68." Ph.D. diss., University of California, Berkeley, 1972.

Citrin, Jack, Herbert McClosky, J. Merrill Shanks, and Paul M. Sniderman, "Personal and Political Sources of Political Alienation." *British Journal of Political Science* 5 (January 1975).

Coleman, Richard, and Lee Rainwater. *Social Standing in America*. New York: Basic Books, 1978.

Converse, Philip. "The Nature of Belief Systems in Mass Politics." In *Ideology and Discontent*, ed. David Apter. New York: Free Press, 1964.

Crozier, Michel. *The Bureacratic Phenomenon*. Chicago: University of Chicago Press. 1964.

Csikszentmihalyi, Mihaly, and Eugene Rochberg-Halton. *The Meaning of Things: Domestic Symbols and the Self*. Cambridge: Cambridge University Press, 1981.

Curti, Merle. *The Roots of American Loyalty*. New York: Columbia University Press, 1946.

Dahl, Robert. *Pluralist Democracy in the United States*. Chicago: Rand McNally, 1967.

————. *Political Oppositions in Western Democracies*. New Haven: Yale University Press, 1968.

Davis, Mike. "The Barren Marriage of American Labor and the Democratic Party." *New Left Review* 124 (November-December 1980):43–84.

Dean, John. "The Ghosts of Home-Ownership." *Journal of Social Issues* 7 (1951):59–68.

Dingemans, J. "Urbanization of Suburbia: Renaissance of the Row House." *Landscape* 20 (1975):19–31.

DiPrete, Thomas, and Whitman Soule. "Status Boundaries, Labor Markets and the Structure of Mobility: A Case Study in the U.S. Federal Government." Paper presented at the Annual Meeting of the American Sociological Association, Detroit, September 1983.

Doeringer, Peter, and Michael Piore. *Internal Labor Markets and Manpower Analysis*. Lexington, Mass.: Heath, 1971

Dolan, Jay. *The Immigrant Church: New York's Irish and German Catholics, 1815–1865*. Baltimore: Johns Hopkins University Press, 1975.

Dollard, John. "The Dozens: Dialectic of Insult." *American Imago* 1:3–24.

Donzelot, Jacques. *The Policing of Families*. New York: Pantheon, 1979.

Duncan, Graeme, and Steven Lukes. "The New Democracy." *Political Studies* 11 (1963):156–77.

Duncan, Otis, and Beverly Duncan. "A Methodological Analysis of Segregation Indexes." *American Sociological Review* 20 (1955):210–24.

————. "Residential Distribution of Occupational Stratification." *American Journal of Sociology* 60 (1955):493–503.

Duncan, Otis Dudley, David Featherman, and Beverly Duncan. *Socioeconomic Background and Achievement*. New York: Seminar Press, 1972.

Dunlop, John. *Industrial Relations Systems*. New York: Holt, 1958.

Durkheim, Emile. *The Elementary Forms of the Religious Life, trans.Joseph Swain.* New York: George Allen and Unwin, 1915; reprint ed., New York: Free Press, 1965.

————. L'individualisme et les intellectuels." *Revue Bleue* 10 (1898); trans. S. and J. Lukes as "Individualism and the Intellectuals," *Political Studies* 17 (March 1969):14–30.

Durkheim, Emile, and Marcel Mauss. *Primitive Classifications*, trans. Rodney Needham. Chicago: University of Chicago Press, 1963.

Economic Policy Council and Office of Economic Policy. *Fifteenth Annual Report.* Trenton: State of New Jersey, 1981.

Edelman, Murray. *The Symbolic Uses of Politics.* Chicago: University of Illinois Press, 1976.

Edwards, Richard. *Contested Terrain: The Transformation of the Workplace in the Twentieth Century.* New York: Basic Books, 1979.

Elias, Norbert, and Eric Dunning. "The Quest for Excitement in Unexciting Societies." Paper presented at the Annual Conference of the British Sociological Association, London, 1967.

Ellis, Leonard. "Men among Men: An Exploration of All-Male Relationships in Victorian America." Ph.D. diss., Columbia University, 1982.

Evans-Pritchard, E. E. *Nuer Religion.* New York: Oxford University Press, 1956.

————. *Theories of Primitive Religion.* Oxford: Clarendon Press, 1965.

————. *Witchcraft, Oracles and Magic among the Azande.* Oxford: Clarendon Press, 1937.

Farley, Reynolds. "The Changing Distribution of Negroes within Metropolitan Areas: The Emergence of Black Suburbs." *American Journal of Sociology* 75 (1970):512–29.

————. "Residential Segregation in Urbanized Areas of the United States in 1970: An Analysis of Social Class and Racial Differences." *Demography* 14 (November 1977):497–518.

Fawcett, Howard H., and W.S. Wood. *Safety and Accident Prevention in Chemical Operations.* New York: John Wiley. 1965.

Feagin, J.R. *Subordinating the Poor.* Englewood Cliffs, N.J.: Prentice-Hall, 1975.

Foresta, Ronald A. "The Evolution of the Modern Urban Core: The Implications of Newark's Late Nineteenth-Century Housing and Population Patterns." In *New Jersey's Ethnic Heritage*, ed. Paul A. Stellhorn. Trenton: New Jersey Historical Commission, 1978.

Frankovic, Kathleen. "Public Opinion Trends." In *The Election of 1980*, ed. Marlene Pomper. Chatham, N.J.: Chatham House, 1981.

Freidson, Eliot. *Profession of Medicine.* New York: Dodd, Mead, 1972.

————, ed. *Professions and Their Prospects.* Beverly Hills, Calif.: Sage Publications, 1974.

Frenkel, Richard L., W. Curtiss Priest, and Nicholas Ashford. "Occupational Safety and Health." *Monthly Labor Review* 103 (August 1980):11–40.

Freud, Sigmund. *The Interpretation of Dreams*, trans. James Strachey. New York: Basic Books, 1959 (originally published 1900).

————. *Totem and Taboo: Resemblances between the Psychic Life of Savages and Neurotics*, trans. James Strachey. New York, Norton, 1952, (originally published 1912–13).

Friedman, Andrew. *Industry and Labor.* London: Macmillan, 1977.

Frith, Simon. *Sound Effects.* New York: Pantheon, 1981.

Funnell, Charles. "Atlantic City: Washbasin of the Great Democracy." In *Urban New Jersey since 1870*, ed. William C. Wright. Trenton: New Jersey Historical Commission, 1975.

Gallie, Duncan. *In Search of the New Working Class*. Cambridge: Cambridge University Press, 1978.

Gans, Herbert. *The Levittowners*. New York: Vintage Books. 1967.

———. *Popular Culture and High Culture: An Analysis and Evaluation of Taste*. New York: Basic Books, 1971.

———. "Symbolic Ethnicity." *Ethnic and Racial Studies* 2 (January 1979): 1–20.

———. "Urbanism and Suburbanism as Ways of Life: A Re-evaluation of Some Definitions." In *Human Behavior and Social Processes*, ed. Arnold Rose, Boston: Houghton Mifflin, 1962.

———. *The Urban Villagers*. New York: Free Press, 1962.

Gellner. Ernest. *Nations and Nationalism*. Ithaca: Cornell University Press, 1983.

Gess, Karol. "The Vanished Glory: A Problem in International Psychology," *Psychoanalytic Review* 37 (1950):345–50.

Giddens, Anthony. *The Class Structure of the Advanced Societies*. New York: Harper and Row, 1973.

Ginsberg, Benjamin. *The Consequences of Consent*. Reading, Mass.: Addison-Wesley, 1982.

Ginzberg, Eli. "The Job Problem." *Scientific American* 237 (November 1977):43–52.

Ginzberg, Eli, and H. Berman. *The American Worker in the Twentieth Century*. New York: Free Press, 1963.

Glazer, Nathan, and Daniel Patrick Moynihan. *Beyond the Melting Pot*. Cambridge: MIT Press, 1963.

———, eds. *Ethnicity: Theory and Experience*. Cambridge: Harvard University Press, 1975.

Glenn, Norval, Adreain Ross, and Judy Corder Tully. "Patterns of Intergenerational Mobility through Marriage." *American Sociological Review* 39 (October 1974):683–700.

Gluckman, Max. *Order and Rebellion in Tribal Africa*. London: Cohen and West, 1963.

———. *Politics, Law and Ritual in Tribal Society*. Chicago: Aldine, 1965.

Goldthorpe, John, David Lockwood, Frank Bechhofer, and Jennifer Platt. *The Affluent Worker: Industrial Attitudes and Behavior*. Cambridge: Cambridge University Press, 1968.

———. *The Affluent Worker: Political Attitudes and Behavior*. Cambridge: Cambridge University Press, 1968.

———. *The Affluent Worker in the Class Structure*. Cambridge: Cambridge University Press, 1969.

Goode, William. "Community within a Community: The Professions." *American Sociological Review* 22 (April 1957): 194–200.

Gramsci, Antonio. *Modern Prince and Other Writings*, trans. Louis Marks. New York: International Publishers, 1967.

Greeley, Andrew. *Crisis in the Church: A Study of Religion in America*. Chicago: Thomas More Association, 1979.

Greeley, Andrew, and William McCready. *Ethnicity in the United States: A Preliminary Reconnaissance*. New York: John Wiley, 1974.

Gutman, Herbert. "La politique ouvrière de la grande entreprise américaine de 'l'âge du clinquant': Le cas de la Standard Oil Company." *Mouvement Social* 102 (January–March 1978):67–99.

————. *Work, Culture and Society in Industrializing America*. New York: Alfred Knopf, 1976.

Haig, Marie. "Social Class Measurement and Women's Occupational Roles." *Social Forces* 52 (September 1973):86–98.

Hall, Richard. *Occupations and the Social Structure*. Englewood Cliffs, N.J.: Prentice-Hall, 1975.

Hamilton, Richard. *Class and Politics in the United States*. New York: John Wiley, 1972.

————. "The Income Difference between Skilled and White Collar Workers." *British Journal of Sociology* 14 (December 1963):363–73.

Handel, Gerald, and Lee Rainwater. "Changing Family Roles in the Working Class." In *Blue-Collar World*, ed. A. Shostak and W. Gomberg. Englewood Cliffs, N.J.: Prentice-Hall, 1964.

————. "Persistence and Change in Working-Class Life Style." In *Blue-Collar World*, ed. A. Shostak and W. Gomberg. Englewood Cliffs, N.J.: Prentice-Hall, 1964.

Hayden, Dolores. "What Would a Non-sexist City Be Like? Speculations on Housing, Urban Design, and Human Work." *Signs* 5 (Spring 1980):170–87.

Heinz, Katherine McMillan. *Retirement Communities*. New Brunswick, N.J.: Center for Urban Policy Research, 1976.

Herberg, Will. *Protestant—Catholic—Jew: An Essay in American Religious Sociology*. New York: Anchor Books, 1960.

Hicks, George, and Philip Leis. *Ethnic Encounters: Identities and Contexts*. North Scituate, Mass.: Duxbury Press, 1977.

Hidy, Ralph, and Muriel Hidy. *History of the Standard Oil Company*. Vol. 1. *Pioneering in Big Business, 1882–1911*. New York: Harper, 1955.

Higginson, John. "A Hazardous Society? Individual versus Community Responsibility in Cancer Prevention." Paper presented at the 103d Annual Meeting of the American Public Health Association, Chicago, November 1975.

Higham, John. *Strangers in the Land: Patterns of American Nativisim, 1860–1925*. New York: Atheneum, 1963.

Hiller, Dana, and William Philliber. "The Derivation of Status Benefits from Occupational Attainments of Working Wives." *Journal of Marriage and the Family* 40 (1978): 63–69.

Hodge, Robert, and Donald Treiman. "Class Identification in the United States." *American Journal of Sociology* 73 (January 1968):535–47.

Holmstrom, Lynda L. *The Two-Career Family*. Cambridge, Mass.: Schenkman, 1972.

Honeyman, A. Van Doren. ed. *History of Union County New Jersey, 1664–1923*. New York: Lewis, 1923.

Horsfall, Alexander, and Conrad Arensberg, "Teamwork and Productivity in a Shoe Factory." *Human Organization* 8 (Winter 1949):13–25.

Huber, J., and W. H. Form. *Income and Ideology*. New York: Free Press, 1973.

Hunt, Morton. *Her Infinite Variety: The American Woman as Lover, Mate and Rival*. New York: Harper and Row, 1962.

Huntington, Samuel P. *American Politics: The Promise of Disharmony*. Cambridge: Harvard University Press, 1981.

Ippolito, Dennis, Thomas Walker, and Kenneth Kolson. *Public Opinion and Responsible Democracy.* Englewood Cliffs, N.J.: Prentice-Hall, 1976.

Jackson, J. B. *The Necessity for Ruins.* Amherst: University of Massachusetts Press, 1980.

Jackson, Kenneth T. "Race, Ethnicity, and Real Estate Appraisal: The Home Owners Loan Corporation and the Federal Housing Administration." *Journal of Urban History* 6 (August 1980):419–52.

——"Urban Deconcentration in the Nineteenth Century: A Statistical Inquiry." In *The New Urban History*, ed. Leo Schnore. Princeton: Princeton University Press, 1975.

Jacobs, Jerry. *Fun City: An Ethnographic Study of a Retirement Community.* New York: Holt, Rinehart and Winston, 1974.

Janowitz, Morris. *The Last Half-Century: Societal Change and Politics in America.* Chicago: University of Chicago Press, 1978.

Jensen, V. *Strife on the Waterfront: The Port of New York since 1945.* Ithaca: Cornell University Press, 1974.

Kanter, Rosabeth Moss. *Men and Women of the Corporation.* New York: Harper, 1977.

Katzman, David. *Before the Ghetto: Black Detroit in the Nineteenth Century.* Chicago: University of Illinois, 1973

Katznelson, Ira. *City Trenches: Urban Politics and the Patterning of Class in the United States.* New York: Pantheon, 1981.

Keniston, Kenneth. *All Our Children: The American Family under Pressure.* New York: Harcourt Brace Jovanovich, 1977.

Keynes, J. M. *The General Theory of Employment, Interest and Money.* London: Macmillan, 1936.

Kirchheimer, Otto. "Private Man and Society." *Political Science Quarterly* 71 (March 1966):1–24.

Kluegel, James, and Eliot Smith. "Beliefs about Stratification." In *Annual Review of Sociology*, vol. 7, ed. Ralph Turner and James Short. Palo Alto: Annual Reviews, 1981.

Kohn, Melvin. *Class and Conformity.* Chicago: University of Chicago Press, 1977 (originally published 1969).

Komarovsky, Mirra. *Blue-Collar Marriage.* New York: Vintage Books, 1967.

Kornblum, William. *Blue-Collar Community.* Chicago: University of Chicago Press, 1974.

Kornhauser, Arthur. *When Labor Votes.* New York: University Books, 1956.

Labov, William. "Rules for Ritual Insults." In *Studies in Social Interaction*, ed. David Sudnow, New York: Free Press, 1972.

Ladd, Everett C. "The Brittle Mandate: Electoral Dealignment and the 1980 Presidential Election." *Political Science Quarterly* 96 (Spring 1981):1–24.

Landau, Ralph, ed. *The Chemical Plant from Process Selection to Commercial Operation.* New York: Reinhold, 1960.

Lane, Christel. *The Rites of Rulers: Ritual in Industrial Society—the Soviet Case.* Cambridge: Cambridge University Press, 1981.

Lane, Robert. *Political Ideology: Why the American Common Man Believes What He Does.* New York: Free Press, 1967.

Lazarsfeld, Paul, Bernard Berelson, and Helen Gaudet. *The People's Choice.* New York: Columbia University Press, 1944.

Leach, Edmund. *Political Systems of Highland Burma: A Study of Kachin Social Structure*. Boston: Beacon Press, 1954.

Leggett, John. *Working-Class Consciousness in Detroit*. New York: Oxford University Press. 1968.

LeMasters, E. E. *Blue-Collar Aristocrats*. Madison: University of Wisconsin Press, 1975.

Lipset, Seymour Martin. *The First New Nation*. New York: Basic Books, 1963.

———. *Political Man: The Social Bases of Politics*. New York: Basic Books, 1963; reprint ed., Baltimore: Johns Hopkins University Press, 1981.

Lipset, Seymour Martin, and Reinhard Bendix. *Social Mobility in Industrial Society*. Berkeley: University of California Press, 1960.

Lipset, Seymour Martin, and Earl Raab. *The Politics of Unreason*. New York, Harper and Row, 1970.

Lipset, Seymour Martin, and William Schneider. *The Confidence Gap*. New York: Free Press, 1983.

Lively, Edwin. "Toward Concept Clarification." *Journal of Marriage and the Family*, 31 (February 1969):108–14.

Llewellyn, Richard. *How Green Was My Valley*. New York: Macmillan, 1940.

Locksley, Anne. "Social Class and Marital Attitudes and Behavior." *Journal of Marriage and the Family* 44 (May 1982):427–40.

Lockwood, David. "Sources of Variation in Working Class Images of Society." *Sociological Review* 14 (November 1966):249–67.

Lortie, Dan. *Schoolteacher*. Chicago: University of Chicago Press, 1977.

Lubell, Samuel. *The Future of American Politics*. New York: Harper and Row, 1965.

———. *The Future While It Happened*. New York: Norton, 1973.

Lukes, Steven. *Emile Durkheim: His Life and Work*. New York: Harper and Row, 1972.

———. *Essays in Social Theory*. New York: Columbia University Press, 1978.

———. "Political Ritual and Social Integration." *Sociology* 9 (May 1975):289–308.

Lynd, Robert, and Helen Lynd. *Middletown*. New York: Harcourt, Brace and World, 1929.

MacAloon, John J. "Sociation and Sociability in Political Celebrations." In *Celebrations: Studies in Festivity and Ritual*, ed. Victor Turner. Washington, D.C.: Smithsonian Institution Press, 1982.

McCaffrey, David. "Work Related Amputations by Type and Prevalence." *Monthly Labor Review* 104 (March 1981):35–40.

McClosky, Herbert. "Consensus and Ideology in American Politics." *American Political Science Review* 58 (June 1964):361–82.

Mackenzie, Gavin. *The Aristocracy of Labor: The Position of Skilled Craftsmen in the American Class Structure*. Cambridge: Cambridge University Press, 1973.

———. "The Economic Dimensions of Embourgeoisement." *British Journal of Sociology* 18 (March 1967):29–44.

Mallet, Serge. *La nouvelle classe ouvrière*. Paris: Editions du Seuil, 1969.

Mann, Michael. *Consciousness and Action among the Western Working Class*. London: Macmillan, 1975.

———. "The Social Cohesion of Liberal Democracy." *American Sociological Review* 35 (June 1970):423–39.

———. *Workers on the Move*. Cambridge: Cambridge University Press, 1973.

Marcuse, Herbert. *One Dimensional Man*. Boston: Beacon Press, 1968.

Mauss, Marcel. "Parentés à Plaisanteries." *L'Annuaire de l'Ecole des Hautes Etudes*, section des sciences religieuses, Paris, 1928; reprinted in Marcel Mauss, *Oeuvres*, 3:109–35. Paris: Editions de Minuit, 1969.

Mayer, Kurt. "The Changing Shape of the American Class Structure." *Social Research* 30 (Winter 1963):458–69.

Miller, Arthur. "Political Issues and Trust in Government: 1964–1970." *American Political Science Review* 68 (September 1974):951–72.

———. "Rejoinder to 'Comment' by Jack Citrin: Political Discontent or Ritualism?" *American Political Science Review* 68 (September 1974):989–1001.

Miller, Delbert, and William Form. *Industrial Sociology*. New York: Harper and Row, 1964.

Miller, Henry. *Tropic of Cancer*. New York: Grove Press, 1961.

Miller, S. M. "Comparative Social Mobility," *Current Sociology* 9 (1960):1–89.

Miller, S. M. and Frank Reissman. "Working-Class Authoritarianism: A Critique of Lipset." *British Journal of Sociology* 12 (September 1961):263–76.

Miller, Warren E. "Disinterest, Disaffection, and Participation in Presidential Politics." *Political Behavior* 2 (1980):7–32.

Mills, C. Wright. *White Collar: The American Middle Classes*. New York: Oxford University Press, 1951.

Modell, John, and Tamara Hareven. "Urbanization and the Malleable Household: An Examination of Boarding and Lodging in American Families." In *Family and Kin in Urban Communities, 1700–1930*, ed. Tamara K. Hareven. New York: New Viewpoints, 1977.

Montgomery, David. *Workers' Control in America*. London: Cambridge University Press, 1979.

Moskos, Charles. *The American Enlisted Man*. New York: Russell Sage, 1970.

Mott, Paul, and F. Mann. *Shift Work*. Ann Arbor: University of Michigan Press, 1965.

Mueller, John E. "Presidential Popularity from Truman to Johnson." *American Political Science Review* 64 (March 1970):18–34.

———. *War, Presidents and Public Opinion*. New York: John Wiley, 1973.

Nairn, Tom. *The Break-up of Britain*. London: New Left Books, 1977.

Namier, Lewis. "Pathological Nationalisms." *Manchester Guardian*, 26 April 1933.

New Jersey County and Municipal Government Study Commission. *Housing and Suburbs: Fiscal and Social Impact of Multifamily Development*. Trenton: State of New Jersey, 1975.

Nichols, Theo, and Huw Beynon. *Living with Capitalism*. London: Routledge and Kegan Paul, 1977.

Novak, Michael. *The Joy of Sports*. New York: Basic books, 1976.

———. *The Rise of the Unmeltable Ethnics*. New York: Macmillan, 1971.

Oppenheimer, Valerie Kincade. *The Female Labor Force in the United States: Demographic and Economic Factors Governing Its Growth and Changing Composition*. Berkeley, Calif.: Institute of International Studies, 1970.

———. "The Sociology of Women's Economic Role in the Family." *American Sociological Review* 42 (June 1977):387–406.

Orden, Susan, and Norman Bradburn. "Dimensions of Marriage Happiness." *American Journal of Sociology* 73 (May 1968):715–31.

Orwell, George. "England Your England." In *A Collection of Essays by George Orwell*. New York: Doubleday, 1954 (originally published 1941).

Parsons, Talcott. "The Kinship System of the United States." *American Anthropologist* 45 (January–March 1943):22–38.

———. "The Social Structure of the Family." In *The Family: Its Function and Destiny*, ed. Ruth Anshen. New York: Harper and Brothers, 1949.

Patterson, Horace Orlando. *Ethnic Chauvinism*. New York: Stein and Day, 1977.

Pennings, J. M. "Work Value Systems of White Collar Workers." *Administrative Science Quarterly* 15 (1970):397–405.

Pfeffer, Richard. *Working for Capitalism*. New York: Columbia University Press, 1979.

Pigors, P., and F. Pigors. *Human Aspects of Multiple Shift Operations*. New York: Addison-Wesley, 1944.

Pilcher, William. *The Portland Longshoremen*. New York: Holt, Rinehart and Winston. 1972.

Pomper, Gerald. *Voters' Choice*. New York: Harper and Row, 1975.

Popham, Robert. "The Social History of the Tavern." In *Research Advances in Alcohol and Drug Problems*, ed. Yedy Israel. New York: Plenum Press, 1978.

Poulantzas, Nicos. *Classes in Contemporary Capitalism*. London: New Left Books, 1975.

Pred, Allen. "The Intrametropolitan Location of American Manufacturing." In *Internal Structure of the City*, ed. Larry Bourne. New York: Oxford University Press, 1971.

Quinn, Robert, and Graham Staines. *The 1977 Quality of Employment Survey*. Ann Arbor: Institute for Social Research, University of Michigan, 1979.

Radcliffe-Brown, A. "On Joking Relationships." In *Structure and Function in Primitive Society*. New York: Free Press, 1965.

Rainwater, Lee, Richard Coleman, and Gerald Handel. *Workingman's Wife*. New York: Oceana Publications, 1959.

Reich, Wilhelm. *The Mass Psychology of Fascism*, 3d ed. New York: Simon and Schuster, 1970.

Remarque, Erich Maria. *All Quiet on the Western Front*. Greenwich, Conn. Fawcett, 1958 (originally published 1929).

Richards, Katherine Lambert. *How Christmas Came to the Sunday Schools*. New York: Dodd, Mead, 1934.

Ritter, Kathleen, and Lowell Hargens. "Occupational Positions and Class Identifications of Married Working Women: A Test of the Asymmetry Hypothesis." *American Journal of Sociology* 80 (January 1975):934-48.

Ritti, R. *The Engineer in the Industrial Corporation*. New York: Columbia University Press, 1971.

Robinson, John. *How Americans Use Time*. New York: Praeger, 1977.

Rodriguez, Clara. "Puerto Ricans: Between Black and White." *Journal of New York Affairs* 1 (1974):92–101.

Roebuck, Julian, and Raymond Kessler. *The Etiology of Alcoholism*. Springfield, Ill.: Charles C. Thomas, 1972.

Roethlisberger, F. J., and J. Dickson. *Management and the Worker*. Cambridge: Harvard University Press, 1939.

Rothbaum, M. *The Government of the Oil, Chemical and Atomic Workers Union*. New York: John Wiley, 1962.

Royal Institute of International Affairs, *Nationalism*. London: Oxford University Press, 1939.

Ruben, George. "Major Collective Bargaining Developments—A Quarter Century Review." *Current Wage Developments* 26 (February 1974):42–54.

Rubin, Lillian Breslow. *Worlds of Pain: Life in the Working-Class Family*. New York: Basic Books, 1976.

Runciman, W.G. *Relative Deprivation and Social Justice*. London: Routledge and Kegan Paul, 1980.

———. "The Sociological Explanation of 'Religious' Beliefs," *Archives Européennes de Sociologie* 10 (1969):149–91; reprinted in W. G. Runciman. *Sociology in Its Place*. Cambridge: Cambridge University Press, 1970.

Safilios-Rothschild, Constantina. "Family and Stratification." *Journal of Marriage and the Family* 37 (November 1975):855–60.

———. "Family Sociology or Wives' Family Sociology?" *Journal of Marriage and the Family* 31 (1969):290–301.

Sager, Clifford. *Marriage Contracts and Couple Therapy: Hidden Forces in Intimate Relationships*. New York: Brunner-Mazel, 1976.

Sayles, Leonard, and George Strauss. *The Local Union*. New York: Harper and Row, 1953.

Schumpeter, Joseph. *Capitalism, Socialism, and Democracy*. New York: Harper, 1950.

Sears, David, and Jack Citrin. *Tax Revolt*. Cambridge: Harvard University Press, 1982.

Shorter, Edward. *The Making of the Modern Family*. New York: Basic Books, 1975.

Shostak, A. *Blue-Collar Life*. New York: Random House, 1969.

Shostak, A., and W. Gomberg, eds. *Blue-Collar World*. Englewood Cliffs, N.J.: Prentice-Hall, 1964.

Sickel, H. S. J. *Thanksgiving: Its Source, Philosophy and History*. Philadelphia: International Printing Company, 1940.

Smigel, Erwin. *The Wall Street Lawyer*. New York: Free Press, 1964.

Smith, Anthony. *Nationalism in the Twentieth Century*. New York: New York University Press, 1979.

Smith, Robertson. *Lectures on the Religion of the Semites*. Aberdeen University, 1888–89; reprint ed., New York: Meridian Books, 1959.

Snyder, Louis. *Varieties of Nationalism*. Illinois: Dryden Press, 1976.

Sombart, Werner. *Warum gibt es in den Vereinigten Staaten keinen Sozialismus?* Tübingen, 1906; trans. P. Hocking and C. Husbands as *Why Is There No Socialism in the United States?* New York: International Arts and Sciences Press, 1976.

Stanner, W. E. H. "Reflections on Durkheim and Aboriginal Religion." In *Social Oranization: Essays Presented to Raymond Firth*, ed. M. Freedman. Chicago: Aldine, 1967.

Steinberg, Stephen. *The Ethnic Myth: Race, Ethnicity and Class in America*. New York: Atheneum, 1981.

Stellman, Jeanne M., and Susan M. Daum, *Work Is Dangerous to Your Health*. New York: Pantheon, 1970.

Stewart, A., K. Prandy, and R. M. Blackburn. *Social Stratification and Occupations*. London: Macmillan, 1980.

Stone, Katherine. "The Origins of Job Structures in the Steel Industry." *Review of Radical Political Economics* 6 (Summer 1974):113–73.

Stone, Lawrence. *The Family, Sex and Marriage in England, 1500–1800*. New York: Harper and Row, 1977.

Stouffer, S. A. *American Soldier*. Vol. 2. *Combat and Its Aftermath*. Princeton: Princeton University Press, 1949.

Strasser, Susan. *Never Done: A History of American Housework*. New York: Pantheon, 1982.

Sullivan, John J., George E. Marcus, Stanley Feldman, and James Piereson. "The Sources of Political Tolerance." *American Political Science Review* 75 (March 1981):92–106.

Sullivan, John J., James Piereson, and George E. Marcus. *Political Tolerance and American Democracy*. Chicago: University of Chicago Press, 1982.

Suttles, Gerald. *The Social Construction of Communities*. Chicago: University of Chicago Press, 1972.

Tarbell, Ida. *The History of the Standard Oil Company*. New York: Harper and Row, 1966 (originally published 1904).

Taylor, Frederick. *Scientific Management*. New York: Harper and Row, 1911.

Taylor, Graham. *Satellite Cities: A Study of Industrial Suburbs*. New York: Appleton, 1915.

Terkel, Studs. *Working*. New York: Pantheon, 1972.

Thernstrom, Stephan. *The Other Bostonians*. Cambridge: Harvard University Press 1973.

Tichy, Noel. "An Analysis of Clique Formation and Structure in Organizations." *Administrative Science Quarterly* 18 (June 1973):194–207.

Toit, Brian M. du. *Ethnicity in Modern Africa*. Boulder, Colo.: Westview Press, 1978.

Touraine, Alain. *L'évolution du travail ouvrier aux usines Renault*. Paris: Centre National de la Recherche Scientifique, 1955.

———. *Workers' Attitudes to Technical Change*. Paris: Organization for Economic Cooperation and Development, 1965.

Treiman, Donald, and Kermit Terrell. "Women, Work and Wages: Trends in the Female Occupational Structure since 1940." In *Social Indicator Models*, ed. Kenneth Land and Seymour Spilerman. New York: Russell Sage Foundation, 1974.

United States Department of Health, Education, and Welfare. *Work in America*. Cambridge: MIT Press, 1973.

United States Department of Labor. *How American Buying Habits Change*. Washington, D.C.: Government Printing Office, 1959.

Usher, A. P. *A History of Mechanical Inventions*. Boston: Beacon Press, 1959.

Vanneman, Reeve, and Fred Pampel. "The American Perception of Class and Status." *American Sociological Review* 42 (June 1977):422–38.

Walker, Charles. *Steeltown*. New York: Harper, 1950.

Walker, Charles, and Robert Guest. *The Man on the Assembly Line*. Cambridge: Harvard University Press, 1952.

Warner, Sam Bass. *Streetcar Suburbs: The Process of Growth in Boston, 1870-1900*. Cambridge: Harvard University Press, 1962.

———. *The Urban Wilderness: A History of the American City*. New York: Harper and Row, 1972.

Warner, W. Lloyd. *American Life: Dream and Reality*. Chicago: University of Chicago Press, 1953.

———. *The Living and the Dead*. New Haven: Yale University Press, 1959.

————. *Social Class in America: A Manual of Procedure for the Measurement of Social Status*. Chicago: Science Research Associates, 1949.

Warner, W. Lloyd, and Leo Srole. *The Social System of American Ethnic Groups*. New Haven: Yale University Press, 1945.

Warren, Donald. *The Radical Center: Middle Americans and the Politics of Alienation*. Notre Dame, Ind.: Notre Dame Press, 1978.

Warren, Donald, and J. Low. *The Social System of the Modern Factory*. New Haven: Yale University Press, 1947.

Weber, Max. *Economy and Society*, ed. Guenther Roth and Claus Wittich. New York: Bedminster Press, 1968.

Whyte, William H. *The Organization Man*. New York: Simon and Schuster, 1965.

Widick, B. J., ed. *Auto Work and Its Discontents*. Baltimore: John Hopkins University Press, 1976

————. *Detroit: City of Race and Class Violence*. Chicago: Quadrangle, 1972.

Wilensky, Harold. "Mass Society and Mass Culture." *American Sociological Review* 29 (April 1964):173–97.

Williamson, J. B. "Beliefs about Motivation of Poor and Attitudes toward Poverty Policy." *Social Problems* 21 (1974):634–48.

————. "Beliefs about Welfare Poor." *Sociology and Social Research* 58 (1974):163–75.

Wilson, Harold. *The Story of the Jersey Shore*. Princeton: Van Nostrand, 1964.

Wilson, John. "Sociology of Leisure." *Annual Review of Sociology* 6 (1980):21–40.

Wolin, Sheldon. *Politics and Vision*. Boston: Little, Brown, 1960.

Woodward, Joan. *Industrial Organization: Behavior and Control*. London: Oxford University Press, 1970.

Wright, Erik Olin. *Class, Crisis and the State*. London: New Left Books, 1978.

Wright, Erik Olin, Cynthia Cosello, David Hachin, and Joey Sprague. "The American Class Structure." *American Sociological Review* 47 (December 1982):709–26.

Wright, Gwendolyn. *Building the Dream*. New York: Pantheon, 1980.

Wright, John. "Some Measures of Distribution." *Annals of the Association of American Geographers* 27 (December 1937):177–211.

Writers Project. *Entertaining a Nation: The Career of Long Branch*. Bayonne: Jersey Printing Company, 1940.

Young, Michael, and Peter Willmott. *The Symmetrical Family*. New York: Pantheon, 1973.

Zaretsky, Eli. *Capitalism, the Family and Personal life*. New York: Harper and Row, 1976.

Zussman, Robert. *Mechanics of the Middle Class: Work and Politics among American Engineers*. Berkeley: University of California Press, forthcoming.

Zweig, Ferdynand. *The Worker in an Affluent Society*. New York: Free Press. 1961.

Index

Abercrombie, N. S., 337n.2
Abrahams, Roger, 324n.9
Abramson, Paul, 337n.14
Acker, Joan, 318n.22
Afghanistan, 199, 239
Age and life cycle: and homeownership, 30–32; and job choice, 86–88, 118–19, 125–26, 142; and layoffs, 162–63; and leaving Imperium, 159–61, 166; and leisure, 35–46, 313nn.8, 10; and marriage, 70–71; generalizing from one stage, xii, 68, 318n.22, 338n.9; and political party identification, 245, 332n.2
Alba, Richard, 335n.4
Alcoholism, 62–65
Aldrich, John, 337n.14
Alt, John, 298–300, 338n.4
Anderson, Michael, 313n.11
Anshen, Ruth, 317n.13
Applebaum, Herbert, 324nn.1, 6
Apter, David, 326n.6
Arensberg, C., 320n.3
Argentina, 231
Ariès, Philippe, 312n.29, 315nn.2, 4, 337n.10
Aronowitz, Stanley, 323n.7
Asbury Park, xv, 27, 311n.24
Ashford, Nicholas, 325n.1
Assembly work, 80–81, 146–47, 322n.1; packagers, 80, 132–33
Atlantic City, 193, 312n.27
Automated plants: automation defined, 88–89; batch production in, 82, 95–102, 115–18; danger in, 109–15, 129, 245; doing research in, xvi-xviii; job hierarchies in, 83–84, 151–59; knowledge and, 119–25, 133–38; leisure in, 138–42; process production in, 82, 91–95, 115–18; production workers in, 81–83, 105–26; shift work in, 115–19, 172–73; struggle for control in, 119–25; support

workers in, 83–84, 127–44; theories about work in, xii, xiv, 80–81, 145–47
Automobile. *See* Suburbs, post–World War II

Bahr, Howard, 315n.20
Barth, Ernest, 318n.22
Batch production, 82, 95–102, 115–18. *See also* Automated plants
Bebout, John, 309n.14
Belloc, Nedra, 321n.7
Bendix, Reinhard, 323n.13
Berelson, Bernard, 332n.1
Berger, Bennett, 3, 17, 30, 167, 228, 307n.2, 308n.9, 309n.17, 313n.1, 314n.15, 326n.5, 329n.6, 330n.10
Berlin, Isaiah, 232, 330n.1
Berman, Harold, 321n.2, 323nn.5, 10
Beynon, Huw, 320nn.1, 2, 3, 11, 322n.4, 323n.12
Birnbaum, N., 336n.2
Blackburn, R. M., 325n.2
Blacks: distinguished from ethnics, 270; race and class consciousness, 189–90, 247–49; residential segregation, 26–31, 226, 302, 310n.21, plates 1, 2, 15, 16; seen a economic parasites, 212–14, 226–27; as victims of nativism, 236–37. *See also* Elizabeth, old port of
Blau, Peter, 307n.5, 309n.15, 318n.21, 323n.13
Blauner, Robert, 319n.1, 320nn.1, 3, 321n.4, 322n.1
Boas, Franz, 324n.9
Bourne, Larry, 308n.8
Bradburn, Norman, 316n.8
Braverman, Harry, 81, 320n.2, 325n.2
Bright, James, 83, 320nn.4, 6, 8, 11
Brooklyn, xiv, 28
Bryce, James 326n.2

Buchanan, William, 327n.1
Burawoy, Michael, 324n.1, 332n.5
Burgess, Ernest, 315n.2, 317n.8
Business: seen as running country, 190–95, 234–35; small business as escape from factory, 166–67, 304
Butler, Jon, 335n.14
Byrne, Brendon (governor of New Jersey), 192, 193, 196, 197, 204, 290

Cahalan, Don, 63, 317n.16
Campbell, Angus, 325n.2, 337n.15
Cantril, Hadley, 327n.1
Caplow, Theodore, 54, 315nn.3, 5, 20, 322n.4, 333n.2, 336nn.2, 5
Carr, E. H., 232, 331n.4
Carter, James, 193, 242, 331n.6; and 1976 and 1980 presidential elections, 245–46
Carteret, xv
Catholicism, 64, 236, 253–69, 311n.21, 331n.1, 333n.3, 335nn.4, 14, plates 31 and 32. See also Religion
Centers, Richard, 190, 325n.5, 327n.1, 330n.10
Chadwick, Bruce, 315n.20
Children: occupations of, 68–70; and parades, 284–87
China, 199, 238, 239
Chinoy, Ely, 30, 149, 312n.26, 322n.2, 323n.12
Chodorow, Nancy, 318n.22
Christmas, 251, 282. See also Holidays, national occasions, and cults
Churchill, Winston, 234–35
Cisin, Ira, 317n.16
Citrin, Jack, 325n.2, 329n.6
Clark, xv, xviii, 9, 16, 26, 29
Class consciousness: and American dream, 69–70, 169–70, 213, 246, 332n.5; based on life outside workplace, 10, 18–19, 24–26, 76–77, 203, 220–30, 242–49, 292, 296–97, 332n.6; based on work 202–14, 218–19, 242–49; and historical materialism, 229, 244, 297; methods of studying, 202–4, 230; and national consciousness, 242–49; populist form of, 233–35, 246, 292; and race and gender consciousness, 190, 247–48, 332n.7; theories of, 189–90, 246–49, 292–301
Class structure: of occupational world, xiii, 186–87, 306n.17; of residential America, 3–23, 308n.7
Clerical workers. See White-collar workers, lower-white-collar sector
Coleman, Richard, 229, 315n.5, 323n.13, 326n.5, 327n.3, 329n.8, 330n.9, 335n.6
Colts Neck, xv, 9, 24, 309n.15
Constitution, American, 198

Converse, Philip, 326n.6, 337n.15
Cosello, Cynthia, 325n.2
Cosmologies: contradictory, 76, 279; defined, 260; set of mediocre, 268-69, 270-71; types of, 266–68
Cranbury, xv
Cranford, xv, 9, 26
Crossley, Helen, 317n.16
Crozier, Michael, 325n.2
Csikszentmihalyi, Mihaly, 313n.8
Cuba, 199, 239
Cults: contradictory, 278–81; defined, 277; partial, 281; politically anesthetized, 281–88; trivialized, 281–88
Curti, Merle, 331n.4

Dahl, Robert, 325n.4, 326n.5, 327n.9
Danger in the workplace. See Automated plants, danger in
Davis, Mike, 326n.5
Dean, John, 308n.8
Democracy: belief in among the working class, 197–201, 300–301, 326n.6; and elections, 191–93, 288–91
Democratic party, 204, 331n.6; workers' identification with, 244–46
Detroit, 200, 314n.13
Dickson, J., 320n.3
Dingemans, J., 309n.11
DiPrete, Thomas, 325n.2
Doeringer, Peter, 321nn.9, 10
Dolan, Jay, 335n.14
Dollard, John, 324n.9
Donzelot, Jacques, 336n.4
Duncan, Beverly, 308n.7, 310n.21, 323n.13
Duncan, Graeme, 326n.1
Duncan, Otis, 307n.5, 308n.7, 309n.15, 310n.21, 318n.21, 323n.13
Dunlop, John, 321n.6
Dunn, Thomas (mayor of Elizabeth), 243
Dunning, Eric, 306n.14, 314n.15
Durkheim, Emile, 251–53, 260, 277–78, 281, 331n.6, 333n.1, 337n.2
Dying, in Western world, 32

East Brunswick, xv
Eatontown, xv
Edelman, Murray, 326n.1, 337n.12
Edison, xv, 9, 15, 311n.24
Education: attitude to teachers, 48–50, 207–9; bilingual, 226; and busing, 226, 242–43; and choice of leisure, 48–50, 313n.8; drugs in schools, 226; and job aspirations, 169–70, 295; of mechanics, 130–32; and tolerance, 326n.6; of wifes, 59–62, 66–68

Edwards, Richard, 321n.13, 332n.7
Elections, 191, 244–26, 280–90
Elias, Norbert, xii, 314n.15
Elizabeth: anger at property taxes in, 243; old port of, 3, 5–9, 21, 26, 27–30, plates 1 and 2; preautomobile industrial suburb of, xi, xiv-xv, xviii, 7, 9–14, 25–26, plate 3; rich section of, 24
Ellis, Leonard, 336n.5
El Salvador, 199
Embourgeoisement, xiii-xiv, 306n.15
Environment, workers' concern about, 225
Ethnicity, 270–76: ethnic composition of Imperium workers, 4–5, 303; and joking relations, 181; melting pot theory of, 270, 276; "new ethnicity," 190, 276; and parades, 285; in perceptions of pre–World War II neighborhoods, 10; symbolic, 274–76. See also Cosmologies; Pope; Rituals
Evans-Pritchard, E. E., 264, 334nn.8, 11
Exxon refinery, xi, 5

Falkland Islands, 231
Family. See Marriage
Fanwood, xv
Farley, Reynolds, 308n.7, 310n.21, 311nn.22, 23
Feagin, J. R., 328n.11
Featherman, David, 323n.13
Feldman, Stanley, 327n.6
Ford, Gerald, 193; and 1976 presidential election, 245–46
Ford, Henry, 243
Foresta, Ronald, 318n.6
Form, William, 322n.4, 328n.11
Franklin, xv, 15, 27–28, 312n.24
Frankovic, Kathleen, 331n.13
Freedman, M., 334n.8
Freedom, 198–200, 238–39
Freehold, xv
Freidson, Eliot, 325n.3, 328n.9
Frenkel, Richard, 325n.1
Freud, Sigmund, 324n.10, 334n.8
Friedman, Andrew, 322n.6
Frith, Simon, 315n.20
Funnell, Charles, 312n.27

Gallie, Duncan, 320n.4, 321nn.4, 6, 323nn.5, 8
Gans, Herbert, 314n.13, 315n.19; on ethnicity, 275–76, 335n.5; on suburbia and Levittown, 269, 308n.8, 310n.20, 328n.5, 329nn.4, 5; on working class, 311n.23, 313n.1, 314nn.15, 19, 317n.9, 324n.8, 328n.9, 333n.7
Garwood, xv, 9
Gaudet, Helen, 332n.1
Gellner, Ernest, 331n.7

Gender: consciousness, 205, 211–12, 214–18, 247–48; and differences in leisure, 35–42, 75, 281; and differences in occupational structure, xiii, 306n.17, 318n.19; and joking relations, 182–83; and politics, 245–46. See also Class consciousness, based on work; Marriage
Gess, Karol, 330n.2
Giddens, Anthony, 329n.1, 338n.10
Ginsberg, Benjamin, 326n.1
Ginzberg, Eli, 317nn.17, 19, 321n.2, 323nn.5, 10
Glazer, Nathan, 335nn.3, 6, 7
Gluckman, Max, 336n.8
Goldthorpe, John, xiv, 228, 314n.16, 320n.1, 323nn.5, 14, 329n.6, 338n.9
Gomberg, W., 308n.9
Goode, William, 325n.3, 328n.9
Gramsci, Antonio, 297–300
Grant, Ulysses, 312n.27
Greeley, Andrew, 326n.5, 333n.4, 336n.7
Grele, Ronald, 309n.14
Guest, Robert, 321n.5, 322n.2
Gutman, Herbert, 307n.4

Hachin, David, 325n.2
Haig, Marie, 318n.22
Hall, Richard, 322n.4, 323n.4, 325n.2
Halloween, 282, 286. See also Holidays, national occasions, and cults
Hamilton, Richard, 3, 17, 307n.2, 309n.15, 310n.17, 323n.14, 326n.5, 327nn.1, 2
Handel, Gerald, 308n.9, 313n.1, 314n.14, 315n.5
Hareven, Tamara, 308n.6
Hargens, Lowell, 318n.22
Hazlet, xv, 9, 13
Heinz, Katherine, 312n.28
Herberg, Will, 269, 334n.13, 335nn.5, 15, 336n.7
Hidy, Muriel, 307n.4
Hidy, Ralph, 307n.4
Higham, John, 331nn.9, 10
Hill, Reuben, 315n.20
Hill, S., 337n.2
Hiller, Dana, 318n.22
Hillside, xv, 30
Hispanics, 5–9, 26–30, 212–14, 226, 236, 302, 310n.21
Hodge, Robert, 327nn.1, 2
Holidays, national occasions, and cults, 251–52, 272, 277–91, 301
Holmdel, xv
Holmstrom, Lynda, 315n.18
Homeownership: extent and economic importance of, xiv, xvi, 3, 11–14, 302, 308n.9; maintenance and improvement of house, 43; second home and retirement, 30–32, plates 17, 18; size, style,

Homeownership *(cont.)*
and value of homes, 11, 15, 19–23, 25, 304, plates 8–12; social and political effect of, 3, 220–29, 302, 329n.6; types of houses, 19–22; and willingness to divorce, 72–73
Homosexuality, 181–83
Honeyman, A., 307n.6
Horsfall, A., 320n.3
Huber, J., 328n.11
Hunt, Morton, 315n.1
Huntington, Samuel, 325n.2

Imperium Oil and Chemical Company, xiv
Imperium workers: earnings, 86; ethnic and racial composition, 303; fathers' occupations, 4; homeownership among, 12; kin relations among, 5; number of, xvi; occupations, 84; overtime, 86; political party identification, 244; residence, 10, map 1; wage structure, 85
Income: and class identity outside workplace, 220–30; overlap between blue- and white-collar workers, 16–19, 60–63, 74–75, 220–30, 294–95, 309n.15
Inflation, 75, 177–78, 246
Integration, social. *See* Working class, integrated or revolutionary
Iran, and American hostages, 200, 231, 235, 239–41, 246, 292, 331n.6
Irvington, xv
Israel, Yedy, 313n.2
Israel, 239, 246

Jackson, J. B., 337n.8
Jackson, Kenneth T., 307n.6, 308n.8, 311n.21
Jacobs, Jerry, 312n.28
Janowitz, Morris, 325n.2, 329n.6
Jersey City, xv
Jews, 195–96, 253, 269, 275, 303, 311n.21, 331n.1
Johnson, Lyndon, 234
Joking relations, 180-85

Kanter, Rosabeth, 59, 216, 314n.16, 315n.19, 317n.11, 323n.4, 325n.3
Katzman, David, 308n.8
Katznelson, Ira, 329n.1, 332n.6
Keniston, Kenneth, 315n.3
Kennedy, Edward, 331n.6
Kennedy, John, 206, 275
Kessler, Raymond, 317n.16
Keynes, J. M., 299, 338n.7
Kirchheimer, Otto, 326n.5
Kissinger, Henry, 239
Kluegel, James, 327n.3
Kohn, Melvin, 314n.14, 319n.22

Komarovsky, Mirra, 53, 308n.9, 315nn.5, 6, 316n.7, 317nn.9, 12, 13, 318n.22
Kornblum, William, 313nn.1, 3, 9, 320nn.4, 11, 324n.8

Labov, William, 324n.9
Lacey, xv, 9, 15
Ladd, Everett, 332n.3
Lance, Bert, 193, 242, 246
Landau, Ralph, 321n.3
Lane, Christel, 336n.2
Lane, Robert, 323n.13, 328nn.6, 11
Lazarsfeld, Paul, 332n.1, 337nn.13, 15
Leach, Edmund, 334n.8
Leggett, John, 328n.8
Leis, Philip, 336n.7
Leisure: and class consciousness, 74–77, 292–96; among older workers, 44–46; saloons and restaurants, 35–39, 43–44, plates 19–23; sports, 39–42, 44, 281, 287, plates 28–29; at work, 121, 124, 138–42
LeMasters, E. E., 324n.6, 328n.11
Levittown, 269, 310n.20, 311n.23
Life cycle. *See* Age and life cycle
Linden, xv, xviii; black section of, 9, 26–28; preautomobile industrial suburb of, xi, xiv-xv, xviii, 4, 7, 9–14, 74, plates 25, 28, 29; property taxes in, 329n.2
Lipset, Seymour, 319n.22, 323n.13, 325n.2, 326nn.5, 6
Little Silver, xv, 9, 24
Lively, Edwin, 316n.8
Llewellyn, Richard, 323n.1
Locke, Harvey, 315n.2
Locksley, Anne, 317n.13
Long Branch, xv, 27, 312n.27
Lortie, Dan, 325n.3
Lower-white-collar workers. *See* White-collar workers, lower-white-collor sector
Lubell, Samuel, 328n.4, 331n.12
Lukes, J., 331n.6
Lukes, Steven, 326n.1, 331n.6, 333n.5, 334n.8, 336n.2, 337n.3
Lynd, Helen, 325n.1
Lynd, Robert, 325n.1

MacAloon, John, 336n.2, 337n.11
McCaffrey, David, 324n.1
McCarthyism, 231
McClosky, Herbert, 200, 325n.2, 327n.8
McCready, William, 326n.5, 336n.7
Mackenzie, Gavin, 308n.9, 309n.15, 313n.1, 314n.15, 328n.6, 330n.9
Mallet, Serge, 320nn.1, 3, 11, 321n.4, 323n.6

Managers. *See* White-collar workers, upper-white-collar sector
Manchester, xv, 9
Manhattan, xv
Mann, F., 321n.6
Mann, Michael, 314n.16, 321n.1, 323n.11, 325n.4, 326n.5, 336n.8, 338n.10
Marcus, George, 327n.6
Marcuse, Herbert, 298–300
Marlboro, xv, 15
Marriage, 53–73; after children leave home, 70–73; conflicts with other ways of living, 55–59; content and discontent in, 55; difficulty of researching, 316n.7; features of modern marriage, 53–54; husbands' social status, 59–62; occupations of children, 68–70; occupations of wives, 65–68; problem drinking in, 62–65; and working-class personality, 318n.22
Marxism: and historical materialism, 297, 337n.2; and working class, xiv, 189–90, 297–300, 318n.22, 337n.1
Masculinity. *See* Gender
Matawan, 15
Mauss, Marcel, 324n.9, 337n.2
Mechanics, 83–88, 127–32, 138, 165–69, 173–74, 320n.7
Memorial Day, 283, 286, 336n.2. *See also* Holidays, national occasions, and cults
Metuchen, xv
Middle class. *See* White-collar workers, lower-white-collar sector; White-collar workers, upper-white-collar sector
Middletown, xv
Miller, Arthur, 325nn.2, 3, 327n.6
Miller, Delbert, 322n.4
Miller, Henry, 237
Miller, S. M., 319n.22, 323n.13
Miller, Warren, 332nn.2, 3, 336n.6, 337n.14
Mills, C. W., xiii, 325n.2
Milpitas, California, 309n.17
Modell, John, 308n.6
Mondale, Walter, 246
Montgomery, David, 322n.6
Moskos, Charles, 322n.3
Mott, Paul, 321n.6
Mountainside, xv
Moynihan, Daniel, 335nn.3, 6, 7
Mueller, John, 331n.13

Nairn, Tom, 330n.1
Namier, Lewis, 331n.5
Nationalism, 190, 203, 231–49, 292, 296, 302; definitional questions, 231–33, 240–41, 331n.6; in holidays and national occasions, 282–87, 296–

97; and nativism, 235–37; and populism, 233–35; in presidential elections, 246. *See also* Class consciousness
Nativism, 235–37, 302
Neptune, xv
Newark, xv, 27–28, 193, 312n.27
New Brunswick, xv, 26, 28, 30, 312n.24
New Jersey: chemical industry in, xi; Meadowlands, 40, plate 27; oil refining in, 4; partial layoffs in, 163–65; plant closures in, 159–60; retirement communities in, 32, 312n.28
New Jersey County and Municipal Government Study Commission, 329n.3
New Providence, xv
New York City, 10, 36, 40, 60, 69, 176, 312n.27, plates 26, 30
Nichols, Theo, 320nn.1, 2, 11
Nixon, Richard, 193, 198, 245
North Brunswick, xv, 9
North Plainfield, xv, 311n.24
Norval, Glenn, 318n.20
Novak, Michael, 335n.6, 336n.5

Ocean Grove, 311n.24
Oil, Chemical and Atomic Workers Union, xvi, 175
Old Bridge, xv, 9, 15
Olympic Games, 287, 292
Oppenheimer, Valerie, 309n.12, 317nn.13, 18, 318nn.19, 21
Orden, Susan, 316n.8

Packagers, *See* Assembly work
Pampel, Fred, 326n.5, 330n.10
Parades, 284-88, plate 33. *See also* Holidays, national occasions, and cults
Parsons, Talcott, 317n.13
Patterson, Horace, 336n.7
Pennings, J. M., 316n.16
Personality. *See* Working class, personality
Perth Amboy, xv, 9, 27, 28, 311n.24
Pfeffer, Richard, 332n.5
Philadelphia, 312n.27
Philliber, William, 318n.22
Piereson, James, 327n.6
Pigors, F., 321n.8
Pigors, P., 321n.8
Pilcher, W., 324n.6
Piore, Michael, 321nn.9, 10
Piscataway, xv, xviii, 9, 15, 21, 24, 329n.2; black section of, 30, 311n.24, plates 15, 16
Plainfield, xv; black section of, 9, 26, 28, 311n.23, 312n.24; wealthy section of, 9, 24

Polish workers: and Solidarity, 274–75; and Polish pope, 272. *See also* Ethnicity

Politics: derived from neighborhood and home-ownership, 225–28, 245; derived from work setting, 219; mistrust of politicians, xiv, 189–90, 191–93, 281–91; party identification, 244–46, 332nn.2, 3; perceived composition of power structure, 194–96; political system, attitude toward, 189–90, 201, 248–49; popular interest in, 281; presidential elections, 242–47, 296, 332n.4

Pomper, Gerald, 332n.3

Pomper, Marlene, 331n.13

Poor, attitude toward, 213–14, 225, 235–37, 248–49

Pope, 254, 272

Popham, Robert, 313n.2

Populism, 190, 233–35, 243, 292, 302. *See also* Class consciousness

Poulantzas, Nicos, 337n.1

Prandy, K., 325n.2

Pred, Allen, 308n.8

Priest, Curtis, 325n.1

Princeton Township, xv, 9, 24

Princeton, xv

Process production, 82, 91–95, 115–18. *See also* Automated plants

Professionals. *See* White-collar workers, upper-white-collar sector

Property tax, 13–14, 225–29. *See also* Home-ownership

Protestants, 64, 253

Quinn, Robert, 325n.1

Raab, Earl, 326n.6

Race. *See* Blacks

Radcliffe-Brown, A., 180, 324nn.4, 7

Rahway, xv, xviii, 9, 16, 26, 28, 193

Rainwater, Lee, 229, 308n.9, 313n.1, 314n.14, 315nn.5, 6, 318n.22, 323n.13, 326n.5, 327n.3, 329n.8, 330n.9, 335n.6

Reagan, Ronald, 193, 199, 223, 234, 238, 243; and 1980 and 1984 presidential elections, 246

Red Bank, xv

Reich, Wilhelm, 318n.22, 331n.5, 337n.1

Reisman, David, 30

Religion, 253–69; and atheism, 253, 333n.3; belief in life after death, 260–62; defined, 253, 333n.1; and magic and science, 334n.9; meaning of God, 264–66; and political party identification, 331n.1; religious beliefs, defined and classified, 260, 266–68; religious rituals, defined and classified, 254, 258–60; sacred/profane dichotomy, 333n.8; and secularization debate, 334n.14. *See* *also* Catholicism; Cosmologies; Jews; Protestants

Remarque, Erich, 231, 313n.4, 331n.3

Republican party, workers' identification with, 244–46

Retirement communities, 32, 312n.28

Richards, Katherine, 336n.7

Richmond, California, 309n.17

Riessman, Frank, 319n.22

Ritter, Kathleen, 318n.22

Ritti, R., 321n.1

Rituals: defined, 254; classified, 258–60

Robinson, John, 42, 52, 313n.6, 314n.13, 315n.20

Rochberg-Halton, Eugene, 313n.8

Rockefeller, 204, 243

Rodriguez, Clara, 311n.21, 335n.2

Roebuck, Julian, 317n.16

Roethlisberger, F. J., 320n.3

Room, Robin, 317n.16

Rose, Arnold, 308n.8

Roselle, xiv, xv, xviii, 14–15; black section of, 7, 9, 26, 28, 30, 242

Roselle Park, xiv, xv, xviii, 7, 14–15, 242

Roosevelt, Franklin, 234–35, 288

Ross, Adreain, 318n.20

Rossi, Alice, 315n.2

Roth, Guenther, 329n.1

Rothbaum, M., 323n.8

Ruben, George, 313n.11

Rubin, Lillian, 54, 313n.1, 314n.15, 315nn.5, 6, 318n.22

Rumson, xv, 9, 24, 309n.16

Runciman, W. G., 334nn.9, 12, 338n.6

Safety at work. *See* Automated plants, danger in

Safilios-Rothschild, Constantina, 314n.16, 316n.7

Sager, Clifford, 71

Saint Patrick's Day, 337n.8. *See also* Holidays, national occasions, and cults

Salespeople. *See* White-collar workers, lower-white-collar sector

Sayles, Leonard, 324n.2

Sayreville, xv

Schneider, William, 325n.2

Schnore, Leo, 308n.8

Schools. *See* Education

Schumpeter, Joseph, 326n.1

Scotch Plains, 9, 16, 24, 26–27, 309n.16

Scranton, Pennsylvania, 213

Sears, David, 329n.6

Secretaries. *See* White-collar workers, lower-white-collar sector

Shanks, J. Merrill, 325n.2

Shift work. *See* Automated plants, shift work in

Short, James, 327n.3
Shostak, A., 308n.9, 324n.14
Sickel, H. S. J., 337n.9
Skilled workers. *See* Mechanics
Smigel, Erwin, 325n.3
Smith, Anthony, 331n.7
Smith, Eliot, 327n.3
Smith, Robertson, 333n.1
Sniderman, Paul, 325n.2
Snyder, Louis, 331n.6
Socialism, 199–201, 218–19, 301
Sombart, Werner, 3
Soule, Whitman, 325n.2
South Amboy, xv, 9, 29, 311n.24
South Brunswick, xv, 311n.24
South Plainfield, xv
Soviet Union, 199–200, 238
Sports. *See* Leisure, sports
Sprague, Joey, 325n.2
Springfield, xv
Srole, Leo, 335n.1
Staines, Graham, 325n.1
Stanner, W. E. H., 334n.8
Staten Island, xv, 9; black section of, 26, 28, 30
Steinberg, Stephen, 335n.6
Stellhorn, Paul, 308n.6
Stewart, A., 325n.2
Stokes, Donald, 337n.15
Stone, Katherine, 322n.1
Stone, Lawrence, 315nn.2, 4
Stouffer, S. A., 331n.3
Strachey, James, 334n.8
Strasser, Susan, 315n.3
Strauss, George, 324n.2
Suburbs: defined, 308n.8; house types in, 19–25; post–World War II, xi, xiv, 15–30, 75, 244, 309n.17; pre–World War II, 9–15, 34–35, 44, 244; racial segregation in, 26–30, 311nn.22, 23; voting behavior of workers in, 244
Sudnow, David, 324n.9
Sullivan, John, 327n.6, 336n.8
Summit, xv, 9, 24
Supervision, 139–41, 155–58
Suttles, Gerald, 333n.7

Tarbell, I., 307n.4
Taverns, 35–39, 313n.3
Taylor, Frederick, 80, 81, 146, 320n.3, 321n.13
Taylor, Graham, 308n.8
Technicians, laboratory, 133–38
Terkel, Studs, 328n.7
Terrell, Kermit, 318n.19
Thanksgiving, 283, 288, 337n.9, plate 33. *See also* Holidays, national occasions, and cults

Thernstrom, Stephan, 323n.13
Thomas, Mary, 315n.2
Tichy, Noel, 314n.16
Tinton Falls, xv
Toit, Brian M. du, 335n.1
Toms River, xv, 9
Touraine, Alain, 319n.1, 322n.1, 323n.6
Treiman, Donald, 318n.19, 327nn.1, 2
Trenton, 26, 28
Tully, Judy, 318n.20
Turner, B., 337n.2
Turner, Ralph, 327n.3
Turner, Victor, 336n.2

Unemployed, attitude toward, 213–14, 225, 235–37, 245, 248–49
Union, xv, 9
Union Beach, xv, 9
Unions: AFL–CIO, 3, 300–302; at Imperium, xvi, 171–80; as part of power structure, 195–97; and Reagan administration, 246; taking job with, 167–68
Usher, A. P., 320nn.8, 9

Vanneman, Reeve, 326n.5, 330n.10
Voting, 191–95, 244–46, 288–91. *See also* Politics

Walker, Charles, 321n.5, 322n.1, 323n.4, 328n.7
Wallace, George, 198
Ward, Peter, 309n.15
Warehouse workers, 142–44
Warner, Sam Bass, 307n.6, 308n.8, 310n.19
Warner, W. Lloyd, 203, 251, 326n.5, 327n.3, 332n.1, 335n.1, 336n.1
Watchung, xv
Watson, Walter, 318n.22
Weber, Max, 329n.1
Westfield, xv, 9, 16, 24, 26, 309n.16
White-collar workers, lower-white-collar sector: attitudes toward, 209–12; characteristics of jobs, 186–87; defined, xiii; income level, 16, 19; marriage and leisure, 42, 50–52, 66–70, 74–77, 292–97, 301–2
White-collar workers, upper-white-collar sector: attitudes toward, 207–9; characteristics of jobs, 186–87; defined, xiii; income level, 16, 19; marriage and leisure, 42, 50–52, 58–59, 64, 66–70, 74–77, 292–97, 301–2; proportion in residential areas, 6–19
Widick, B. J., 322nn.4, 5
Wilensky, Harold, 48, 312n.27, 313n.13
Williamson, J. B., 328n.11
Williamson, Margaret, 315n.20, 332n.2, 336nn.2, 5
Willmott, Peter, 50, 314n.17, 315nn.2, 20, 317n.10

Wilson, John, 315n.20

Wittich, Claus, 329n.1

Wolin, Sheldon, 281

Women: in labor force, xiii, 306n.17, 318n.19; wives of blue-collar workers, 61–62, 65–68; working woman, concept of, 214–18. *See also* Gender; Marriage

Woodbridge, xv, xviii, 9, 23

Woodward, Joan, 319n.1, 321n.1

Work. *See* Automated plants; White-collar workers, lower-white-collar sector; White-collar workers, upper-white-collar sector; Working class

Workaholism, 50–51, 57–59

Working class (blue-collar): characteristics of jobs, 186–87, 293; conflicts between workers, 171–85; culture, debate over, 34–35, 51–52, 74–75, 294–96; defined, xiii; and education, 48–50, 59–62, 66–68, 130–32, 169–70, 207–9, 295, 313n.8, 326n.6; instrumentalism of, 338n.9; integrated or revolutionary, xiii-xiv, xvi, 189–90, 201, 248–

49, 297–301; job security, 159–65; as middle class, xi-xiv, 293–97; and occupational mobility, 149, 152–58, 165–70; personality, 318n.22; privatization of, xiv, 338n.9; proportion in residential areas, 6–19; social relations at work, 171–85; social relations outside workplace, 46–48; tolerance among, 326n.6; working man, concept of, xvii, 202–19, 292–97; working woman, concept of, 214–18. *See also* Automated plants; Class consciousness

World War II, participation in, 233–35

Wright, Erik Olin, 306n.17, 325n.2

Wright, Gwendolyn, 307n.1

Wright, John, 310n.21

Wright, William, 312n.27

Young, Michael, 50, 314n.17, 315nn.2, 20, 317n.10

Zaretsky, Eli, 315nn.3, 4

Zussman, Robert, 321n.2, 325n.3, 329n.7

Zweig, Ferdynand, 298–300, 321n.6, 338nn.5, 8